CULTURAL REVOLUTION IN RUSSIA, 1928–1931

Studies of the Russian Institute, Columbia University

CULTURAL REVOLUTION IN RUSSIA, 1928–1931

Edited by Sheila Fitzpatrick

Indiana University Press • Bloomington and London

Published in Canada by Fitzhenry & Whiteside Limited, Don Mills, Ontario

Manufactured in the United States of America

The Russian Institute of Columbia University sponsors the *Studies of the Russian
Institute* in the belief that their publication contributes to scholarly research and
public understanding. In this way the Institute, while not necessarily endorsing their
conclusions, is pleased to make available the results of some of the research conducted under its auspices.

Library of Congress Cataloging in Publication Data
Main entry under title:
Cultural revolution in Russia, 1928–1931.
   (Studies of the Russian Institute, Columbia University)
   "The conference at which these papers were originally
presented was jointly sponsored by the Research and
Development Committee of the American Association for the
Advancement of Slavic Studies and the Russian Institute,
Columbia University.
   Includes index.
   1. Russia—Intellectual life—1917–
Congresses. I. Fitzpatrick, Sheila. II. American
Association for the Advancement of Slavic Studies.
Research and Development Committee. III. Columbia
University. Russian Institute. IV. Series: Columbia
University. Russian Institute. Studies.
DK266.4.C86   301.5'92'0947   77-74439
ISBN 0-253-31591-3   1   2   3   4   5   82   81   80   79   78

Contents

073959

ACKNOWLEDGMENTS

The conference at which these papers were originally presented was jointly sponsored by the Research and Development Committee of the American Association for the Advancement of Slavic Studies and the Russian Institute, Columbia University. Preparation of the manuscript was facilitated by a further grant from the Research and Development Committee and by the cooperation of the Russian Institute and its staff, especially John Hanselman and Nora Beeson, whose assistance was greatly appreciated.

The editors and contributors wish to make particular acknowledgment of the contribution of fellow scholars who participated in the conference: Stephen F. Cohen, Robert C. Tucker, Loren R. Graham, Peter Juviler, and Joel Shapiro, who acted as formal discussants: Seweryn Bialer, Alexander Erlich, and William Harkins, who chaired the three sessions; Alexander Dallin, who gave the address; Leopold Haimson, George Collins, and others who took part in the general discussions. Robert V. Daniels and William Rosenberg read the papers while the manuscript was in preparation and made valuable and detailed comments.

To our regret, the conference paper presented by Kendall E. Bailes could not be included in this volume because of its prior publication in his book *Technology and Society under Lenin and Stalin* (Princeton, 1977). Katerina Clark's paper is published here in condensed form.

The editor owes special gratitude to Frederick Starr, who first encouraged her to organize a conference on the cultural revolution and subsequently acted as liaison with the Research and Development Committee of AAASS, and to Loren Graham, for his support, advice, and enthusiasm throughout.

CULTURAL REVOLUTION IN RUSSIA, 1928–1931

Editor's Introduction

"Cultural revolution" is a term most familiar from the upheaval in China in the 1960s. But, whether or not the Chinese Communists were aware of it, their cultural revolution had a precedent in Soviet history. During the First Five-Year Plan, and particularly in the years 1928–31, the old Russian intelligentsia was buffeted by a militant movement in which Communist youth were particularly prominent. Students challenged their professors, forcing them to undergo "reelection" to their positions. In the professions, established authorities were overthrown by younger, more militant, Marxist groups, and scholars were urged to focus their research on topics that were of practical relevance to society and the economy. Along with a drive to link the whole educational process with the "real life" of industry, kolkhoz agriculture, and the political campaigns of the day, Communist and working-class students were recruited to higher education in unprecedented numbers. Cultural revolutionaries attacked "bureaucratic" administrative forms, proposing instead new organizational methods to which they gave military-sounding names—"light cavalry" charges, production "brigades," "campaigns" of the "cultural Army." In the climate of cultural revolution, radical experimentation flourished, and blueprints were drawn up for the socialist cities and "collectivization of life" appropriate for the new world in the making.

This kind of cultural revolution was quite unlike the process that Lenin had envisaged under that name. Lenin's idea of cultural revolution was a gradual and nonmilitant raising of cultural standards, achieved without direct confrontation with the old intelligentsia and involving above all the expansion of mass education and the spread of basic literacy.[1] Lenin's usage was the one to which Stalin returned in the late thirties, and the one now accepted by Soviet historians.[2] Contemporary Soviet writers do not dwell on the outburst of militancy called "cultural revolution" in the First Five-Year Plan (and, similarly, they deny that the Chinese "cultural revolution" deserves that title or has a legitimate place in the normal process of socialist development).

The First Five-Year Plan period in general presents difficulties to Soviet historians. The foundations of Soviet economic development were laid at this time, but so, clearly, were the foundations of Stalin's "cult of personality." Soviet historians must balance the achievements of the period against its "excesses." Among the "excesses," perhaps, were the regime's harsh dealings with the non-Party intelligentsia during the cultural revolution. Among the achievements was the creation of a new "Soviet intelligentsia," largely recruited from the working class and the Communist party.

This is, indeed, a period of contradictions, and we cannot begin to understand the First Five-Year Plan cultural revolution without considering the political and economic context in which it took place. The decision to undertake a program of rapid industrialization—unsupported by foreign credits or even by extensive foreign trade, and without the internal capital accumulation that many thought a prerequisite—was made after long debates in 1927–28. It was assumed, rightly or wrongly, that the peasantry would have to take the burden, and that the resources necessary for industrial investment would have to be "squeezed" out of the agricultural sector. At the first sign that the peasantry might resist the squeezing process—that is, refuse to market grain for the low prices set by the state—the Party leadership reacted with something like panic. Stalin insisted that force should be used against peasant "hoarders." When this proved insufficient, the policy of immediate and, as far as possible, universal entry of the peasantry into collective farms was adopted as a solution to the related problems of state grain collection and political control.

The effect of these measures was to provoke a direct confrontation between the state and the peasantry—or, as it was described, between the "proletarian dictatorship" and the kulak "class enemy." At the same time, conflict between the Stalin and Rykov-Bukharin groups in the Politburo produced a top-level political crisis. Even before these events, real or imagined fears of foreign intervention had led to the development of a siege mentality. Faced by actual crisis, the fears of external and internal enemies intensified. The potential enemies within included the kulak, the urban businessman and trader, the old (non-Communist) intelligentsia, and the remnants of defeated political parties and Communist opposition groups. The period was marked by an increase in political coercion of all kinds and an expansion of the sphere of Party intervention and control.

However, the social consequences of the new policies were by no means all negative. A high level of urban unemployment, especially of youth, coupled with limited opportunities for peasants to find seasonal or permanent employment in the cities had characterized NEP. There had been a feeling among Communists and Komsomols of lost momentum and lack of direction—a suspicion that the leadership no longer had the dynamism to undertake radical social and economic change. The Five-Year Plan restored the Communist sense of purpose and released a considerable charge of energy and enthusiasm for its accomplishment. At the same time, it eliminated urban unemployment and (although the new kolkhozy formally restricted the departure of their members) created the conditions for a massive population movement of peasants from rural areas into towns and the new construction sites. Some of the movement was involuntary, a product of the deportation of kulaks. Nevertheless, from the viewpoint of a social historian, the First Five-Year Plan must be regarded as a period of enormous upward social mobility, as peasants moved into the industrial labor force, unskilled workers became skilled, and skilled workers were promoted into white-collar and managerial positions and higher education.

It was, of course, the upward movement from the working class that was stressed as a positive achievement by the regime at the time, and has since been stressed by Soviet historians. Hundreds of thousands of workers and Communists were "mobilized" for study in technical schools and higher educational institutions. Newly trained "Red specialists" moved into the engineering jobs created by industrial expansion (as well as those vacated by arrested "bourgeois wreckers"). The Communist party itself was conducting large-scale recruitment in the factories and becoming, as it had never been under Lenin, a predominantly working-class party.

There was an analogy to this process in the intellectual and cultural world, although it often appeared a contrived and artificial one. Groups of Communists established "proletarian hegemony" in various intellectual and cultural professions, and for a few years exercised a belligerent, exclusive, and oppressive dictatorship over their professional colleagues. In fact these Communist groups were usually not proletarian in any real sense, although they made strenuous efforts to establish contact with a mainly indifferent working-class opinion. The two centers of the intellectual "proletarian" movement—the literary association RAPP and the Communist Academy—were faction ridden and, in most practical ways, unproductive. Despite their services in attacking "rightism," the Party leadership had little patience with them.

It is this latter aspect of cultural revolution that has attracted most attention from Western scholars.[3] The scholarship has been largely focussed on the persecution of the old intelligentsia and the extension of political controls over cultural life. It has treated the First Five-Year Plan period primarily as a transition, arbitrarily and abruptly separating the NEP period of relative tolerance and cultural diversity from the Stalin period of repression and cultural stagnation. The Party, or Stalin himself, has often been seen as holding the levers of change and manipulating them almost at will to reach preconceived goals.

In this volume, we have made the first attempt to see the cultural revolution as a whole, and to consider it not simply as a transition but as a discrete phenomenon with its own special characteristics. Instead of concentrating exclusively on the theme of Party intervention in culture (the major theme of previous Western studies), we have looked at what was happening *within* the cultural professions and sought to relate this to contemporary social and political changes, including the movement for worker promotion (*vydvizhenie*) into the intelligentsia.

The genuinely proletarian component of "proletarian cultural revolution"—working-class upward mobility into professional and white-collar occupations—is discussed in the articles by Fitzpatrick, Lewin, and

Lapidus. Cultural revolution as an antibureaucratic and iconoclastic youth movement is described by Fitzpatrick. In regard to the old intelligentsia, contributors discuss the impact of cultural revolution both on cultural/ intellectual debate and on the conditions of professional life. The "visionary planning" and utopian expectations characteristic of the period are described by Starr, Sharlet, and Lapidus: Starr's study of the town planners gives us a particularly interesting example of regime endorsement of such visionary planning and its partial implementation in practice; Sharlet and Lapidus deal respectively with the theories of "withering away of the law" and "withering away of the school," which achieved wide acceptance during the cultural revolution and were based in part on the observable disintegration of traditional legal and educational institutions.

Clark discusses the writers' efforts to reconceptualize their own role in a changing society, comparing their search for contact with the working-class masses with the Russian intelligentsia's "movement to the people" in the 1870s. Joravsky, looking at the psychoneurologists, describes a process of cultural impoverishment as the profession accepted increasing restrictions on the scope and quality of intellectual debate. Internal and generational conflicts within professions are examined by Solomon, for the rural scholars, and Enteen, for the historians. In the case of the rural scholars, both Marxist and non-Marxist schools were concerned with the precollec- tivization, small-farming peasantry, and the regime's adoption of a policy of all-out collectivization brought their enquiries to an abrupt end. In the historical profession, on the other hand, Marxists waged a successful strug- gle against "bourgeois" historians and then themselves split into warring camps. The internecine struggle among the Marxists that followed is well documented, and gives us an unusual insight into the political processes and implications of in-fighting in a Communist-dominated profession.

On the historical continuum, Fitzpatrick investigates the connection between the First Five-Year Plan cultural revolution and the social and political tensions of NEP. Lewin's article describes the complex social situa- tion of the 1920s and 1930s, relating the flux and chaos of the First Five-Year Plan period to similar characteristics of the Great Purge years of the later thirties. Joravsky also relates the "great break" of 1928–29 to subsequent developments in the Stalin period, but at the same time points to a continuity in intelligentsia/regime relations through the Soviet period as a whole. The "great break" produced an outright confrontation between the interests of the regime and those of the intelligentsia, he argues, but even under Lenin the regime's demands and assumptions were incompatible with free intellectual enquiry. A contrast between Joravsky's view of cultural revolution and Fitzpatrick's is drawn by Solomon in her article on the rural scholars.

In conclusion, Hough considers the implications of our emerging picture of First Five-Year Plan cultural revolution for Western models of Soviet development, with particular reference to modernization (also discussed by Lapidus in her article on education), "Great Retreat" (Timasheff's image of repudiation of revolutionary ideals in the 1930s), and the totalitarian interpretation of state/society interaction in the Stalin period.

The appropriateness of the totalitarian model was, in fact, one of the questions most frequently raised in discussion at the conference at which these papers were originally presented. A major point of debate was the applicability of the notion of "revolution from above" to the process of cultural revolution. "Revolution from above" has been used to characterize the rapid industrialization drive, collectivization, and the political transformation of the First Five-Year Plan period. The term emphasizes the voluntarist nature of the policies adopted by the Party leadership. The implication is that social and economic forces played a relatively insignificant part; that an activist regime imposed its will on a passive society; and that the Party leadership acted without constraint or encouragement either from the society or from its own rank-and-file.

In the cultural sphere, the debate hinges on the extent to which cultural revolution was a movement initiated and controlled by the Party leadership (or by Stalin's group within it) for its own ends. The argument for cultural revolution as "revolution from above" is supported by the leadership's initiative in staging the Shakhti trial of 1928, which set the pattern for anti-intelligentsia action in other areas; the intervention of the leadership in various episodes of the cultural struggle (for example, Stalin's 1929 speech to the Agrarian Marxists and his 1931 letter to the editors of *Proletarskaia revoliutsiia*); the cultural revolutionaries' attacks on Stalin's "rightist" opponents; the high degree of politicization of the movement; and the claim invariably made by militant groups to be acting "for the Party" or, in some cases, with a mandate from the Central Committee.

It has also been argued, however, that there were important elements of "revolution from below" in cultural revolution. This argument—which has implications beyond the cultural sphere—points to the existence during NEP of strong pressures within the Communist Party, the Komsomol, and the industrial working class for more militant and radical policies. It stresses the instability of NEP society and politics, the Communist doubt that the revolution had been irrevocably won, and the continuing force of resentment against the educated and privileged classes of the old regime. The argument is supported by evidence that the Party's "instruments" in harassing the old intelligentsia were essentially self-appointed and often insubordinate to higher authority; that in attacking the old intelligentsia the cultural revolutionaries were overthrowing what they regarded as the cultural "establishment," and this reflected their general mood of hostility toward constituted authority; and that the radical ideas that cultural revolution brought into prominence—in particular the theories of the "withering away" of state, school, and law—were both unacceptable to the Party leadership and inappropriate to its purposes.

Those (including the present writer) who argued for elements of "revolution from below" tended to reject the dichotomy of state and society and the idea of untrammeled political voluntarism. Cultural revolution, in their view, was not only generated by forces within the society but also served to create societal support (as well as societal opposition) for the regime. The support came from what has been labelled the "new class"— the predominantly working-class and peasant group promoted and trained during the First Five-Year Plan that moved into managerial positions in the thirties and has dominated the Soviet political scene virtually to the present day.

Like all good arguments, this one remains unresolved. It hardly needs to be pointed out that its relevance is not limited to cultural history. In recent years, scholars have been trying to break away from the spell of the totalitarian model, and find new frameworks for understanding the October revolution and the period of NEP. But there has been little reinterpretation of the period from 1929, which, in more senses than one, remains the dark ages of Soviet history. Stalin's Russia is still almost uncharted territory for the historian.[4] This volume, dealing with the formative first years of the Stalin period, suggests some possible lines of reinterpretation of the period as a whole. We hope that the questions we have raised will prove provocative enough to stimulate further research and debate.

Cultural Revolution
as Class War

Sheila Fitzpatrick

In the First Five-Year Plan period, the term "cultural revolution" was used in a special sense, different from earlier or later Soviet usages. It described a political confrontation of "proletarian" Communists and the "bourgeois" intelligentsia, in which the Communists sought to overthrow the cultural authorities inherited from the old regime. The aim of cultural revolution was to create a new "proletarian intelligentsia." The method of cultural revolution was "class war."

The concept of class war depended on a definition of the old intelligentsia as "bourgeois" and the Communist party as "proletarian." All Communists agreed on this definition, but not all thought it necessary to make culture a battleground. In the first ten years of Soviet power, the Communist leadership had tended to avoid outright confrontation with the intelligentsia. Lenin had rejected the idea that cultural power, like political, could be seized by revolutionary action. Culture, in his view, had to be patiently acquired and assimilated; Communists must learn from "bourgeois specialists," despite their identification with an alien social class; and refusal to learn was a sign of "Communist conceit." During NEP the leadership as a whole had treated harassment of specialists (*spetseedstvo*) as a regrettable byproduct of revolutionary zeal rather than a mark of developed proletarian consciousness.

In 1927, on the eve of the industrialization drive, the leadership was still talking in terms of a nonantagonistic relationship with bourgeois specialists. The Party's task, Stalin told the Fifteenth Party Congress in December, was "to strengthen the bond (*smychka*) of the working class with the toiling Soviet intelligentsia of town and country," and industrialization would only tend to reinforce the alliance, since the technical intelligentsia, "being closely linked with the process of production, cannot but see that the Bolsheviks are leading our country forward to better things. . . ."[1] On the same occasion, the future "rightist" Rykov and future "Stalinist" Molotov agreed that in the interests of successful industrialization it would be necessary to make a substantially increased investment in culture, particularly in the priority areas of primary education, technical education, and the campaign against illiteracy.[2] *Pravda* used the term "cultural revolution" in its Leninist sense (see p. 2) to describe the nonmilitant development of mass education that industrialization would require:

> Industrialization—our general course—is unthinkable without rationalization. But rationalization, in its turn, is unthinkable without a raising of the cultural level: both the cultural level of "cadres" and the cultural level of the masses. The demand to raise the cultural level of the worker-peasant masses, the demand to carry out a broad and profound *"cultural revolution"* in the country is evident: it is now really "in the air."[3]

The switch to a class-war concept of cultural revolution came abruptly a few months after the Fifteenth Party Congress, in an atmosphere of rising political tension. In January 1928 Stalin visited Siberia, where grain procurements had been small in spite of a good harvest, and decided that it was necessary to resort to coercion of the peasantry and confiscation of hoarded grain. This was the beginning of the policy of "class war" against the prosperous peasant, which subsequently led to the forced collectivization of agriculture. In March 1928 the State Prosecutor announced the forthcoming trial of a large group of mining engineers and technicians from the Shakhty area of Donbass on charges of conspiracy and sabotage. The trial, which took place in Moscow in May and June, received maximum publicity and was preceded by a highly organized public discussion and condemnation of the accused. This was a turning point in Soviet policy toward the bourgeois specialist. From this time, the technical intelligentsia ceased to be seen as the Party's natural ally in industrialization, and became a potentially treacherous group whose real allegiance was to the dispossessed capitalists and their foreign supporters.

The purpose of the Shakhty trial, according to an NKVD official quoted by Medvedev,[4] was " 'to mobilize the masses,' 'to arouse their wrath against the imperialists,' 'to intensify vigilance.' " This vigilance was directed against the intelligentsia *as a class enemy*. The necessary condition of successful industrialization was no longer (as Rykov and Molotov had thought in December) more engineers and a more literate population, but more *proletarian* engineers and a population alert for signs of wrecking and sabotage among the bourgeois intelligentsia.

The new concept of cultural revolution was defined by Krinitskii, head of the agitprop department of the Central Committee, at a special meeting on cultural questions held while the Shakhty trial was in progress. Under present conditions, Krinitskii said, cultural revolution was inconceivable without class war, and the proletariat must fight "against bourgeois elements which are supported by the remnants and survivals of the influence, traditions and customs of the old society." These bourgeois elements had mounted an attack on the cultural front, "struggling to increase their share, fighting for their own school, their own art, their own theatre and cinema, trying to use the state apparatus for that purpose." Communist cultural administrators (particularly those in Narkompros [Commissariat of Enlightenment of the RSFSR], under the tolerant leadership of the Old Bolshevik intellectual Anatolii Lunacharskii) had failed to recognize the threat, being disarmed by "an anti-revolutionary, opportunist conception of cultural revolution as a peaceful, classless raising of cultural standards—a conception which does not distinguish between bourgeois and proletarian elements of culture, . . . and does not see the fierce struggle of the proletariat against the class antagonist in everyday life, the school, art, science and so on. . . ."[5]

The period of official sponsorship of class-war cultural revolution in the Soviet Union can be dated from the Shakhty trial (early summer 1928) to

Stalin's statement of reconciliation with the old technical intelligentsia three years later (June 1931). Subsequently, from the standpoint of Soviet discussion, the episode was buried—indeed, class-war cultural revolution became a theoretical impossibility, as the Leninist definition of cultural revolution was taken back into Soviet usage from the late thirties. Western historians, regarding the First Five-Year Plan period in culture as essentially a transition from the relative permissiveness and pluralism of NEP to the regimentation of "Stalinism," have usually treated the class-war terminology simply as camouflage for the basic process of Communist intimidation of the intelligentsia.

However, cultural revolution was not only a more complex phenomenon than this scheme suggests, but also one of peculiar importance for the understanding of Soviet political and social development. This was the period in which the social and generational tensions of NEP came to a climax in an onslaught (which the leadership only partly controlled) on privilege and established authority. But these were also the first and formative years of the Stalin era. We are accustomed to the idea that the First Five-Year Plan laid the foundations for Stalinist industrialization, just as collectivization laid the foundations for Stalinist agriculture. It should surely be recognized that cultural revolution was an equally important part of what has been called the "Stalin revolution." The substance behind the rhetoric of class war was large-scale upward mobility of industrial workers and working-class Party members into higher education and administrative and managerial jobs. Cultural revolution was the vehicle for training the future Communist elite and creating the new Soviet intelligentsia.

This feat of social engineering—unprecedented and unrepeated in Soviet experience—was accomplished in the midst of a cultural upheaval, some aspects of which were directly manipulated by the Party leadership, others outside the range of leadership vision. Cultural revolution had many facets. It was a worker-promotion movement linked to a political campaign to discredit the "Right Opposition" within the Party. It was an iconoclastic youth movement directed against "bureaucratic" authority. It was a process whereby militant Communist groups in the professions established local dictatorships and attempted to revolutionize their disciplines. It was, finally, a heyday for revolutionary theorists and "hare-brained schemers," whose blueprints for the new society not only attracted disciples among the Communist cultural militants but also in many cases gained solid institutional support.

I

Cultural revolution was initiated as a revolution from above. The Shakhty trial—and the subsequent show trials of the "Industrial Party" (1930), the Mensheviks (1931), and other groups accused of conspiracy and sabotage—can be seen as a mobilization strategy designed to create an atmosphere of crisis and to justify the regime's demands for sacrifice and extraordinary efforts in the cause of industrialization. The trials built on the popular fears aroused by the war scare of 1927, and purported to demonstrate that the "wreckers and saboteurs" of the bourgeois intelligentsia were potential allies of the encircling capitalist powers in the event of a renewed military intervention. The wreckers also served as scapegoats for economic failures, shortages of consumer goods, and a general fall in urban living standards as resources were channeled into the priority area of heavy industry.

In cultural revolution, as in the earlier war scare, the mobilization strategy had the additional purpose of discrediting Stalin's opponents in the Politburo. From the beginning of 1928 Rykov and Bukharin had opposed Stalin on the crucial political issues of use of force against the peasantry and industrialization tempos. Through 1928 a great deal of the energy of the propagandists of class-war cultural revolution was devoted to demonstrating that the same Party "Rightists" who were inclined to conciliate the kulaks were also conciliators of the bourgeois intelligentsia, and thus opponents of cultural revolution.

This was certainly true of Rykov, who, as head of the Soviet government (chairman of the All-Union Sovnarkom), was seen by contemporaries as the major political figure of the Right. Rykov objected to introducing the "class issue" in the discussion on training of engineers that followed the disclosure of the Shakhty wrecking;[6] and, by quoting Lenin's statements on the need to work with bourgeois specialists, he tried to convince the Politburo that persecution of engineers was the wrong policy.[7]

But Rykov's position may not originally have been a factional one. He was the only Rightist leader with a background in industry, and it was the "industrialists" of the Party leadership who best knew the value of the bourgeois engineers and were most likely to defend them. Like Rykov, the present and future heads of Vesenkha (Kuibyshev and Ordzhonikidze) both reacted to the announcement of the Shakhty trial with public warnings against the danger of *spetseedstvo*. [8] But, since Kuibyshev and Ordzhonikidze were clearly Stalin supporters committed to high tempos of industrialization, their doubts were evidently practical and not ideological or motivated by factional interest.

In contrast, Tomskii—the Rightist head of the trade unions—expressed no concern for the bourgeois specialist or opposition to the principle of class-war cultural revolution. It was, indeed, as natural that the representative of organized labor should support cultural revolution, as a policy offering workers the chance of upward mobility, as that he should oppose the increased powers of management *vis-à-vis* labor that were a concomitant of high-speed industrialization. Throughout 1928 Tomskii behaved more as trade-union spokesman than as a member of a unified Rightist group. The trade unions, for example, were at odds with Narkompros on the question of labor training. In mid-1928, when Rykov and Bukharin were making support for Narkompros one of the issues of contention with the Stalinist group in the Politburo,[9] Tomskii joined the cultural-revolutionary attack on the commissariat.[10]

Bukharin's relation to the new doctrine of cultural revolution was more complicated. His official positions as head of the Comintern and editor of *Pravda* gave him no institutional interest in defending the bourgeois specialists; and he does not in fact seem to have expressed early objections to the Shakhty trial. His record on the issue of cultural class war was contradictory. On the one hand, he had opposed the "proletarian" RAPP and defended the "bourgeois" non-Party writers in the literary debate of 1924–25; and in doing so he had expressed what was then a leadership consensus that "our policy in general does not follow the line of fanning class war but, on the contrary, goes some way to damp it down".[11] On the other hand, he was the only member of the Party leadership who had been actively involved in the earlier "proletarian" movement in culture (the Civil War Proletkult), and, unlike Rykov, he was capable of taking at least a rhetorically threatening Communist stance toward the bourgeois intelligentsia. [12]

Stylistic evidence points to Bukharin as the author of *Pravda*'s first editorial statement on the cultural implications of the Shakhty trial, which advocated a militant proletarian isolationism in culture, very much in the spirit of the old Proletkult manifestoes. The proletariat and proletarian Party needed an "armor of proletarian culture" to protect themselves from "alien class influences, bourgeois degeneration, petty-bourgeois waverings, dulling of revolutionary vigilance in the face of the more cultured class enemy," *Pravda* stated. [13]

If this was in fact Bukharin's position, it was closer to class-war cultural revolution than to conciliation. But it became clear very quickly that, whatever Bukharin's opinion of the moment, he was going to be labelled as an opponent of cultural revolution. A few days after the *Pravda* editorial, the agitprop department of the Central Committee held a meeting on current cultural tasks. Lunacharskii and other known conciliators of the bourgeois intelligentsia were attacked. In an unusual omission, the *Pravda* editorial was not cited in the keynote speech by Krinitskii, head of the agitprop department. Instead, Krinitskii went out of his way to suggest that Bukharin opposed the new policy—not mentioning him by name, but referring to his well-known statement of 1925 against "fanning the class war" in culture. "Some comrades," Krinitskii said, "may perhaps reproach me: have I not talked too much about the revival of class war, the attempts at bourgeois counter-attack against the triumphant march of the proletariat, the need to give a decisive rebuff to each and every kind of bourgeois maneuver? Isn't this 'fanning the class war'?..." [14]

It is doubtful, therefore, that the three Politburo Rightists took a united stand on the issue of class-war cultural revolution in the spring of 1928. But in political terms this issue was secondary. The important thing was that the Rightists disagreed with Stalin on industrialization tempos and the peasant question. Because of this, Stalin no doubt wished to discredit them by all available means; and, as will be argued later in this essay, "softness" on the bourgeois intelligentsia was a position that the working-class majority of rank-and-file Party members were likely to condemn.

From the fact that class-war cultural revolution was used to discredit Stalin's political opponents, it seems probable that the initiative in introducing the new policy came from Stalin or his supporters. The evidence, however, is largely circumstantial. One source states, evidently on the basis of contemporary Party rumors, that the decision to stage the Shakhty trial was made by Stalin over the objections of Rykov, Kuibyshev, and Iagoda, the head of the GPU.[15]

In the second half of 1928, during Stalin's battle with the Rightists in the Politburo and the Moscow Party Committee, cultural revolution received remarkably detailed coverage in the press, with the commentaries that persistently associated the "counterrevolutionary" tendencies of the bourgeois intelligentsia with the "rightist danger" within the Party. Since "rightist danger" in effect meant opposition to Stalin, the association was presumably made on Stalin's behalf, if not on his personal initiative.

The press coverage of 1928 was heavy with innuendo, since the exact location of the political "rightist danger" had not yet been disclosed. Only one cultural Rightist was clearly identified, and that was Sviderskii— removed from the Russian Commissariat of Agriculture because of policy disagreements in the spring of 1928, and from that time head of the Narkompros arts administration. At Narkompros, Sviderskii had no real line because he had no expertise: he was convicted in advance of cultural "rightism" because he had been a Rightist in agriculture.[16]

Lunacharskii and his colleagues at Narkompros were also accused of cultural "rightism," although, with the exception of Krupskaia, they were not in fact politically associated with Stalin's opponents in the Politburo. However, between April and July 1928 the Central Committee was discussing the question of transfer of control of higher technical schools from Narkompros to Vesenkha; and on this issue Rykov and Bukharin apparently supported Narkompros, while Stalin and Molotov supported Vesenkha.[17] In the summer of 1928 Khodorovskii, the head of Narkompros's technical-education administration, was dismissed, and Vyshinskii appointed in his place.[18] Since Vyshinskii had just served as presiding judge at the Shakhty trial, there was the disturbing possibility that his Narkompros assignment was in the same line of duty—and in fact the second of the show trials (the "Industrial Party" trial of 1930) featured Vyshinskii as prosecutor, charging a number of experts formerly sympathetic to Narkompros's position on engineering training with "wrecking," and citing a volume edited for Narkompros by Khodorovskii as one of the basic documents on which the prosecution had built its case.[19]

These links were enough to connect the cultural "rightism" of Narkompros with the political "rightism" of Rykov and Bukharin and the wrecking activities of the bourgeois specialists. Stalin's supporters did not neglect to point this out. What was the "rightist danger in art"? Krinitskii offered two answers. On the one hand, it was the danger of bourgeois influence, or of excessive Communist susceptibility to such influence. On the other, it was "the rightist danger in the ranks of the Party transferred into the language of art."[20]

As the cultural revolution gathered momentum, it became clear that Bukharin was to be its exemplary victim among the political Rightists. This was probably because Bukharin, unlike Rykov or Tomskii, actually was an intellectual with literary and artistic interests and some bourgeois literary friends. He could plausibly be included in the category of "Communist *literati*" of whom Stalin spoke contemptuously both before and after the cultural revolution—those who "sat for years in [European] cafes, drank beer, and were nevertheless unable to learn Europe or to understand it,"[21] and who, on returning to Russia, lacked the stamina to remain in the leadership during successive periods of crisis.[22] Bukharin, moreover, was on bad terms with the leading vigilantes of cultural revolution: both the RAPP leadership and the Komsomol Central Committee had taken the brunt of his sarcasm and no doubt had personal scores to settle.[23]

As Communist scholars in the professions established ascendancy over the local bourgeoisie, their tendency was to fall into warring factions exchanging accusations of political deviation. The deviations most frequently mentioned were "Trotskyite-Menshevist" and "Bukharinist." The scholarly attacks on Bukharin began in the Communist Academy's Institute of World Economy and Institute of Philosophy in 1929.[24] A few months earlier, Bukharin had been appointed head of the Vesenkha administration of scientific and technical research institutes. This was not only a politically unrewarding post but a compromised one: Bukharin replaced an earlier opposition leader, Kamenev; Kamenev moved to the still less desirable position of head of the Chief (Foreign) Concessions Committee formerly held by Trotskii;[25] and Trotskii had just been expelled from the Soviet Union altogether. These appointments provided an apt illustration—and, given Stalin's cast of mind, probably not an accidental one—of the downward path: oppositionism led to association with the bourgeois intelligentsia, then to dealings with international capitalism, and finally to disgrace and exclusion from Communist society.

The leadership struggles of the twenties had developed the politics of rumor, smear, and guilt by association into a fine art. These techniques were fully in evidence in the cultural-revolutionary campaign against the Right. The anti-Right propaganda created the image of a continuum running from the Politburo Right through Narkompros and the bourgeois intelligentsia to the Shakhty wreckers. As scientific research chief at Vesenkha, Bukharin was virtually bound to associate himself in some way with a "technocratic interest,"[26] thus discrediting himself further. Lunacharskii, who left Narkompros in the autumn of 1929, became the victim of rumors that portrayed him as a kind of Communist cultural Nepman, corrupted by privilege, foreign travel, and the good life.[27] Both Bukharin and Lunacharskii were elected to the Academy of Sciences (under Party pressure)[28] at a time when their political fortunes were at their lowest ebb and the Academy itself was being pilloried in the press as the last refuge of aristocratic internal emigres.

Cultural revolution carried the message that conciliators of the peasantry, conciliators of the intelligentsia, bureaucrats (the press represented Narkompros as the archetypal "bureaucratic" commissariat), Nepmen, kulaks, cafe-haunting *literati*, wreckers, expropriated capitalists, and foreign spies were all on the same side in the political struggle and collectively represented the "rightist danger" to the Party. Stalin's political opponents were not yet accused of direct communication with foreign espionage agents, as they were to be in the show trials of the late thirties. But for a potential Communist leader, the suggestion of association with the privileged and anti-Communist bourgeois intelligentsia was damaging enough.

II

Our discussion so far has dealt with an aspect of cultural revolution that appears directed and manipulated from above. But this is only one part of the picture. Cultural revolution also involved a response on the part of the leadership to pressures within the Communist movement and the society as a whole. The class-war concept of confrontation between proletariat and bourgeoisie reflected real social tensions between the materially disadvantaged and the privileged. The antibureaucratic drive of cultural revolution—often verging on an attack on established authority per se—

reflected real grievances of the younger generation. Within the professions, Communists and non-Communists tended to gather in potentially antagonistic camps: the appeal for "proletarian hegemony" in scholarship and the arts did not originally come from the Party leadership, but from groups within the professions and scholarly institutions. The specific forms that cultural revolution took in different areas were largely determined by existing tensions and conflicts. From this perspective, cultural revolution was not only an attempt to resolve the contradictions of NEP, but a product of those contradictions.

The class-war component of cultural revolution was built on a solid foundation of working-class and Communist tradition. In this connection, it is important to remember that in the period after Lenin's death both Party and Komsomol took in large new enrollments of workers. By the First Five-Year Plan period, they were mass organizations with predominantly working-class membership: in 1930, 56.3 percent of Party members were of working-class origin and 46.3 percent were workers by current occupation.[29] This may have made them more amenable to manipulation by politically sophisticated leaders, as is often suggested in the Western literature, but it surely also made the leaders more sensitive to the working-class opinions and grievances expressed within their Party constituency.

A militant class-war tradition in the Party, however, predated the mass recruitment of workers after Lenin's death. It developed during the Civil War—another big period of lower-class recruitment—when the Party became a fighting organization that identified its enemies in class terms. Besides the foreign interventionists, the "class enemies" of the Bolsheviks during the Civil War were the capitalists, the kulaks, the clergy, and the intelligentsia.

Despite the revolutionary tradition of the Russian intelligentsia, almost none of its members supported the Bolsheviks in the first months after October. Even students were overwhelmingly opposed to the October revolution; teachers in Petrograd and Moscow went on strike; professional associations refused to recognize Soviet power. During the Civil War, the provincial intelligentsia largely supported the Whites, and many followed the retreating White armies. Large numbers of prominent cultural figures drifted south from the capitals: some later left the Crimea with the evacuation of Wrangel's army, while others, still doubtful and suspicious of the new regime, returned to Moscow or Petrograd.

The Old Bolsheviks were surprised and indignant at the solid hostility of the intelligentsia, but remained cautious about classifying the intelligentsia as an outright enemy of the revolution. However, this was not the attitude of the Civil War recruits to the Party, nor probably of the post-Civil War Party as a whole. Rank-and-file Communists continued to regard the intelligentsia as a class enemy, despite the leadership's policy of conciliation of the "bourgeois specialist," introduced at the beginning of NEP.

Throughout NEP, many Communists regarded the toleration of bourgeois specialists as a limited and revocable tactic, similar to that governing the Party's relations with kulaks, Nepmen, and priests. The ambivalent attitude of the Old Bolshevik leaders was, indeed, a difficult one to communicate to Communists of the post-October generation. The intelligentsia was described as "bourgeois," yet its members—unlike Nepmen, kulaks, and priests—had the vote, and were supposed to be respected for their skills. In the mid-twenties, the Party leaders sometimes went to considerable lengths to assure the intelligentsia of their goodwill.[30] But they did not repudiate the idea of class war. The NEP policy, in Bukharin's words, was not to fan the flames.

One of the reasons that members of the intelligentsia were officially referred to as "bourgeois specialists" was that in Communist usage the term "intelligentsia" was pejorative. Proletarian and Communist students in Soviet universities during NEP were warned against succumbing to *"intelligentshchina."* The Communist students who voted for Trotskii in 1923–24 were held to be corrupted by *intelligentshchina* and the "petty-bourgeois environment" of NEP. The youth cult of the poet Esenin after his suicide in 1925 was condemned in similar terms.

NEP provided further grounds for resentment, since in social terms it meant an acceptance of privilege and inequality. The Civil War had acted as a leveller by temporarily reducing the entire urban population to near subsistence conditions. The effect of NEP was to make at least some sections of the population more prosperous. But at the same time there was widespread unemployment in the towns, affecting primarily unskilled workers and the young, but also intermittently touching skilled workers, trade unionists, and Party members.

With some exceptions, the intelligentsia rose quickly from the poverty of the Civil War years. By the mid-twenties, the old intelligentsia of the capitals clearly constituted a privileged group that, in material terms, was part of an emerging "Soviet bourgeoisie." Specialists employed by government agencies earned very high salaries. Professors, despite their vociferous complaints of ill treatment, had high salaries and a number of special privileges in areas like housing priority and access to higher education for their children. White-collar workers as a group earned more than industrial workers, were less liable to unemployment, and were better housed.[31]

To many Communists—especially those whose standards of living had not risen with those of the professionals and "bureaucrats"—the cafes and cabarets of the NEP city symbolized a shameful retreat from revolutionary ideals. The clientele of these cafes—Nepmen, Soviet bureaucrats, members of the literary and artistic intelligentsia[32]—combined those apparently disparate categories of the urban population that came under heaviest attack during the cultural revolution.

In discussing cultural revolution as a response to social grievances, it is also necessary to consider the cultural revolutionaries' claim that in 1927–28 the Soviet system was threatened with an actual "bourgeois attack" (*nastuplenie*). To some extent, of course, this can be related to the supposed external threat provoking the war scare of 1927. But there were other specific causes of concern. In 1927–28 there was an outburst of anti-Communist organization by schoolchildren, sometimes overtly political, sometimes aggressively apolitical as in the case of the Esenin cult.[33] The schools most affected were the "bourgeois" urban secondary schools. In the countryside, contemporary Soviet sources reported that the churches were making an unprecedented number of converts among peasant youth. Two million young people were said to be enrolled in religious youth organizations in 1928, and the Baptist "Bapsomol" and Mennonite "Mensomol" supposedly had more members together than the Soviet Komsomol.[34]

The Shakhty trial itself represented a response to an alleged bourgeois threat. No evidence to support the concrete allegations of sabotage and conspiracy has been produced by Soviet historians in the post-Stalin period, and some Soviet accounts come close to saying outright that the trial was fraudulent. Nevertheless, the possibility remains that, in a more general sense, rank-and-file Communists were inclined to believe that such a threat existed, and even perhaps to suspect the Party leadership of falling dangerously under the influence of its bourgeois specialists.

This suspicion was not totally implausible. For example, at a congress of the scientific intelligentsia held early in 1927, Academician S. F. Oldenburg and Professor N. Ia. Marr launched a violent attack on Lunacharskii for not trying hard enough to raise scientific budgets and academic salaries. The scientists seemed to be implying that if Narkompros failed to satisfy them, they were confident of obtaining high-level Party support. Not only did Lunacharskii bear the attack meekly, but, when the incident was mentioned at a meeting of the Congress of Soviets shortly afterwards, a damper appeared to be put on criticism of the scientists.[35] All this was reported in the daily press, leaving readers free to conclude that leaders of the organized non-Party intelligentsia thought that their irreplaceable skills allowed them to negotiate on equal terms with Soviet power, and that at least some persons in the Party leadership agreed.

A few months later, in an article published in November 1927, Lunacharskii wrote in guarded terms of the revival of the prerevolutionary concept of *"narodnicheskaia intelligentokratiia"*—an almost untranslatable coinage suggesting a meritocracy of non-Marxist intellectuals. The intelligentsia, Lunacharskii said, were "awaiting a call from Soviet power to bring the most valuable elements of the aristocracy of the mind into the highest organs of the government." This was a dangerous situation, because there were people who "would like to create a conflict on the issue of participation of 'chosen intellectuals' in power." If such a conflict occurred, Lunacharskii warned, the bourgeois specialists' confidence that Narkompros and their other government employers could protect them might turn out to be misplaced.[36]

III

It may be that genuine fears of an emerging and politically ambitious *intelligentokratiia* were in part responsible for the arrests and prison sentences that were one aspect of cultural revolution. If so, the Party leadership's fears evidently centered on the engineering profession and, to a lesser extent, the Academy of Sciences. In the Academy, more than one hundred workers—including a few Academicians, a number of historians, and Secretary Oldenburg's assistant—were arrested in 1929 and 1930, and many of these spent the remainder of the cultural revolution period in exile or imprisonment.[37] The engineers suffered *en masse*. The Smolensk Archive contains a report, dated June 1928, that twenty out of forty local engineers were under GPU suspicion, together with a request that "if possible, specialists should not be pulled out in bunches but gradually, so as not to denude industry."[38] Kendall Bailes[39] quotes contemporary estimates of arrests of engineers ranging from two thousand to seven thousand—most of them presumably coming from the group of university-trained engineers currently working in large-scale industry and numbering somewhat over ten thousand. Arrest, of course, was not necessarily followed by imprisonment. But a report of April 1929 from the engineering union VMBIT stated that "after the Shakhty affair the number of engineers in production jobs declined by 17%,"[40] evidently through imprisonment and the flight of engineers fearing arrest.

Another kind of purge—not involving arrest, but dismissal from a job or expulsion from a school—was going on at the same time. Its victims were "bureaucrats" and "social aliens," and for a number of reasons it deserves to be considered as a phenomenon distinct from the police purging, despite an area of overlap. The main difference between the two (besides the obvious difference to the individual victim between being fired and being arrested) was that antibureaucratic and social purging was to a large extent a product of local initiative and an expression of strongly felt grievances against privilege and the "bureaucratic degeneration" of the revolution.

One could, of course, point to the existence of such grievances against the "bourgeois engineer" in the factory: workers commonly resented the privileges offered to persons associated with the old regime, and Communist directors often clashed with non-Party chief engineers. But the post-Shakhty arrests of engineers were not in any direct sense products of these grievances. Local authorities took action against the engineers as a result of central instructions. If they did not take action, they were rebuked, and in uncovering "wrecking and sabotage" they were expected to follow the Shakhty model quite closely.[41]

The pattern of antibureaucratic and social purging was different. Here, central initiative and instructions *followed* widespread local practice, and sometimes contradicted it. There was no original central model for local authorities to imitate. The decisions of the leadership that did most to stimulate social purging—for example, the high "proletarian percentages" recommended to universities and technical schools after the July 1928 plenum of the Central Committee, or the tightening of franchise qualifications for the Soviet elections of 1929—were framed with other policy considerations in mind, and at most could only be said to imply a tolerance of social purging of institutions.

But social purging seems to have been an activity that required only absence of discouragement from the center to flourish, for good Communists had always been suspicious of "bureaucrats" and "class aliens." Cultural revolution produced an upsurge of a condition that had been chronic since 1917 and remained so through the 1930s. (On purging as an endemic phenomenon of Soviet life, see Lewin, this volume, pp. 56, 77.) Like most chronic conditions, this one had a tendency to flare up under stress. A society undergoing rapid industrialization, faced with food procurement problems, and aware of the possibility of foreign intervention, war, and internal collaboration with the enemy was under a high degree of stress. The result was that the activists of the society turned on those whom they had traditionally suspected, using the familiar method of the institutional purge.

The Komsomol initiated the antibureaucratic movement with its "light cavalry" raids on the government *apparat* during the rationalization campaign of 1927. These were mainly directed against corrupt and incompetent bureaucrats, but the offense was naturally judged more harshly if committed by an old *"chinovnik"* (Tsarist employee) of doubtful social origin. From 1928 purges of the *apparat* were conducted locally by whatever organization—Komsomol, Party, soviet or worker-peasant inspection—considered itself particularly vigilant. These purges are described by a Soviet historian as "spontaneous" and conducted essentially on the basis of social criteria. He reports that in the Irkutsk okrug, for example, "800 persons—former officers, policemen and *chinovniki*—were driven out of government institutions. In their places 130 persons, mainly Communists and workers from industry, came to work."[42]

Local Party committees conducted extensive purges of the universities, expelling sons and daughters of kulaks, priests, merchants, Tsarist officers, and (less frequently) intellectuals and state employees. These purges come into a special and rather peculiar category, in terms of the source of initiative: they were more or less secretly sponsored by the Party Central Committee and more or less openly opposed by the republican education commissariats.[43]

Spontaneous local purging of the secondary schools followed. Government condemnations of social purging were published in the central press, including *Pravda*, but had little effect. In early 1929, however, the situation became extremely complicated when *Pravda* published an editorial that, in somewhat Aesopian language, appeared to sanction school purging.[44] This heartened local Komsomol groups, which were in the forefront of the school purging movement, and discouraged local *apparatchiki* of the educational departments who were trying to follow Narkompros instructions. In Smolensk, for example, the education department had just succeeded in convincing the local Party committee *not* to purge the schools when the *Pravda* editorial appeared. Soon after, "a group of young people turned up in the education department and announced that we had to start a purge."[45]

There was a functional explanation for the school purges, in that local authorities were under pressure to improve the "proletarian percentage" in the schools, and it was easier to expel or refuse to admit "socially alien" children than to recruit children of workers. But there were various and conflicting pressures on local authorities, and the actions of local Communists were often determined by their own assumption that only workers had an absolute right to education, while the rights of other groups—like their right to vote—were conditional and subject to instant withdrawal. The Russian Narkompros took a principled stand against social purging, but in doing so felt that it opposed the will of the working-class and Communist majority. As V. N. Iakovleva, the deputy commissar of education, remarked with unusual frankness, "If we educational leaders are going to say 'yes' to all these decisions which the masses demand, and are not going to stand up for our point of view energetically, . . . then the masses will not even learn from their mistakes. . . . It is a question of cultural leadership, and our country is uncultured."[46]

The most lively antibureaucratic campaign was conducted by the Komsomol, whose activities resembled those reported of the "Red Guards" in the Chinese cultural revolution of the 1960s. The Komsomol was a traditional enemy of bureaucracy, but for most of the NEP period its antibureaucratic enthusiasm was regarded with some suspicion by the Party leadership, since it was associated with a tendency to support Party Oppositions and accuse the leadership of "bureaucratic degeneracy." Stalin, it is true, encouraged the Komsomol attacks on bureaucracy in 1928, probably because the campaign against the "bureaucratic" trade union leadership, in particular, was serving a useful purpose from his point of view.[47] But it would be a considerable over-simplification to see the Komsomol simply as a Stalinist tool in its cultural revolution campaign against bureaucracy. *Komsomol'skaia pravda* was firing in every direction, but its main targets make sense in terms of Komsomol priorities, not Stalin's: the newspaper spent more space in 1928 denouncing the (presumably "Stalinist") bureaucrats of Vesenkha for their stand on adolescent employment and training than it did in attacking the "Rightist" bureaucrats of the trade unions; and its favorite Rightist target was the politically insignificant conductor of the Bolshoi Theatre orchestra—the "bourgeois specialist" Golovanov, who was later to be a recipient of a Stalin Prize.

The Komsomols were enthusiasts of cultural revolution, which they understood in the most iconoclastic sense as an overturning of "reactionary" and "bureaucratic" authority. They treated cultural revolution as a replay of the October Revolution and Civil War, in which many of them had been too young to participate. It sometimes seemed that they were engaged not so much in class war as in a class war game: "fortresses" like the traditionalist Bolshoi Theatre and the Academy of Sciences had to be "stormed"; cultural "fronts" had to be defended against bourgeois counterattacks; popular illiteracy had to be liquidated by a "Cultural Army" with the aid of "cultural ambushes" (*kul'tzasady*), "cultural bombs" (*kul'tbomby*) and "cultural espionage" (*kul'trazvedka*).[48]

It was characteristic of the Komsomol that its chief cultural-revolutionary initiative—the "cultural campaign" or *kul'tpokhod* against illiteracy[49]—should have been conducted in quasi-military style, and been directed not only against illiteracy but against the educational bureaucracy that had so far failed to cope with the problem. Adult education, including the teaching of literacy, came under the jurisdiction of local education departments. The departments, which were part of the local Soviet *apparat* with appointed officials, were regarded by the Komsomol as quintessentially bureaucratic organizations. As an alternative organizational form, the Komsomol Central Committee first proposed reviving the popularly elected "educational soviet" with which Narkompros had briefly experimented in 1918.[50]

However, the 1928–29 *kul'tpokhod* against illiteracy produced its own organizational form—the "cultural General Staff" or *kul'tshtab*. This was established on an ad hoc basis, if possible under the patronage of the local Party committee, to recruit volunteers for the teaching of literacy and to raise funds for the purpose by eliciting voluntary contributions from the population and subsidies from local organizations like the trade unions, the cooperatives, and industrial enterprises.

The *kul'tshtaby* had no paid officials and no budget. But in certain areas, like Saratov, their achievements in the literacy campaign of 1928–29 were considerable, and they were praised by the Party leadership for their energy, enthusiasm, and low-cost results.[51] The Party leadership clearly had no thought of dismantling the existing education departments and replacing them with improvised *kul'tshtaby*. But this was the objective of the *kul'tpokhod* enthusiasts. As the Saratov organizer put it, "we began [our] work outside the education system. . . . And that work was in fact an attack on the education authorities and an attempt to reorganize the education system on new bases."[52]

The education departments had dual subordination to the local soviets and the central Narkompros. Narkompros might have been expected to react very negatively to demands for the abolition of local departments, but in fact—partly because the departments were not very effectively subordinated to Narkompros, partly because the Narkompros leadership itself was susceptible to arguments against bureaucracy and in favor of revolutionary popular participation in government—the reaction was relatively sympathetic.

A popular mass movement for cultural revolution had developed outside the educational bureaucracy, Narkompros informed its local departments in an excited and somewhat incoherent document of mid 1929.

> Like every revolution, it proceeds spontaneously (*stikhiino*) to a considerable extent. Many of us did not understand, and some of us to this day do not understand, that the very cultural revolution which we urged and of which we talked so much is already developing before our eyes. Many people imagined cultural revolution as a process coming from above. . . .

[But] in fact the cultural revolution, like all revolutions, arose and is developing as a mass movement, a movement which is continually changing its form....[53]

Shortly afterwards, *Pravda* called for mass initiative in the rooting out of "bureaucratic methods," and the Party leadership approved the creation of educational soviets as advisory bodies to the education departments.[54] These were essentially not policies of leadership initiative, but of leadership response to what was already going on. Narkompros's response went even further. Early in 1930 it was considering abandoning its departments altogether in favor of soviets with partly elected, partly delegated membership.[55]

However, with official sponsorship the spontaneous and potentially anarchic elements of antibureaucratic cultural revolution tended to disappear. The *kul'tpokhod* was warmly praised for its achievements in literacy at the Sixteenth Party Congress in the summer of 1930, but meanwhile the Central Committee had found a fine bureaucratic solution to the question of local forms of educational organization: the departments (*otdely narodnogo obrazovaniia*) were to remain, but they were now to be called *organy narodnogo obrazovaniia* to indicate repudiation of their past bureaucratic tendencies.[56]

The same waning of spontaneity can be observed in the movement of social purging. After a year of sporadic and disorganized social purging of institutions, the Sixteenth Party Conference (held in the spring of 1929) decided to authorize a formal purge of the entire government bureaucracy. The central commissariats were purged in the winter of 1929–30 by commissions of Rabkrin (the Commissariat of Worker-Peasant Inspection), backed up by brigades of workers from Moscow factories. Throughout the country about a million and a half Soviet employees went through the purge, and 164,000 were fired.[57] The purge was described as part of the general campaign against Rightism, exemplifying the militant proletarian class line. But it was in fact a bureaucratic purge of bureaucracy, quite efficiently conducted by Rabkrin in a spirit of organizational rationality.[58] The theme of class enemies was comparatively little emphasized, at least in the center, and voluntary participation and initiative were almost completely absent.

I V

The nature of cultural revolution within the professions was complex. "Class war" in this area was conducted by and on behalf of groups that only *claimed* to be proletarian, but in fact consisted of Communist intellectuals of overwhelmingly white-collar or intelligentsia background. The Communist intellectuals were often extremely aggressive, but at the same time unsure of their own credentials. They tended to question their own value to society, suggest that factory workers could do their jobs better, and waver on the brink of demanding liquidation of the intelligentsia as a class. What one observer called "the disease of self-flagellation in a collective of intellectuals"[59] became epidemic during cultural revolution.

In essence, cultural revolution in the professions meant that Communists were encouraged to go for all-out victory in existing professional conflicts. To some extent, these conflicts were already perceived in class-war terms—particularly in the universities, where the so-called proletarian nucleus of students really was predominantly working-class, and the professors often emphasized their own "bourgeois" or prerevolutionary orientation.

During NEP, from the standpoint of Communists in the professions, there was a confrontation of the new Communist culture and the "establishment" culture of the old intelligentsia. The old intelligentsia, however, saw no such cultural confrontation, but only a political threat to culture per se. (The threat, as the old intelligentsia saw it, came from the regime rather than from the Communist professionals, most of whom were young, former students, and not to be taken seriously.) Thus, paradoxically, both Communist and "bourgeois" intellectuals regarded themselves as underdogs during NEP, each group considering that the other had special and undeserved advantages.

The most striking example of an existing and already politicized professional conflict was in literature—probably the only profession where it could be claimed that Communists achieved power during cultural revolution almost entirely as a result of their own efforts. The Communist militants' group was RAPP, an association founded by young intellectuals in the early twenties for the promotion of proletarian literature. By 1924, RAPP was already clamoring for a mandate from the Central Committee to establish the hegemony of "proletarian" Communists over "bourgeois fellow-travellers," and the 1925 Central Committee decree on literature was in effect a refusal of such a mandate.

RAPP's original base was the Komsomol, and in particular the Komsomol journal *Molodaia gvardiia*. This connection is important, for in many respects RAPP's development in the twenties is best understood not in the context of literary debate but in that of generational conflict within the Communist movement. Both RAPP and Komsomol leaderships were chronic sufferers from the disease that Bukharin called "revolutionary avant-gardism." They tended to suspect the older generation of succumbing to the temptations of power, losing revolutionary momentum, and falling into bureaucratic lethargy. They were potential supporters of any "revolutionary" opposition (and, by the same token, enemies of any moderate opposition to a revolutionary leadership). Even after thorough purging of Trotskyites and Zinovievites, the RAPP (then VAPP) and Komsomol Central Committee position on social and cultural questions was hard to distinguish from the platform of the 1926–27 Opposition in its criticism of social privileges and inequality, emphasis on the grievances of working-class youth, contempt for "bourgeois" literature and "bourgeois" schools, and calls for Communist vigilance and class war.[60]

Nevertheless, the RAPP leaders commended themselves to the Party leadership by repenting their former Oppositionism and savagely attacking oppositionist tendencies (real or imagined) in other literary groups. By 1928 RAPP, still lacking a formal mandate, had assumed leadership in the campaign to unmask the "rightist danger" in the arts and scholarship. Between 1928 and 1932, the RAPP leaders exercised a repressive and cliquish dictatorship over literary publication and criticism. This dictatorship, supposedly in the name of the proletarian Party, was in fact not under effective Central Committee control.[61]

During the cultural revolution, there was intense competition between the RAPP leaders and the Communist radicals of the Communist Academy and Institute of Red Professors ("schoolboys playing professors" [*professorstvuiushchie shkol'niki*], as a RAPP leader unkindly described them[62]). Protagonists on both sides had political ambitions within the Party and attempted to discredit each other by accusations of political deviation. This tendency was widespread among Communist intellectuals, and was, of course, encouraged by the use of cultural revolution as a weapon against the Right Opposition in the Party. (The accusations of "left deviation," made in 1930 and 1931 against those who had been too extreme in attacking the "rightist danger" or had former Trotskyite connections, reflected a rather heavy-handed attempt by the Party leadership to subdue the militant cultural revolutionaries and normalize the atmosphere in the professions.)

The relationship of the Party leadership to the activists of cultural revolution has puzzled both Western and Soviet historians. The activists usually claimed to have a Party mandate, but it was rare that anything resembling a mandate was actually published or even written down. One of the best descriptions of the relationship came from the first of RAPP's Communist victims (Voronskii, editor of the literary journal *Krasnaia nov'*), who wrote indignantly to the Central Committee press department: "You have unleashed the young comrades, given them such rights and privileges that they have lost all sense of proportion, lost humility. . . . You have unleashed them, comrade Gusev."[63]

The image of "unleashing" can be applied to groups other than the young Communist militants. Cultural revolution also unleashed the "visionaries" (as Frederick Starr describes them in this volume) and "cranks" (David Joravsky's term) of the NEP period, many of whom are memorably described in Fulop-Miller's *The Mind and Face of Bolshevism*.[64] These characters were usually outsiders in their professions, excited by the revolution but not necessarily Communists, with a radically innovative theory and a small group of committed disciples.

In the 1920s, all Communists shared to some degree a vision of the future society, transformed by collective spirit, rational scientific organization, and technology. In the Civil War period, and again during the cultural revolution, this vision tended to become intensified and at the same time divorced from practical reality.

Communist visions of Utopia and peasant visions of the coming of Antichrist (frequently reported during the First Five-Year Plan period) arose from the same perception that the familiar world was being destroyed. Until Stalin explicitly denied it in the middle of 1930,[65] many Communist intellectuals thought—as they had during the Civil War—that Engels' prophecy of the withering away of the state was already being realized. Pashukanis's theory of the withering away of law (see Sharlet, this volume) and Shulgin's theory of the withering away of the school (see Lapidus, this volume) gained great impetus from cultural revolution simply because legal and educational institutions seemed to have begun a spontaneous process of self-liquidation. It was observation, not authority or theoretical argument, that gave such ideas currency.

Because cultural revolution was, among other things, an attack on accepted ideas, most of the ideas that flourished under its auspices were radical, and some were distinctly eccentric. Every Communist with a private blueprint, scheme, or invention felt that cultural revolution spoke directly to him. This was also true of non-Communist intellectuals whose projects had previously been ridiculed or ignored. Even government institutions, urged to throw off habits of bureaucratic conservatism, responded to cultural revolution by subsidizing the innovators.

Radical plans for the Socialist City were devised by architects and accepted by planning organizations and building trusts (see Starr, this volume). A government commission considered plans for calendar reform, and some enthusiasts counted 1917 as Year One of the new era. The Institute of Labor, run by a working-class poet, contracted with Vesenkha to train a new labor force on the principles of conditioned reflex. Kagan-Shabshai, a private entrepreneur in the field of engineering training with a grudge against what he called "engineering intellectuals," made very profitable contracts with the industrial trusts to train engineers at "shock-work" tempo. Professor Marr's unorthodox Japhetic theory of language was exalted. Professor Iavorskii's theory of "melodic rhythm," ignored by the reactionary professors of the Moscow Conservatory, was championed by Komsomol music students. The pedologists, who had been struggling to establish a new discipline on the borders of pedagogy and psychology, finally broke down the barriers to their professional establishment in the schools.[66]

Communist intellectuals had tended to have an uneasy relationship with their own disciplines, as was natural both for the Old Bolshevik generation, whose first profession was revolution, and for the young Communists, who felt themselves to be professional outsiders. They might tend toward intellectual abolitionism in their own discipline, like Pokrovskii in history; they might become reductionists, like the literary "sociologists" or the reflexologists in psychology; they might recommend the transformation of literature into journalism or theater into "biomechanics." Cultural revolution brought these transformational and abolitionist tendencies to a climax. Communist intellectuals began to predict the imminent merging of town and countryside, education and industrial production, art and life. These predictions were a kind of running commentary on contemporary processes of institutional disintegration and social flux. They were predictions in which hope and fear were mingled: the cultural revolutionaries' favorite concept of "withering away" (*otmiranie*), however optimistic in Marxist terms, was still in Russian translation a way of dying.

V

We come finally to the movement for "proletarian advancement" (*vydvizhenie*), which was the positive corollary of the campaign against the "bourgeois" intelligentsia and the social purging of the bureaucracy. This theme, very much emphasized in the Soviet literature on "the forming of the Soviet intelligentsia," has been almost ignored in the Western literature. One of the reasons, undoubtedly, is that a great deal of Western research has concentrated on the cultural professions, in which the attack on "bourgeois" authorities was carried out by Communist intellectuals whose only claim to be "proletarian" was their Party membership.

Cultural revolution had, indeed, both pseudoproletarian and genuinely proletarian aspects. In the sphere of pseudoproletarianism, Communist intellectuals sought to make contacts with industrial workers in order to establish their own legitimacy, and Soviet institutions put themselves under the patronage of local factories in order to avoid accusations of bureaucracy. In the rhetoric of cultural revolution, working-class opinion was the touchstone of good and evil, and working-class participation was essential to the success of any undertaking. Thus writers began to read their latest works before factory audiences and worked as consultants on collective histories of industrial enterprises (see Clark, this volume). Universities invited workers to participate in the reelection of professors. Factory brigades were organized to assist the Rabkrin purge of government commissariats. After receiving delegations of Moscow workers (organized by the Komsomol) protesting against its policy of "class neutrality" in education, the collegium of Narkompros began holding its meetings in factories to hear proletarian criticism of its decisions.[67]

The substantive proletarian aspect of cultural revolution was the promotion of workers into responsible jobs and their recruitment to higher education. This was a period of enormous expansion of high-status professional and administrative jobs. Between the end of 1928 and the end of 1932, the numbers of engineers employed in the civilian sector of the Soviet economy rose from 18,000 to 74,000, while the number of professionals employed in administration, government, and exchange rose from 63,000 to 119,000.[68] The policy of the Soviet leadership was to promote industrial workers and Communists of working-class origin into these jobs. The process of promotion usually involved training at a technicum or higher technical school and was often accompanied by entrance into the Party. The radical reorganization of Soviet higher education in the First Five-Year Plan years was in large part determined by the worker-promotion policy and the new emphasis on technical training. The scope of worker promotion through education cannot be judged with complete accuracy because forged documents of social origin were in use, and children of white-collar and peasant families could become "proletarian" by working for a few years in a factory after leaving school. But, even allowing for exaggeration, the figures are impressive: over 120,000 university students in 1931 were classified as workers or children of workers, as against 40,000 in 1928.[69]

By the beginning of the Second Five-Year Plan (1933), half the directors of industrial enterprises and their deputies were former workers.[70] But this was only the top stratum of upwardly mobile workers within industry. As the number of jobs at all levels increased, the plants organized their own training schemes and promoted from within. Unskilled workers moved into skilled jobs; skilled workers became foremen, masters, and technicians; technicians became engineers.

The school system was also reorganized in a way that maximized working-class access to secondary and higher education. For a few years during the First Five-Year Plan, the "bourgeois" general secondary school virtually ceased to exist, while the working-class factory apprenticeship (FZU) schools expanded their enrollment from 1.8 million in 1928 to 3.3 million in 1931.[71] The FZU schools, established in the early twenties to train adolescents entering industry, were supposed to be serving the same purpose during the First Five-Year Plan. In practice, however, the majority of apprentices took the opportunities offered to them as working-class students with secondary education, and went on to technicums and universities.[72]

The worker-promotion policy was clearly part of the "revolution from above." But there is at least a *prima facie* case for seeing the policy as to some extent a leadership response to working-class grievances of the NEP period. According to Narkompros reports of the twenties (based on substantial though unsystematic sampling of public opinion), workers viewed university education as a right won for the working class by the revolution. When working-class access to university was limited, as it was during NEP, this was regarded as a betrayal of promises. But working-class families were unwilling to keep their children in the upper grades of the "bourgeois" general secondary school. Young adult workers should have the opportunity to go to university through the rabfak, and receive a stipend. For working-class adolescents, the preferred school was the FZU, which taught a trade, paid students an industrial wage, and was free of "bourgeois" influence.[73]

The education system that emerged during the First Five-Year Plan—highly irrational from many points of view, including that of industry—corresponded closely to this pattern. But its most striking feature was the emphasis on recruiting adults without a full secondary education to university. This requirement was dictated by the decision of the leadership to send the Party to school. The typical Party member in 1928 was a former worker with primary education.[74] Earlier in the twenties it had been assumed that the future Communist elite should be trained in Marxist social science. But the First Five-Year Plan decision was to train Communists—especially former workers, and including future administrators—in the engineering schools. The imperative in this situation was an education system that allowed adults with primary education to enter higher technical schools and gave priority in enrollment to working-class Communists.

VI

Stalin's rehabilitation of the bourgeois engineers (June 1931)[75] and condemnation of the fruitless theorizing of Communist intellectuals (in the letter to the editors of *Proletarskaia revoliutsiia* published a few months later[76]) mark the end of official sponsorship of cultural revolution. In some areas, this intervention brought ongoing developments to a jarring halt. In others, the revolutionary impulse had already exhausted itself and combatants were locked in bitter scholastic disputes and mutual denunciation.

With or without intervention, there was a natural time limit on cultural revolution as an enthusiastic dismantling of the institutions and conventions of NEP. The pressures for a restoration of order and rebuilding of institutions were, even in the comparatively short run, irresistible.

The finite limits on cultural revolution are particularly evident in the sphere of worker promotion—not the promotion of working-class Communists, which continued at a high level for some years, but the promotion of workers from the factory bench. By 1931, when the factories took the first steps to tighten labor discipline and pull workers back from outside activities,[77] schools and universities were already finding it difficult to meet their proletarian quotas. Recruitment at the factory encountered increasing resistance from the enterprises, which were experiencing an acute shortage of skilled labor. The young workers willing and able to go on to higher education had already volunteered. The traditional working class (now called *kadrovye* or *potomstvennye rabochie*) was depleted by promotion and assignment to the new construction sites, and was swamped by the vast influx of peasants into the industrial labor force.

There were not only practical but also conceptual problems in fighting cultural class war on behalf of a proletariat whose members were to a large extent peasants recently uprooted by collectivization. The imagery of the early thirties was not of battle but of passing on the torch. The Komsomol no longer spoke of *kul'tpokhod* but of *kul'testafeta*, or cultural relay-race. In the factories and new construction sites, experienced workers became exemplars and teachers (*shefy*) to the new arrivals, verbally transmitting the necessary skills and traditions of the industrial working class.

Social discrimination was gradually dropped in educational admissions. The education system was reorganized along lines that were conservative and traditionalist even in comparison with NEP, let alone the ultraradicalism of the cultural revolution. In literature, predictably, the militant proletarians proved difficult to displace, but in 1932 RAPP was dissolved, and by 1934 a new Union of Soviet Writers incorporating all Communist and "bourgeois" groups had been created. In scholarship, the Communist Academy—center of cultural-revolutionary activity— gradually conceded authority to the Old Academy of Sciences and the reconstituted universities. Formerly disgraced "bourgeois" scholars were rehabilitated. Formerly arrested "bourgeois" engineers were released, usually to occupy positions comparable with those they had involuntarily left.

There are three groups whose fate after cultural revolution is of particular interest to us—the Communist intellectuals who had carried out the cultural revolution, the non-Party intellectuals who had suffered from it, and the promoted workers and worker-Communists who formed the core of the new "Soviet intelligentsia."

The Communist intellectuals, suffering the proverbial fate of those who go for a ride on a tiger, turned out to be the ultimate victims of cultural revolution. The general assumption during the cultural revolution had been that the militant radicals had the endorsement of the Stalinist leadership: when Bubnov, for example, replaced the conciliatory Lunacharskii as head of Narkompros in 1929, he found it natural to turn to Shulgin (theorist of the withering away of the school), not because he knew anything about his ideas, but because of the Communist "fighting spirit" he sensed in him.[78] Yet it has already been pointed out that the Stalinist endorsement, if it existed at all, was really a very cautious one. On a few occasions Stalin encouraged belligerent activity against Rightists and bourgeois intellectuals,[79] but he also took occasional action to protect bourgeois victims like the writer Bulgakov, and in a private letter expressed the opinion (which at the time nobody else could possibly have expressed) that the whole campaign against "rightism" in art was based on an absurd premise.[80]

In many fields, the Communist faction-fighting during cultural revolution discredited and demoralized the participants, distracted them from their real work, and ended some promising professional developments of the NEP period. The Communist intelligentsia was far too deeply involved in ideological and factional politics to respond to leadership demands for practically useful work. In fact, it was "politicized" to the point of being virtually useless to the Soviet regime, except in the fields of journalism and agitprop.

In the aftermath of cultural revolution, those of the Communist intellectuals who were not permanently excommunicated as "left" or "right" deviationists were left to make the best of professional careers among presumably hostile ex-bourgeois colleagues and *vydvizhentsy* of completely different life experience and outlook. A few former cultural revolutionaries—the philosophers Iudin and Mitin of the Communist

Academy, the writer Fadeev of RAPP—held prominent positions through the Stalin period, but many more suffered premature eclipses in the purges of the late thirties. In general, the young Communists trained for leadership during NEP in such institutions as the Sverdlov Communist University and the Institute of Red Professors turned into something of a lost generation. What was required of a future Communist leader in the Stalin period was not Marxist social science and polemical skill, but technical training and experience in industrial administration.

The old intelligentsia came out of cultural revolution in better shape than its members had probably expected, or than Western historians have generally recognized. A very large number of "bourgeois" engineers served time in prison or at work under GPU supervision; some distinguished historians died in exile; and many more intellectuals underwent psychological suffering as a result of the cultural revolutionaries' attacks. However, the old intelligentsia as a whole had not been subject to mass arrest, like priests, or mass deportation, like peasants. Its members (except for the relatively small number of engineers working as convict specialists) were not sent out of the capitals to the new construction sites or to the countryside to teach in rural schools, as apparently happened in the Chinese cultural revolution. No form of labor conscription was ever proposed, even for such socially useful specialists as doctors, teachers, and agronomists. Despite the social purging of scholarly institutions, the acute shortage of specialists in all fields meant that only in exceptional circumstances was a "purged" specialist left without professional employment.

The result was that, when the cultural revolution ended and the regime was ready to offer compensation, the old intelligentsia was in a position to receive it. The immediate improvement—not only in comparison with the period of cultural revolution, but also in comparison with NEP—was that the "bourgeois" non-Party intellectuals were no longer subject to attack within their professions by organized Communist groups, or to harassment on grounds of social origin. In many fields, the old professional "establishment" won back its previous authority. Arrested and exiled specialists returned to responsible jobs (sometimes even the same jobs they had held at the time of arrest). Scientific leadership returned to the Academy of Sciences. Traditional artistic institutions like the Bolshoi Theatre recovered preeminence.

But there were more positive gains. As part of a general process of social differentiation in the thirties, the privileges of the intelligentsia relative to society as a whole greatly increased. The leaders of the cultural intelligentsia became part of the highest Soviet elite. The "cultural achievements" of the Soviet Union—which essentially meant the achievements of the old "bourgeois" intelligentsia during the thirties—were acclaimed and rewarded by the regime.[81] A genuine poll of intelligentsia opinion taken, say, in 1934, would surely have recorded increased satisfaction with the regime (not only in comparison with 1929, but also with 1924) and expectations of further improvement to come.

But the "class war" of cultural revolution was waged on behalf of the proletariat, and it was surely the proletarian *vydvizhentsy* (and to a lesser extent *vydvizhentsy* from the peasantry) who emerged as its chief beneficiaries. During cultural revolution, hundreds of thousands of workers from the factory and Communists of working-class origin were promoted into technical jobs, management, and administration, or recruited to higher education.[82] Working-class children were taken into secondary vocational schools in unprecedented numbers, and the vocational schools in this period acted as channels to higher education.

In the years after the cultural revolution, the Soviet Union—like other societies in the process of industrialization—continued to provide great opportunities for upward social mobility simply because of the expansion in numbers of skilled labor and professional and managerial jobs. Although children of white-collar parents had a much better statistical chance of entering higher education during the thirties and forties than children of workers (and children of peasants were in a definitely inferior position), the expansion in higher-status jobs was great enough to leave ample room for the talented and ambitious children of all social classes; and the network of evening and correspondence schools established from 1932 provided additional opportunities for those who had not entered higher education directly.

Nevertheless, the generation promoted during the cultural revolution remained unique in many respects. It was the only group whose promotion—from skilled industrial work, or lower-level political and administrative positions—was the result of a conscious leadership policy and an intensive general campaign. Furthermore, it was the group that was the primary beneficiary of a second social upheaval, the great purge of 1937, which removed much of the top stratum of Communist managerial and administrative personnel. The careers of Aleksei Kosygin and Dmitrii Ustinov (the present Minister of Defence)—both working-class *vydvizhentsy* of the First Five-Year Plan period, graduating respectively in 1935 and 1934, and by 1941 holding ministerial appointments in the government of the USSR—exemplify, if in extreme form, the dizzying rise of thousands. The First Five-Year Plan *vydvizhentsy* are, in fact, the "Brezhnev generation"—the core of the sub-Politburo elite in the forties under Stalin, and of the top political leadership of the fifties and sixties. This is the generation that, more than any other, has influenced the evolution of Soviet political and social culture over almost four decades.

It is appropriate to speculate, in conclusion, on the ways in which the experience of cultural revolution may have influenced the attitudes of this generation to culture and social control. The *vydvizhentsy* were a very different group from the Communist intelligentsia formed during NEP, which provided the militant activists of cultural revolution. Those sent to university during the First Five-Year Plan were in a position to observe the cultural revolutionaries' activities first hand, and it seems likely that many of their observations were unfavorable. The *vydvizhentsy*, by all accounts, were a highly motivated and practical-minded group, interested in acquiring useful knowledge as efficiently as possible. Their studies were undoubtedly made more difficult by the methodological experimentation and organizational chaos produced in the universities by cultural revolution.

The militants of cultural revolution were not only experimenters on the grand scale, but also ideological hair-splitters and obsessive faction-fighters. It would not be surprising if many *vydvizhentsy* came to the conclusion—reinforced by the post-1931 decisions of the Party leadership—that intellectuals of the cultural-revolutionary type were a dangerous breed: factious, vicious, anarchic, and totally lacking in common sense. Certainly the Party leadership of the thirties and forties, of which the "Brezhnev generation" was an increasingly important part, seemed inclined to such an opinion and determined to avoid any repetition of the chaotic "unleashing" of the First Five-Year Plan period.

In the course of the thirties, the *vydvizhentsy* rose into responsible positions and, in most cases, assumed the life style appropriate to a social elite. The new elite's aspirations towards the *kul'turnost'* of classical ballet and orange lamp shades in the postwar period have been vividly described by Vera Dunham.[83] These aspirations were already evident in the second half of the thirties: a landmark of changing attitudes was the 1936 meeting of "wives of industrial managers," attended by Stalin and other Politburo members, at which women of the new elite described their philanthropic efforts to introduce *kul'turnost'* into the factory barracks and communal dining rooms.[84]

Promotion of the "Brezhnev generation" was the major product of cultural revolution, and the subsequent embourgeoisement of the new elite formed the very unrevolutionary cultural climate of the Stalin period. But one cannot discount the importance of the First Five-Year Plan cultural revolution in establishing a model for radical social change. When Khrushchev—one of the older of the First Five-Year Plan *vydvizhentsy*— sought to initiate such change in the late fifties, he not only revived ideas and terminology characteristic of the cultural revolution but also (notably in the education realm) mobilized some former cultural revolutionaries to the task. Like all complex phenomena, the cultural revolution left a complex legacy. But it is a legacy whose understanding is crucial to our interpretation of Soviet historical development.

Society, State, and Ideology during the First Five-Year Plan

M. Lewin

The period 1929–33 is probably one of the most momentous quinquennia in the history of Russia, indeed in modern history. The scholar is astounded by the incredible intensity and scope of the transformation of society, not to speak of the bewildering effect those years had on contemporaries. This was a unique process of state-guided social transformation, for the state did much more than just "guiding": it substituted itself for society, to become the sole initiator of action and controller of all important spheres of life. The process was thus transformed into one of "state building," with the whole social structure being, so to speak, sucked into the state mechanism, as if entirely assimilated by it.

The pace and violence of the changes were breathtaking. In a matter of a few years much of the previous social fabric, Tsarist and Soviet, was dispersed and destroyed. With the destruction came the creation of new patterns, which, although they emerged very rapidly, became permanent. The sense of urgency in the whole upheaval is baffling: the pace imposed suggests a race against time, as if those responsible for the country's destinies felt they were running out of history. The appearance of a new social hierarchy in the thirties was a similarly speedy and contradictory affair: the emerging ruling strata were kept in a state of perpetual tension and were several times knocked out and partly destroyed before they were allowed to settle down. Most of the makers of the upheaval were themselves transformed, engulfed, and annihilated in this prolonged Walpurgis night, thus giving to those years the traits of a real "total drama": nobody was left unharmed, and all the survivors became thoroughly disfigured. This was not surprising. The new world being built was not the better and freer world of the dreamers but a Caliban State. That a progressive ideology, initially intended to enhance human freedom and to create higher forms of community, came to serve a police state is one of the peculiarities of the period and an important phenomenon to study.

1. BEFORE THE PLANS

The Tsarist Heritage

The strictly dramatic point of view would suggest that our study should begin at some idyllic moment before the storm, perhaps 1926. But more prosaic scholarly interests will be better served by starting at about 1922, immediately after the great famine that was the culmination of years of war, revolution, and civil strife. This starting point serves to highlight the fact that the lull between the end of one catastrophe and the onset of a new one (quite different in character) lasted a mere seven years: Russia's body social, shattered in our century by a series of cataclysmic events, has shown an amazing capacity to recover.

The period 1914–21 was unquestionably a demographic earthquake. At the end of it, Russia's population was about thirty million less than would normally have been expected: the shortfall included about sixteen million dead in war and civil war, famine, and epidemics, with the remainder accounted for by the calamities that befell potential parents.[1] These figures are relevant to an understanding of the stresses of the thirties, for the thirty million missing out of the 1923 population contributed to the later serious gaps in the labor force and military manpower.

Before war and revolution, Tsarist Russia had seen a significant advance in industrialization and urbanization, with its cities growing faster than the total population. But the whole urban sector comprised no more than about 18 percent of the population, and the modern industrial sector was even smaller than that: less than one in five of the population lived in towns (most of which were quite small provincial backwaters), and only two in one hundred were employed in manufacturing and mechanical industries, compared to 11.6 in one hundred in the United States.[2] Thus most of the cities were dominated by rather small producers. The educated professional and intellectual segment was also small, and it included more bureaucrats and officers than managers, teachers, scientists, and artists.

Rural Russia was bedeviled by poverty, land hunger, and irritating remnants of the old regime of serfdom, and was in the throes of the social unrest created by the Stolypin reforms. These reforms led to the development of a consolidated smallholder class among the peasantry and to the shattering of the communal system, but the hardship they caused the peasants had painful effects.

Official and educated Russia was notoriously detached and isolated from illiterate and semiliterate rural Russia, though the peasants came to the towns in millions in search of seasonal or full-time employment and formed the bulk of the armed forces. This was a symptom of Russia's "underdevelopment," and one of the most profound.

The top layers of the Russian social and political structure, some 4 percent of the population, presented an intriguing and complicated pattern. They included the top bureaucracy, considered by some (including Lenin) to be the real rulers of Russia—organized, socially cohesive, and highly instrumental in ensuring the stability of the state. But there was a fundamental weakness: decisions on who was to head the bureaucracy and the government were made by a quite antiquated institution, the imperial court. The court, a product of centuries of absolutism, was incapable of making the most of the talent, growing experience, and skills accumulating among the abler elements of the bureaucracy. An important social prop of the system, the nobility, was a decaying class, heavily dependent on the favors of the Tsar and his officials (themselves part of the top stratum of the nobility), deeply in debt, and constantly losing its lands and its economic and political power.

The entrepreneurial classes, developing before and during the war in the wake of an impressive industrial expansion, came to play an important role, especially during the war, but were still inhibited by their low culture, dependence on state tutelage, and political immaturity.

The Civil War

Revolution and civil war brought economic life almost to a standstill and destroyed the old social structure. The landowners, bourgeoisie, top officials and, on the whole, army officers ceased to exist as classes or groups. Death and emigration also carried away much of the middle class—the administrative, managerial, and intellectual talent that Russia had begun to develop and use before the war. The whole modern sector of urbanized and industrialized Russia suffered a severe setback, as becomes obvious from the population figures. The entire population of the country fell from its 1917 level by many millions, but the cities—still only a modest sector in Russia—were particularly badly hit. By 1920, city dwellers had fallen from 19 percent of the population in 1917 to 15 percent. Moscow lost half its population, Petrograd two-thirds.[3]

The social structure of the cities also changed. Moscow and Petrograd population figures for 1920[4] show that the middle classes and small producers—members of the free professions, merchants, artisans, and craftsmen—were depleted, while déclassé elements, such as servants of masters who had fled or been killed, stood almost untouched, and with them the quite indestructible criminal demimonde that could not but thrive on the prevailing conditions of dislocation. Two groups now stood out as strongest in these towns: the working class and the category described as "state employees" (sluzhashchie). In the latter, probably, was a mass of lower Tsarist officials who had flocked into the new Soviet offices, as well as many new recruits from the former privileged classes who, being literate, could get office jobs and some kind of haven. A survey prepared for Lenin[5] claimed that in 1920 a typical Soviet institution would shelter, for every fifteen hundred officials, some nine hundred from the former "working intelligentsia," two hundred and fifty former workers, and about three hundred former landowners, priests, officers, top managers or "bourgeois specialists," and high Tsarist officials. All these people got into a lot of trouble in later years; the label of "byvshie liudi" (people from the past) turned out to be ineradicable.

The working class, especially the hard core that the Soviet system considered its mainstay, dwindled by more than half. Some six hundred thousand served in the Red Army, one hundred eighty thousand were killed, many went into the state and Party *apparat* and others—some seventy-five thousand—into food squads. Many more returned to their native villages in order to survive, or became déclassé in various ways.[6] Those who remained in the factories were diluted by an influx of "foreign elements" from other social strata conscripted for labor. This admixture contributed to the general industrial demoralization and unrest an element that, as Soviet writers stated, was "purely peasant": demands for an end to the forced requisition of grain and cattle and the confiscation of "peasants' domestic objects" (sic).[7] It was alleged that this was a result of the "corrupting influence of petty-bourgeois anarchy [stikhiia]" on the working class.

As industry came to a standstill, some three million people were fired in an enormous purge of offices and factories. The state could not employ them and could offer them no rations. They included two hundred sixty thousand industrial workers, 27.7 percent of Vesenkha's (i.e., Supreme Council of the National Economy of the USSR) work force.[8]

The peasantry was the class that survived the upheaval best. It absorbed many of the fleeing city dwellers, quite a number of whom—characteristically for Russia—had not yet severed their connections with their native villages. It is important to note the so-called levelling out (*poravnenie*) of the peasantry. Many of the richer peasants disappeared, or lost part of their farms and economic strength, and many poor peasants received land and, at least for the statistician, moved into the category of the "middle" peasant.

The Civil War left the cities shattered. Russia became much more rural and smallholding than it had been before the storm—a considerable setback in terms of social and economic development. Significantly, Russia's historical "heartland"—the most developed and populated central regions—was also badly battered. As Lenin's stronghold, the "heartland" survived the onslaught of the peripheries, but it was bled white and in great need of a respite to recover from the bleeding.

The New Economic Policy

The respite was provided by the New Economic Policy (NEP), which allowed a limited restoration of private enterprise and reestablished market relations between town and country. This helped restore economic activity to prerevolutionary levels and bring the population figures up to and above those of old Russia. It was the tide of robust peasant fertility that made it possible for the country to recover from the war wounds. The cities also grew, regaining or surpassing the prerevolutionary population level by 1926. Working class numbers were back at, though not above, prewar level by the end of NEP.

Restoration of the country's industrial-administrative stronghold earned the new political system a breathing spell, but without producing any important structural changes that might have overcome Russia's backwardness. If anything, this structure was less developed than the Tsarist one. Eighty-two percent of the population still lived in rural areas, and 77 percent earned a livelihood directly from agriculture; 86.7 percent of the employed population lived on agriculture. This was, in crude terms, the level of development of India or Turkey, though Russia was better equipped in terms of administrative and industrial experience. The social structure that emerged in the NEP period was characterized, first of all, by nationalization of the key sectors of the economy, hence a larger role for the state. A parallel novelty, in the political sphere, was the Party and its leadership. This new factor had important social implications too, as the role, status, and well-being of individuals and groups would increasingly be determined by their place in the state apparatus and the Party, not by wealth or birth. This utterly new and momentous fact was not yet fully perceived, because of the continued existence of private sectors and people with money.

The Party, the new linchpin of the system, was in the process of transformation. The old revolutionary organization of political intellectuals and politically active workers (there were no peasants in the Bolshevik party before the revolution, and not many just after) was steadily being eliminated, and a "secretarial machinery," reflecting the impact of Civil War and NEP recruits on the social composition of the Party, was coming into the ascendant. The lower and middle ranks of the Party, and to some extent the upper ranks, began to draw in semieducated recruits from the milieus of industrial workers and junior government employees, and this important new pool of officials could not fail to make an imprint on the outlook of the party and to penetrate the higher echelons. For some time to come, the very top Party posts would still be held by the former professional revolutionaries—but it was precisely this category that was continually weakened by dissent and pushed out. A crucial role in the state machinery was played by professional experts, the so-called bourgeois intellectuals, who had acquired their skills before the revolution. Only the few who joined the Party before or during the revolution had the privilege of having the "bourgeois" stigma removed. Their weight was a tribute to the strength of the pool of professional talent that Tsarist Russia already possessed but had not managed to put to full use. Their important role in restoring industry, organizing the state administration, and teaching Russia's youth was parallel to the role peasants played in restoring the country's livelihood and human stock. They would soon, however, have to play the very different role of scapegoat.

The urban population of NEP Russia was made up of a growing working class (estimated at 4.5 million in 1926–27); an army of unemployed, reaching at least the million mark; and the increasingly large and influential group of government employees (reaching 3.5 million at the same period), partly composed of former Tsarist officials and refugees from the former privileged classes. Some seven hundred thousand artisans and half a million small merchants, mainly self-employed, formed a fairly small supply-and-services private sector. To complete the picture, there was a maze of smaller, picturesque underworld elements; an amazingly large number of "servants" (339,000), middlemen, and speculators (the heroes of Zoshchenko and Ilf and Petrov[9]); and a very small but immensely creative artistic intelligentsia. As for the Nepmen or "bourgeoisie"— entrepreneurs and merchants employing hired labor—they constituted only 75,600 people (284,000 together with their families), according to one source.[10] Such figures could be inflated by including the small merchants under the heading of "bourgeoisie,"[11] giving the still unimpressive total of 855,000 people (2,705,000 with families). This shows how small the private sector was, even after the quite inadmissible inclusion, common in the official statistics, of peddlers and people renting out a room in an apartment in the category of "entrepreneurs."

An assessment of the taxable earnings of all groups and classes of NEP society made by a special committee of Sovnarkom[12] showed that the category called "small, semicapitalist entrepreneurs" earned per capita only slightly more than Soviet officials, and even this figure was pushed up by the numerically smaller but richer group of merchants belonging to the "big bourgeoisie." Artisans employing hired labor similarly earned per capita slightly more than workers or officials. But it was only the few big entrepreneurs and merchants who earned considerable sums, though these were certainly less impressive after tax. The scope of private entrepreneurial activity under NEP can further be seen from figures on the labor force employed by the bourgeoisie. The bulk of private employment was concentrated in the small, basically craft industries, which had 230,400 workers, while the big capitalist entrepreneurs employed only 67,200 people.[13] One would not quarrel with the Soviet statistician who stated that the NEP bourgeoisie was "suffering from a wasting disease" (*khudosochnaia*).[14]

Under NEP, the peasantry was to a great extent left to its own devices, coming into contact with cities through the usual ways of the marketplace and part-time work, and with the state at the time of tax assessment and payment. Grain procurement was another area of contact fraught with potential conflict, but in the heyday of NEP this was still a commercial operation. The peasantry was relatively peaceful and not particularly antisoviet. Nevertheless, the Russian peasants, true to their traditions, distrusted the state and its officials—particularly the tax collector, who was for them the symbol of the state. For the peasant, what was "state" (*kazënnyi*) came to be seen as the product of a foreign, soulless, and oppressive force.[15]

The phenomenon of *otkhod*—seasonal departure of peasants in search of work—reappeared with NEP after a prolonged absence during the Civil War, and grew to a stream of several million *otkhodniki* per year. This put pressure on the towns and increased their unemployment rate, but helped the peasant family make ends meet and allowed the cities to get the indispensable labor force for many difficult jobs. The *otkhodnik*, a product of rural overpopulation, occupied an intermediary rung between the farmer and the urban worker or artisan; and in this category, probably, were many of the most literate and competent elements of the peasantry.

The social "levelling" that the revolution caused in the countryside was not significantly disturbed during the NEP years. The most cautious assessments[16] show 2,300,000 farmhands, but of these only 44 percent—about one million people—worked in the private farms, the rest working for the state or for peasant communities. At the other pole of rural society were the "rural entrepreneurs" (kulaks), holding 750–760,000 homesteads or about 3.4 percent of all farms. By definition, they were supposed to have prospered through systematic exploitation of hired labor.[17] However, the "systematic exploitation" was hardly impressive, considering that 750,000 rural entrepreneurs were employing only about a million laborers. The most prosperous peasants, according to a large 1927 survey, had two to three cows and up to ten hectares of sowing area, *for an average family of seven people.*[18] Sovnarkom's taxation committee computed that such an entrepreneur made 239.8 rubles a year for each member of his family, compared to a rural official's 297 rubles. Though the kulak still made twice as much as the middle peasant,[19] Soviet rural "capitalism" barely existed. The state could curb the richer peasants at will; indeed, it did so in 1928–29, when, under pressure of taxation and forced procurements, this stratum shrank very substantially,[20] and rural "capitalism" began to melt like wax. In defiance of the official class analysis of the peasantry, the attempt at the end of NEP to identify and squeeze out kulaks immediately had adverse effects on the peasantry and agriculture in general; many "middle" peasants were badly affected, and their economic activity began to dwindle.[21]

The Cultural Lag

NEP and its class structure, though quite aptly characterized as a "mixed economy," was not a mixture of "socialism" and "capitalism." Basically the society and the economy were dominated by the rural sector and small-scale producers and merchants, with a small, highly concentrated and influential large-scale industrial sector, and a state administration employing quite a cohort of officials and putting to good use a smaller administrative and professional stratum.[22] This society was spared such familiar phenomena of underdevelopment as absentee landowning and moneylending classes with a plethora of servants and luxurious, conspicuous spending. But it had its own stigmata of backwardness—a greedy, uneducated, and inefficient officialdom and a maze of offices in which a simple citizen, especially a peasant, felt entirely lost and quite unceremoniously mistreated. "Bureaucratism" was officially attributed to "survivals of the past" and was combatted under this heading. Linked to the bureaucratic source of corruption were the "infected spots" (*gnoiniki*) resulting from unholy alliances of officials (especially in the supply networks) with private merchants on big illegal operations with government goods. The press was full of such stories of large-scale corruption, and now and again the whole leadership of a district or even a republic would be purged for having tolerated or participated in such affairs. NEP thus had its share of venality, crooked business deals, and ways to spend the profits, including night-clubs, *cafés chantants*, gambling dens, and houses of prostitution.

In the background lay discrepancies very menacing to the system's future. There was the disparity between the Party's ideology and aspirations and the frustrating reality of a petty-bourgeois country, aptly described by a recent historian as "large scale theories versus small scale realities."[23] As the government, not unnaturally, strove to revive and develop the economy, it allowed the cultural front—mass education and the fight against illiteracy—to trail dangerously: the economic recovery had not yet become a cultural one as well. Although the industrial specialist was relatively well off and the white-collar employee in big industry earned almost twice as much as the worker in the period 1926–29, teachers—lowest on the pay scale, especially in elementary schools—were the most neglected part of the "intelligentsia" in income and status[24] and earned no more than 45 percent of their prerevolutionary salaries.[25] Investments in "culture" were lagging heavily behind investments in the economy, and Lunacharskii complained to the Fifteenth Party Congress that he had at his disposal less money for schools than the Tsarist educational system had. Some of the top leadership were painfully aware of the problem. Rykov stated at the same congress that without sufficient cultural advance further economic progress would become blocked.[26]

With the proportion of elementary-school pupils per thousand inhabitants even lower than that in many poorly developed countries—and with lower per capita expenses on culture and average duration of schooling in the countryside and in towns[27]—the current expression "Asiatic lack of culture" (*asiatskaia beskul'turnost'*) had its justification. "Vodka is squeezing out culture!" a Party writer exclaimed dramatically,[28] though he still did not admit that it was too early to talk of a "new culture," let alone a proletarian one. It was one of the peculiarities of Party life that obvious facts about society became distorted in the mirror of Party struggles and ideological juggling. Trotskii had to be attacked for having stated the truth that as long as the "clutches of dictatorship existed," no new culture would emerge.[29]

The "clutches of dictatorship" would soon be used to spread popular education, but the higher levels of culture, as well as the bearers of that culture, were to go through serious troubles. The party had made a concerted effort, partly successful, to get more workers and peasants into higher education. In 1926, however, limitations on university entry for white-collar and other nonproletarian social groups were eased, and the university became relatively accessible even to sons of "alien classes," especially those of the "bourgeois intelligentsia."[30] But the NEP world, dominated as it was by the mass peasant background, the rapacious moneymaking Nepman, the sternly ideological Party militant, and the conniving, corrupt state official, did not make for any buoyancy in the intelligentsia and student circles. Vodka was widely used among the moody Russian educated people; and among student youth in particular there were "manifestations of despair culminating in suicide" at and after the time when the poet Esenin took his life, and "mischievous behavior culminating in crime," as Lunacharskii put it.[31]

In contrast to the oversensitive intellectual Oblomovs[32] and talented but gloomy Esenins was the current urban type of the ordinary "soviet lad"— poorly educated, but dodgy and shrewd, semicynical, and semiparasitic. His collective portrait was sketched by Bukharin as follows: a good drinker and a good fighter who can raise hell and swear like a trooper; a lad who won't work too hard and knows how to look after himself.[33] These "smart fellows" were products of a semideveloped society, on the border of a static and uninspiring rural world and a corrupting urban (usually small-town) world of petty affairs. They were to flock into the clean and unexacting jobs of lower (and often higher) officialdom, into the supply networks, into the criminal world and—why not?—into jobs as police investigators.

In sum, the cultural deprivation of the NEP population—with its working class crammed into a diminishing living space, its massive illiteracy, its tricksters and Oblomovs, its brilliant top layers and crude and ambitious rulers—gave substance and lent credibility to the fears for the fate of the revolution and the future of the state. The danger of degeneration (*pererozhdenie*) of the Party and its leadership—a cry raised by the Party oppositions—was taken up by Bukharin, though somewhat ambiguously since he himself was still one of the leading official spokesmen: if there was no cultural rise of the masses, no constant influx of workers to universities, degeneration was to be feared, as this would certainly push the leading cadres "to close in upon themselves, to harden into a separate layer, with a tendency to form a new ruling class."[34]

Bukharin's suggestions for avoiding such an outcome were clearly insufficient. Speedy and half-baked mass education may tend to make people more vulnerable to propaganda and indoctrination[35] and enhance the grip of the leadership and the controllers, rather than make the leaders more open to the pressure of the masses. This was, in fact, what happened after the shattering of NEP society and its furious reshaping during the subsequent "revolution from above," when mass schooling and crash courses did not prevent the hardening and self-seclusion of the ruling groups, or an unprecedented degree of alienation of state from society.

2 . THE BIG DRIVE

Ruralization of the Cities

The all-out drive for industrialization from 1928 opened a period in which so many things happened simultaneously that one could aptly describe it as the birth pangs of a world. There was, to begin with, a huge population movement, with millions milling around the country, building and rebuilding, flocking to towns, searching for a way out of material and other miseries, and with many ending up in the growing concentration camps. At the same time, a massive cadres formation process was launched, bringing in its wake a hectic restructuring of society—a growing industrial working class, sprawling bureaucracies and offices, managements, a scientific establishment, a new hierarchy of status, privilege, and power, and an ominously growing security and coercion establishment that tried to match the energy of the builders by furiously ferreting out and destroying numerous social categories of the past as well as many of the newly formed groups. In the countryside, it was an upheaval as elemental as a hurricane—the old rural structures and ways of life were shattered to their very roots, with uncountable consequences for society and state alike.

The whole explosion was, once more, damaging for population growth. Population growth did not stop, to be sure, but was certainly slowed down, especially in the countryside, by the collectivization terror and the famine in the southern parts of the country in 1932–33. The rural birthrate fell from 49.1 in 1913 (31.7 in cities) to 42–43 in 1923–24 and, finally, to 32.2 in 1935 (24.6 in cities). Material hardship and the turmoil of collectivization were among the main reasons for this trend[36] and, according to a number of sources, Gosplan expected by 1937 a much greater population than was actually found in the 1937 census. [37] Without entering into the complex problem of how high a price in human lives was paid for Soviet development policies, there is no doubt that, as a result of the internal battles of the Five-Year Plans, the Soviet Union was approaching the war—another terrible bloodletting—with many combat divisions missing.

Industrialization was launched on such a scale that the sudden demand for labor flooded the planners and government offices and for a long time threw the whole machinery out of gear. The peasantry had to provide, at short notice, millions of people for the construction sites and the new cities. This in itself was no problem for the notoriously overpopulated countryside. Peasants were used to the quite unorganized but fairly steady *otkhod*, the seasonal departure for work along well-trodden historical routes. But at first the newly created and shaky *kolkhozy* (collective farms) tried to retain the labor force, fearing the prospect of remaining without the labor indispensable for the still unfamiliar tasks of a collective organization. However, governmental measures and the urge of the peasants to leave the *kolkhozy* soon broke down all impediments. [38] During 1926–39 the cities grew by some thirty million people at least, and their share in population grew from about 18 percent to 24 percent (reminding us that by 1939, 76 percent of the population was still rural). During the First Five-Year Plan alone the cities grew by 44 percent, almost as much as during the whole period 1897–1926, and the salaried labor force (workers and officials) more than doubled, growing from 10.8 to 22.6 million. [39] There is no doubt that the bulk of this growth was made up by peasants. If during the years 1928 and 1929 about one million new migrants came to live in the cities, during the next three years three million came each year. The Moscow and Leningrad regions alone each received 3.5 million new inhabitants during the First Five-Year Plan. In 1931 a staggering figure of 4.1 million peasants joined the city population; and for the years 1929–35 the total was 17.7 million.[40] This does not yet give the whole measure of the mass movements and changes, since in addition to those peasants who came to stay in industry, cities, and construction sites, millions of seasonal *otkhodniki* went, with or without contracts, to build roads, canals, and factories. In the remarkable year of 1931 alone, about seven million *otkhodniki* moved around the country.[41]

In the cities, the inordinate and unanticipated growth transformed a strained housing situation into an appalling one, creating the specifically Soviet (or Stalinist) reality of chronically overcrowded lodgings, with consequent attrition of human relations, strained family life, destruction of privacy and personal life, and various forms of psychological strain. All this provided a propitious hunting ground for the ruthless, the primitive, the blackmailer, the hooligan, and the informer. The courts dealt with an incredible mass of cases testifying to the human destruction caused by this congestion of dwellings. The falling standards of living, the lines outside stores, and the proliferation of speculators suggest the depth of the tensions and hardship. Soon the cumulative results of such conditions were to cause widespread manifestations of neurosis and anomie, culminating in an alarming fall in the birthrate. By 1936, in fact, the big cities experienced a net loss of population, with more children dying than being born, which explains the alarm in government circles and the famous laws against abortion proclaimed in that year.

Once the initial urgent need for labor was satisfied and the authorities realized the damaging effects of the chaotic influx into cities, passports and the *propiska* system of obligatory registration with the local police were introduced (by law at the end of 1932 and in practice during 1933). These were methods of controlling movement of the rural population, especially during the hungry winter of 1932–33, when starving peasants trying to save their lives crawled into the cities without permission. A peasant received a passport only if the authorities were satisfied that he was needed in some employment and the *kolkhoz* was ready to let him go.

It was during those years of mass mobilization that the government and managers acquired the characterisically Soviet habit of shuffling the labor force around like cattle. With their eyes fixed only on their targets, they forgot some elementary human needs. This attitude, which was not born in the camps but predated them, served as a background to the growing camp system of the GPU and the "reeducation through labor" of its inhabitants.

A single term to characterize the process would be "ruralization" (*okrest'ianivanie*) of the cities. One of the results of this ruralization was the breakdown of labor discipline, which saddled the state with an enormous problem of educating and disciplining the mass of the crude labor force. The battle against absenteeism, shirking, drinking in factories during working hours, and breaking tools was long, and the Soviet government played no "humanistic" games in this fight. Very soon, methods such as denial of ration cards, eviction from lodgings, and even penal sentences for undisciplined workers were introduced. The same harshness was applied in the fight against deterioration in the quality of industrial products (*brak*); here the fight was directed not only against workers but also against managers and technicians, and the weapons were special laws put in the hands of the prosecutors.

"Tekuchka"

As traditionally happened in times of stress and catastrophe, peasant Russia was turning into *Rus' brodiazhnaia*, a country of vagrants. Massive and rapid labor turnover (*tekuchka*) was characteristic of the early thirties. The factory labor force, hard pressed by working and living conditions, moved around to find something better, encouraged by real or fictitious differences in pay or food. The workers were often (illegally) lured by promises from the managements of construction sites and enterprises, who were forever anxious to have labor reserves to meet crises of plan fulfillment.

It was all too easy to explain this phenomenon by insisting on the petty-bourgeois character of the new working classes, with its concomitant anarchism, self-seeking, lack of discipline, attachment to property, and slovenliness, to use the morally charged vocabulary of Soviet sources. That it was this same petty-bourgeois mass of parasites which actually built the country is one of the paradoxes of this type of class analysis. Factories and mines in these years were transformed into railway stations—or, as Ordzhonikidze exclaimed in despair—into one huge "nomadic gypsy camp."[42] The cost of the turnover was incredible. Before they had managed to learn their job, people had already given their notice or done something in order to get fired.

But more: the same process, and on a large scale, was going on among managers and administrators, specialists and officials. At all levels of the local administration and Party *apparat*, people adopted the habit of leaving in good time, before they were penalized, recalled, brought in for questioning, downgraded, fired, or arrested.[43]

Thus workers, administrators, specialists, officials, party apparatus men, and in great masses, peasants were all moving around and changing jobs, creating unwanted surpluses in some places and dearths in others, losing skills or failing to acquire them, creating streams and floods in which families were destroyed, children lost, and morality dissolved. Social, administrative, industrial, and political structures were all in flux. The mighty dictatorial government found itself, as a result of its impetuous activity during those early years of accelerated industrialization, presiding over a "quicksand" society.

It is not difficult to imagine the despair of the rulers and their fierce resolution to put an end to this situation and introduce law and order into the chaos. The stern traits of the disciplining effort soon became viciously contorted. That the drive pressed hard on the judiciary—itself "leaking" like everything else—was a foregone conclusion. The secret police (GPU) was allowed to swell its empire to enormous proportions. Constant purges (*chistki*)—a paradoxical method, not unfamiliar in medicine, of dealing with an illness by injecting the same microbes—were undertaken and contributed considerably to the flux. After the early period of "proletarianization," two additional strategies were used to stabilize the body social: first, creation and consolidation of a network of supervisors in the form of hierarchies, apparatuses, and elites; and then, from about 1934, the adoption of policies that the sociologist Timasheff[44] described as "The Great Retreat"—a set of classical measures of social conservatism, law and order strategies complete with a nationalist revival, and efforts to instill values of discipline, patriotism, conformism, authority and orderly careerism. That such a policy should be accompanied by another shattering set of purges, in the later thirties, is one more enigma, amazing even for one who is already well versed in the vagaries of Soviet history and policies.

During the Five-Year Plan frenzy (1928–32), all social groups and classes were in a state of flux and shock, partially or totally "destructured" and unhinged. One can say that for a short span of time, some years ahead of the happy announcements of the coming of a socialist society, Russian society was indeed "classless"—all its classes were out of shape, leaving a free field for the state and its institutions, themselves very considerably shaken, to act and grow.

3. CLASS WARFARE

The "Aliens"

Industrialization, collectivization, and the formation of cadres were not the only factors in the shaping of the new social structure. Social policies of a quite complex and often contradictory pattern were factors too. One can tentatively speak of an initial period of "proletarianization," which could also be called the "production" (*produktsionnyi*) period, when workers were given preference and drafted through special mobilizations into universities, schools, and administrations. Parallel to this process went *spetseedstvo* (specialist-baiting), overwhelming emphasis on social origin, and the transformation of academies and universities into "production brigades." The frenzied "proletarianization" often emptied the factories of their most experienced and reliable workers and pushed many of them into a hostile environment of officialdom or, on the basis of social origin or Party loyalty alone, into the stressful situation of being enrolled in institutions of higher learning without appropriate academic preparation.

From 1931, this line began to change. Recruitment of workers to offices was formally forbidden at the end of 1930, and somewhat later university enrollment returned to a basis of some ability and academic preparation. A temporary halt to the cruder forms of *spetseedstvo* also occurred at this time. With the fight for labor discipline in factories, *kolkhozy*, and offices, a new strategy was adopted for instilling stability and productivity, which entailed creating a new and strong layer of bosses. This kind of "elitist" policy would continue, not without some baffling reversals, throughout the thirties.

That mass terror was permeating all these phases is a well-known fact.

The first target of the security "organs" were those who had belonged to the former privileged classes before the revolution ("class enemies"). Later the terror would be turned against the growing elite itself: most of the top layers in Party and state administrations were to be totally renovated by an influx of new recruits from the universities or the lower ranks of the bureaucracy.

One important factor that ought to be strongly emphasized is that for millions there was upward mobility and social promotion in the midst of the whole upheaval. This statement needs to be qualified. Peasants going to factories could not see it then as promotion—for many, the factories meant a drop in their standard of living and self-respect. But it may have been different for the great number who became officials, however low the rank and bad the pay. For those who went to universities and to responsible jobs, or acquired new skills, the social advance was undeniable and the new possibilities were seized on eagerly.

Urban social groups and classes, freshly formed to a great extent, were obviously not yet stabilized in their new jobs and settings, and it would take some time for the new patterns to solidify. Flux remained part of the social landscape for most of the Stalinist period. No wonder that the state, which turned into a Leviathan and kept extending its domination, met no countervailing forces or checks. The state presided imperiously over the social changes and ruled society—but this does not mean that the influencing and shaping was a one-way affair. Though the mighty state machinery was in no direct way accountable to the masses, the social milieu, however passive and defenseless, might exert an influence not unlike that which the conquered sometimes have on their conquerors. But this is a problem that must be left open for further discussion.

Of all social groups, the most defenseless were those destined for "liquidation as a class." This could mean anything from simply being squeezed out of one's business and allowed to hide in some office or factory to imprisonment in camps or shooting. The biggest such group, with more than a million homesteads, was that of the kulaks. "Dekulakization," which consisted of exiling the kulak families to uninhabited territories (plus some straight prison sentences and shootings), was equivalent in its scale to the uprooting of a small nation. It was an economic disaster, with incalculable long-term effects and insignificant, even ridiculous, immediate gains: officially, one hundred seventy million rubles worth of property (or up to four hundred million, according to a reassessment)[45] were confiscated, that is, between one hundred and seventy and four hundred rubles per household. What meager assistance the *kolkhozy* gained from the destruction of "rural capitalism"! It is probable that even the uncharitable but unavoidable expenditure on resettlement of these people, after shattering them and thinning out their numbers, cost more.

But kulaks were not the only victims of the "anticapitalist revolution." All members of the relatively modest sectors of private activity and initiative under NEP now fell into one of the imprecise categories of "nonlaboring," "alien," or "déclassé element," or were *lishentsy*—deprived of civil rights. In the RSFSR alone, 1,706,025 people or some 3.9 percent of all potential voters were *lishentsy*, and in 1932, 3.5 percent were still on the black list.[46] But these figures probably do not express the full numbers of those who got into trouble by virtue of belonging to one category or another of "people from the past" listed in the edict that instructed authorities on who should be deprived of the right to vote.[47] The methods of dealing with these groups were not restricted to the quite platonic deprivation of the right to vote. Such deprivation was often followed by denial of lodging, food ration, and medical services,[48] and especially by exile. One of the better known aspects of the antibourgeois campaign was the mass arrest of people supposed to have possessed valuables like gold and silver. Another was a huge purge of "undesirable persons" from the cities in 1932, just before the introduction of passports.[49]

The "squeezing out of the private businessman" (*vytesnenie chastnika*) consisted of the eviction of about half a million ex-merchants (1.5 million with families), most of whom were small-timers working without employees. Their shops in the countryside, where most of them operated, were assessed in 1927 as having a capital value of 711 rubles per shop.[50] The effects of this eviction operation, as well as similar action against artisans and craftsmen, were momentous. As merchants closed their shops and went to factories, offices, and camps, there arose a deplorable situation of "commercial desert," a development the state and cooperative sectors were not equipped to cope with. Even the meager goods available could not be distributed. New shops and commercial organizations were quickly founded to cope with the emergency, but their quality remained lamentable and their numbers insufficient for more than a generation. As the lines outside the stores grew, so did the plague of speculation, black markets, and rackets. The fight against speculation—now counting among its victims many people with impeccable class origins—brought a mass of new criminal offenses into the overcrowded and overworked courts: personal and mass embezzlements, theft in supply networks, fictitious accounting, illicit dealings in ration cards, and so on.[51] A fiercely repressive law of 7 August 1932 against theft in *kolkhozy* was later broadened to embrace all, other sectors and became the state's main weapon for protecting its property. Mass thefts were in fact taking place as the economic situation, especially food supplies, deteriorated. The GPU could help neither in supplying food nor in rooting out theft. The nation, disrespectful toward state property, seemed to have been transformed into a nation of thieves.

The Working Class

For the development of the working class, some figures can provide a telling picture (Table 1). Growth was phenomenal in the First Five-Year Plan period and still considerable in the second, but slowed almost to a standstill as far as industrial and construction workers were concerned in the years 1937–40 (when the increase was mainly in the "employees"

TABLE 1.

	(in thousands)			
	1928	1932	1937	1940
Total employment (workers and employees)	10800	20600	26700	31200
Workers only (total)	6800	14500	17200	20000
Workers in industry	3124	6007	7924	8290
Workers in construction	630	2479	1875	1929
Workers in *sovkhozy* and other state farms	301	1970	1539	1558

Sources: A. B. Mitrofanova, in D. L. Baevskii, ed., *Izmeneniia v chislennosti i sostave sovetskogo rabochego klassa*, M. 1961, p. 220; and same author, in R. P. Dadykin, ed., *Formirovanie i razvitie sovetskogo rabochego klassa* (1917–1961), M. 1964, pp. 55–56.

sector). The growth, as already stated, was based on a mass influx of peasants. But even in the pre-Plan period the peasant influence in the working class had been strong, especially in the Ukrainian mining regions. A survey of industrial labor carried out in 1929 showed that 42.6 percent of the workers were of peasant origin, and 20.6 percent had land in the countryside.[52]

Not unexpectedly, the professional level and educational standards of the crude labor force were extremely low. As late as 1939, when things had largely settled down, only 8.2 percent of the workers had an education of seven grades or more.[53] The working class had also become much younger. It included not only a mass of inexperienced and often bewildered peasants, but also many women new to industrial jobs: by 1936 women constituted 40 percent of the work force.

For the managers, for the state, and especially for the workers themselves, the problems arising from such rapid growth were formidable. At the beginning, many of the newly enrolled peasants experienced cultural and psychological shock, manifested, for example, in drinking, hooliganism, criminal behavior, breaking the expensive and unfamiliar machinery, and "a colossal growth of industrial traumatism."[54] The problem of labor turnover has already been discussed. The bewildered administrations sometimes tried to placate the workers and sometimes reacted with "administrative methods"—a flood of fines, dismissals, and repression.

The constant seesaw of short periods of liberalism and long waves of *goloe administrirovanie*" (crude administrative methods) was by now firmly embedded in Soviet politics. Mass repression was not, as the party liked to put it, some aberration of local officials, but party policy. The harshness of the methods used against absenteeism can be illustrated by a law of 15 November 1932, supplemented a few months later, prescribing dismissal, denial of food rations, denial of access to food shops, and eviction from lodgings regardless—as the text emphasized—of the time of year.[55] Factory administrations were now allowed to starve people in order to ensure their presence in the factories. A single day of "unjustified absence" was defined as absenteeism, punishable according to this law (in 1938, twenty minutes' absence or lateness would constitute absenteeism).

The overall strategy, of course, was more complex and included more than sheer repression. Trade unions and Party cells were mobilized to serve the needs of production and the plans, and this was supplemented by inculcating in the managers a taste for the pleasures of power. Tough leadership became the style preached by the Party, with Kaganovich teaching the manager to behave in such a way that "the earth should tremble when the director walks around the plant."[56] The NEP "triangle" of Party, trade unions, and management was abandoned in 1929 and replaced by fierce one-man rule (*edinonachalie*). A further method in the struggle to raise the productivity of labor was the enforcement of piece work; spreading of the pay differential; and promotion and offer of better food and priority in lodging, vacations, and school admission for the outstanding worker (*udarnik*) and his children, and for those who stayed long enough on the job. It never seemed sufficient, however, and the fight against the proponents of new categories of morally reprehensible behavior (castigated by the propaganda as "flitters," "idlers," "disorganizers," "absentees," and so on) always included those "indiscriminate mass repressions" that Kaganovich, the chief architect of the strategy, pretended to regret in 1936.[57]

From time to time, almost as an afterthought, an Ordzhonikidze or Kirov would appeal to the managers to stop neglecting their workers and to improve their attitude towards them.[58] But the fact was that once the "triangle" was gone and the Party and trade union turned their "face to production," they had to turn their face against the workers.

The Peasants

In the countryside, a state of major crisis and warfare existed between the government and the peasants. There was nothing like "dekulakization" in regard to the workers, even in the heat of the ruthless fight to instill discipline in their ranks, and (except in the prewar period) the most repressive bills against labor absenteeism did not abolish the freedom to leave the workplace after giving due notice, though many obstacles were put in the way of doing so. Salaries and social benefits paid out to workers, however meager, nevertheless remained an obligation that the state accepted and fulfilled. In the cities, the government's effort to stem disorder was to some degree bearing fruit, and workers, however sluggish and apathetic many of them might be, did learn trades, improve productivity, and yield to more orderly patterns.

In the countryside, the effects of collectivization were of a different kind. For the peasants it was a revolution, a violent destruction of a system of production and of a life pattern. Although even here, after an initial period of shock lasting, probably, from 1930 to 1934, the peasants acquired some working habits and accepted some routines; long-term phenomena persisted, and some have not been overcome even today.[59]

At the root of the difficulty of the *kolkhoz* system lay the fact that the peasants' previous experience, way of life, and educational level in no way prepared them to accept and run the system that was now being imposed on them. It was this contradiction, a Soviet writer stated, that made imperative the state's interference in[60]—or rather takeover of—all aspects of running the *kolkhoz* system. In addition, the strains caused by forcing on a conservative and mostly illiterate people[61] an abrupt change of age-old life patterns were compounded by an attack on their religion—an act of incredible folly, and quite irrelevant to the problems of *kolkhoz* production. Its futility was demonstrated by the later admission of the head of the antireligious crusade that by the end of the thirties two-thirds of the peasants were still believers.[62]

At the very beginning of the process some leaders honest enough to raise a fuss in public predicted the essence of things to come. S. I. Syrtsov, Premier of the government of the RSFSR, sounded the alarm.[63] There could already be observed, at the beginning of 1930, a dangerous "explosion of consumerist moods": as the regulators and stimulants of his previous life and production were lost, in fact violently repudiated, the peasant's usual urge to save and accumulate was replaced by an equally strong urge to consume everything (*proedat'*); his usual care and worry about the state of affairs on his farm was replaced by apathy and "a nihilistic attitude toward production" (*proizvodstvennyi nigilizm*). The peasant was now waiting to be guided, expecting to be told what to do. But the state did not know what to do or how to do it, and its agencies in the countryside were in confusion and disarray.

Loss of interest in production was part of the larger problem of loss of identity and self-respect. In the previous system, the peasant was the master (*khoziain*) on his farm and with this, however poor the farm, went the sense of dignity of a free agent. The new situation deprived the peasants of status and freedom: their main objection to the *kolkhozy* was that they would be "put on a ration system," which would mean a loss of independence. When this happened the peasants, as we have seen, became eager to get away from the *kolkhoz* into towns—a reaction, among other things, against the phenomenon of "statization" (*okazënivanie*).[64]

The first steps of *okazënivanie* were not part of a deliberately planned strategy. The government was forced, or felt itself forced, to undertake salvage operations that led it ever deeper into the trap of growing interference in all phases and details of agricultural production and organization. The one big step that can be regarded as strategy was the removal of machinery from the *kolkhozy* to the government MTS (Machine Tractor Stations),[65] but much else in government policy at the beginning had the character of ad hoc reactions.

Because the state's needs in grain and other products were urgent and immediate, it pressed on its officials and local administrations to get what was necessary from the peasants. Quite soon the *kolkhoznik* and *kolkhoz* managements found themselves gagged and at the mercy of an all-powerful network of local officials making searches and seizures, judging, punishing, expelling, and, in particular, arresting freely, making liberal use of the meaningless label of *podkulachnik* (kulak's hireling). Ia. A. Iakovlev, the Commissar for Agriculture, formally protested, apparently, at the Central Committee meeting in July 1931 against what he called the "mass of anti-kolkhoz actions" by local administrations, saying that the *kolkhoznik* had become "an object of sheer arbitrariness." But in the same year one of his Central Committee colleagues, B. P. Sheboldaev, gave the key to the situation and to the policy of the hardliners who were more powerful than Iakovlev. The *kolkhozy*, he stated, "have too little goodwill towards the interests of the state," and there was no justification for "idealizing the *kolkhoznik*." The old wisdom of rulers—coercion—had to be resorted to without qualms.[66] This attitude totally disregarded the interests of the several million peasants. The concerns of the government were epitomized in the procurement (*zagotovki*) squeeze, "that touchstone on which our strength and weakness and the strength and weakness of our enemy were tested," as Kaganovich said in a sentence crucial to the understanding of government strategy and the relations between *kolkhoz* peasantry and the state.[67] "The enemy" here were truly legion. Hence the shrill demands coming from the Central Committee to punish "without mercy" not only reluctance to part with grain but also what was called "a maliciously careless attitude to work";[68] hence the suggestions to local authorities that bad work should be called "kulak sabotage" and that lenience toward transgressors would be considered as help given to the enemy.

Krylenko's[69] typology of "contravention of socialist legality" in regard to peasants and the *kolkhoz* included such "arbitrary treatment of the peasantry as . . . illegal searches and arrests, confiscations, pre-emption of property, illegal fines and the like."[70] The capriciousness of the accusations of "sloppily careless work" and sabotage becomes clear when we examine the kind of "guidance" the state was giving the *kolkhozy*. Obviously the local Party committees knew nothing about agriculture in general, and even less about their pet idea—large-scale agricultural production. Stalin taught that, since the *kolkhozy* were inexperienced, they had to be run from above by minute party interference. But as Kirov stated in a moment of despair and truth: "I myself, sinful man, don't see clearly in agricultural matters,"[71]—this after having given the most ignorant orders to peasants, and then ordering or approving mass arrests of those who refused to comply[72] before discovering that he was on a false track.

The more honest Stalinists were more and more despairing of the state of affairs and were groping for changes. Kirov, who sometimes seemed utterly disappointed in 1933, called for change and made an appeal to go and learn from the *kolkhoznik*—a telling statement of the failure of government methods. But it was at about the same time that Stalin issued stern instructions to meddle, in effect, with every detail, because the *kolkhozniki* did not know how to run their affairs.[73]

The peasants were fettered and "bureaucratized," and well knew that they had lost the independence they had had as producers and citizens under NEP. There was a whole system of discrimination, amounting to a special legal and social regime for the *kolkhoz* peasantry. If lack of legally guaranteed rights was to be the trait of the system in regard to all classes, the peasant was particularly vulnerable because of the ideological formula of the regime, which considered him suspect in terms of his class origin, in terms of the inferior status of *kolkhozy*, in terms of the purity of socialism in comparison with state-run institutions. Whereas the worker earned a salary—more or less state controlled, but independent of the total output of the industry or of the industry's efficiency—the *kolkhoznik* was paid from the residual of *kolkhoz* income after the crop had been gathered and the state had taken its share. This income was both insecure and, as was formally acknowledged, insufficient to feed the peasant's family; hence the concession to the peasant allowing him a private plot and a cow (small enough not to make him too happy and forgetful of the *kolkhoz*, but big enough to provide for some of his family's, and the whole country's, essential needs). This allowance, of course, was one of the factors keeping the old peasant alive in the *kolkhoznik*, thereby providing an additional argument for doubting his socialist credentials.

In addition to insecurity of income, the peasants were denied the benefits of social security that the state guaranteed its workers and employees.[74] The peasants were subject to several state corvées—road building, timber hauling and so on—whereas city dwellers had long ago forgotten this remnant of the middle ages. The peasant did not have the freedom of movement, however qualified, that the worker had. His travels were controlled by the passport system and the *propiska* (the document indicating registered place of residence), and also by the law of 17 March 1933 stipulating that a peasant was not allowed to leave the *kolkhoz* without a contract from a prospective employer, duly ratified by the *kolkhoz* management. At about the same time, the USSR Procurator Akulov ordered peasants to be punished by up to six months in prison for not respecting a contract with a state employer. Akulov was reminded by one writer (with unknown results) that introducing criminal law into a basically civil transaction like a labor contract was contrary to the principles of Russian and European labor law.[75] But this was precisely the point: disregarding the interest of "the state" was all too easily becoming a criminal or, even worse, a political offense. This was one of the attributes of "Stalinism."

Here, then, was the system of "military-feudal" exploitation of the peasantry that Bukharin had fearfully anticipated in 1929, and "statism" at its purest. A producer (not to say citizen) so strongly fettered and discriminated against could not be efficient. On the contrary, he lost the incentive to exert himself on the job, unless this happened to be his own plot, and became demoralized both as a producer and as a person. "We are not our own men but the *kolkhoz's*," the peasants often repeated. This summed up the whole process. Before they had been their own men; now they belonged to the *kolkhoz*, but the *kolkhoz* did not belong to them.

Over the years, slow and not unimportant changes took place within the *kolkhoz* peasantry, such as the emergence of numbers of managers and administrators who did not exist at all in NEP agriculture. Growing numbers of tractor drivers made their appearance, as did a sprinkling of "rural intelligentsia"—but according to a Soviet sociologist, by the end of the Five-Year Plans this so-called rural intelligentsia was barely distinguishable by its level of education from the mass of *kolkhozniki*.[76] The mass was still composed of peasants, and they were at the bottom of the social ladder, just as the *muzhik* had been in former times. The only means of social promotion was to move out. Millions did so whenever they could, and in so doing probably influenced Soviet society, culture, and the state much more deeply than is sometimes realized.

4 . THE EDUCATED AND THE RULERS

"Spetseedstvo"

The so-called intelligentsia is a problem of considerable complexity, and its story during and after the "big drive" is crucial for understanding the social structure that was in the making. Here too we have a state action carried out with great speed and urgency. The First Five-Year Plan created an enormous demand for technicians, administrators, and scientists of all sorts, and the existing training facilities and governmental institutions were overwhelmed by the task. It is significant that very soon the whole problem of the "intelligentsia" became a problem of "cadres" in the hundreds of thousands and even millions, administered and bureaucratized by a network of "departments of cadres," established "as we go along," as Ordzhonikidze put it.[77] Improvisation of a social and professional process of such importance is a trait we keep meeting in this period, not only in the domain of cadres.

The attitude toward the intelligentsia in this and previous periods was shaped by contradictory factors and under changing circumstances. From the very first days of the regime, the party needed educated people to run the economy and the state (a dependence that was somehow not anticipated: the party leaders, intellectuals themselves, were busy understanding "history" and political strategy, not running an economy). However, the intelligentsia en masse, including the so-called popular (*narodnaia*) intelligentsia, actively opposed Bolshevik takeover, in the massive strikes of late 1917/early 1918. This opposition, in its overt forms, was quite quickly put down, but the shadow kept hanging over relations between the Party and the intellectuals.

With all the disdain for Oblomovs and *"intelligenty"* that Bolsheviks sometimes encouraged (the notorious "makhaevite tendencies"), an urgent need arose to foster respect for members of the intelligentsia. It was not an easy task. The conundrum can be studied in two statements by Lenin: he declared on the one hand, "they must be given work, but they must be carefully watched; commissars should be placed over them and their counterrevolutionary schemes suppressed"; he appealed on the other for respect for culture and those who possessed it, and issued the injunction to "command less, or rather not to command at all."[78] That this contradictory attitude would produce zigzags in political tactics and mar relations is obvious. Lenin knew that he could not take a step without experts, and he acknowledged frankly after the Civil War that the Red Army, for example, would not have existed at all without the ex-Tsarist officers who helped create it.[79] But the same was true of the universities, the State Planning Commission (Gosplan), and all the important economic ministries as well. The great dream of preparing "our own" intelligentsia could not be achieved without the old one cooperating in the job.

NEP settled down to an uneasy acceptance of this situation. The intelligentsia was basically still, at the end of NEP, the "old" one, non-Bolshevik in its majority. In October 1929 a third of all specialists working in the national economy and a majority of those with higher education were from the old intelligentsia, as were 60 percent of teachers in higher education. The mass of new specialists being prepared under Soviet rule would not just be trained by these instructors, but also undoubtedly politically influenced by them.[80]

The Shakhty affair[81] came as a warning and a demonstration that the "old" would not have it their way in shaping the profile of the immense mass of new trainees. It opened a period in Soviet history that was not only a tragedy for the old intelligentsia but also amounted to a furious destruction of many cultural values. The hectic creation of instruments for the diffusion of culture—schools, higher schools, universities—was to be accompanied by an unbelievable display of obscurantism and attacks on anything sophisticated or refined. The universities, for example, were almost completely destroyed before a new approach, from about 1934, helped to save them.

During the Shakhty trial and thereafter intellectual circles were panic-stricken and depressed, in a not unjustified expectation of a wave of *spet-seedstvo* and mass repressions.[82]

One central idea that the key leaders wanted to "explain" by the Shakhty trial was that neutrality in politics—that is, toward party policies—could lead to sabotage. This message was now presented in a new way: by a stage production with a recognizable signature on it.

Lenin had earlier been irked by the attitude of educated specialists who claimed noninvolvement in politics as part of a moral and professional ethic. This implied, from Lenin's point of view, that they would work as specialists for the new regime without endorsing it or identifying with its aims. Lenin was prepared to accept this compromise, but Stalin's policies refused any such accommodation. His objective, in common with that of the Inquisition, was to force thinking people to desist from their independent thoughts and moral principles and to identify with a party and with policies felt to be unacceptable or questionable. The most unacceptable was precisely what they were asked to do: to prostrate themselves, to turn their guts out in fervent repentance—or else be declared treasonable. The equation "doubt = treason" was one of the most deadly tools of the moral and cultural reaction that hit the country at the height of its economic and military construction. Why this presumably optimistic surge of creativity was darkened by such a deeply pessimistic attitude to men and culture is one of the unanswered questions. In any case, the quasi-mystical "disarm yourself before the Party and repent" was self-defeating. Even the most dedicated and blind follower of the Party line could not prove that he had really never had any doubts.

The singling out of the "bourgeois intelligentsia" for this treatment was a catastrophe. The country's development could not proceed without the participation of the best professionals, who were badly needed amid the now enormous mass of inexperienced and ignorant newcomers and with the deficit of specialists still growing. Some were mercifully allowed to "redeem their crimes"—that is, their alleged sabotage—by working "honestly," inventing or designing in their prison cells or on the site, but with the status of convict. To encourage them to invent machinery and weapons, big salaries and the best food in a hungry country were sometimes given to these men, but at the same time they were kept as prisoners and promised freedom at the price of compliance.

The policy certainly did not have the full approval of all top leaders. Within the framework of a new line initiated in 1931 to stop some of the damage of *spetseedstvo*, Ia. E. Rudzutak explained officially that many lower technicians were too ignorant to be able to distinguish "wrecking" from the normal professional risk taken by an engineer;[83] but he certainly knew that the problem was not one of "ignorant technicians." It was a problem of Party policy throughout, otherwise the excesses of the "proletarianization" period could not have taken place. There were waves of purges, dismissals, and arrests of "alien elements" and, in particular, of their children, taking place in universities and institutions. The numerous "social purges of students" enhanced the anxiety and panic among the intelligentsia and even produced suicides—not to speak of candidates to build the canals.[84] Mass expulsions of students drew a protest from Lunacharskii, who, in a letter to Stalin that was found in the Central Party Archives, considered it unacceptable to persecute sons for the sins of their fathers, especially when the sin was no more than the wrong "social origin."[85]

The treatment meted out to old specialists was scarcely beneficial to the rest of the engineers, including the party members, who were not under suspicion. The onslaught on the old engineers hurt the system across the board. Lack of initiative, a tendency to avoid responsibility and hide behind somebody's back, putting the blame on somebody else, and the philosophy that "it's no business of mine" (*moia khata s kraiu*) came to permeate institutions and whole layers of society.

The Intelligent and the Less Intelligent

The figures on the growth of the "intelligentsia" during the thirties are staggering. From modest beginnings at the end of NEP it is claimed that there was a leap by 1939 to ten or eleven million employed, amounting to 13–14 percent of the whole population[86]—in itself an important structural change. Numbers of university students grew from 169,000 in 1928–29 to 812,000 in 1940–41, and there was an impressive growth of students in secondary technical schools. In the early years, however, it was not the school system that supplied students for the university and men for professional jobs: in the proletarianization period this was done by mobilization of party members, workers, and peasants through short courses, workers' faculties, *vydvizhenie* (advancement of workers to positions in the apparat or higher education), and so on. In fact, like everything else, the school system was in turmoil during these years, and the quantitative strides were not the whole story. This was especially true of the universities, whose hectic expansion and initially lax admission standards created large numbers of unviable institutions producing graduates whose level of qualification was no higher than that of secondary school. The crash campaign for cadres was costly and to some degree ineffective. Later, measures were taken to stabilize the system and, with the development of secondary schools, mobilizations and discrimination on class grounds ceased. But the effect of such measures on the quality of specialists and officials subsumed under the label of "intelligentsia" could not be felt quickly. In 1930 a survey of industrial cadres showed that more than half the engineers and technicians in industry were *praktiki* (persons working as engineers and technicians without the appropriate formal training and diplomas) with low education and sometimes without even a crash course. Only 11.4 percent of the engineers and technicians had higher education. The same applied to the whole mass lumped together into the category of "leading cadres and specialists" in industry at large. A survey taken in 1933 showed that of 861,000 people in this category, some 57 percent had neither higher nor specialized secondary education.[87]

We should examine the general problem of the "intelligentsia" from yet another angle. The statistical concept used by official publications was faulty and did not express social realities. The term itself hid a set of social policies and a maze of special groups comprising (a) the creative intelligentsia, old and new; (b) the specialists, old and new, covered by the concept of "engineering and technical workers"; (c) lower officialdom in the various apparats; (d) the higher administration; and (e) the top ruling oligarchy. The last two can be grouped together in the somewhat larger concept of a sociopolitical elite.

This classification makes it clear that the story of the intelligentsia involves more than creating a layer of educated professionals. Hiding or

camouflaging the realities of power in statistical or ideological construc-
tions is not an exclusively Soviet phenomenon, but a universal one that
takes on different forms in different circumstances. Categories like "employees" (*sluzhashchie*) or "intelligentsia" conceal far more than they dis-
close.

The millions listed as "intelligentsia" also included an overwhelming
majority of officials with little education and a low level of professional
skill—three such officials to one educated professional.[88] The lumping
together of these unspecialized and poorly educated people with the educated specialists and literati was intended to create the impression of a
cultural leap and grossly overstated the true situation. In reality this mass of
badly paid officials was an addition to the social structure that did not
necessarily elevate it, but, on the contrary, provided a convenient milieu
for the spread of irrational and obscurantist tendencies. The category of low
officials overlapped only partly with that of *praktiki*, many of whom, although not formally educated, were men of ability. The majority of the
low officials were, as a Soviet sociologist put it, quite "unpromising" (*bes-
perspektivnye*), though many of them filtered through the Party into quite
high places in the influential apparats. Many such people were incorporated into the category of Party members listed as "employees," and they
certainly contributed to the moral and cultural decadence of the Party in
these years.

Our intention here, it should be said, is not to link degrees of education
with moral standards. But we are dealing with a political climate that
promoted or appealed to irrational and baser instincts, and that probably
received a better response from an inexperienced, uninformed, untrained,
and disorientated mass than it would have from the more cultivated, politically alert population.

Exalting this mass that was overcrowding the offices to the glamorous
category of "intelligentsia" was a spurious gesture. The junior officials in
any case did not gain much from the policy of promotion and improvement in salary and prestige that was applied to specialists. This policy
gained momentum in the process of the fight against wage-levelling (*uravnilovka*). The spread of salaries increased, first among the workers themselves, on the basis of skill and piece-rate norms, and second (at the same
time, from 1931 on) when the average salaries of engineers began to grow

and to move away from the hitherto privileged norms of industrial workers' earnings. In August 1931 an important formal step was taken to remove discrimination against the technical intelligentsia: full equality of the technical intelligentsia with industrial workers—including admission of children to higher education, food norms, and rights to sanatoria—was introduced in areas where the industrial workers had had priority. The technical intelligentsia was also given the all-important right to accommodation on equal priority with industrial workers, with the further right—hitherto reserved only for the privileged category of senior officials (*otvetrabotniki*)— of extra space for a study.[89] A year later, a special government committee was created to watch over the construction of housing for engineering and technical workers and scientists.

The position of equality with industrial workers did not last for long. since the status of technical and other specialists continued to rise. During the "proletarianization" period, the social composition of the university student body had included over 50 percent from the working class, with the "employee" category falling to 32.8 percent. But in the course of the thirties, class limitations on entrance to universities and the party were removed, and the sons of employees (including specialists) came back in force. In universities, the employee group allegedly rose to 42.2 percent, with the workers dropping back to their position under NEP, 33.9 percent.[90] Obviously sons of workers and peasants were now in the universities in great numbers. But the growing trend in favor of the children of the already educated was unmistakably part of a new scale of values of the policy maker, and of society at large.

From 1934 on, the professional, the specialist, and the administrator would begin to get orderly and guaranteed fixed monthly salaries; and after the quiet removal in 1932 of the *partmaksimum*, which kept salaries of party members at about two hundred fifty to three hundred rubles a month, the gate would be open for the creation of a real pyramid of income and privilege.[91]

The Bosses and their "Apparats"

The cadre problem was not just one of getting enough specialists and managers, but of promoting a powerful class of bosses—the *nachal'stvo*, composed of top managers in the enterprises and top administrators in state agencies. The *nachal'stvo*, the state's ruling stratum, was the principal group that the system kept fostering—though we must not forget that in Stalinist terms "fostering" always meant, even for the most privileged, constant beating.

Nevertheless, the rewards for being admitted to this group were very considerable, especially in a country in a condition of penury, and the power over subordinates was very great. Some privileges—a car, a special pension, separate eating places—were public knowledge. But much was hidden, like the special stores, special warrants, graduated scale of expense accounts, housing privileges, special well-sheltered resorts, and finally the "sealed envelope" with money over and above the formal salary. All these slowly developed into a formally stratified and quite rigid ladder of importance and power.

The *nachal'stvo* class was born of the principle of one-man direction (*edinonachalie*) as it developed after 1929. The creation of a hierarchical scaffolding of dedicated bosses, held together by discipline, privilege, and power, was a deliberate strategy of social engineering to help stabilize the flux. It was born, therefore, in conditions of stress, mass disorganization, and social warfare, and the bosses were actually asked to see themselves as commanders in a battle. The Party wanted the bosses to be efficient, powerful, harsh, impetuous, and capable of exerting pressure crudely and ruthlessly and getting results "whatever the cost." Rudeness (*grubost'*) became a virtue and, more significantly, the boss was endowed with quasi-police power in the workplace: among his prerogatives were fines and dismissals, which meant deprivation of lodging and food, and he had the further resource (even more corrupting) of the local security organs and the public prosecutor. The formation of the despotic manager was actually a process in which not leaders but *rulers* were made. The fact that their own jobs and freedom were quite insecure made the tyrannical traits of their rule probably more rather than less capricious and offensive.[92]

The Flood of Paper ("bumazhnyi potok")

All the apparats—central and local, party and state—were affected by rapid growth and rapid turnover, purges, low educational and professional standards, and the dysfunctions associated with over-centralization and "administrative methods."

Centralization of decision making, coupled with concentration of power, prerogatives, and resources in a few hands at the top, was paralleled by similar tendencies in every single administration. At all levels power went to the top few, and often in the hands of a single boss. We have already discussed this creation of "small Stalins" in the factories. The phenomenon became all-embracing. But its overall results were only partly calculated and sought for. The policy makers were guided by the idea that in conditions of scarce resources, scarce talent, and not too much commitment in the growing socioeconomic organism, one should concentrate power in fewer, but more competent and reliable, hands. This was reflected in the fostering of the *nachal'stvo, edinonachalie,* and, at the summit of the edifice, the "cult of the individual." But much of the trend was spontaneous, under the combined impact of policy and those numerous unplanned but tenacious elements, inherent in the bureaucratic world of a dictatorial state, that fitted no strategy and nobody's intentions. These elements might separately be identified as "deficiencies" by Politburo members, journalists, or inspectors of the apparat; but in fact the "deficiencies" were so persistent that there was no escape from the conclusion that they amounted to permanent features of the system.

Among them were the "flood of paper" (*bumazhnyi potok*), the proliferation of officials and offices, and (incredible as it may sound for such a centralized state) multicentrism. A study of Mikoian's commissariat of foreign and internal trade, to take an example, found the whole ministry to be, characteristically, in a state of crisis in 1930. But submergence in details, a flood of 2,500 "papers" a day, and loss of control of essential policy matters and their coordination[93] was not only young Mikoian's problem. Another study[94] of the apparats of local soviet executive committees found the following unpalatable traits: firmly entrenched distrust of lower organs, lack of clarity in the division of functions, multicentrism, parallelism, enormous multiplicity of channels all the way down the line from Moscow to the raions, harassment and pettifogging supervision of the lower level by the higher, and constant delays.[95] Red tape and the bureaucratic style of operation, castigated by the top leaders themselves as "formalistic paper work" (*kantselarshchina* and *formal'no-bumazhnoe rukovodstvo*), became phenomena from which there was no escape. The leadership and the public alike were bewildered and, in fact, helpless. Stuchka (a leading jurist, theoretician, and Supreme Court judge), for instance, seemed quite astonished to discover what every official knew already, that government departments were engaging in fierce in-fighting: it was real "class warfare," he said, in which the parties behaved like enemies and genuine competitors.[96] He could only sigh.

The leadership clearly did not understand what was happening or why. Ordzhonikidze, when still head of the commissariat of state inspection, lamented that every time reductions of personnel and financial economies were decreed the result was bigger expenditure and an increase in the number of officials.[97] It was impossible, he went on, to get through the maze of cumbersome and top-heavy apparats and wrench realistic date out of them,[98] and he appealed for a study of the tendency of the apparats to distort government decisions. It was, in fact, an impossible task. Officials formed "families" and engaged in every kind of mutual protection.

The growing bureaucratic Moloch not only menaced the country but terrified the top leaders as well. They reacted, true to style and tradition, by pressuring and purging the apparats. The general idea was to make the officials feel "the firm and controlling hand" and, in addition, "to come down hard on some, as an example to the others" (bol'no stuknut' kogo sleduet, v primet i nauku drugim).[99] As the leadership increased control and terror, "centralization" was also strengthened and kept breeding more and more of the same phenomena. Facing such pressure from above, officials felt compelled to defend themselves by padding, cover-up, and "hand in glove" policies—and by redirecting the pressure downwards to get some results.

In this atmosphere, the type that thrived and prospered was precisely the cunning and dodgy character, unscrupulous and conformist, who had learned the hard way the disadvantages of taking any initiative without orders from above. Soon the habit would become second nature, and the system of "counter-incentives" would mobilize more energies to blocking orders and plans from above than to fulfilling them. Syrtsov, chief of the state machinery of the RSFSR, knew what he was talking about when he commented: "We bind a man hand and foot with all kinds of agreements; we drive him into a bottle, cork it up and put a government stamp on it; and then we go round saying: 'Why doesn't this man show any energy or any initiative?'"[100] He did not mention terror, but this was obvious. His appeal to solve the problem "by letting people out of the bottle" led him into trouble the very same year.

Four years later Kaganovich, one of the promoters and practitioners of the method of "coming down hard," listed the factors responsible for the devastating turnover of personnel in the Party and other apparats: those at the top "hit from the shoulder," and dismissals and punishments were so frequent that many local party officials, even if highly successful for some time, took it for granted that normality could not last and, in order to avoid catastrophe, decided: better clear out (*nado smyvat'sia*) while the going's good. [101]

The "logic" of the centralized machinery led to putting the blame only on the lower ranks: if only the oblast committees knew more about their cadres and looked after them better, a Kaganovich would complain. But he could also resort, when necessary, to a broader view: the "class analysis." Tsarist officials still in service and all the other "socially alien, . . . bankrupt, degenerate hangers-on" could be invoked to carry the blame.

These were, in fact, the terms used to guide the mammoth purge of the state apparats ordered by the party in 1929. [102] To purge (*chistit'* or, more lovingly, *podchistit'*) became another expression of the current "art of ruling," and had far-reaching and well-known effects for everyone. The purge of officialdom begun in 1929 dragged on for a full two years, disorganized and disorientated the administrators, dismissed every tenth official who was checked—and then petered out with a decision to stop the whole thing and never return to the method of "wholesale purges" (*poval'nye chistki*). [103] As the 160,000 purged officials left (many probably found their way back later) and all the disturbing phenomena remained, including inflation of personnel, the government decreed a new move: not a purge but a "reduction of personnel," in which a further 153,000 officials were apparently fired in the winter of 1932–33. [104]

This was not going to be the last word. The *chinovnik*, Trotskii thought, was going to swallow the dictatorship of the proletariat if the dictatorship did not swallow him in good time. The prophecy was not quite accurate. The *chinovnik* was "swallowing" the masses, the state was swallowing those same *chinovniki*, and the proletariat was quite irrelevant to the question. The whole thing was simply the *modus operandi* of a police state, beating the country into a modernity of its own definition and catching some morbid diseases in the process.

Educational Strategies and Cultural Revolution: The Politics of Soviet Development

Gail Warshofsky Lapidus

To an observer of Soviet political development, the unfolding of the Great Proletarian Cultural Revolution in China in the mid-1960s was not altogether without historical precedent. The sweeping assault on the cultural remnants of the past and on its bourgeois representatives unleashed by the Party leadership and pressed by a coalition of militant cadres and youthful zealots evoked the atmosphere of revolutionary enthusiasm and political militance that swept the USSR between 1928 and 1932.

These two dramatic episodes, so widely separated in time and space, differed in several important respects.[1] The scope of cultural revolution in China was far broader and its methods and goals more systematic and comprehensive than those of its Soviet counterpart. Indeed the entire task of cultural transformation occupied a more distinct and central place in

I should like to express my appreciation to the National Fellows Program of the Hoover Institution, Stanford University, and to the Institute of International Studies and the Center for Slavic and East European Studies of the University of California at Berkeley for their research support.

Maoist revolutionary strategy. In the Soviet Union, the Cultural Revolution of 1928–32 was stamped by the dramatic socioeconomic transformation that it accompanied, the crash programs of industrialization and agricultural collectivization inaugurated by the First Five-Year Plan. This compression was missing from the pattern of Chinese development. Agrarian revolution largely preceded the political seizure of power, while the Great Leap Forward antedated the Great Proletarian Cultural Revolution by a decade. The tasks of cultural revolution therefore took on an independent and defining importance in China, by contrast with the Soviet treatment of cultural change as largely derivative, a function of the redefinition of economic, political, and social domains.[2]

Yet the parallels are suggestive. Soviet and Chinese Communist elites brought similar orientations and dispositions to the tasks of revolutionary transformation in a number of critical respects. They shared an apocalyptic vision of the future as well as a strong interventionist propensity, which was expressed in an intense concern with uprooting antecedent attitudinal and behavioral patterns, and a preoccupation with the fundamental transformation of human nature itself. Though they adopted different strategies for this purpose, both conceived the process and tasks of revolutionary transformation to extend beyond the destruction and reconstitution of political and economic institutions; they envisioned a decisive alteration of traditional cultural norms and the creation of a new Communist man.[3]

Moreover, in both milieus cultural revolution came to the forefront in the context of similar political and developmental needs. It represented a short-lived but intense eruption of revolutionary militance unleashed at the center as a weapon in factional conflicts over alternative developmental strategies. It permitted the release of accumulated tensions generated by conflicting ideological and developmental imperatives. And it accompanied a shift of power within the political elite, a reconstruction of political coalitions, and a basic redefinition of organizational and political priorities. These parallels are sufficiently striking to suggest that the scope, implications, and limits of cultural revolution in Russia might be illuminated by a broader comparative perspective that treats it not merely as a unique combination of historical circumstances peculiar to the early history of the Soviet regime but as an expression of generic developmental problems in the evolution of Communist systems.

EDUCATION AND DEVELOPMENT:
A CRITIQUE OF CONVENTIONAL
INTERPRETATIONS

While a broadly comparative treatment remains beyond the scope of this paper, a more detailed exploration of the relationship between cultural revolution and developmental strategies in the Soviet Union provides a useful starting point for further discussion. A focus upon educational policy offers a particularly fruitful approach to these larger issues. For the USSR as for China, education was the key to the cultural revolution that would create a society at once socialist and modern. It would inculcate the scientific knowledge and practical skills that would transform a backward agrarian society into a modern industrial order. It would serve as a channel of social mobility for previously disadvantaged groups, undermining traditional hierarchical and ascriptive patterns of social organization and facilitating the creation of an egalitarian community. Finally, education would transform the values, attitudes, and behavior of the population itself, creating the new men and women, the future citizens, of a modern socialist society. Educational policy was therefore intimately bound up with patterns of economic and political development in the larger society, and changing orientations in education reveal much about the broader redefinition of organizational and developmental priorities that accompanied the evolution of both Communist systems.

In the Soviet Union, as in China, the Cultural Revolution coincided with a dramatic reorientation of educational policy. Yet this shift has been partially obscured by the conventional periodization of Soviet political and social development. Typically, treatments of the early evolution of Soviet education emphasize the abrupt repudiation, in the early 1930s, of the utopian and experimental educational policies of the 1920s, and the restoration under Stalin of a more traditional and authoritarian educational system.[4] The standard explanation for this Great Retreat is a functionalist one, which emphasizes the adaptation of the educational system to new economic and political needs. As Merle Fainsod put it, "The educational reforms of the early thirties with their emphasis on the restoration of discipline, the reinforcement of the authority of the teacher, and the teaching of fundamentals represented a first adjustment of the educational system to the needs of the industrial order."[5]

The broader implications of this approach are developed more explicitly by Richard Lowenthal, who interprets the evolution of Communist polities in terms of the tension between utopian and developmental goals.[6] The gradual erosion of revolutionary utopian values, he argues, is the inevitable concomitant of the modernization of Communist systems. Stalinism, in this view, expresses the universal functional requisites of modernization, a necessary if deplorable stage in the transition to modernity.

Yet this analytical framework poses a false dichotomy. The presumed antithesis between "utopian revolutionary ideology" and "developmental needs" itself rests upon a series of unstated propositions that deserve further exploration. When applied to the evolution of the Soviet educational system it imposes rigid and misleading categories upon a more complex reality. Not two but three distinct stages can be identified in the evolution of the Soviet educational system. For the conventional emphasis upon 1931 as the turning point in educational policy obscures the dramatic assault on the educational system unleashed by the Cultural Revolution and the mixture of destructive and constructive changes that it inaugurated.

The Cultural Revolution launched in 1929 marked a dramatic departure from, and indeed repudiation of, the educational practices and priorities of the 1920s, introducing a brief period of educational radicalism that brought to the fore educational undercurrents submerged during NEP, while simultaneously laying the foundation for subsequent developments. The Great Retreat that began in 1931 involved a series of measures directed against these very currents and policies and not merely against the educational practices of Narkompros in the 1920s. The Cultural Revolution, therefore, forms the crucial and missing link in understanding both the history of Soviet educational policy in particular and the evolution of the Soviet system more broadly. Thus a closer examination of these three distinct phases in the development of the Soviet educational system will call into question conventional interpretations of Stalinism, clarify the redefinition of political and developmental needs that it precipitated, and permit a fresh interpretation of the pattern of modernization in the USSR and the place of cultural revolution in this larger developmental process.

THE EDUCATIONAL STRATEGY OF
NARKOMPROS: 1917–1928

In their efforts to transform the schools "from the weapon of bourgeois class domination into a weapon for the total destruction of class divisions within society... [and] the Communist regeneration of society,"[7] the leaders of the new Soviet state sought to transform both the structure and the ethos of the educational system inherited from the Tsarist regime. Its elitism, scholasticism, and authoritarian atmosphere were viewed as obstacles to social and economic progress, creating individuals with skills, values, and personalities ill suited to a modern and socialist society. Bolshevik critiques of the Tsarist educational system owed much to the views of prerevolutionary educational reformers. The stratified and hierarchical structure of the Tsarist school system, its critics had long claimed, offered little opportunity for mobility based on achievement. The scholasticism of the educational curriculum, influenced as it was by classical literary culture and Orthodox doctrine, was irrelevant to the scientific and technological needs of a modern society. The extreme authoritarianism of the school environment, with its emphasis on rote learning, destroyed intellectual curiosity and initiative and produced stunted conformists fit only for staffing the gigantic bureaucracy of the autocratic state. Under the leadership of Anatolii Lunacharskii, a philosopher-poet and revolutionary enthusiast who once described himself as "an intellectual among Bolsheviks and a Bolshevik among intellectuals," the new Commissariat of Enlightenment (Narkompros) attempted to construct an educational system on entirely new foundations.

The democratization of educational opportunities was a first priority. In place of the fragmented school system of Tsarist Russia Narkompros proclaimed the establishment of a unified network of schools of a single type, open to all without restriction, in which a student could move without interruption from the bottom to the top of the educational ladder. In theory, access was to be equally available to all. As Lunacharskii himself put it: "In principle, every child of the Russian republic enters a school of an identical type and has the same chances as every other to complete the higher education."[8]

In practice, however, resources were severely limited. With massive educational expansion foreclosed by economic constraints, the allocation—not the extension—of educational opportunities became the crucial issue. The criteria of selection became the subject of heated controversy. Particularly in higher educational institutions, an exclusive emphasis on achievement would exclude precisely those social strata whose mobility the new regime sought to encourage. On the other hand, if excessive weight were given to the social composition of educational institutions, the consequent erosion of academic standards would threaten the training and supply of skilled specialists so desperately needed for economic reconstruction. The utilization of preferential admissions policies therefore responded to the changing economic and political priorities of the leadership, and attempted to balance the goals of proletarianization against competing economic and social needs.[9]

But preferential admissions policies were not the only device available for shaping the social composition of the school population. Indeed the Commissariat introduced a wide range of innovative measures designed to widen the access to education of previously disadvantaged social strata. The creation of *rabfaks* (workers' faculties) attached to higher educational institutions and designed to provide a rough but rapid equivalent of a secondary education, played a central role in this effort. By 1928 rabfak graduates formed almost one-third of the total of incoming students in higher educational institutions, contributing substantially to the rise in worker representation in higher education from 15 percent in 1923–24 to over 26 percent in 1927–28.[10] Narkompros thus identified itself with efforts to widen access to existing institutions rather than radically to transform their role in social selection.

A second feature of the new educational system that distinguished it from its Tsarist predecessor was its effort to achieve a "close unity of education and socially productive work."[11] The objective of the Narkompros leadership was to construct an educational curriculum that would avoid the twin pitfalls of academic formalism on the one hand—a bookish and intellectual learning divorced from real life—and excessive vocationalism and narrow specialization on the other. Even at the primary level, the new school was to be a labor school. Learning would begin with the immediate environment of the child and his or her direct experience, proceeding outward in a series of concentric circles to encompass an ever wider natural and social universe.

At more advanced levels the curriculum would combine general education with polytechnical training. This elusive but important concept was the key to socialist educational thought. By contrast with the narrow vocationalism that capitalist societies imposed upon working class children, a genuinely socialist education would offer broad and comprehensive training. Polytechnical education would prepare these children for participation in a modern and changing industrial economy whose future shape was not yet fully known by equipping them with a broad understanding of modern industrial processes and the principles underlying all science and technology. In practice, "polytechnicalism" was a loose term that came to encompass everything from workshops to laboratories to apprenticeship training; indeed, as one observer remarked, anything short of a lecture or text. But the objective was central to a genuinely socialist education, and the Narkompros leadership was outspoken in its defense of broad and theoretical training against pressures for early vocationalism and production practice.

Yet a third objective of the new educational system was to develop new values and patterns of behavior. "Socialism," wrote Krupskaia, "will be possible only when the psychology of people is radically changed. To change it is the task standing before us."[12] Thus the school was conceived as a microcosm of the larger social universe, capable of socializing children into the new roles and behaviors suitable to a socialist society. If the hierarchical and authoritarian features of the Tsarist schools had suppressed spontaneity and initiative, the new Soviet schools would give them every encouragement. Maturation replaced training as the goal of educational efforts, and traditional pedagogical methods that emphasized the authority of the teacher, formal lectures, compulsory homework, and individual evaluation through examinations were swept away in favor of an emphasis on independent activity and collective goals. The libertarian strain in early Bolshevism found a congenial environment in the Commissariat of Enlightenment.

But other, more contradictory, aims were also assigned to the new Soviet school. It was expected to foster cultural secularism and a critical scientific outlook among its students while simultaneously cultivating the development of a proper Communist world view. Although the distinction between upbringing and indoctrination was insisted upon in pedagogical theory, it proved difficult to maintain in practice.

With the gradual consolidation of Soviet power and the emergence of new institutions and priorities in economic and political life, the ideological and political premises of early educational policy were called into question. Both the internal organization of the early Soviet school and its relation to local social organizations were influenced by a syndicalist image of socialism as a free association of self-regulating communes. Educational populists like Krupskaia sought to encourage decentralization and popular participation in school affairs, both within the school itself and in the relations of the school with social groups outside it. They envisioned local communities playing an active role in the direction of school affairs through a Soviet equivalent of American school boards. But the emergence of a centralized and hierarchical state bureaucracy overwhelmed these goals and created an increasing lack of congruence between the patterns of authority within the school and those of the larger political and social environment.

If the visions that guided the efforts of Narkompros were often remote from the realities of school life, the Commissariat leadership was itself profoundly aware of the gap between aspirations and possibilities. The fault lay not merely with its misplaced values and administrative incompetence, as critics tended to charge, but above all with the cultural backwardness of Russian society and with the priorities of a leadership unwilling to commit to education the resources for which these apostles of enlightenment continually pleaded. For the Party leadership, political and economic issues were of transcending significance, while educational and cultural matters were secondary, indeed tertiary, given their designation as the "Third Front." Only in 1928, when educational backwardness constituted a growing impediment to the regime's ability to implement new economic priorities, did educational needs receive more direct attention. Yet in their concern for equality of opportunity, for individual autonomy, and for a more democratic structure of authority, the educational policies of Narkompros in the 1920s were far more congruent with many contemporary definitions of modernity than were those that would be adopted later.

THE CRITICS OF NARKOMPROS:
ALTERNATIVE STRATEGIES

If the Narkompros leadership was dismayed by the continuing gap between vision and reality, it could nonetheless take pride in many of its accomplishments. The new education of the Soviet republic represented, for all its shortcomings, a decisive break with the past and a real stride forward in the direction of a modern, socialist school system, based upon a genuinely Marxist-Leninist pedagogical theory.

This satisfaction was not shared by its critics. To them, the policies and priorities of Narkompros were altogether too timid, its leadership too conservative, the schools too reminiscent of the elitism and scholasticism of the past. Not only was a revolutionary transformation of education still to be accomplished; the evolution of educational policy in the late 1920s was in some respects a step backward. The elaborate trappings of the new pedagogy in fact concealed a retreat from revolutionary goals.

Yet the critics of Narkompros shared no single definition of educational goals. They represented a rather diverse coalition of interests, were animated by conflicting priorities, and urged very different solutions to the problems that they raised. It would be difficult to classify them in any scheme based upon the dichotomy of "socialism" and "modernity," or to divide them neatly into political categories. They were all, in different ways, concerned with how best to construct a society that would be at once socialist and modern, and how to educate technical cadres at once "red" and "expert." They held different views of the requirements of each, which carried very different implications for educational policy.

The critics included, first of all, the advocates of more radical proletarianization. Urging that education be considered a privilege of the working class, and that the schools be used to assure its dominance, the proletarianizers urged more drastic efforts to alter the social composition of the schools. Pressing what one recent study has called the "hard line" in cultural policy,[13] they demanded the abolition of the general secondary school, whose clientele included only a small fraction of children of worker or peasant background, and the direct recruitment of workers and peasants into higher educational institutions. The reliance on competitive examinations to regulate admissions served to limit the access of workers' children, they argued, and should be eliminated.

The supporters of more radical proletarianization were concentrated within the trade union movement, the Komsomol, and the lower ranks of the Party. It was a movement marked by the mentality of the Civil War, eager to perpetuate an atmosphere of crisis and class struggle, impatient with compromise and fearful of bourgeois restoration. It represented a psychology as much as a political program. Yet it was not a movement hostile to expertise itself. Rather, it was concerned with assuring the dominance of the proletariat among the new Soviet experts. Both the invocation of class war and the respect for expertise emerge together in the characteristic alarm of Preobrazhenskii, who came to the defense of further proletarianization during his brief involvement in the educational controversies of 1921:

> The bourgeois and intellectual strata of the population are frantically trying to maintain themselves and their children at the level of education and social position reached in the pre-revolutionary period. This, of course, is quite understandable. But the proletarian state will never allow the parents and children of the former privileged classes to decide the question of the numbers and social origins of the future specialists we train in our schools. At the moment there is a genuine class war at the doors of the higher school between the worker-peasant majority of the country, which wants to have specialists from among its own kin in its own state, and the governing classes and strata linked with them. The proletarian state openly takes the side of its own people. [14]

What the Party opposition feared most was the revival of influence of "unreconstructed" social and cultural forces over the definition of educational goals. Not intrinsically hostile to expertise but eager to thwart a potential bourgeois restoration, it pressed for more far-reaching measures to assure the social and political domination of the schools by representatives of the proletarian dictatorship.

Criticism of yet another kind came from an alliance of economic and technocratic interests centered in the economic commissariats and in Vesenkha. Their chief preoccupation was with the supply of technical specialists needed for economic reconstruction. Although the Narkompros leadership was sensitive to the urgent need for large numbers of skilled workers, the value attached to general education, and, more broadly, to literary and humanistic culture, was an obstacle to the real expansion of a network of vocational schools. The advocates of vocationalism consequently sought to wrest control of technical education from Narkompros and transfer it to the economic commissariats. While they tended to resist measures that would erode academic standards in higher educational institutions, they advocated the massive expansion of vocational programs at the expense of secondary general education.

Although this group of critics differed in composition and orientation from the first, and was far more concerned with the economic conse-quences of educational policy than with its implications for social and political structure, the two approaches often overlapped. The tendency for the advocates of proletarianization to favor increased vocationalization as well, and to draw a connection between the two, is exemplified in the views of O. Iu. Schmidt, who, as deputy head of Glavprofobr, had fought unsuccessfully for a change of policy within Narkompros, and who favored both the wider use of class quotas in higher educational admissions and a speeding-up of the training of engineers. Preobrazhenskii was voicing the common concern of this loose alliance when he insisted:

> Only that part of the national income can be spent on enlightenment which corresponds to the given level of development of socialist produc-tion. And that part which is spent must be distributed according to the importance of this or that branch of enlightenment for the whole economy of the country in general. In any case, higher education must be highly diminished in favor of lower; and, in lower education, the general branch must be enormously diminished in favor of what is urgently important for industry and agriculture. [15]

Preoccupied with the wish to speed the training of middle-level specialists and skilled workers, this group tended to advocate a shortening of instruc-tional programs and the intensification of production training within the schools along lines that were already being practiced by the Ukrainian Commissariat of Education under G.F. Grinko. Narkompros shared some of its general objectives, but placed them in a different time perspective. A long-term strategy for scientific and technical education, Lunacharskii in-sisted, should not be sacrificed to more immediate needs. To lower the level of training of Soviet engineers would be politically and economically counterproductive. [16]

Yet a third group of critics emerged from a cultural left that expressed in educational terms the implications of radical Communism. Drawing on the anarchistic strains of Lenin's *State and Revolution*, they envisioned a society in which the spontaneous initiative of the masses would create new communal and associational forms. Educational theorists like V. N. Shulgin and M. V. Krupenina gave eloquent expression to an instinctive suspicion of formal educational institutions. Schools were inherently elitist and divorced from life and would "wither away" in a future Communist society. [17] These advocates of "deschooling" proposed that participation in socialist construction replace formal school attendance.

Although the views of the educational radicals added fuel to the criticisms of Narkompros policy expressed by the other two groups, and although some of their objectives did indeed overlap, the radicals were more concerned with challenging the fundamental premises of the emerging educational system than with influencing the course of educational policy. Krupskaia herself was sympathetic to many of their concerns, and her journal *Na putiakh k novoi shkole* offered a forum for their views, but they remained marginal in the development of educational theory and practice until a new political climate gave them a new significance.

THE CULTURAL REVOLUTION IN EDUCATION, 1928–1931

A sequence of political events abruptly altered the environment in which educational policy was shaped, and called into question its fundamental premises. The Fifteenth Party Congress held in December 1927 had called for the mobilization of economic resources on behalf of industrialization, and appeared to lend support and encouragement to the long-standing efforts of Narkompros to extract a greater share of resources for educational programs. Lunacharskii reported with satisfaction on the results of the Party Congress. Its special significance, he commented, was that the Party leadership had finally acknowledged the degree to which further economic advances were dependent upon progress in the cultural sphere. [18] Industrialization increased the demand for skilled cadres, and if manpower needs were to be met, then massive investments were needed for the expansion of the educational system at all levels.

The advocates of a "soft line" in cultural affairs were further heartened by the rebuff given to their enemies. The Congress rejected the opposition's warnings that a bourgeois offensive constituted a serious threat to Party control and required intensified warfare. Finally, to the special satisfaction of Narkompros, the pressures for the transfer of higher technical education to the economic commissariats had once again been resisted. The Congress appeared to confirm the view that cultural revolution was a gradual process, a steady enhancement of the level of literacy, culture, and technical-scientific knowledge of the population. The leadership of Narkompros in this process had been affirmed.

Lunacharskii's contentment was to be short-lived. The Shakhty affair in the spring of 1928, involving the arrest and trial of fifty-five engineers and technicians on charges of sabotage, touched off an assault on the bourgeois specialists that was followed by a massive ideological campaign against class enemies. The term "cultural revolution" was redefined to incorporate the left oppositionist view of cultural revolution as class war. As the head of the Central Committee agitprop department now warned, "The most dangerous distortion of the Party line in cultural work . . . comes from an opportunist, anti-revolutionary conception of cultural revolution as 'peaceful' cultural development . . . irrespective of class war and class contradictions."[19]

The period from 1929 to 1931 saw a dramatic reorientation of educational policy that was neither a solution to the accumulating problems of the late 1920s nor the first step in the direction that educational policy would take thereafter. It proved to be a reorientation that the educational policies of the 1930s would largely undo. The defeat of Bukharin in the economic debates and Stalin's adoption of radical economic programs represented a major shift in the balance of power and policy within the central Party leadership. In its aftermath, Stalin associated himself with the critics of Narkompros, espousing their call for more radical proletarianization of educational institutions, the transfer of higher technical education to the economic commissariats, and a reorganization of Narkompros itself. Class war on the cultural front, long advocated by the Party opposition, had become official policy.

The new political climate affected educational institutions and policies in three critical areas. First, the shift from class conciliation to class war was a signal to the Komsomol and Party advocates of radical proletarianization that the Party leadership had now given formal sanction to their position. It touched off a vast wave of purges at all levels of the educational system, which the Narkompros leadership tried in vain to halt.[20]

Proletarianization and politicization were inextricably linked. At institutions of higher education widespread purges of faculty and students were accompanied by drives to enhance ideological purity. The Smolensk Archives document in fascinating detail the process by which the universities were brought under more direct Party influence.[21] At Smolensk State University the Cultural Revolution was launched in the spring of 1929. Party organs forced the replacement of key administrators with trusted Party figures and ordered the new leadership to improve the social composition of the student body, to communize the leading organs and scientific workers of the university, and to create conditions "which would aid to the maximum the task of training cadres of real builders of socialism."[22] A special commission of the Smolensk *obkom* appointed to review the execution of these directives noted with approval the dismissal of fifteen scientific workers characterized as conservative types unsuitable for a Soviet university and their replacement by a new group with substantial Party representation. Party members now dominated the governing board of the university as well as the faculty of social sciences. The Party cell was nevertheless accused of insufficient political vigilance and urged to overcome its "right-opportunist attitudes" and to press forward with expulsions of "socially alien and hostile students and reactionary scientific workers." Further purges of "reactionary" faculty followed. A linguist accused of "wrecking" for having spent five hundred rubles of state money to acquire a copy of "The Lay of Prince Igor," "a memorial to the great princely chauvinism of the twelfth century," was among those dismissed, as was a librarian described as socially passive for his refusal to subscribe to the State Loan, and excessively "formal" in his relationships with students. Although it proved impossible to dispense completely with the services of the older intelligentsia in university faculties, the older generation of non-Party professors was being increasingly displaced from positions of administrative and political importance.

Students as well as faculty fell victim to the purges of higher educational institutions. Massive expulsions of students of intelligentsia and bourgeois origins took place. The purging appeared to have official sponsorship and sanction although it was the subject of considerable controversy and bureaucratic conflict. At Smolensk University in 1929–30, the Archives report, a number of the students expelled as "alien elements" were subsequently reinstated by the Oblast Department of Public Education. As the new rector complained to the Party unit, "The reinstatements... bring students to the conclusion that there exist two Soviet powers in Smolensk—one, the 'bad' one, in Smolensk State University, and the other, the 'good' one, in the Oblast Department of Public Education...."[23]

The expulsion of large numbers of students whose social origins were suspect was accompanied by intensive efforts to increase the representation of students of proletarian background. The extension of rabfaks designed to prepare poorly educated workers for entrance into the university and the effort to recruit students of designated social background or political affiliation to fill assigned quotas began to have a dramatic impact on educational statistics. The proportion of students of working class background rose from 30 percent of the total in 1928–29 to a high of 58 percent by 1932–33.[24]

The purges extended from the universities and secondary schools to even the lowest levels of the school system, given added impetus by the anti-kulak campaign that accompanied collectivization. Lunacharskii and Krupskaia protested in vain the punishment of children for the social status of their parents. The purges controverted what was to them the very function of the schools, to reshape and reeducate the nonproletarian masses of the population.[25] For Krupskaia, socialism was synonymous with popular enlightenment, and she repeatedly expressed her incomprehension that a Communist should wish to deny anyone the right to education and development.

The new political climate affected not only the social composition of the schools but also their educational function. The imposition of a radical and indeed technically unfeasible version of the Five-Year Plan meant the abandonment of rational long-term planning of education as well, and the reorientation of education to serve immediate economic needs. In education as in economic life, crash programs became the order of the day, designed to achieve dramatic results—such as the liquidation of illiteracy—in extremely short periods of time. Educational institutions were further disrupted by the frequent mobilizations of students for social work. The establishment of exaggerated goals without provision of adequate resources submerged the schools in a flood of enrollments, for which they lacked both physical space and trained personnel. The system of formal education began to collapse under the weight of pressures for the rapid training of skilled workers.

A major reorganization of higher education completed the process of subordinating education to immediate economic and political needs. Higher educational institutions were broken into separate and narrowly specialized fragments, and the authority of Narkompros over them was diluted by their subordination to Vesenkha or related economic commissariats.[26] By 1931–32 just eleven universities remained of the twenty-one in existence in 1924–25. Some seventy new institutions of higher education had meanwhile been formed, offering in 1932 some nine hundred different specializations.[27]

The secondary schools were either transformed into vocational institutions with shortened courses of study or became mere adjuncts of local enterprises or collective farms. Even the primary schools shifted to a campaign style in which productive labor replaced formal learning. Shulgin's enthusiasm at the prospect of the imminent "withering away" of the schools offered an optimistic rationalization of educational chaos.

Finally, the structure of authority and decision-making in education was shattered by the shift of power at the center. The assault on the right opposition within the Party weakened the position of the Narkompros leadership itself and made it vulnerable to attacks not merely for administrative incompetence but for political deviation. In the fall of 1929 Lunacharskii was replaced by Bubnov, a former political commissar who brought to Narkompros the military style of the Civil War period, and whose mission was to purge the Commissariat of rightist deviation and to make it a more reliable instrument for carrying out the directives of the Party leadership.

In this turbulent political atmosphere obsessed with ideological deviation and class warfare, yet permeated by apocalyptic visions of a socialist utopia, radical proposals met with new receptivity. It was a climate in which the educational ideas of Viktor Nikolaevich Shulgin might be suddenly, if briefly, welcomed. Shulgin himself exercised no real leadership in the formulation or execution of educational policy. He was less a leader than an observer and interpreter of events inspired and directed by others, and his views in any case had little in common with those of the more pragmatic Bubnov. His numerous and rather repetitive contributions to educational philosophy express a mood more than a concrete program. As one of his critics delicately noted, his writings are characterized by an unfortunate "lack of clarity of expression,"[28] and it is impossible to distill from them a coherent and comprehensive educational theory. Yet his efforts to develop a "pedagogy for the transition period" deserve attention as an authentic expression of the cultural revolution and of the vision of an imminent socialist utopia inspired by the gigantic upheaval of the First Five-Year Plan. At the same time, the fate of his endeavors demonstrates that the revival of cultural radicalism, though encouraged briefly by the new political and economic needs, was useful for instrumental purposes but fundamentally incompatible with the new society that was emerging.

V. N. SHULGIN AND THE "WITHERING AWAY" OF THE SCHOOL

Shulgin's enthusiastic reception of the First Five-Year Plan as the long-awaited fulfillment of the Revolution of 1917 reveals the formative imprint of his anarcho-communist involvement during the Civil War period. A member of the Moscow camp in educational circles in 1918, he was an early supporter of the view that existing school institutions should be converted into "school-communes," in which pupils, teachers, and service personnel would form an ecomonic as well as educational collective. While the NEP had a sobering effect on much early radicalism, for Shulgin it was merely a breathing spell. As Director of the Institute of School Methods he sought to use this temporary lull to lay the foundations for a new revolutionary breakthrough. In a succession of essays written during the 1920s addressing the problems that preoccupied both Narkompros and its critics, Shulgin defended and elaborated upon these early views.[29]

Shulgin shared many of the fundamental concerns of Lunacharskii and Krupskaia, and his critical attitude toward the new educational system gave voice to a malaise they themselves often shared. Educational democratization was a first and fundamental concern. Shulgin was critical of Narkompros's efforts to widen access to educational institutions as a way of ultimately reallocating social status, for he rejected the entire system of social selection on which a formal system of education rested. Any system of formal education, he implied, was inherently elitist, and no reform limited to the question of access would accomplish the goals of democratization. The problem, as he defined it, went beyond the social composition of the schools. It extended to the very meaning of education itself.

Shulgin shared the hostility of the proletarianizers to the urban 7- and 9-year schools. The dominance of socially alien groups was paralleled by the dominance of alien values. He was alarmed by the pervasive influence of reactionary ideologies, anti-Semitism, and sexual promiscuity among students revealed in the surveys conducted by his institute. In his view, the school environment of NEP, far from educating the younger generation in the spirit of socialism, exerted a harmful influence on its intellectual and moral development. The school environment stood in stark contrast to the healthy influence of the wider social environment, and of factories and Communist youth organizations in particular.

So long as schools were concerned with the transmission of an accumulated store of knowledge, so long as learning was a bookish enterprise divorced from the larger struggles for economic productivity and social progress, the formal educational system would perpetuate the division between intellectual and manual labor. This division could only be overcome, in his view, by a fundamental reorientation of the school curriculum to emphasize production training, and participation in the larger struggle to create a Communist society.

In writings of the mid-1920s addressed to the internal reforms that might improve the effect of the school environment, he emphasized the need to make the labor of the child the core of educational programs. He was opposed to the invention of school tasks for children to perform, but sought to integrate children into the work of the community. More extensive provisions for workshops within the schools were needed, but the more active participation of children in the daily struggles of the larger community was essential to Communist upbringing. By the late 1920s, in his enthusiasm for the economic and social transformation of Russian society promised by the Five-Year Plan, his writings increasingly blurred the distinction between education and production and between education and social struggle. Indeed, it was precisely the merger of education and production that would accomplish the ultimate democratization of the former. In a society in which all members, children as well as adults, were engaged in productive work and learning simultaneously, society itself would become an educational enterprise and all its members therefore students. No mechanism of selection would be required at all; education was indistinguishable from citizenship.

The merger of learning and production was crucial not only to the democratization of education but to its very definition. Shulgin's views superficially echoed those of the technocrats in calling for a reorientation of the curriculum to emphasize vocational training. But where the technocrats emphasized the contribution of such measures to the supply of skilled manpower, Shulgin was more concerned with their moral and educative effect. His faith in the purifying nature of labor has its contemporary counterpart in the assignment of Chinese cadres to the May 7 schools in rural areas for reeducation. For Maoism shares with Shulgin a profound conviction that immersion in production exercises a cleansing effect on social and moral development.

Shulgin's conception of education was essentially utilitarian. The knowledge he valued was knowledge that could serve some immediate use, and indeed arose out of immediate practical concerns. The more completely education and production were joined, the more closely education approached his vision. In 1929 Shulgin hailed the emergence of the enterprise-school in urban areas and the kolkhoz universities in rural regions as the realization of his vision of new institutions in which education and work would merge.

It was a vision that deemphasized the role of the school as a distinctive social institution with a distinctive educative mission. Education, he insisted, was not a process confined to the four walls of a school or club but a process that was inseparable from life itself. Not formal educational institutions but the soviets, the Party, professional associations, mass organizations, these were for Shulgin the real "school of the masses." His views represented an educational counterpart to the view of the state developed by Lenin in *State and Revolution*. For Shulgin the school, like the state, was a temporary historical phenomenon that would "wither away" with the advent of a communist society. In 1928, that prospect seemed imminent. It was not only the school that lost its exclusive educative function. Shulgin's vision called into question the special role of the teacher as well. Specific pedagogical tasks were dissolved in a social universe where the mechanic, agronomist, engineer, indeed anyone with any skills at all, had something of value to communicate. The tasks of pedagogy expanded to include the understanding and utilization of the entire natural and social environment. Shulgin's universe, in short, was one in which all distinctions based upon function, expertise, and even age seemed to dissolve. Children, adolescents, and adults were ultimately indistinguishable, all engaged in a simultaneous and identical process of learning and working together.

There was, clearly, a major problem of coordination of this undifferentiated and elemental wave of spontaneous mass activity. Shulgin was aware of the problem; indeed, his writings are permeated with a concern for unified and centralized control. But his suggestions on how this should be achieved lack clarity and coherence. Although the Party, soviets, youth organizations, and other associations were assigned important educative roles, Shulgin did not propose a type of centralization based on existing institutional hierarchies. Instead—like many other writers of the period— he offered "planning" as the solution for the conflicting requirements of centralized control and local spontaneity. The educational plan would be sensitive to needs and possibilities at a local level. At the same time, it would serve the function of ideological coordination and integration of environmental influences.

The amorphous quality of Shulgin's vision suggests the central dilemma of the cultural revolutionaries more generally. They offered a sweeping criticism of prevailing institutions and priorities without being able to elaborate a comprehensive and coherent program of their own. Caught up in the momentum of vast changes whose implications they only dimly perceived, they mistook reality for the fulfillment of their hopes. Just as Shulgin's writings had previously crystallized in new form the opposition of very different groups to the policies pursued during the 1920s, they now welcomed the upheavals of 1928 as the long-awaited vindication of his views.

His views, however, had more concrete political utility in the new climate created by the redefinition of cultural revolution as class war. The defeat of Bukharin and Stalin's shift to the left drew into the larger political vortex controversies over pedagogical matters that had remained relatively independent of politics. The acceleration of industrialization, with its extreme emphasis on voluntarism, had fundamental implications for philosophy, which in turn impinged directly upon pedagogical issues. Shulgin became a useful instrument for an attack on the Right in educational theory and practice, indeed for an assault on the educational establishment more broadly.

Shulgin had been a major participant in the continuing debates of the 1920s over the nature of Communist education. In contrast to educational theorists such as Pinkevich and Kalashnikov, who insisted that the major theoretical problems had already been resolved, or to others like Shatskii, who argued that general theory had little to offer of practical utility, Shulgin insisted upon the need for a comprehensive Communist pedagogical theory. Sound educational practice, he argued, could not rest upon the fragmentary contributions of bourgeois educational theorists. The time had come to formulate a comprehensive and genuinely Marxist pedagogy.

Shulgin's views were given the opportunity for a formal airing at an enlarged meeting of the Narkompros collegium in December 1928 attended by two hundred leading pedagogues and school authorities of the RSFSR.[30] His opening report, full of characteristically military imagery, assaulted the theory and practice that had guided Soviet education, leading Lunacharskii to comment that Shulgin resembled an Indian on the warpath looking for victims to scalp. The policies of Narkompros were defended by a succession of distinguished Marxist educational theorists, who took Shulgin to task for exaggerating the significance of small differences of definition and methodology. His own work, they pointed out, had serious defects: it confused spontaneous with purposive educational influences, where only the latter were the proper subject of pedagogy. Moreover, his excessively broad definition of education, they argued, had the effect of downgrading the role of both school and teacher. Above all, they took Shulgin and his allies to task for treating methodological differences as political deviations. In a letter addressed to the meeting Pinkevich protested as "unprincipled" the practice of labelling his own work, and that of other colleagues, "bourgeois" or "Menshevik."[31]

In subsequent months, however, it became clear that educational issues could no longer be treated independently of larger political struggles. The attack on right positions came to focus upon the work of Kalashnikov, who was accused of incorporating Bukharin's mechanistic theses into his pedagogical theory. An excessive emphasis on the determining role of biological factors was incompatible with the voluntarism that had now come to the fore. Kalashnikov's mechanistic, positivist approach to social adjustment, insisted his critics, failed to appreciate the significance of class struggle and to maintain a properly dialectical sensitivity to the interaction of man and his environment, while his skepticism about the degree to which an educational superstructure could advance ahead of its socioeconomic base represented an unwillingness to utilize pedagogy as a weapon for social transformation.

The resistance to a purge of Narkompros was unavailing, although the "unmasking" of right deviationists took a comparatively dignified form. The scope and limits of the purge were neverly clearly defined, and the attack on the Narkompros leadership was further complicated by the relative invulnerability of Lunacharskii and Krupskaia, given their own sympathy for many aspects of educational radicalism. But Shulgin's influence in any case was far greater in his role as critic of educational policy than it was as a builder of the new Soviet school. His newly named Institute for Marxist-Leninist Pedagogy was briefly the ideological center of the educational Cultural Revolution. Ultimately, however, the economic and social transformation wrought by the Five-Year Plan affected the educational system in ways far different from anything Shulgin had anticipated or intended. His advocacy of the "withering away of the school" was fundamentally incompatible with the growing role of the political superstructure in Stalinist Russia, and was shortly to come under attack. By 1931 left deviation was already being singled out as the main danger.

THE REORIENTATION OF
EDUCATIONAL POLICY AFTER 1931

The disintegration of the system of formal education in the wave of mobilization for industrialization and cultural revolution was a secondary, and to some extent unintended, consequence of the forces loosened by shifting political alliances at the center. With the initial breakthroughs in industrialization and collectivization accomplished, the Right Opposition defeated, and Party control over educational and cultural institutions tightened, the alliance with cultural radicalism had served its purpose. The Party leadership was free to turn its full attention to a whole range of substantive policy issues and to approach them on their own terms without reference to broader ideological and political implications. Beginning in the spring of 1931, in education as in other areas, a series of Central Committee decrees attacked the basic premises of the Cultural Revolution and laid out the new direction that policy would take in subsequent years. [32]

The reorganization of educational institutions and the reorientation of educational policy in the course of the 1930s has often been described as a "Great Retreat," a return to the traditional, authoritarian educational system of prerevolutionary Russia. Yet it would be a mistake to view these changes as if they were nothing more than a return to the *status quo ante*. As Kenneth Jowitt has argued more broadly, Leninist political systems "are interested in the selective reintegration of tradition only *after* the political relevance of tradition has been decisively altered."[33] The events of 1928 to 1931 had decisively and irrevocably transformed the political, economic, and social foundations of Soviet life. On virtually every conceivable economic and social indicator, these years stand out as a watershed in Soviet development. The reorientation of educational policy represented a new synthesis, a selective adaptation of traditional elements within the context of a radically new educational system, different from its Tsarist antecedents as well as from the child-centered schools of the 1920s. It entailed new approaches to the problems of social selection, technical training, and political socialization different from those pursued by Narkompros in the 1920s as well as from those of the cultural revolutionary period.

The First Five-Year Plan period had brought a vast expansion of the educational network at all levels. Almost two million additional pupils were attending primary and secondary schools by the end of the plan period. As Table 1 indicates, enrollments in higher educational institutions tripled between the years 1927–28 and 1933–34. In secondary specialized institutions they more than quadrupled. A dramatic shift in emphasis had also occurred, with increasing proportions of students enrolled in engineering-industrial programs.[34] This massive extension of

TABLE 1.

	1927–28	1933–34
Preschool		
Institutions	2,155	19,611
Enrollments (in thousands)	107,500	1,061,700
Primary and Secondary Schools		
Institutions	118,558	166,275 (1932–33)
Enrollments	7,896,000	9,656,000 (1932–33)
Secondary Specialized Institutions		
Institutions	1,037	3,509
Enrollments	189,400	723,700
Higher Educational Institutions		
Institutions	148	714
Enrollments	168,500	458,300

Educational Expansion during the First Five-Year Plan, USSR. Sources: Tsentral'noe statisticheskoe upravlenie, *Narodnoe obrazovanie, nauka i kultura v SSSR* (Moscow, 1971), pp. 44–45, 151; *Kul'turnoe stroitel'stvo SSSR* (Moscow, 1956), pp. 232–34, 208–11.

educational opportunities created a new foundation for Soviet educational efforts.

Accompanying this expansion was a new philosophy of education, which offered very different solutions to the questions of who should be educated, with what skills, in what kind of a social setting. Stalin's repudiation of "petty-bourgeois egalitarianism" signalled the the end of admissions policies designed to give preferential treatment to children of working-class or poor peasant background. The use of objective socioeconomic categories as criteria for educational preferment was abandoned in favor of the far more flexible criterion of "social worth." This new definition of merit encouraged the reward of technical expertise as well as political loyalty, and would readily merge with a functionalist rationalization of inequality.

The new emphasis on individual achievement was strengthened by the restoration of examinations and grades, and their use as criteria for promotion, thus reinforcing the link between advantaged family background and educational opportunity. The practice of compiling statistics on the social origins of students was abandoned in the late 1930s, in part, no doubt, because they revealed a sharp decline in the proportion of students of working-class background and a rise in the proportion of employees. The image of socialism as an egalitarian proletarian democracy was supplanted by another image that equated socialism and meritocracy, albeit in a plebiscitarian framework.

The abandonment of a commitment to equal educational opportunity was also expressed in a more fundamental reorganization of the educational system, which abandoned the elusive goal of a unified and uniform educational experience for all children in favor of a system of educational streaming. The expansion of educational opportunity at the primary and junior secondary level was accompanied by the creation of two distinct and separate educational channels, one permitting a small proportion of students the opportunity of a complete academic education and the other channeling the majority into vocational instructional programs closely tied to industrial enterprises that offered little opportunity for rapid upward mobility. The educational foundations of a division of labor that early educational reformers had tried so hard to undo was thus recreated in new form in the Stalin period.

This process was facilitated by a reorganization and stabilization of the curricula of all educational institutions along lines that differed both from the combination of general with polytechnical education in the schools of the 1920s and from the extreme vocationalism of 1928–32. It emphasized the formal and academic content of the programs of the general schools, adding a strong ideological component to the curricula, while turning over vocational functions for which the schools were poorly equipped to special programs closely linked to production. Genuine polytechnicalism was never fully realized in practice and was essentially abandoned.

Finally, the reorientation brought with it a dramatic shift in the ethos of the entire educational system. The experimentalism and diversity that had been encouraged by the decentralization of educational administration in the 1920s ended, as the Party took an increasingly active role in shaping the fundamental direction of the schools. The emergence of more uniform policies was accelerated at higher levels of the system by the creation of a central State Committee for Higher Education. A child-centered approach to education came under direct attack from the Central Committee, which saw its emphasis on environmental determinism as the quintessence of fatalism. At a time when dramatic departures in economic and social policy required enormous efforts to *transform* the environment, an excessive preoccupation with natural laws of development was tantamount to counterrevolution.[35] Shulgin was accused of a leftist deviation that exaggerated the role of environmental influences and underestimated the importance of consciousness and purpose, prompting Krupskaia to complain that once again the proverbial baby was being thrown out with the bath water. Not maturation but training was henceforth to be the central concern of Soviet educators.

The libertarian ethos of an earlier epoch succumbed to an authoritarianism that stressed the disciplined subordination of hierarchical units rather than the automatic solidarity of collectives.[36] The new ethos and values were elaborated in new textbooks whose images of socialism were dramatically different from those of the 1920s, and were communicated by means of an increasingly formal system of political indoctrination.

To interpret these changes, as some analysts have done, as a response to the universal functional requisites of modernization is to substitute a theoretical model for the exploration of empirical reality. The shifts in educational policy that began in 1928 represented less the triumph of universal developmental laws than the destruction by Stalin of the political and institutional bases of alternative developmental paths. Whether the policies adopted after 1931 were more "modern" or more "functional" than those pursued earlier is a question that requires a more precise definition of those terms. In many respects, the educational values held by Narkompros in the 1920s were more congruent with current definitions of modernity than were those that permeated educational policy from the mid-1930s, with their stress on dogmatic ideology and on unquestioning obedience to external authority. Precisely because Stalinism joined a radical transformation of the economic, political, and social bases of Soviet society to a system of values and a pattern of authority relations with powerful traditionalist and authoritarian components, it gave a very special character to Soviet patterns of modernization. Without a criterion of functionality and a specification of the range of policies that would meet it, the imputation of universal developmental requisites to Stalinist policy obscures the reality of social and political conflict and the policy processes through which it is mediated.

The orientation of educational policy during the Cultural Revolution, viewed in relation to the policies that preceded and followed it, emerges in sharper focus. It was neither a solution to the accumulating educational problems of the late 1920s, nor an anticipation of the direction education would take in the mid-1930s. It represented, rather, the secondary effects upon education of a shift to militant leftism shaped by the economic and political conflicts that engulfed the Party leadership, effects that later educational policies were designed to undo. But, despite the special character of educational theory and practice during this period, the Cultural Revolution did prepare the way for later policies in two important respects. By facilitating the more direct subordination of educational efforts to short-term economic needs, and by injecting direct, if crude, political criteria into the evaluation of educational theory and practice, the cultural revolution destroyed the limited autonomy that Narkompros had achieved, and its vision of an education that joined social needs to individual development.

The Construction of the Stalinist Psyche

David Joravsky

I

In September 1919, when the Bolsheviks seemed on the verge of losing the Civil War, Lenin wrote an angry reply to Gorky, who had protested the arrest of dissident intellectuals. "The intellectual forces of the workers and peasants," Lenin boasted, "are growing stronger in the struggle to overthrow the bourgeoisie." As for the intelligentsia, he dismissed them as "accomplices [of the bourgeoisie], lackeys of capital, who fancy themselves the nation's brain. In fact they are not the brain but the shit."[1]

That explosion of angry contempt for the intelligentsia, that overcompensating boast of intellectual forces growing among workers and peasants, are the essence of the cultural revolution, as far as Solzhenitsyn is concerned, with little or no distinction among the Leninist, Stalinist, and post-Stalinist phases.[2] Of course, Solzhenitsyn is a passionately biased witness, but his passion is itself important evidence for the historian of the cultural revolution. Such outrage, kept alive more than half a century after

I wish to thank the NSF, the NEH, and the ACLS for support that made this research possible.

the Civil War by the Soviet leaders' continuing determination to suppress dissident intellectuals, is evidence that Solzhenitsyn may be right. The cultural revolution may be an excruciatingly protracted process. It may be an endlessly self-perpetuating effort of the single ruling Party to join the ice of monolithic unity with the fire of modern culture, shutting the mouths that say a choice must be made—and continually making the choice, for the ice of unity rather than the dissolving fire of modern culture.

Although the official Soviet view is drastically different from Solzhenitsyn's in emotional coloration—and in its astonishing capacity for willful amnesia—the two perspectives are remarkably similar in historical interpretation. Both emphasize the continuity of the historical process from 1917 to the present. Both brush aside the relative freedom and cultural diversity of the twenties as an ephemeral anomaly, incompatible with Communist goals, which required the transformation of the fractious "bourgeois" intelligentsia into a class of a new type, the disciplined Soviet intelligentsia, dutifully executing the Party's command.[3]

There is something to be said for that interpretation. Taken as a whole, the cultural revolution *can* be described as beginning not in 1928 but in 1917, or even earlier, when "critically thinking individuals" found themselves in a minority among growing numbers of educated people who were more dedicated to paid professional careers than to critical thought. The word "intelligentsia" has undergone a basic change in meaning, which undoubtedly corresponds to a change in social reality. From a relatively small group of disaffected intellectuals the intelligentsia has been transformed into an enormous mass of professionals and white-collar workers. From autonomous critics of the existing system, seeking an integral understanding of the universe and of human destiny as the first step to reform or revolution, the intelligentsia has been transformed into a class of obedient servants of the existing system, performing specialized mental labor for specified rates of pay. Their massive silence in response to isolated angry critics like Solzhenitsyn underscores the transformation, as Amalrik has gloomily argued.[4]

So there is truth, I think, in that global picture, whether painted with the self-congratulatory rouge and the amnesiac chalk of the Soviet establishment or with the furious hues of the muckrakers. But it is a seriously deficient truth, for it ignores the great paradox of the cultural revolution, the combination of modernization and thought control. If modern specialization of function is the essence of the long-run process, why have the specialists in political rule tried so long and hard to keep all the scattered areas of modern culture subordinated to a single way of thought, a comprehensive ideology maintained by state power? The historian's most difficult problem is to explain the weird combination of the one and the other, the Bolshevik effort to push Russia into the fragmented culture of modern times while reviving the ancient subordination of culture to the unifying creed of an established church. Why—to take the example of the psychoneurological sciences—did the Bolsheviks vigorously promote the development of diverse specialties and schools of thought and then seriously impair their development by thought control, by forceful imposition of a single viewpoint, which was so crude as to be almost meaningless?

One response is to call the promotion of modern culture Leninist, the imposition of thought control Stalinist; in other words, to deny that the cultural revolution has been a single, long-term process. I suppose that is one of the things the editor of our volume had in mind when she singled out 1928–31 as *the* cultural revolution: that was the time when the hundred flowers of the Leninist stage gave way to the rectification campaigns of Stalinism. I see the point of her synecdoche, but I fear the confusion and question-begging it may entail. After all, Lenin was urging a cultural revolution right after his political revolution, and Bogdanov was urging it even earlier, on the grounds that the working class could not manage a political revolution until it had experienced a cultural revolution. And quite aside from the intentions of individual leaders, the odd combination of efforts to promote modern culture with efforts to regiment it can be found in the period before 1928. We may not simply assume that Stalin introduced this paradox in 1928 or '29.

To avoid confusion, I prefer to name the five-year convulsion that began in 1928 or '29 with one of the phrases Stalin bestowed on it at the time: the great break (*velikii perelom*), the revolution from above, or the all-out assault on capitalism along the whole front. But names matter less than the things named. I am inclined to agree that there was such an abrupt acceleration of certain trends in 1928–31, and such an abrupt reversal of others, as to constitute a break with the past. *Partiinost'* and *praktika* as the main criteria of truth were not invented in that period, but they were given such drastically new meanings, charged with such intense exigency, pressed upon so many new fields, with such fundamental and enduring change resulting, that I will not quarrel further with Professor Fitzpatrick's designating the transformation of culture in 1928–31 as *the* cultural revolution, just as she may wish to call the collectivization campaign of the same years *the* agrarian revolution, and the final transformation of opposition into a heinous crime instead of a limited right *the* political revolution. Names aside, what happened?

On all sectors of the cultural front—note the revived Civil War manner of speech—the great break brought angry insistence on an end to idle theorizing, on a turn to "practice" as the supreme criterion of truth, with the Party chiefs, and Stalin personally, hailed as the ultimate judges of practical utility and thus of truth. There was wholesale "unmasking" of previously respected Marxist thinkers, now exposed as "pseudo-Marxists" who had been trying to smuggle "bourgeois" modes of thought into the Communist camp. Henceforth Soviet learning was to be unique, distinguished from "bourgeois" trends in foreign lands by the transforming power of Marxist-Leninist principles, which were to be drawn from three dead "classics" (Marx, Engels, Lenin) and from their one living continuer, Joseph Stalin, now acclaimed the "coryphaeus" of thinkers and artists (their choirmaster, in plain English) no less than the "chief" (*vozhd'*) of the toiling masses. As for the intellectual substance of this unique, new, practical Marxist-Leninist Soviet culture, it was so crude, so heavy with *proizvol*, willful illogic, that anxious scholars tended to confine themselves to small safe subjects, waiting to hear from above the large new truths they were supposed to be seeking. And everywhere the status of cranks and militant ignoramuses rose sharply. Their isolation from the mainstreams of their disciplines, their eagerness to solve complex problems at one easy stroke, could now be interpreted as evidence of revolutionary uniqueness, the very thing that Marxist-Leninists were supposed to be seeking in all fields of learning.[5]

This characteristic turmoil engulfed the psychoneurological sciences during Stalin's great break, but it was less intense there than it was in agronomy or biology or the philosophy of science, not to speak of such terror-stricken disciplines as economics and Party history. I read the scale of intensity in various fields as an indicator of levels of frenzy in the

Bolshevik mentality of the time. Rational examination of the Party's past record of diversity, or of the sky-high targets of industrial growth, had become quite intolerable to the Stalinist mentality. Arguments over ways to increase crop yields—or to recover from the sharp declines that attended collectivization—were perceived as subversive postponements of practical action, all the more vexing if the learned arguers got involved in esoteric issues of plant physiology and genetics. It may seem strange to find the philosophy of science fairly high on the scale of Bolshevik concern, as evidenced by vehement articles in *Pravda* and by Stalin's personal intervention, with a decree soon following from the Central Committee.[6] The plain hard explanation was repeatedly given—in this declaration, for example, by Ernst Kol'man, a leading agent of the great break in philosophy and science:

> Now it is clear to everyone that the basic lesson of the philosophical discussion is this: philosophy, and every other science as well, cannot exist in the conditions of the proletarian dictatorship separate from Party leadership. Now it is clear to everyone that all efforts to think of any theory, of any scholarly discipline, as autonomous, as an independent discipline, objectively signify opposition to the Party's general line, opposition to the dictatorship of the proletariat.[7]

That new definition of the relationship between scholars and bosses was far more important to the new Stalinist culture than any substantive issue in the psychoneurological sciences. Indeed, the turmoil in those sciences whirled about a void, the lack of a Marxist-Leninist position, and the nagging question, finally repressed, whether there was a theory of the psyche that could fill the void.

In the twenties it was self-evident to Soviet Marxists that they had no distinctive position in the psychoneurological sciences.[8] That was indeed the initial premise of the campaign to create a Marxist psychology, which was launched by A. B. Zalkind and K. N. Kornilov about 1923.[9] The plain fact that Marxists and psychoneurologists had shown no interest in each other until the 1920s[10] was subsequently obscured by two legends, one rising directly out of the great break, the other indirectly, in the late thirties and forties. The first insists that the writings of Marx, Engels, and Lenin do contain a distinctively Marxist-Leninist view of psychology and neurophysiology. The second equates that Marxist view with Pavlov's doc-trine (*uchenie*), which is also pictured as the culmination of a Russian radical tradition founded by comrades Chernyshevsky and Sechenov in the late 1860s. These legends, now widely accepted in the West as well as the Soviet Union, render the tumult of the great break incomprehensible. If the "classics" contain a distinctive view of the psychoneurological sciences, it is impossible to understand why Soviet Marxists were blind to it until harsh scolding in 1931 forced them to open their eyes.[11] If Pavlov's doc-trine was the realization of the dialectical materialist view and the outcome of the Russian radical tradition, it is impossible to understand why Soviet Marxists failed to see that until 1950–51, when they were castigated for their failure at the "Pavlov Sessions" of the Academy of Sciences and the Academy of Medical Sciences.[12]

These difficulties are the unnecessary result of accepting legends.[13] When the legends are set aside, the historian's real puzzle emerges: Why did the Bolsheviks bother? Until 1917 they had been overwhelmingly indifferent to the psychoneurological sciences in general, and to Pavlov's doctrine in particular. One might think that the new burdens of ruling Russia would have occasioned a shrinking rather than an expansion of intellectual commitments. Yet the twenties witnessed extensive efforts to create a Marxist approach to psychology (not yet to neurophysiology). The *intellectual* reasons for the venture were obvious and persuasive: the varied explanations of human nature offered by various schools of psychology were an implicit challenge to the adequacy of Marxism as *the* science of human nature. It is the social and political reasons that are puzzling. Until they took power the Bolsheviks seemed to be drifting toward the narrow preoccupations characteristic of twentieth-century politicians. Once in power they strove against the tide, trying not only to revive the broad intellectual concerns of Marx and Engels but also to expand into areas like experimental psychology, which had hardly interested even Marx and En-gels.

The solution to the puzzle, as I have argued elsewhere, is to be found in the change that the seizure of power caused in Bolshevik relations with the intelligentsia.[14] An anxious sense of mutual dependence and hostility stimulated efforts at explanation and accomodation; rulers and scholars tried to reconcile their different approaches to a scientific understanding of human nature. The initial result was a series of philosophical reformulations of existing schools of psychology. There were Soviet Marxist Freudians, Soviet Marxist Gestaltists, Soviet Marxist behaviorists, and Soviet Marxist reflexologists (divided between a large majority of Bekhterevians and a small minority of Pavlovians).[15] The leading theorist of the twenties, K. N. Kornilov, was a product of Wundtian training who was moving toward behaviorism in his own work, while seeking, in his role as leader, an ecumenical rally of all the schools under the capacious banner of Marxism.

The great break brought harsh denunciations of all such philosophic reformulations of existing science. They were a masked surrender to "bourgeois" pseudoscience. Bolsheviks were given the staggering job of revolutionizing science itself, at the very time they were supposed to be collectivizing peasants and pushing industrial output to impossible levels. Once again, only much more so than in the aftermath of 1917, a great increase in the burdens of rule was accompanied by a paradoxical expansion of intellectual commitments rather than the contraction one might logically expect. What is most perplexing about this great leap forward in all directions at once is the explanation that the Bolsheviks endlessly repeated: *practical* considerations obliged them to move from philosophizing about the sciences from without to revolutionizing them from within. To the retrospective outsider it seems incredible that a country as backward as Russia had exhausted the potential benefits of existing science, and required a new, higher-level science to solve the practical problems of a new, higher-level society. But we must bear in mind that the Bolsheviks who carried through the Stalinist revolution from above were not retrospective outside observers. They were passionate activists whose vehement insistence on practicality can hardly be suspected of insincerity. We must take them at their word, and try to see the relationship between science and practical problems as they did.

II

Professional autonomy was the first practical problem the Bolsheviks attacked, in the Biblical sense of attacking a problem: plucking out the offending eye, cutting off the offending hand or foot. As early as 1927 the

Communist organization (*komfraktsiia*) in the Moscow Institute of Neuropsychiatric Prophylaxis opened a campaign against the Moscow Society of Neuropathologists and Psychiatrists.[16] The initial appeal was not so much to Party spirit as to rivalry between status groups. Membership in the society was exclusive, limited to specialists who had published works of sufficient merit to be elected by the existing membership. As a result, only eighty or a hundred—the reports vary—of the four hundred neurologists and psychiatrists in Moscow belonged.[17] They met in private, appointed the editors of the country's leading professional journal, dominated the psychoneurological sections of the *Great Medical Encyclopedia,* and organized the conventions open to the profession at large. The handful of Communist professionals failed repeatedly in their efforts to change this traditional pattern. At one large conference in 1928 they were dismayed by a counterattack: the professional associations were called on not to surrender their autonomy, but to strengthen it by defending the material and professional interests of psychiatrists and neurologists. It was not until November 1929, when the terrorization of scholars was being revived, that the Moscow Society gave in. The requirement of publication was dropped, three hundred new members were elected en masse, along with a new slate of officers, half of them Communists, the other half members of VARNITSO (the All-Union Association of Workers of Science and Technology for Aid to the Construction of Socialism).[18]

This upheaval, paralleled in every other scientific society of the time, changed little of substance at the outset. The old guard's fears of a lowering of standards seemed groundless, for the time being. The new guard made grand declarations about a sharp turn to dialectical materialism and to practical service of socialism, but their only significant step in that direction was to print articles on the Behavioral Congress of January 1930 and on the mental health movement, where they saw the main chance for psychiatrists and neurologists to aid the construction of socialism.[19] (Note that the base from which the Communists launched their takeover campaign was the Moscow Institute of Neuropsychiatric *Prophylaxis.*)

In part, "psychohygiene," as the mental health movement was called by its Soviet advocates, was their version of a worldwide effort, especially admired in its American manifestation. The object was to substitute prevention for cure, or rather, for the institutional confinement that notoriously fails to cure mental illness. In part the "psychohygiene" movement was a reaction to a peculiarly Soviet problem. Eight years of war, social upheaval, economic collapse, and famine, 1914–22, had done enormous damage to mental health. Psychiatrists used various terms to describe what they saw in their clinics and heard from their colleagues. Some spoke of mass neurasthenia, others of mass schizoidization, or the widespread appearance of autistic symptoms, or simply of "Soviet *iznoshennost'*" (exhaustion, or premature aging).[20] Dr. P. B. Gannushkin, one of the leaders of the Moscow Society until the Bolsheviks dislodged him, coined a new term: "early acquired invalidism" (as opposed to congenital invalidism and to the disability that comes with age).[21] Whatever terms were used, there was general agreement on a great increase in the number of psychically bruised and worn-out people, tending to shrink into themselves, to become apathetic, or to lose the capacity for work at an early age.

Party activists were a class of special concern, as the upper stratum of any population is to psychiatrists. Repeated studies showed that they suffered from an especially high incidence of neuroses, hypertension, and other cardiovascular disorders. As Dr. L. L. Rokhlin put it: *"To, chem zhivet partaktiv—mozgom i serdtsem—tem on bol'she vsego boleet."* ("That by which the Party *aktiv* lives, the brain and the heart, that is what ails them most of all.")[22] In the twenties Party leaders reacted with sympathetic concern, annually referring nervous comrades to psychiatrists during the lull after the spring campaigns, commissioning special investigations of such sample populations as the activists sent to study at Party schools, and most of all fostering open talk, advising the *aktiv* how to take proper care of themselves. Dr. A. B. Zalkind, the chief Party expert in the psychoneurological sciences until the great break, set the tone in lectures, *Pravda* articles, pamphlets, and books.[23] Commonsense realism was the characteristic viewpoint. The *aktiv* were warned against the widespread habit of crowding too many hours into a working day, skipping a regular day off, grabbing irregular and poorly balanced meals. Concerning other threats to mental health the experts could do little but point warning fingers. Crowded apartments, to take the most serious threat, allowed the *aktiv* no place to do their paper work or studying, or simply to relax in quiet, or to have a normal sex life.[24] The psychiatrists also noted the special problems of those activists—the overwhelming majority—who were shifting from manual to mental work with no formal education beyond grade school. Wracked by repressed fears of inadequacy, unaware of the sedentary worker's need for periodic breaks and physical exercise, a large percentage of such activists developed neurotic symptoms, while a minority suffered breakdowns.[25]

The initial impact of the great break was to intensify the drive both for preventive and for remedial measures. The newly Bolshevized journals published shocking figures on the insufficiency of hospital beds for the mentally ill, on the massive need for *vytrezviteli* ("sobering stations," where alcoholics could be dried out, releasing hospital beds and psychiatric personnel for more serious cases), even on the need for a campaign to stop rural people from chaining and beating the mentally ill.[26] There were intensified appeals for an end to "penitentiary psychiatry," with its "factories producing chronic inmates."[27] To a large extent that was the kind of appeal one constantly hears from concerned psychiatrists all over the world. But there were also elements of revolutionary utopianism in the appeals of Soviet psychiatrists during the first part of the great break: socialist society would now accomplish what could only be dreamed of by "bourgeois" psychiatrists. Early in 1931, for example, Dr. L. M. Rozenshtein, who was then joining the Party, forecast "the creation of working, semi-therapeutic 'phalansteries', somewhat like *kolkhozy*, in the vicinity of agrotowns (*agrogoroda*), and especially the creation of forms of light work in socialist town-communes, in *sovkhozy* of an industrial sort, and so on."[28]

But most of all the stress was on prevention. The mental health movement so much admired in the United States for its extensiveness would become a genuinely mass movement under socialism. Its aim would be not only the elementary "struggle for culture, against drunkenness, for a real liquidation of illiteracy, for labor consciousness and labor discipline among the working masses and the peasantry."[29] Dr. Rokhlin quoted that characteristic formula from Party resolutions, and spelled out further dreams of his own. During times like the Civil War, he explained, one could hardly speak of "carefully measured labor, of the culture and rationalization of work and everyday life, of the culture of the personality." When the Soviet republic had been in danger "the maddest expenditure of oneself was justified." But now, with the construction of socialism, the cultivation of the personality through careful organization of work and everyday life was becoming a practical matter.[30]

It takes no great perspicacity for the outsider to see Dr. Rokhlin's gross misreading of the new age and the psychiatrist's role in it. The all-out construction of socialism brought a return of the maddest expenditure of individual selves, not the final leap to utopia. Even before the great break some specialists had been apprehensive of possible backlash against the mental health movement. Dr. Gannushkin, for example, confessed that he deliberately selected an obscure journal for his first articles on "early acquired invalidism," because he did not want to provoke undue alarm.[31] His students, speaking on the subject at the Behavioral Congress of January 1930, were anxious to explain that Gannushkin intended no criticism of the revolution by his frank examination of its psychic costs.[32] In February *Revolution and Culture*, a publication of the Central Committee, gave Gannushkin and another psychiatrist space to offer more explanations and reassurances. They insisted that the mental health movement did not call into question the power of intensive work to invigorate, if it is performed under socialism rather than capitalism.[33] The same theme echoed in critical notes that the newly Bolshevized journals appended to articles on mental health: the articles were one-sided in their reports of mental illness, blind to the mental health achieved by socialist labor, but they raised issues that required discussion.[34]

Apologies and explanations proved unavailing. In the spring of 1931 the bosses stopped the mental health movement. The new Commissar of Health, M. F. Vladimirskii, told a conference on medical education that it was a mistake to publish stuff like Gannushkin's or Rokhlin's, with or without editorial disclaimers.[35] The Commissar's directive provoked no backtalk, for professional autonomy had been denied in principle, and sharply limited in fact, by the installation of Bolshevik officers and editors in the professional societies and journals. The offending authors and editors hastened to make amends, in the harsh new spirit generated by Stalin's condemnation of "Menshevizing idealism." (In December 1930 Stalin put that subversive label on the tendency to "separate theory from practice," that is, to keep intellectual culture separate from direct service of the Party line.) No matter that the Party had been encouraging, as recently as 1930, what it condemned in 1931.[36] Inoperative policies were henceforth to be charged as mistakes or crimes against the individuals who had carried them out, not against the Party that had ordered or tolerated them.

Under the headline, "For a Bolshevik Offensive on the Theoretical Front of Psychoneurology," a former leader of the mental health movement apologized for his sins, such as the assertion that socialist inspiration reduces the worker's *feeling* of fatigue. It reduces the *reality* of fatigue, he now perceived.[37] As usual his self-criticism was mild by comparison with his criticism of others. "Only a conscious or subconscious enemy of socialist construction" could write, as another specialist had, that activists transferred from manual to mental labor experienced special problems.[38] There were even harsher words for Dr. V. A. Giliarovskii, an eminent psychiatrist, who had lectured the Behavioral Congress on the problems created by rapid urbanization, such as "early arteriosclerosis, premature invalidism, Soviet exhaustion (*iznoshennost'*)":

> So-called "Soviet exhaustion [*iznoshennost'*]" does not exist in reality. What exists is merely a reactionary mania [*bred*], by which they are trying to pit the proletariat against its revolutionary tempos, and by sowing fear of non-existent difficulties to hold back our movement forward. This whole theory of Professor Giliarovskii is a theory of bourgeois restoration.[39]

N. I. Grashchenkov, who was emerging as one of the top three new Party leaders on the psychoneurological front,[40] revoked the previous admiration that Soviet writers had expressed for the mental health movement in the United States. He found it hopelessly "bourgeois" in character. "In our country," by contrast, the movement "must be an instrument for mobilizing the masses for the execution of the tasks of construction, an instrument for creating a personality that fully meets the requirements of socialist society [*polnotsennaia lichnost' sotsialisticheskogo obshchestva*]."[41]

That formulation was a bit vague. M. B. Krol, another of the new top three Party leaders on the psychoneurological front, was more specific. In his celebration of the Revolution's fifteenth anniversary, he argued that the mental health of workers and collectivized peasants was assured by their dedication to labor as a matter of honor, glory, and heroism; by their participation in the sociopolitical life of the native land. Those were the chief means for achieving the *ozdorovlenie*, the health improvement, of the nervous system. What then could specialists contribute? Krol offered a concrete example. An "express brigade" (*skvoznaia brigada*) from the Belorussian Institute of Health Care had gone to a factory and persuaded a group of workers to use five minutes of their lunch break for calisthenics. The result was an increase in their productivity as well as an improvement in their mental health.[42] Another authority tells of a nationwide movement in 1931–32 for calisthenics during rest periods.[43] "We have no figures at hand," Krol confessed in November 1932. "But every neurologist and every physician will confirm that nervous disorders, functional ones in particular—hysteria, neurasthenia—show a clear tendency to decline."[44] Indeed. Psychoneurological specialists would have had to be crazy themselves to withhold confirmation.

That was how the great break revolutionized the psychoneurological sciences in order to solve the practical problem of widespread mental illnesses such as "Soviet exhaustion."[45] At least two eminent specialists who had been studying functional disorders shifted to organic illnesses, the consequences of brain damage, during the great break. It is hard to resist the inference that they were moving from the characteristic preoccupations of comfortable classes in advanced countries to the more elemental problems of Stalinist Russia.[46] A thorough history of the Soviet psychiatric and neurological professions would show, I think, that their dominant emphasis all along had been on organic illnesses.[47] The great break intensified that emphasis, made it almost exclusive—with schizophrenia as the big exception that may or may not prove the rule, since it may or may not be an organic disease, or indeed a single disease.[48]

Whether it is a sensible strategy for a backward country to concentrate its psychoneurological expertise on the most serious organic disorders is an interesting issue for academic theorizing about modernization. It is hardly relevant to the peculiarly Stalinist way of achieving such a concentration. Concern for functional disorders—such things as neurasthenia or "Soviet exhaustion," which are less serious than aneurysms or tumors or a crushed skull—was not consciously postponed to a more affluent future. It was denounced as a subversion of shock-brigade tempos, a counterrevolutionary challenge to the invigorating effects of "built-in-battles socialism."[49] Numerous violent mystifications of that sort were propagated during the great break, bequeathing to future generations the torments of demystification, the blind struggle with self-deception, that are painfully evident in the Soviet Union today.

The case of the mental health movement was paralleled in the other fields where the psychoneurological sciences find practical application. (Neuropathology—e.g., the study of brain lesions—was a major exception. It avoided serious mystification until 1950, a delayed consummation lying so far beyond the years of the great break that I cannot consider it here.) Wherever professional expertise clashed with the intuitive judgments of practical bosses, the professionals were obliged to quit the field or learn to echo the bosses. "Psychotechnics"—the application of physiology and psychology to problems of industry, the military, and the like—moved to a peak of eager endeavor in the first years of the great break, only to be summarily destroyed by the mid-thirties.[50] Its major sins were its concentration on studies of fatigue and on testing as the objective way to get the right persons in the right positions. Some leaders in industrial psychology had the courage (or stupidity) to point out that they were seeking optimum, not maximum, work loads. One of them even used the word "exploitation" in arguing that too great an increase in tempos of production might have the self-defeating effect of lowering productivity by inducing chronic fatigue.[51]

With respect to *testy*, a borrowing from English to indicate placement tests in education and industry, it is important to note that psychologists led the way in pointing out the notorious shortcomings of those supposedly objective measurements of abilities and preferences. Such tests, as we all know, tend to be biased against the lower classes and the disfavored nationalities.[52] The specialists cautioned against that bias and set themselves the research task of devising tests that would distinguish more effectively between the basic characteristics of the individual and the superficial characteristics of his class, nationality, or race.[53] That very effort was used to support accusations of snobbism, nationalism, and racism against the psychologists.[54] The growing annoyance of the Party bosses derived not only from the faults of testing, which the specialists called attention to, but also from the contradiction between objective methods of placement and *vydvizhenchestvo* (pushing up workers and peasants into higher positions). One can perceive here the Soviet version of a worldwide phenomenon: bosses are annoyed by egghead interference in their sacred power of placement, of arranging people in hierarchies. One specialist in psychotechnics was careful to argue that "psychotechnics does not in any way try to replace the political leadership of social life."[55] He made no impression. By the mid-thirties all institutes and journals in psychotechnics were abolished. In 1936 the Central Committee administered the coup de grace to *testy* in education, with the well-known decree against pedology.[56] Educational psychology was not destroyed. It became virtually the only field of applied psychology to survive the great break; indeed, it became the field of obligatory choice for psychological science as a whole. But it was a peculiarly Stalinist psychology, "characterized by fear of experiment. Developing almost exclusively as a part of pedagogy, psychology became a purely descriptive science"—descriptive, that is, of the intuitive judgments of school administrators and their political bosses.[57]

The military field of applied psychology presents the neatest little revelations of the conflicting attitudes that prompted fellow-travelling specialists to offer practical assistance and Stalinist bosses to spurn it. During the twenties the Red Army referred many cases of suspected malingering to a psychiatrist, who summarized his findings in a 1931 article that provoked instant condemnation.[58] He was trying to tell Soviet military physicians and other officers how to deal with a worldwide problem. He found conscious faking to evade service to be extremely rare. Soldiers who complained of invisible illnesses were usually unbalanced, he concluded, and he warned that accusations of malingering and rough orders to shape up accomplished nothing, except perhaps to precipitate a physical attack on the accuser. This "narrow-minded specialist" received the familiar Stalinist rebuke: he did not see the problem as a whole. He failed to appreciate the therapeutic value of the Red Army's training and indoctrination, and thus had come to recommend psychiatric coddling of malingers.[59]

Analogous irritation was directed against Iu. P. Frolov, who was emerging as one of Pavlov's most prolific students. He had been doing conditioned-reflex studies of soldiers to determine the nature of human endurance of military stress.[60] Tolerated, perhaps considered useful when first published in 1928, his studies were sharply attacked in 1930–31, from two sides. Marxist psychologists who disapproved of Pavlov's biological approach to human behavior were joined by Party militants in condemning Frolov's alleged degradation of Red Army men to the level of Pavlovian dogs, his failure to see that indoctrination and morale, not reflexes, determine the soldier's ability to withstand stress.[61] Frolov himself was hardy enough to keep on offering professional help to the military, but he had the sense to switch from the investigation of stress to toxicology.[62]

It is tempting to sum up the whole process very simply: because the times changed, the ordinary pursuits of the professionals suddenly outraged the politicians. The great break stimulated professionals to intensify their previous efforts at the solution of practical problems, but it also stimulated the bosses to read a new meaning into the universal insistence of bosses that specialists must be on tap, not on top. The Stalinist concepts of *partiinost'* and practicality were born, heavily anti-intellectual, quite authoritarian, crippling a number of autonomous disciplines, including the psychoneurological sciences.

There is certainly much evidence to support such a generalization. The most starkly revealing is the publication curve of journals in the psychoneurological field, which rose to a peak of sixteen in 1928–31, and dropped to near zero by 1934.[63] For more than two decades following there was no journal in any field of psychology, whether theoretical or applied, none in neurophysiology, one in psychiatry and neuropathology, and one in pedagogy. Those two survivors were severely chastened; dangerous topics were either avoided altogether or treated only from the crude viewpoint of the bosses.[64]

III

The evidence leaves no doubt that anti-intellectual pragmatists nearly crushed the psychoneurological sciences as autonomous professions during the great break. But this is not the whole truth. The Bolsheviks, if I may paraphrase Stalin, were anti-intellectual pragmatists of a special sort. They demanded not only practical service from the professionals, but also theoretical service, a Marxist-Leninist explanation of the psyche. We may call that demand practical, in the sense that the Bolsheviks came to it only after their seizure of power, as an aspect of their problem of legitimacy, part of their ideological need to convince the sullen intelligentsia that the Party was entitled to rule by virtue of its one true universal philosophy. We may be appalled by the crudely anti-intellectual nature of the demand in the years following 1931, which reached the ultimate absurdity of insisting that Pavlov's imaginary neurophysiology is the Marxist explanation of the psyche. Nevertheless, however ideological in origin, however crude in its Stalinist phase, the Bolshevik demand for a psychological theory was quite genuine and very dangerous. In the thirties it reached a peak of intensity, and the psychoneurological sciences were almost destroyed. Since the mid-fifties the politicians' interest has been slowly withering away, and the psychoneurological sciences have been reviving as autonomous disciplines. Certainly that is a paradox, but it should surprise no one who has noticed the dependence of intellectual freedom on the modern politicians' disdainful indifference to the world of the intellect. The Bolsheviks have been taking a long time reaching that indifference.

If our volume were devoted to philosophy, it would be appropriate to examine the various approaches to a Marxist psychology that were proposed in the twenties and reached their climax in 1928–30.[65] In their diverse ways they shed considerable light on the protean nature of Marxist philosophy and on the insuperable fragmentation of psychological schools. One even finds a superbly imaginative essay on the social and intellectual origins of that fragmentation: "The Alienation of Action," by the humanistic philosopher and historian of science T. I. Rainov.[66] But for the great break, Soviet Marxists would probably have rivaled or surpassed German and French thinkers in creative development of the Marxist intellectual tradition. But our focus is on historical realities, not philosophical possibilities. Our concern must therefore be with the intellectually barren viewpoint that triumphed in 1931, rather than the creative rivals that it crushed.

In theoretical psychology, as in applied, Marxist specialists responded to the great break by intensifying their previous efforts—until they provoked wholesale rejection by the leaders they were trying to serve. Conferences were summoned and resolutions adopted at an accelerating pace, in an effort at unity that intensified the rivalry of the schools. At the end of 1927 and beginning of 1928 a Pedological Congress seemed to enthrone Kornilov's school.[67] The Marxist reflexologists tried to organize a conference that would achieve unity on the basis of *their* views. *Glavnauka*, the office of Lunacharskii's Commissariat in charge of higher learning, intervened on behalf of greater breadth. The organizational bureau of the reflexologists' projected congress was directed to get together with the Communist Academy, where Pavlovian views were dominant, and with the Institute of Experimental Psychology at Moscow University.[68] That was the main center of efforts to create a Marxist psychology, where Kornilov's reactology, "a Russian variant of American behaviorism,"[69] coexisted with Marxist versions of Freudianism, Gestalt, and the eclectic "historico-cultural" approach of Vygotskii and Luriia. During 1929 "Marxist seminars" were organized all over the country to prepare for the unifying congress.[70] One can only guess how realistic Dr. Zalkind was in perceiving "an organic urge [tiaga]" toward participation.[71] Even skeptics, he told the opening session on January 25, 1930, could see that this First All-Union Congress on the Study of Human Behavior was not " 'ordered,' not artificially 'created.' "[72]

Poor Zalkind may have been trying to find some reassuring explanation of the ominous coolness at the Party summit. Although three thousand people gathered in Leningrad for the week-long Congress,[73] neither *Pravda* nor *Izvestiia* nor *Bol'shevik* gave it a line of attention. The highest official to address the Congress was Lunacharskii, who had recently lost his position as Commissar of Education and came to speak, not on the central issue—the way to a unified, practically useful, Marxist psychology—but on the psychology of art.[74] Karev and Luppol, the philosophers who gave the main methodological speeches, were already under attack by Stalin's young zealots for separating theory from practice, that is, for keeping philosophy somewhat separate from direct service of the Party line.[75] In short, the organizers of the Congress were either in the process of losing the support of the highest Party leaders, or had never had it to lose. Soviet Marxist psychologists, making their greatest concerted effort to unite in the service of socialism, were offering something, on the theoretical as well as the practical level, that the Party leaders were finding increasingly obnoxious. At the end of 1930 Stalin put the name of "Menshevizing idealism" on scholarship that did not directly serve the Party line, and within a few months a well-disciplined "discussion," openly guided by a spokesman of the Central Committee (Kol'man), condemned all previous discussions and theorists. They had claimed to be seeking a Marxist psychology, but they had actually produced "mountains of rubbish, rising on the ground of a scholastic and unprincipled quarrel."[76]

On a very abstract level, some of the principles affirmed at the Behavioral Congress of January 1930 survived the damnation of 1931. The psyche was held to be a product both of biological and of social evolution, and was supposed to have an independent quality reducible neither to biology nor to sociology, but requiring a separate science of psychology. Since all the competing efforts to make those principles scientifically meaningful had been condemned as "bourgeois," the principles were condemned to be scientifically meaningless. This simultaneous insistence on a science and paralysis of it had been foreshadowed in the relatively free twenties by the stunting of social psychology. There had been widespread agreement that social psychology would be the field where Marxists would make their greatest contribution, and there was equal agreement that Marxists were failing to enter the field.[77] Mavericks like Bekhterev and Bogdanov offered sweeping theories, but they provoked only irritated rejections from the guardians of orthodox Marxist-Leninist social theory.[78] The most influential Marxist theorists of psychology during the twenties attempted little more than brief, vague suggestions of the ways that orthodox social theory might link up with their versions of individual psychology. At the time of most intense effort to meet the Bolshevik demand for a distinctively Marxist theory of the psyche, in the late twenties and early thirties, an "historico-cultural" psychology was sketched out by Vygotskii and Luriia, and, separately, by Kurazov. But the one derived too obviously from such "bourgeois" theorists as Piaget and Lévy-Bruhl, the other from Bekhterev. They suffered the usual condemnation for reformulating "bourgeois" theories rather than forging distinctively new Marxist views. (Vygotskii and Luria were also found contemptuous of Soviet peasants, whom they had studied as examples of the primitive mentality.)[79]

Social psychology was simply too close to the petrifying ideology of the state, the social theory of Marxism-Leninism. Even in the relatively free atmosphere of the twenties, that theory was becoming a sacred doctrine, increasingly confined to the "classics," excerpted and interpreted under the rigid supervision of the ideological bureaucracy. During the great break that stultifying tendency reached its culmination in *tsitatnichestvo*, "citationism," beading quotations from the classics into patterns set by the latest decrees of the Central Committee and the latest slogans of Stalin. In 1931 that style of worship—one can hardly call it thought—was extended to psychological theory. The ideological bureaucracy began to insist that the classics contained invaluable comments on psychology, which the leaders of pseudo-Marxist psychology in the recent past had perversely ignored.[80] A few scholars then undertook the job of combing the classics for such insights, producing, in 1933–34, little bundles of quotations that could mean virtually anything with respect to the actual problems of psychology, and therefore meant virtually nothing.[81]

S. L. Rubinshtein, who emerged as the chief anthologist and philosopher of psychology, expressed the official view of the resulting deadlock:

> The mechanism of reflexology, the eclecticism of reactology (K. N. Kornilov), the uncritical pursuit of fashionable foreign theories (L. S. Vygotskii), which were presented as Marxist psychology, and the distortions of pedology led psychology into a dead end.[82]

It would be more reasonable to put the blame on the wholesale condemnation of the only psychological theories available. But whoever or whatever is blamed, the existence of an impasse was undeniable. It was most dramatically evident in the sudden disappearance of psychological articles from the chief journals of Marxist-Leninist theory.[83] That happened in 1931, as part of the "discussion" of psychology, and the professional journals of theoretical and applied psychology expired soon after. A hasty glance might suggest that the Party ideologists were discarding their interest in psychological theory. But a closer look reveals a shift rather than a discarding, from a search for a theory in psychology to a search in neurophysiology,[84] foreshadowing the decision that Pavlov's doctrine was the way out of the impasse, the way to a distinctively Marxist theory of the psyche.

It is hard to imagine a greater irony than that outcome. Throughout the twenties and early thirties Pavlov's doctrine was regularly criticized by Marxist psychologists for its one-sided insistence that physiology alone is the way to an objective understanding of animal behavior, with little or no distinction between dogs and humans.[85] "A person," as Vygotskii said, "is not at all a sack of skin filled with reflexes, and the brain is not a hotel for a series of conditioned reflexes accidentally stopping in."[86] Pavlov's doctrine was not only at odds with the Marxist conception of humans as social beings, historically determined. It was also at odds with physiology. The realization was beginning to spread among specialists that Pavlov's conceptions of brain function were imaginary, increasingly set aside by the progress of genuine neurophysiology.[87] His famous experiments on conditioned reflexes were ingenious correlations of stimulus and response, with little or no way or proving the intervening neural processes that he hypothesized. In short, he was doing "black-box" experimental psychology while insisting that he was doing physiology, and drifting, in the process, further and further from the mainstreams of both disciplines.

In philosophy and ideology Pavlov occupied an even stranger position. His explicit denials that his doctrine was materialist[88] did not stop Bukharin and other Communist ideologists of the twenties from insisting that Pavlov's doctrine furnished an important weapon for "the iron arsenal of materialist ideology."[89] Largely ignored or briefly dismissed by the sophisticated Marxists seeking a new psychology, Pavlov's doctrine appealed to Bolshevik ideologists. Vygotskii's gibe about a sack of skin filled with reflexes may have been inspired by Bukharin's metaphor of a person as "a sausage skin stuffed by environmental influences."[90] Pokrovskii, the old Bolshevik historian and chief of higher learning in the twenties, told the Communist Academy that

> the study of the brain according to Pavlov's method is the last word of materialism, expressed quite unintentionally by the old idealist Pavlov. Sometimes it happens that way, that a man will express a new word at odds with his personal world view.[91]

Pokrovskii had a very simple reason for insisting that materialism is implicit in Pavlov's doctrine: "It abolishes the spirit (*dukh*); in the most obvious manner it abolishes the very concept of the soul (*dusha*)."[92] That remained the crudely theoretical appeal of Pavlov to Bolshevik officials—that, and his unique standing as the only Nobel laureate in the Soviet Union—even when he defied their regime and ridiculed Marxism.[93]

These paradoxes were compounded in the turmoil of 1929–30, when Pavlov took a firm stand against the Bolshevization of the Academy of Sciences, yet received increased support for his institutes and laboratories.[94] Pavlovians were not included in the official program of the Behavioral Congress in January 1930, but somehow a day was set aside for ad hoc presentations by Pavlovians of diverse ideological persuasions, with L. N. Fedorov presenting the Bolshevik overview in the evening. He was a rare bird indeed. Perhaps the only one of Pavlov's many students who had joined the Red Army and the Communist Party during the Civil War, he would soon become Director of the Institute of Experimental Medicine in Leningrad, the main center of Pavlov's school.[95] The official record of the Behavioral Congress omitted his speech, which argued that Pavlov's doctrine, properly amended and expanded to include social influences, was compatible with Marxism.[96] But Grashchenkov, the Bolshevik who had just won control of the main journal in psychiatry and neurophysiology, focussed on the extraordinary "Pavlov day," and on Fedorov's speech, in his report of the Behavioral Congress.[97] At the Communist Academy in March 1930, Kornilov repeated his previous criticisms of Pavlov's doctrine and virtually called for the old man's arrest: "His recent political speeches have been clearly counterrevolutionary, requiring intervention by the appropriate organs."[98] But Zalkind rebuked Kornilov for diverging from the Central Committee's policy: political struggle with Pavlov, but support for his important scientific work. Zalkind also criticized Kornilov's views on psychology, to some extent continuing the disagreements of the twenties and foreshadowing the denunciations that would fall on Kornilov (and Zalkind too) within a year.[99]

Pavlov's school was criticized in the general condemnation of 1931.[100] But the criticism was less, and less harsh, than that directed at other schools, presumably because Pavlov's school had played a fairly minor role in the efforts to create a Marxist psychology. (This is by no means the only case in Soviet intellectual history of thinkers escaping serious condemnation by avoiding serious involvement in Marxism.) In 1931, as in the past, Pavlov was criticized for his one-sided insistence on physiology as the only way to a scientific understanding of human nature. Little attention was paid to the fatal defect of Pavlov's doctrine as physiology, the growing gap between it and genuine neurophysiology.[101] In any case problems of neuron organization and cerebral localization must have seemed technical trifles to officials concerned either with Marxist ideology or with health care, both now viewed through crude, Stalinist spectacles.

Chance seems to have played a major part in opening the way to the deification of Pavlov. Gorky, newly returned to the Soviet Union and transformed from a critic of Lenin's dictatorship into a propagandist of Stalin's, had somehow conceived a special interest in the Institute of Experimental Medicine.[102] In his apartment on October 7, 1932, Stalin, Molotov, and Voroshilov met with "a group of scientists" from the Institute, undoubtedly including Director Fedorov, the rare Pavlovian Communist.[103] A week later the Council of People's Commissars elevated the Institute to All-Union status, designating it the center for the "all-round study of man," the Magnitostroi or Dneprostroi of the medical sciences, as the press explained.[104] A little later, meeting with writers in Gorky's apartment, Stalin bestowed on them his famous cliché, "engineers of human souls."[105] Whether consciously or not, a major decision had been made on the way to unify psychological theory and practice. The psyche would be explained and cared for on the medical level by physiologists, "above all Pavlov's school,"[106] on the spiritual level—if the word be permitted—by imaginative writers. The science of psychology would be a handmaiden of Pavlov's school, or of Stalinist pedagogy, or nothing.

I have used the advantage of hindsight to pick out elements of a trend that was still not clear in 1932. For a time in the mid-thirties it seemed that one of Pavlov's students, A. D. Speranskii, would get the highest support for his especially crankish version of neurophysiology, which promised medical miracles, as Pavlov did not.[107] But Pavlov himself, at the age of eighty-five, finally made peace with the Soviet regime. He had all along nursed the overcompensating national pride that was becoming one of the strongest elements in Stalinist ideology, and nursed it all the more strongly as he saw his Russian school of physiology becoming increasingly isolated from the cosmopolitan mainstream of brain studies.[108] He had all along disdained politics, which enabled him to take support from a government he disapproved. In 1934–36 he publicly withdrew his disapproval, in a series of messages that rose to explicit approval just before he died. In August 1935, at a large meeting in the Kremlin, he thanked the Soviet regime for its generous support and modestly worried whether he would justify it. Molotov shouted, "We are sure that you will, no doubt about it!"—and Pavlov returned the compliment lavishly:

> As you know, I am an experimenter from head to foot. My whole life has consisted of experiments. Our government is also an experimenter, only of an incomparably higher category. I passionately want to live, to see the victorious completion of this historical social experiment.[109]

Those words were engraved in newsprint, along with "stormy applause," Pavlov's toast "To the great social experimenters," and a photograph of the fantastic neurophysiologist Pavlov side by side with the fantastic social experimenter Molotov. Pavlov was transformed in the handouts of the ideological bureaucracy. He ceased to be pictured as a mechanistic physiologist with a one-sided concentration on the neural basis of the psyche and an unfortunate ideology. He became a Soviet patriot and the discoverer of the dialectical materialist way to an understanding of the psyche. [110]

That denouement lies beyond the temporal limits of the cultural revolution, as defined in our volume. But it must be mentioned, for it helps to reveal, as ultimate consequences can, the essential elements of the cultural revolution as an intellectual process. Let me state those essentials in four propositions:

1. In our century a rational, comprehensive world view has become intellectually impossible. To put the matter more concretely, it has become impossible to keep the sciences of nature and of human nature integrated with humanistic and artistic visions, and with the ideological beliefs that hold together such groups as political parties and governments.

2. That central fact of modern intellectual history was politically intolerable to the Soviet regime.

3. Therefore the Soviet regime fostered a synthetic world view, in both senses of the word synthetic: pulling everything together, and artificial, ersatz.

4. The great break was the time when the Soviet regime moved from fostering to forcing, achieving a synthetic vision by suppression of rational discourse, so synthetic—in the sense of phony—as to be a tragicomic scandal.

The first three propositions form a sequence that has some appearance of logic, some suggestion of reason, if only reason of state. The fourth, the leap from fostering a synthetic world view to forcing an absurd caricature of one, defies even the semblance of logic. I find myself staring, in the last analysis, at the wild irrationality that confronts the historian of collectivization and of mass terror. I can see how the Stalinist mentality worked, but I cannot find a rational explanation for it.

Rural Scholars and
the Cultural Revolution

Susan Gross Solomon

The intellectual and social pluralism that had characterized Soviet cultural life in the 1920s was brought to an end by the so-called cultural revolution or the seizure of power in culture by "proletarian" intellectuals, which began in late 1928.[1] When the revolution had spent its force less than four years later, Soviet cultural life bore but a superficial resemblance to what it had been for most of the NEP period. The cultural institutions that had enjoyed a fair measure of autonomy in the administration and conduct of their work were firmly under the control of the Party. The intellectual community had been purged of many of its most brilliant members, non-Party and Party alike; these men had been replaced by individuals whose names were on the whole unknown in the arts and scholarship. And the content of most fields of culture had been radically altered; traditional concerns now deemed "counterrevolutionary" were set aside in favor of new preoccupations that fit the Party's definition of truth and beauty.

Among Western students of Soviet history, it has been customary to regard the cultural revolution of 1928–31 as imposed from above, brought about primarily by the intervention of the Communist party in the conduct of the arts and scholarship.[2] According to this view, there were important debates within the cultural professions in the 1920s, but the fundamental hostility in Soviet cultural life in the NEP period was that *between* the cultural professions, which were struggling to preserve their autonomy, and the Communist party, which was gradually extending its hegemony over every sphere of Soviet life. The proponents of this view have contended that at the end of the twenties the Party changed its tactics, turning, as David Joravsky has put it, "from fostering to forcing."[3] From 1928 on, the Party bent every effort to control culture and, in the face of such intense political pressure, the intelligentsia capitulated.

This traditional view has recently been challenged by Sheila Fitzpatrick. On the basis of her research on the politics of Soviet literature and education in the NEP period, Fitzpatrick suggests that much of the initial impetus for the harnessing of the cultural professions came from below, that is "from within the lower ranks of the party, the Komsomol, and Communist vigilante groups such as the proletarian writers and the militant atheists (Militant Godless)."[4] In developing this idea, Fitzpatrick draws attention to the conflicts between "bourgeois" and "proletarian" intellectuals that divided the cultural professions throughout the 1920s. According to her, these conflicts were bitter because, more often than not, divergent political commitments were overlaid with differences in the professional standing and orientation of the disputants; in many a profession, young Communist intellectuals new to their field and somewhat ambivalent about its norms found themselves subordinate to non-Communist intellectuals who occupied the most important posts and who regarded themselves as the guardians of professional standards.[5] In Fitzpatrick's view, the in-fighting within the cultural professions was inherently explosive. It was contained in the pre-1928 period only because the Party discouraged the escalation of conflict; as soon as the Party ceased its policy of active discouragement in 1928, the young Communist intellectuals, aggrieved because of their inferior status and position, converted the conflicts into open warfare. Fitzpatrick does not deny the importance of the Party's intervention in cultural life at the end of the twenties, but she places primary emphasis on the tensions that existed within the professions prior to that intervention.

At first glance, the difference between the traditional and the new interpretations of the cultural revolution appears to be one of emphasis. Both interpretations accord some importance to the factors of Party intervention and professional in-fighting; the two accounts differ only over the weight assigned each factor. Further reflection suggests, however, that the difference between the two accounts goes far beyond the question of accent. It is rooted in a fundamental disagreement over the cohesion of the cultural professions in the NEP period. The traditional view seems to assume that the intellectuals who were engaged in the disputes were united by a feeling of professional solidarity that transcended their expressed differences. The new view, on the other hand, implies that the cleavages that gave rise to the intraprofessional disputes were so basic as to outweigh the tendency to professional solidarity. The disagreement on this point is an important one, for it raises the more general question of the viability of the NEP experiment in culture. The more recent interpretation of the events of 1928–31 would suggest that the coexistence of social and intellectual opposites, which was the hallmark of Soviet cultural life in the twenties, was so uneasy that some sort of crisis in culture was likely. The traditional view would imply that the NEP experiment in cultural pluralism did have some chance of success because within the intellectual community there was a sense of solidarity that overrode particular disputes.

Further examination of these important issues would require detailed studies of the controversies that divided intellectuals working in various fields in the 1920s. Optimally, such studies would have a dual focus. First, they would analyze the patterns of cleavage in a cultural profession. How did those working in the field divide according to intellectual position, social profile, professional orientation, institutional affiliation, and political commitments? Were the cleavages overlapping or cross-cutting? And second, the studies would examine the cohesion among intellectuals working in a field. How much substantive consensus was there? On what factors was this consensus based (agreement on theory, method, important questions, criteria of good work)? How much social solidarity was there in the profession? Were the disputants loyal only to their subgroups or did they demonstrate some allegiance to the profession as a whole? What were the bases of solidarity (institutional affiliation, distribution of power and authority among intellectuals, shared professional norms, training)?

The assessment of the intellectual in-fighting within a range of cultural professions is well beyond the scope of any single paper. Here we examine in detail the controversy that divided intellectuals working in one field of scholarship—rural social studies.[6]

RURAL SOCIAL STUDIES IN THE 1920s

In the first decade of Soviet power, the field of rural studies was the scene of great activity. There had been research on the Russian countryside as early as the last two decades of the nineteenth century,[7] but the Bolshevik Revolution of 1917 brought with it unprecedented interest in the rural sector, upon which depended not only the economic prosperity but also the political stability of the new regime. With the Soviet government now assuming the role of patron and client of all the sciences, the field of rural inquiry burgeoned. New teaching and research centers were founded, new journals were created, and talented young people were recruited.

As the field grew, its intellectual content broadened. In the first half of the 1920s (as in the previous decade), the most vital area of rural inquiry was agricultural economics. At mid-decade, the field expanded to include questions characteristic of rural sociology.[8] The intellectual growth of rural inquiry was accompanied by its institutional development. For most of the 1920s the center of the rural studies profession was the Timiriazev Agricultural Academy.[9] With this venerable institution, founded in 1865 on the Petrovsko-Razumovskoe estate outside Moscow, were affiliated a majority of the scholars interested in the study of the Russian countryside. In the course of the 1920s, the Academy expanded its teaching and research activities. It undertook an active policy of recruiting students, so that by mid-decade it was able to boast an enrollment of three thousand undergraduate and graduate students—a figure that made it the largest such institution in all of Europe.[10] Two new research institutes were created within the Academy, one on soil science and the other on agricultural economics.[11] The latter, whose full title was the Scientific Research Institute on Agricultural Economics (*Nauchnoissledovatel'skii institut sel'skokhoziaistvennoi ekonomii*), was responsible for some of the most creative projects undertaken during the NEP period.[12] Despite its prerevolutionary origins and its largely non-Marxist faculty, the Timiriazev Academy had close relations with the Soviet government.[13] The Institute on Agricultural Economics served as the research arm of the Ministry of Agriculture, and the Academy's journal, *Puti sel'skogo khoziaistva*, was published in conjunction with that Ministry.[14] At the end of 1925 a second center for research on the rural sector came into being. In keeping with the regime's new emphasis on the creation of institutions in which a Marxist science of society could be forged,[15] the Communist Academy opened the doors of its Agrarian Section.[16] Within but a few years of its creation, this Section became the most significant center for Marxist research on the rural sector and as such constituted a genuine alternative to the Timiriazev Academy and its institutes.[17]

The scholarship produced in these institutions was well known for its quality both inside and outside Russia. Because rural inquiry was totally state-supported and because the countryside was a major concern of practical policy, the rural scholars' choice of problems for study was often influenced by governmental policy commitments. This did not mean that the studies produced were simply apologies for official policy; in fact, in the period 1921–29, the instances in which a scholar adjusted his findings to support the *substance* of Party policy were exceedingly rare.[18]

For the scholars engaged in the study of the Soviet rural sector, the decade of the 1920s was a turbulent one. Between 1923 and mid-1928 the field was rent by a scientific controversy. The participants in the dispute were divided into two groups: the members of the Organization-Production school (*organizatsionno-produktivnaia shkola*) and the Agrarian-Marxists (*agrarniky-Marksisty*). Though part of a single profession, these two groups were remarkably dissimilar: their members differed from one another in age, professional standing, attitude toward scholarship, intellectual preoccupations, and political sympathies. For most of the decade, the Organization-Production scholars were the undisputed leaders of the field.[19] Agricultural economists of some distinction, these men held major posts in the Timiriazev Academy well before 1917. The Organization-Production scholars were not Marxists by conviction nor did they become members of the Communist party after the Revolution,[20] yet they continued to teach and conduct research in the Timiriazev Academy throughout the 1920s, thus taking a leading role in the training of the first generation of Soviet agricultural specialists. Led by A. V. Chaianov,[21] the youngest member of the group, these scholars were among the principal

contributors to the Timiriazev Academy's journal and to the series of
research reports (*trudy*) issued by the Academy's Institute on Agricultural
Economics. The attitude of the members of the Chaianov group toward
their work was that of "cosmopolitans."[22] Anxious to preserve their reputations for excellence outside as well as inside Russia, they exchanged research findings on a regular basis with foreign colleagues whom they
treated as an important reference group. The second set of scholars, the
Agrarian-Marxists, were younger rural sociologists. With the exception
of their leader, L. N. Kritsman,[23] the members of this group came to
maturity after the Revolution.[24] In the first half of the 1920s, they were still
doing graduate work in the Timiriazev Academy, where they studied with
and worked as research assistants to the members of the Organization-
Production school. The Agrarian-Marxists' careers began effectively at the
end of 1925, when they joined the newly created Agrarian Section of the
Communist Academy.[25] Here they became involved in editing the section's journal, *Na agrarnom fronte*,[26] and in conducting research on peasant social structure. For this research, the members of the Kritsman group
soon acquired reputations in Russia as the foremost Marxist students of the
countryside. In the main, the attitude of these young researchers toward
their work was that of "locals."[27] Unlike their teachers, they evinced little
interest in securing recognition from colleagues abroad.

Even after the controversy was resolved in mid-1928, there was no
peace for the scholars engaged in rural studies. Beginning in late 1928 the
field was engulfed by the cultural revolution. Within short order, Marxist
credentials became a prerequisite for any scholar who proposed to do
research on the Soviet countryside. And the Party was established as the
final arbiter of truth in rural studies.[28] As a consequence of these developments, the most productive period in the history of Soviet rural inquiry
came to a close.

For a consideration of the problems in Soviet history raised at the outset
of this article, the case of rural studies has a major advantage. Within the
course of a single decade, the field experienced both a protracted internal
controversy and the direct intervention of the Communist party in the
conduct of inquiry. This combination of events enables one to assess the
relative impact upon the fate of rural inquiry of the factors of professional
in-fighting and political intervention.

THE CONTROVERSY: 1923 TO MID-1928

The controversy between the Organization-Production and Agrarian-Marxist scholars took place in two distinct stages. The first lasted from 1923 to early 1927; the second began in early 1927 and ended in mid-1928 with the resolution of the dispute. Both the issues and the conduct of the disputants varied considerably from the first to the second stage.

The First Stage: 1923–27

In the first phase of the controversy, the two groups of scholars were engaged in a dispute over the goals for their field. They differed primarily over the ranking of research questions; each school considered its own work primary and that of its rival peripheral.

Throughout their existence as a distinct school of inquiry, the *Organization-Production scholars* focussed their attention on the Russian family farm (*trudovoe khoziaistvo*), a commodity-producing economic unit that functioned without benefit of hired labor. They were interested in explaining the operation of this form of farming, which, according to their estimate, constituted 90 percent of Russian agriculture; and they were concerned with devising methods of streamlining the farm's activities.

This mixture of theoretical and practical objectives that characterized Organization-Production work in agricultural economics had its origins in the early work experiences of the members of this group. During the first decade and a half of the twentieth century, most of the Organization-Production scholars were employed as agronomists by the *zemstva*. [29] Their work in the villages of Russia shaped their social philosophy and defined their intellectual interests. Having witnessed at first hand the limited success of the Stolypin Land Reforms of 1906–10, they became convinced that the redistribution of land would not in itself alleviate agricultural backwardness. What was needed was the thoroughgoing reorganization of farming—the intensification of production, the introduction of complex machinery, and the relegation of certain farm tasks to the rural cooperatives. Such reorganization could not be legislated from above, they insisted; it could be effected only by slow and patient work with the peasantry. Thus it was that these men saw agronomy rather than politics as the means to rural improvement. They demanded of the agronomy in which they placed their faith that it be "scientific," founded on a precise understanding of the principles underlying the organization of agriculture and the behavior of the peasant farmer. Their own observations of peasant life reinforced by the comments of other agricultural officials led them to suspect that the predominant form of agriculture in Russia, the family farm, was an unusual economic unit whose springs of action remained to be discovered. To accomplish this important task, the agronomists turned from practical careers to the full-time study of the family farm.

The Organization-Production scholars approached their subject as microeconomists. They focussed on the internal dynamics of the family farm and paid no attention—at least initially—to the relation of that farm to the rural sector as a whole.[30] In defense of this focus, the members of the Chaianov group argued that without the study of the operation of the individual farm, all research on the countryside would be superficial.[31] Their explanation of the dynamics of the family farm began with an analysis of the psychology of the family farmer. The head of the family farm, so ran the theory, was not acquisitive by nature; he was interested only in satisfying the consumption needs of the members of his family. The pursuit of this objective led the farmer to behave in an unusual way. Until his family's needs were met he would work, often laboring well past the point of diminishing marginal returns; as soon as his family's needs were met, however, the farmer would cease his labors irrespective of the prospects for additional gain.[32] The Organization-Production account of the activity of the family farm was essentially a demographic one. "Consumption pressure," the variable identified as determining the economic activity of the farm, was defined by the members of the Chaianov group as the ratio of consumers to workers in the farming family and was declared to vary in accordance with the age (number of years in existence) of the family unit.[33] All differences in the economic activity between farms were attributed to variations in family composition; no mention was made of the inequities in the distribution of resources or talents.[34]

By 1915 the rudiments of the demographic explanation had been presented. For the next decade, the Organization-Production scholars concentrated their energies on examining every aspect of the farm they had described. They charted the organization of the family farm by studying its resource budget; they explored the effects on the family farm of its participation in rural cooperatives; they isolated the principles underlying the farmer's calculation of the optimum size and patterns of cultivation for his farm; and they traced the evolution of Russian agriculture by examining farming in widely different regions.[35] The results of their research persuaded these men that some of the most important categories of classical economics (wages, profit, rent) could not be meaningfully applied to the operation of the small-scale independent farm. Codifying their observations in 1924, the Organization-Production scholars presented an explanation of the dynamics of the family farm, which they daringly entitled a "theory of non-capitalist economics."[36]

The *Agrarian-Marxists* brought to rural studies a set of concerns that differed substantially from those of their mentors. They concentrated on the economic and social stratification of the peasantry, insisting that only through an analysis of peasant social structure could the evolution of the rural sector be laid bare. As Marxists, they started from the premise that the Soviet peasantry was in the process of evolving to socialism and they devoted their efforts to studying the pattern of that evolution.

In approaching their subject, the members of the Kritsman group were influenced by the fact that they were the first generation of Soviet Marxists to study the Russian countryside. Responding to what they perceived as the demands of this unique position, the young researchers began their work with the declaration that all previous Marxist thinking about the transition of the rural sector to socialism was inappropriate under Soviet conditions.[37] In taking this stand, the group's principal target was the theory, espoused by Western and late nineteenth-century Russian Marxists alike, that on its route to socialism the peasantry had to pass through the stage of capitalism.[38] The Agrarian-Marxists conceded that this law was valid when applied to the countries of Western Europe or even to their own Russia before 1917, but they termed it "outmoded" in a setting in which political power was in the hands of the proletariat.

In place of the Marxist formulations of the past, the Agrarian-Marxists substituted a new theory whose rudiments they extracted from Lenin's last writings.[39] They contended that "under the dictatorship of the proletariat" there were two possible routes to socialism. In addition to the traditional capitalist route, the peasantry could now evolve to socialism via the rural cooperatives; the small and middle peasants could join the rural cooperatives and, as members of these large-scale, horizontally organized institutions, could engage in the struggle with capitalist agriculture. Of the two paths to socialism, the Agrarian-Marxists preferred the cooperative route for a variety of reasons. In their view, the cooperative path would promote the development of a homogeneous economy. Instead of the immediate emergence of socialism in industry, with agriculture moving first to capitalism and then to socialism, the cooperative route would permit both sectors of the economy to develop in tandem. Further, the cooperative route would effect with minimum social cost the dissolution of the major obstacle to socialism, the precapitalist (read "independent") peasantry; now for the first time, the small and middle peasant could avoid the agonies of an unequal contest with the rural capitalist and the almost certain pro-letarianization that would issue from that contest. And finally, the very existence of the cooperative option would testify to the originality—and greatness—of the Soviet experiment.

Their partisanship on behalf of the cooperative pattern did not blind the Agrarian-Marxists to the difficulties that would attend its implementa-tion. While asserting that the hegemony of the proletariat had increased the number of possible paths to socialism, the Agrarian-Marxists admitted that the actual choice of path was dependent upon peasant attitudes toward farming. With this factor in mind, the young researchers predicted that in the initial phase of the dictatorship of the proletariat, both paths to so-cialism would be pursued. While some peasants would choose to enter the cooperatives, others, victims of the traditional attachment to individual farming, would stubbornly cling to their tiny plots and thus contribute to the capitalization of the rural sector. But, insisted the Agrarian-Marxists, as more and more peasants became disillusioned about their prospects of becoming large-scale landowners, they would join the cooperatives, and thus the new route would gradually gain ascendancy over the old.[40]

In its first phase, the controversy between the Chaianov and Kritsman groups was conducted in moderate tones. Each group devoted its efforts to enunciating its own theory and to pursuing those research projects that it deemed consequential. Serious intellectual criticism of either group by the other was rare; when criticisms were launched, they tended to be directed at particular points rather than at the opponent's position as a whole. Social relations between the two schools in this period appear to have have been most cordial. The two groups met frequently, as both were housed in the Timiriazev Academy, and there is no record of any hostile or acrimonious confrontation. Even more revealing, these years saw the initiation of several large-scale research projects that involved the collaboration of members of both schools.[41]

Though not the predominant concern of either school, the dispute over the goals for the field tacitly influenced the research of both. The continued insistence of their students upon the importance of studying interfarm relations eventually led the Chaianov group to move into the arena of "macroeconomics" and to examine the relation of the family farm to the larger rural sector. On the basis of their examination, in 1925 the Organization-Production scholars declared that the unique properties of the family farm to which they had earlier drawn attention would permit the small-scale farm to withstand the process of rural capitalization; indeed, they asserted, over time there would take place a marked transfer of lands from capitalist to family farming.[42] The implications of this position were clear: the Soviet rural sector would not evolve to capitalism, but would for the foreseeable future remain dependent upon the small commodity producer. At the prospect of such a future, the Organization-Production scholars were not at all dismayed. In their view, the family farm—its activity rationalized as a result of the performance of some of its functions by the vertically organized cooperatives[43]—was well suited to serve as the basis of a modern agricultural sector. At about the same time that the Organization-Production scholars concluded that the countryside was not evolving to capitalism, the Agrarian-Marxists modified their original stand with the declaration that the Soviet peasantry was adopting the capitalist path to socialism. The primary reason for this modification was cognitive. When the young researchers turned to study the rural sector, they were confronted with a glaring disparity between the postulates of their theory and actual conditions in the Soviet countryside. Specifically, even their most cautious prediction about the gradual drift of the poor and middle peasants to the cooperatives was proving over-optimistic; the data they collected showed clearly that the lower strata of the peasants were clinging resolutely to their small allotments and that the cooperatives were being used by the better-off peasants for their own purposes.[44] Faced with this reality, the Agrarian-Marxists effected a compromise. They did not repudiate the propositions of the theory they had espoused. They simply structured their research around the hypothesis that the Soviet peasantry was pursuing the capitalist path to socialism; they undertook extensive studies of rural social structure using indicators designed to detect the growing capitalization of the peasantry.[45] This compromise, which had been hammered out by 1926, had two advantages: it allowed the Agrarian-Marxists to conduct empirical inquiry on problems they considered important; and it served to differentiate the young researchers from their mentors and thus constituted an important stage in the Kritsman group's drive to carve a place for itself in the community of Soviet rural scholars.

The Second Stage: 1927 to mid-1928

In the second stage of the controversy, the issues dividing the two schools underwent an important change. The new phase began in early 1927 when the Chaianov and Kritsman groups met in the Timiriazev Academy's Institute on Agricultural Economics to debate the question of rural differentiation.[46] The two groups of scholars came to the meeting with widely divergent views of differentiation in Soviet Russia—its nature, its causes, and its effects on peasant society.

The Agrarian-Marxists considered the most important differences among the peasantry to be social in nature and economic in origin. Beginning with the fact that the means of cultivation were in short supply and were unevenly distributed in the rural sector, the researchers showed that the existence of these inequities generated webs of hire-and-lease transactions, whose objects ranged from inventory and livestock to the land itself. By virtue of these transactions some peasants became dependent upon others for the means of their existence. Thus arose the social relations of subordination and superordination, which, to the members of the Kritsman group, constituted the essence of rural differentiation. According to the young researchers, the process of differentiation would end by transforming the rural sector. The peasantry would become increasingly stratified until the rural population was polarized into two groups: rural capitalists and agricultural wage-workers. The middle, precapitalist peasant would be resolved into one or the other—usually the latter—of the two groups and with him would disappear traditional peasant society.

The Organization-Production scholars took a very different position. They considered the salient variations between peasant farms to be demographic in origin. According to them, the economic activity of each farm was a function of the ratio of consumers to workers on the farm, and that ratio in turn varied with the number of years the family unit had been in existence. The demographic analysis put forward by the Chaianov group led logically to an equilibrium model of rural development.[47] Assuming that the cycle of growth and decay of each farm was determined by the composition of its family, for every farm that expanded its operation there would be another in the process of contracting its activities. Thus any *net* change in the map of peasant social structure was unlikely and the traditional peasant society of the small independent farmer could be expected to endure for some time.

In the course of the discussion in the Timiriazev Institute, it became clear that underlying the schools' dispute over peasant stratification was a disagreement over a more fundamental question—the nature of the Russian family farm. The Chaianov group treated the family farm as a form of biological organism with its own internally determined cycle of growth and decay; external factors were viewed as exerting minimal influence on that cycle. The Kritsman group considered the family farm to be an economic unit that, like other such units, was primarily determined by the socioeconomic environment within which it existed. To be sure, this disagreement had been latent in the schools' earlier divergence over the capitalization of the rural sector. But now the issue of the family farm came to the fore, eclipsing all other points of difference between the two groups. Indeed, from early 1927 on, the controversy in rural inquiry was no longer a disagreement over goals; it had become a dispute on a single point of substance.

The emergence of the issue of the family farm as the center of the rural studies controversy was related to certain shifts of emphasis in the rural policy of the Communist party. Until 1926 the regime courted the individual peasant on the theory that the good will of this figure was necessary, as Soviet agriculture would continue for some time to be based on small-scale units of production. Even the long-range plans for the rural sector drafted during this period reflected this assumption.[48] After 1925, however, there was much less emphasis on conciliating the individual peasant. As the Party began to face the challenge of constructing socialism, calls were issued for the strengthening of the large-scale socialist farm sector and for the expansion of the role of the rural cooperatives.[49] At about the same time, the deficiencies inherent in small-scale farming were becoming increasingly apparent. This confluence of events highlighted the question of the future of the family farm. That the rural scholars were aware of the urgency of that question was clear from the discussion at the Timiriazev meeting.

In addition to the shift in the issues dividing the scholarly community, in the second phase of the controversy there was a noticeable change in the conduct of the disputants. As of 1927, the dispute began to consume most of the energies of the scholars. There was a decrease in the attention devoted by each group to its own work and a corresponding rise in the amount of notice given by each to the research of the other. The intensified scrutiny varied in form. The Agrarian-Marxist scholars conducted a root-and-branch attack upon the Organization-Production position. They undertook extensive research designed to disprove the core propositions enunciated by their teachers[50] and they attempted to challenge the hegemony of the Chaianov group over certain fields of inquiry by proposing alternative approaches to questions traditionally studied by the Timiriazev professors.[51] For their part, the Organization-Production scholars became defensive. They attempted to minimize the novelty of their work on the family farm by drawing links between it and the work done by their students,[52] and they worked to reformulate their research so that it would be relevant to the current concerns of the regime.[53] They did not, however, retract any of their core beliefs or assertions. As each of the schools increased its criticism of the scholarship of the other, social relations between the two groups became strained. Collaboration ceased and it became rare for members of one group to acknowledge with sincerity their intellectual debts to their rivals.[54]

Probably several factors influenced the change in conduct. The Agrarian-Marxists' decision to read and criticize their rivals' work with care was taken primarily in response to the extension of Organization-Production theory into the arena of "macroeconomics". As of 1925, the Timiriazev professors were claiming to have unlocked the secrets of the entire rural sector. Confronted with this sweeping claim, the Kritsman group realized that piecemeal criticism was useless; to best their mentors, the young researchers would have to cast doubt upon at least some of the basic postulates of Organization-Production theory and propose an alternative account of the phenomena explained by the Chaianov group. The Organization-Production scholars were influenced in their decision to adopt a defensive strategy by the shifts in rural policy described above. The extent to which their intellectual position was out of tune with the commitments of the new age was not lost upon these scholars. Concerned lest they lose their status as experts on Soviet agriculture, the members of the Chaianov group began to deflect attention from their work on the family farm and to present their research wherever possible as relevant to the new directions in rural policy.

The changes in the behavior of both sets of disputants were affected by modifications in the professional organization of the rural studies field that occurred at mid-decade. In the first half of the 1920s, the Chaianov group had occupied the major posts in the most prestigious institution, with the Agrarian-Marxists filling the subordinate positions. The founding of the Agrarian Section of the Communist Academy and the move by the Agrarian-Marxists to this new section in 1926 altered the balance of power in the rural studies community. Now the young researchers had the independence they needed to launch a full-scale critique of their teachers and the Chaianov group had to adopt a more cautious line, for it no longer exercised undisputed control over the field. Not only did the new professional organization of the field affect the rivals' intellectual conduct, it also influenced their social behavior. The move by the Agrarian-Marxists to the Agrarian Section brought to an end both the teacher-student relations that had been responsible for the cordiality of the earlier period and the collaborative research that had inhibited the levelling of unrestrained criticism by one school against the other.

Resolution: Spring to Autumn 1928

Between the early spring and the autumn of 1928 the controversy that had divided the rural studies community for over half a decade was resolved. The end came quietly, with no fanfare. The Organization-Production scholars ceased doing research on the family farm and began to study the organization of large-scale state and collective farms.[55] For scholars who had been so convinced of the merits of small-scale independent farms and so skeptical of the viability of large-scale socialist agriculture,[56] the shift to this new topic constituted a *volte face*. Indeed, in setting aside their traditional interests for new concerns, the members of the Chaianov group were effectively conceding that the small noncapitalist farm would not play the role in Soviet agriculture that they had envisaged for it.

The concession by the Chaianov group is open to two very different interpretations. The Organization-Production scholars may have been prompted to alter their research focus primarily because of the tense atmosphere that surrounded the Shakhty trial. The trial of the Shakhty engineers took place in May 1928, but beginning in March of that year extensive publicity was given to the "treason" of the "bourgeois" specialists.[57] It is possible that the Organization-Production scholars conceded their position because they anticipated that, as a consequence of the Shakhty trial, the distrust of non-Communist specialists would spread to those working in cultural fields.[58] Alternatively, it may well have been that the Organization-Production scholars shifted their research focus largely in response to the Party's patent disenchantment with small-scale farming and its growing emphasis on large-scale agriculture as reflected in the resolution passed at the Fifteenth Party Congress enjoining "the gradual transformation of individual peasant holdings into large-scale farming enterprises."[59]

Our evidence suggests that the latter explanation is more appropriate than the former. In mid-1928 the members of the Chaianov group do not appear to have foreseen the suspicion of all bourgeois specialists that followed in the wake of the Shakhty trial. In their studies of socialist agriculture written during the year 1928, the Timiriazev professors made no attempt to style themselves as "proletarian" scholars. Instead, they presented themselves as apolitical experts whose skills were technical and therefore applicable in any political context;[60] only later did the members of the Chaianov group attempt to jump aboard the political bandwagon. But in mid-1928 the Organization-Production scholars *do* seem to have perceived that, as a consequence of their identification with the study of the family farm, their status as experts on Soviet agriculture was in jeopardy. That they looked upon their new work as a means to avert obsolescence was clear from the fact that wherever possible they drew attention to the relevance of their current research for the concerns of the regime. In our view, therefore, the concession of mid-1928 should be interpreted mainly as an intensification of the quest for relevance begun by the Chaianov group in the second phase of the controversy.

RURAL INQUIRY AND THE CULTURAL REVOLUTION: 1928-31

In the second half of 1928, almost as soon as the controversy was resolved, the field of rural inquiry began to feel the impact of the cultural revolution. That revolution affected every aspect of the field—the administration and structure of the major teaching and research institutions, the composition of the scholarly community, and the content of theory and research on the countryside.

The first signs of the change occurred in the professional organization of the field. In September 1928, the Agrarian Section of the Communist Academy was raised to the status of an institute.[61] Officially, the change was made in recognition of the achievements of the section in the study of rural social structure. More likely, the change reflected the Party's understanding that for the hegemony of Marxist theory to be established in rural studies (as per the charge to the Communist Academy of May 1928),[62] the Kritsman group would require additional stature. At about the same time, the Timiriazev Academy was reorganized. In June 1928, a new director, M. E. Shefler, was installed.[63] Shefler, a member of the Communist party since 1917, waited only a month after his appointment before criticizing the workings of the Academy at a session of the collegia of the Commissariats of Agriculture and Enlightenment.[64] Shefler's attack culminated in the drawing up of a five-year plan for the revamping of the academy. For our story, the important aspect of the projected change was the planned bifurcation of the economics faculty into a faculty of state farms and a faculty of collective farms. With the implementation of this change, there would no longer be any faculty in which courses on presocialist (read "family") farming could be mounted. Thus the Organization-Production scholars, who had always done their teaching in the economics faculty, would be deprived of their *pied à terre*. In the last third of 1928 the reorganization of the academy took effect. It was followed closely by an attack on the research institution dominated by the Chaianov group, the Institute on Agricultural Economics. In February 1929, a proposal was made in the Presidium of RANION to integrate that institute with the Institute on Land Consolidation and Migration.[65] The clear purpose behind the proposal was to ease the Chaianov group out without having to close down its institute.

The changes in the professional organization of rural studies were followed almost immediately by alterations in the composition of the community of scholars. These alterations stemmed from the implementation of a policy that required any researcher studying the Soviet countryside to possess credentials as a Marxist. As might have been expected, the first victims of this unwritten rule were the Timiriazev professors. As they became aware of the new policy of "credentialism,"[66] the members of the Chaianov group attempted to retain their positions by "confessing" their errors and pledging to conduct rural inquiry along Marxist lines.[67] Initially, these "confessions" were accepted at face value. However, as the leaders of the Organization-Production school proved unable to adjust their work to the official view of the rural sector, the genuiness of their confessions was called into question by Party officials working in agricultural science, and the repentant authors were denounced.[68] Restrained, monitored, and vilified, the members of the Chaianov group retreated one by one from the field they had once led. By the end of 1929 they had disappeared as a force in rural inquiry. And, *Puti sel'skogo khoziaistva*, the journal in which these scholars had published their most important articles, was replaced by a new journal entitled *Sotsialisticheskaia rekonstruktsiia i sel'skoe khoziaistvo*, which devoted little space to agricultural policy and even less to articles on agricultural economics.[69] For some zealots, the elimination of the Organization-Production scholars from the field was apparently insufficient. For in 1930 the leaders of the school were arrested on the charge (never proven) that they had formed an opposition political party, the Working Peasant Party.[70]

The emphasis on credentials that had led to the elimination of the Organization-Production scholars from rural studies took its toll on the Agrarian-Marxists as well. At the Conference of Marxist-Leninist Scientific Research Institutions held in April of 1929, the Kritsman group found itself facing two charges levelled against them by scholars boasting superior credentials as Marxists.[71] First the attackers claimed that the Kritsman group had allowed the Timiriazev professors to define its Marxism for it. The irony of this charge was bitter. For over half a decade, the Agrarian-

Marxists had staunchly battled their teachers in the name of Marxism; now that the Timiriazev professors no longer constituted a threat, that very service was being turned against Kritsman and his followers. To be sure, there was a grain of truth in the accusation. The Agrarian-Marxists had shaped their research *in part* with a view to refuting their teachers' contention that the rural sector was not evolving to capitalism. Equally important, the Kritsman group had not dismissed out of hand the work of its rivals. In fact, in October 1929—half a year after the April attack—a member of the Kritsman school drew up a proposal for a course in rural studies in which all the major writings of the Timiriazev professors were included as suggested (rather than required) readings.[72] The second accusation directed against the group in the Agrarian Institute was that their views contradicted Party policy on the countryside. In particular, the critics cited the failure of the Kritsman group to discuss the virtues of cooperative agriculture. Rhetoric notwithstanding, the doctrinal element in the April attack was minimal. More than anything else, the attack was a reflection of the struggle for power and prestige that was taking shape within the community of Marxist rural scholars.

With the Organization-Production scholars removed from the field and the Agrarian-Marxists under fire, the stage was set for the last act in the drama—the establishment of the Party as the final arbiter of truth in rural studies. In December 1929, the First All-Union Conference of Agrarian-Marxists convened in Moscow.[73] This Conference, which was the analogue of a similar meeting of Soviet historians held the previous year, brought together some three hundred delegates from all over the Soviet Union. The official purpose of the conference was to foster links between the scholars working at the Agrarian Institute of the Communist Academy in Moscow and Marxist researchers working on the periphery. The evidence suggests, however, that its real aim was to solidify the control of the Agrarian Institute staff over the field of rural studies. In preparation for the December meeting, scholars from the Moscow Institute were sent out to "advise" in the selection of delegates from outlying regions.[74] And no less revealing, well in advance of the conference the members of the institute were designated as the leaders of an All-Union Society of Agrarian-Marxists whose formation was to be announced at the December meeting.[75]

The seven-day conference opened on December 20 against the background of an intensive campaign to make full-scale collectivization an immediate reality. Yet the subject of collectivization did not dominate the meeting.[76] Rather, the sessions were taken up with intricate disputes over credentials. Day after day, the scholar-delegates debated the question of who in the community of rural researchers could be considered an orthodox Marxist.[77]

In these discussions over credentials, there were signs of a growing tendency to assess the value of scholarship on the basis of political criteria. But it was not until Stalin appeared to address the delegates on the seventh and final day of the meeting that the use of such criteria of assessment received official sanction. Stalin's speech to the assembled delegates began rather innocuously. The speaker reminded his audience of the importance of theory in the study of the countryside; to this, he added the not-surprising injunction that only Marxist theory be tolerated in Soviet research on the rural sector.[78] Stalin's rather bland remarks on rural studies proved to be but the prelude to the core of his address—the announcement that the *kulaks* or better-off peasants were to be liquidated as a class.[79] The effect of Stalin's announcement was—in the words of one of the delegates—"electrifying."[80] Suddenly the assembled scholars understood that the discussions of the requirements for Marxist rural studies that had occupied their attention for six days were irrelevant. The final arbiter of truth in rural studies was not to be Marxist-Leninist theory as a body of doctrine, but rather the facts as created by the Communist party through its rural policy. Henceforth, the task of theory would be to celebrate those facts and the task of researchers would be to confirm the correctness of theory.

In retrospect, it is clear that the conference had its most profound impact on the members of the Kritsman group. They had come to the conference prepared to assume the responsibility for securing the hegemony of Marxist theory and research in rural studies; indeed, the transcript of the December meeting showed them eager to take on their posts of leadership in the new All-Union Society of Agrarian-Marxists. With Stalin's appearance on the seventh day of the conference, the terms of their mandate underwent important change. Now the Kritsman group was to ensure that the substance of Marxist rural inquiry was consistent with the policy of the Communist party. For this new task, the group proved itself remarkably unsuited. And consequently, like their teachers before them, the young researchers were forced to leave the field of rural studies. The saga of their departure was no less pathetic than that of their one-time rivals. In September 1930, Kritsman lost his position as editor-in-chief of *Na agrarnom fronte*, although he did retain a seat on the editorial board. Toward the end of that year, the attacks on Kritsman and his group multiplied[81] and some of his younger colleagues issued recantations.[82] The attempts to avoid censure proved futile, however. In early 1932 the entire editorial board of the journal was replaced, an action that was justified as necessary in the face of Kritsman's "anti-Leninism."[83] With this act, the politicization of rural inquiry was complete.

In experiencing politicization, the field of rural studies was far from unique. In the course of the cultural revolution, most fields of social science suffered a similar fate; the fields differed from one another only in the timing and pattern of their transformation. In rural inquiry, politicization began relatively early. The reasons for this are not difficult to surmise. Most of the rural studies conducted during the 1920s reflected the assumptions underlying NEP—the belief in the advantages of a transition period in which agriculture would continue to be conducted by the small commodity producer and the conviction that socioeconomic change in the countryside had to be both gradual and unforced. In late 1928, when they began to think seriously of jettisoning NEP, some Party leaders felt it necessary to harness the field of rural studies lest dissenting—and knowledgeable—voices be raised against the shift in policy. Not only did the politicization of rural inquiry begin early, it was also accomplished with relative dispatch. By early 1930 the Communist party through its spokesmen was in effective control of the field. The comparatively quick takeover of rural inquiry may have been made possible in part by the controversy that divided the field from 1923 to mid-1928. The importance and lengthy duration of the debate over the family farm resulted in the polarization of the community of rural scholars. By 1928 the position of a scholar who was not affiliated with either school had become untenable.[84] Moreover, the shift in the issues of the controversy from a disagreement over goals to a substantive dispute was accompanied by the narrowing of the content of the field; all research not directly related to the disputed issue was set aside as of 1927. By weakening the fabric of the intellectual community and by impoverishing the substance of the field, the controversy may have had the effect of easing the way for politicization.

The fact that the controversy of 1923 to mid-1928 may have facilitated the subsequent politicization of rural inquiry should not lead one to conclude that politicization was simply an intensification of trends already in progress. In fact, the characteristics of the cultural revolution in rural studies—the invocation of "credentialism" as the basis for excluding scholars from the conduct of research and the installation of the Party as the final arbiter of truth in the field—were unique to the period after mid-1928. In the first decade of Soviet power, the instances in which the assessment of a work of scholarship was affected by the political allegiances of the investigator were rare. This was, after all, the period in which the Party was encouraging non-Marxist as well as Marxist scholars to engage in social inquiry.[85] Moreover, in those years agreement between the findings of research and Party policy was not a requirement. To be sure, because rural studies was a field whose subject matter was of concern to practical policy, there was some premium placed on scholarship that would be "useful" in practice; however, until late 1928 "useful" work was defined as research that bore on questions of importance, not as research that supported the policy line of the Party. These conditions underwent radical change over the period 1928–31. For the scholars engaged in the study of the Soviet countryside, the cultural revolution constituted a real break with the past.

CONCLUSION

Our survey of developments in the field of rural studies revealed that although the in-fighting between the Chaianov and Kritsman groups was bitter in the period prior to mid-1928, it stopped short of all-out war. What were the factors that constrained the conflict in this period? In the case of rural inquiry, there is no basis for the conclusion that it was the Party that was instrumental in discouraging the spread of conflict. Rather, the evidence suggests that the in-fighting among scholars was contained because of the existence of intellectual and social cohesion within the profession.

At first glance, it would appear that the intellectual consensus in the field was severely limited. The two schools could not agree on the content of theory, on the methods of research, or even on the ranking of problems in their area of inquiry. The extent of the disagreement between the Chaianov and Kritsman groups should not, however, obscure the fact that the contending scholars did share a common framework of discourse, a framework defined by the assumptions underlying the New Economic Policy. It was by virtue of this shared framework that the disputants talked to—rather than past—one another. So successful was the dialogue between the contending schools that at the end of the 1920s the Agrarian-Marxists were accused of having internalized the perspective of their rivals!

Similarly, the social solidarity among scholars working in rural inquiry was more extensive than appearances would suggest. To be sure, the members of each school were primarily loyal to their own group, particularly as the controversy gathered force in 1927. Despite sectarian loyalties, there was evident among rural scholars of all stripes some feeling of identification with the field as a whole. Neither group sought to break away from the field in order to create a subspecialty in which its concerns would be dominant; nor did either group attempt to have the other excluded from the field.[86] Rather, each school seemed to accept the other as part of its profession. There were most likely several sources of this feeling of solidarity. To begin with, for most of the 1920s the field of rural studies was defined so broadly as to include all serious study of the Soviet countryside. The breadth of this definition made possible the identification of two such diverse groups with a single profession. But more important, the professional organization of the field in the first half of the 1920s encouraged both groups to share certain norms of scholarly work and conduct. Until 1926, it will be remembered, the Agrarian-Marxists studied with and worked as research assistants to the members of the Chaianov group. It seems clear that this early training affected the young researchers profoundly. When they sought to displace their former teachers as the leaders of the rural studies community, the members of the Kritsman group did not suspend the rules of social science method or set aside their commitment to scholarship; instead, they made every effort to outdo their former mentors according to the rules of the game. The young Marxist scholars who conducted research on the rural sector did not have the uneasy relation to their profession that characterized the writers (as described by Fitzpatrick).[87] Far from being hostile to or even ambivalent about the norms of their profession, at a crucial juncture the Agrarian-Marxists demonstrated their commitment to using the established route to success. The abandonment of scholarly norms came only in 1929 with the ascendancy of new cadres of "rural scholars."

It is interesting to speculate about the sources of the difference between rural studies and literature. Some of the variation in the attitude of writers and rural scholars toward their respective professions may well have derived from dissimilarities in the socialization to which novices in the arts and social sciences were subjected.[88] One might hypothesize that there was more encouragement of and scope for originality in the field of literature than in that of rural studies. But there were other factors that contributed to the Agrarian-Marxists' allegiance to traditional norms. For one thing, the long history of the field influenced the type of novice attracted to the study of the countryside; the fact that rural inquiry had been conducted in Russia for nearly half a century discouraged the entrant who was seeking a field with a small body of knowledge that could be easily assimilated. Further, the government's acceptance of rural studies inhibited most potential rebels from overthrowing the established norms of their profession. In the period prior to mid-1928, government agencies regularly commissioned research from leading rural scholars; as we have indicated, the Timiriazev Academy's Institute on Agricultural Economics functioned as the research arm of the Ministry of Agriculture. Thus, young students in the field were educated in the belief that official recognition would be accorded those who extended, rather than destroyed, the corpus of research on the rural sector. The evidence suggests that the Agrarian-Marxists learned their lessons well.

The behavior of the Agrarian-Marxists from 1927 on leads to the conclusion that in the field of rural inquiry, the impulse for the cultural revolution did not come from within the ranks of the Communist intelligentsia. Without doubt, the members of the Kritsman group disagreed vehemently with their mentors, whom they sought to displace from positions of leadership. But the young researchers did not attempt to exclude their senior colleagues from the field. Indeed, as late as October 1929, the Agrarian-Marxists were still acknowledging the value of their teachers' contributions. In the field of rural studies, responsibility for the onset of the cultural revolution must be laid at the door of the Communist party and its minions—men with no scholarly credits but with the requisite willingness to act as ideological watchdogs over those who dared to conduct inquiry.

The fact that our case supports the traditional view of the onset of the cultural revolution should not be regarded as in any way diminishing the value of the new interpretation of the events of 1928–31. Clearly, the transformation of Soviet culture at the end of the twenties did not take place according to any single pattern. In some fields, the young Communist intellectuals chafed at the norms of their profession and therefore, at the first opportunity, converted their disagreements with their non-Marxist (or sometimes Marxist) senior colleagues into all-out war. In other fields, the in-fighting among intellectuals, however bitter, was contained because of the existence of intellectual and social cohesion within the profession; in these cases it was the intervention by the Party and its deputies that set the revolution in motion. With the variations in the development of the cultural professions under NEP an accepted fact, students of the period must now begin the task of identifying the factors that produced those variations.

Such work will, we hope, yield an understanding of the potential of the NEP experiment in culture. The facts of the rural studies case as presented here argue against the view that the coexistence of intellectual opposites under NEP was inherently unstable and that some sort of revolution in culture was therefore unavoidable. Our evidence suggests that although the rifts of 1923 to mid-1928 were serious, there was still an overriding commitment among rural scholars of all persuasions to the continuation of pluralism in the field. The Agrarian-Marxists who might have been thought most eager to eliminate their non-Communist rivals showed themselves disinclined to do so. It would appear, then, that the Agrarian-Marxists were concerned to secure for Marxism (and for their own group) a position of hegemony, not monopoly, in rural studies.

A pluralism in which Marxism was the dominant but not the only approach to social inquiry would have met many needs. It would have satisfied the desire of the regime for research that was sound and supportive; it would have fulfilled the longings of the Marxist scholars for control of their fields; and it would have preserved the diversity of the intellectual community. Regrettably, this form of pluralism was never tried. In the realm of culture, as in other realms, the limits of the NEP experiment were never reached.

Marxist Historians during the Cultural Revolution: A Case Study of Professional In-fighting

George M. Enteen

Even to the nonspecialist, some aspects of the "cultural revolution" in the historical profession are familiar. It is well known that Pokrovskii's group of Marxist historians established its own brand of "hegemony" in the historical field, somewhat comparable to that of the proletarian association RAPP in literature (see Fitzpatrick, this volume). It is also well known that in 1931 Stalin personally intervened in the historical debate with his letter to the editors of *Proletarskaia revoliutsiia,* and that this intervention was followed by an eventual decline in the prestige and influence of the Pokrovskii school.

From these facts alone, one might conclude that the Party leadership first selected an "instrument" for the subordination of the historical profession and later discarded it when it had served its purpose. However, it is the contention of this essay that such an explanation both simplifies and distorts the nature of the cultural revolutionary process in history. The dynamic impulse behind the 1928–31 upheavals in the historical profession seems to have come not only from directives and hints from above, but also from factional struggles generated *within the profession.* Pokrovskii, who occupied a position in the historical profession comparable with that of Pashukanis in law (see Sharlet, this volume), faced a challenge from other Communist historians who (like Vyshinskii in the legal profession) clearly looked to the Party leadership for support in their campaign against the dominant Marxists in the profession, and partially obtained it. At the same time, almost certainly, the challengers were aided in their campaign by the resentment felt by non-Marxists and non-Communists in the profession toward the Pokrovskii group that had earlier humiliated them.

As in the case of law, the logical interest of the Party leadership was probably in conflict with theories of the dominant group of Marxist historians. Pokrovskii's theories were, after all, deterministic, cosmopolitan in spirit, and indisposed to stress the importance of exceptional individuals. But this did not supply the Party leadership with an overwhelming reason to intervene in the historical debate. So long, however, as factional conflict had not been overcome in the Party, the writing of Party history constituted a form of power. The history of the Party was too important to be left entirely in the hands of historians. In this sense the situation resembled that existing, for example, in rural studies (see Solomon, this volume), where collectivization *did* provide a reason for Party intervention. Although the leadership was only intermittently concerned about historical quarrels, regarding them as of secondary importance, individual members of the leadership were probably inclined to favor different historical factions. Once historians became embroiled in factional conflicts of their own and appealed to the Party leadership for support, Party leadership could not overlook political consequences and stand aloof.

The focus of the present essay is on the efforts of rival groups of Marxist historians to win a mandate from the Party Central Committee to guide historical research and publication, to control the staffing of institutions, and to enforce professional norms. This constitutes a case study of infighting within a profession during the period of cultural revolution; and our view is that such a study exposes one of the basic processes of cultural revolution and provides, at the same time, important insights into the political culture of the early years of the Stalin period.

Until 1927, a *modus vivendi* existed between Marxist and non-Marxist historians. But it was a *modus vivendi* in which non-Marxists effectively dominated the profession: despite hardship resulting from the Civil War and losses through emigration, the so-called bourgeois historians continued their pursuits and retained their leadership in the traditional scholarly institutions.

The Marxist historians at first organized themselves separately, and on the periphery of the profession. Leaving the Academy of Sciences to the traditional historians, they organized their own Society of Marxist Historians under the poorer and less prestigious Communist Academy. In RANION[1]—the biggest center for historical research and graduate teaching—the faculty included only a minority of Marxists.

This was a situation of academic pluralism. But it must be remembered that pluralism was no more secure than the mood of compromise and the policy of reconstruction that had engendered NEP, and those involved viewed it as a confrontation of two camps, in which the stronger would ultimately triumph. In 1927 it was already clear that the belligerent spirit was rising. This must partly be attributed to the social and political tensions produced by the "war scare" of that year. But in the field of history, a local factor was also involved: the militance of the Marxist students. Late in 1927 a student wall newspaper in RANION's Institute of History called for an end to "demarxification" and denigration of Lenin, and denounced the aping of Western fashions as the latest word in scholarship. A delegation appeared at the office of Pokrovskii, then head of RANION, demanding remedy of the situation.[2]

Almost simultaneously with this student campaign against the "bourgeois historians" came a political fight within the party organization of the Institute of Red Professors. The students here—an extremely highly politicized group of Communists—were reacting to the first phase of the battle within the Politburo over grain procurements and the pace of industrialization. As early as February 1928, according to a Stalinist account published in 1931, the future Right Oppositionist N. A. Uglanov (then secretary of the Moscow Party Committee) had used the institute as a forum to express a warning about forcing the pace of industrialization and provoking a confrontation with the peasantry. The Party bureau of the institute supported him, but was apparently unseated in March by demonstration of rank-and-file support among Communists of the institute for the tougher line on economic policy associated with Stalin.[3]

In the course of 1928, an increasingly vituperative public campaign was mounted against non-Marxist historiography. The most prominent targets were D. M. Petrushevskii, a medievalist who headed the RANION Institute of History and was soon to be elected to the Academy of Sciences; Academician E. V. Tarle, a specialist in modern history who had hitherto been deemed "progressive"; and Academician S. A. Zhebelev, a specialist in ancient history.[4]

Pokrovskii did not initiate the campaign, and at first even gave some appearance of diffidence in prosecuting it. But by the autumn of 1928, when it was already clear that Stalin was winning his battle with the Politburo Right, Pokrovskii was not only stressing the theme of class conflict in scholarship, but also participating in attacks on specific non-Marxist historians.[5] He may simply have found it expedient to accept the Shakhty trial message that the bourgeois intelligentsia was involved in a conspiracy against Soviet power. But there is also the possibility of real emotional conversion, whether under the influence of his students or (as some evidence suggests) of his experiences at the International Congress of Historians held in Oslo during the summer.[6]

By the beginning of 1929, in any case, Pokrovskii had made a major decision: to attack the institutional base of the non-Marxist historians. At the First All-Union Conference of Marxist Historians, an occasion for celebrating the influence and maturity of Marxist historical scholarship, Pokrovskii agreed to support and champion a proposal to liquidate RANION's Institute of History and create in its place a new institute under the Communist Academy.[7]

The Communist Academy, designated in the summer of 1929 as the national center for research and graduate teaching, came to include all the institutes of the former RANION as well as the Institute of Red Professors.[8] The new Institute of History opened in the autumn of 1929 with a staff of forty and a relatively modest enrollment of thirty-six graduate students. It was governed by a collegium headed by Pokrovskii and including his close associates, some of whom had been his students in the Institute of Red Professors.[9] Beside it in the Communist Academy was the Society of Marxist Historians, the forum for Marxist discussion in the profession and source of many of the attacks on "bourgeois historians." As the most distinguished of Soviet Marxist historians, Pokrovskii dominated the society and exercised great influence over the work of its younger members.

The "Pokrovskii school" dominated the Marxist historians and, from 1929, the Marxist historians dominated the profession through their control of scholarly institutions and journals.

Yet even as circumstances conspired to heighten Pokrovskii's stature and to popularize his historical views, they set obstacles in his path. The Marxist camp was by no means firmly united under his leadership and that of the Society of Marxist Historians. Among those institutions whose work the society aspired to lead and coordinate were Istpart (the Commission for the Study of the October Revolution and the Russian Communist Party), the Lenin Institute, the Marx-Engels Institute, and the Society of Former Political Prisoners and Penal Exiles, which published the journal *Katorga i ssylka*. These institutions were of independent genesis and stood outside the Communist Academy system. The Lenin Institute, merging in 1928 with Istpart to create a large center for the study of party history, established its own facilities for training specialists in 1930, and could scarcely conceal its disdain for the tutelage of the Party Section of the Society of Marxist Historians. The Marx-Engels Institute, headed by the learned and notoriously intransigent Marxist scholar D. B. Riazanov, also failed to express gratitude for projects conceived in the Communist Academy. And the members of the Society of Former Political Prisoners and Penal Exiles, which included both Marxist and populist victims of the Tsarist regime, remained true to their revolutionary tradition by ignoring calls for unity.

Pokrovskii's position became less secure as his power over the historical profession increased. It was the phenomenon known in European diplomacy as a threat to the balance-of-power system: consolidation of the profession under Marxist control enhanced Pokrovskii's authority, but at the same time the possibility of his achieving hegemony brought about an opposing coalition within the Marxist camp.

Even among Marxist historians, Pokrovskii had always had intellectual opponents. Among them was I. A. Teodorovich, an Old Bolshevik who had come to the party via populism, occupied important government posts until 1928, and was currently working as chief editor of the journal *Katorga i ssylka* and head of the new International Agrarian Institute, both of which were outside the Communist Academy system. The major conflict between Teodorovich and Pokrovskii developed out of the fiftieth anniversary celebration of the founding of *Narodnaia volia*—the most famous of all populist revolutionary groups, responsible for the assassination of Tsar Alexander II in 1881. Pokrovskii's view of *Narodnaia volia* was that its ideas had little in common with socialism and that it was essentially a bourgeois party. Teodorovich, on the other hand, saw a political and ideological continuity between the left wing of *Narodnaia volia* and the later Bolshevik movement. [10] The judgment of each man appeared to coincide with his own early revolutionary experience—Pokrovskii as a social-democrat arguing with the populists, Teodorovich as a left populist attracted to the outright revolutionaries among the social-democrats.

Of the two views, Pokrovskii's clearly appeared the more "orthodox" for a Bolshevik. However, it was not ideological orthodoxy that determined the course of the dispute, but something much more like sectarian politics. Pokrovskii's supporters were successful in obtaining a resolution of censure on Teodorovich's view from the culture and propaganda (formerly agitprop) department of the Central Committee. [11] But since the resolution was drafted by a historian of the Pokrovskii school (Tatarov), Teodorovich was not disposed to take it as final. He launched an energetic attack on the cliqueishness (*gruppovshchina*) of Pokrovskii's supporters, notably Gorin, Tatarov, and Fridliand. The *kul'tprop* censure, he suggested, could have been avoided had he but "invited Gorin to a cup of tea." Instead, he had taken the path of "calling the attention of Party society to the need of exposing these Communist mandarins of historical scholarship." [12]

Pokrovskii's behavior did indeed show some signs of the cliqueishness that Teodorovich attributed to his group. He approached intellectual controversies as a political tactician. His former student P. O. Gorin, now academic secretary of the Institute of History, took the brunt of the battle because of Pokrovskii's illness and trips for medical treatment to Europe; but Pokrovskii offered him detailed tactical advice by letter, suggesting which arrangements he should use, warning against certain stylistic devices that left openings for his opponent, and even commenting on his diction. [13]

Pokrovskii saw trouble ahead: "'the signs multiply,' as Lenin once wrote, that a great attack is impending on the right flank." [14] He was alarmed at indications of wavering in his own camp when Malakhovskii (a member of the Society of Marxist Historians specializing in the revolutionary movement) "took fright and decided to make peace" with Teodorovich. He noted with concern that Riazanov, of the Marx-Engels

Institute, showed sympathy with the opposition.[15] There was some reason for concern. Teodorovich had access to the pages of *Bol'shevik*, the party's ideological journal, through his old friend Emelian Iaroslavskii—a senior member of the Society of Former Political Prisoners and Penal Exiles, chairman of the *Narodnaia volia* jubilee commission, and Teodorovich's companion in the Bolshevik underground and Tsarist prison.

Iaroslavskii had political stature equalling and probably exceeding Pokrovskii's—since 1923 he had been Secretary of the Central Control Commission of the Party and a member of the editorial boards of *Pravda*, *Izvestiia*, and *Bol'shevik*. Within the Communist Academy, he had a status junior to Pokrovskii, having become a member only in 1928. But he was, like Pokrovskii, an editor of the journal of the Society of Marxist Historians, *Istorik-marksist*, and he played an important role in the governing bureau of a new section of the society dealing with Party history, Leninism, and the Comintern. This Party Section appears to have been something of a Trojan horse within the society: it is described by Soviet historians as concerning itself with the work of the society as a whole, and leading to the struggle against "revisionism, pseudo-Marxism, and bourgeois doctrine."[16] Iaroslavskii, furthermore, was a member of the governing body of the Lenin Institute—one of those institutions that resisted the tutelage of the Society of Marxist Historians—and chief editor of four weighty volumes of Party history published between 1926 and 1930,[17] which contained criticism of Pokrovskii's ideas.

In the *Narodnaia volia* controversy, Iaroslavskii did not offer an ideological defense of Teodorovich's position, but protested that the Society of Marxist Historians should not label Teodorovich as a revisionist "while being silent... about the errors of other comrades" whose writings contained "no fewer" errors. Sharing Iaroslavskii's position were Bubnov, a member of the Orgburo of the Central Committee and, as RSFSR Commissar of Education, Pokrovskii's superior in the government hierarchy, and the Party historian N. N. Popov.[18]

In response to an appeal from Iaroslavskii "not to mutilate an Old Bolshevik"[19] (that is, Teodorovich), Pokrovskii replied unrepentantly:

> No one is mutilating Comrade Teodorovich. He is being "criticized" [*prorabatyvaiut*] as I was criticized in *Bol'shevik* in 1924, as I have been "criticized"

since then in the Institute of Red Professors (the last time three days ago in the first-year seminar), as I was criticized in the Society of Marxist Historians (the dispute about Chernyshevskii) and most recently in connection with Dubrovskii's book. . . . If you consider the judgment about Teodorovich—[that he] is theoretically close to populist authors—incorrect, . . . you can bring the question before the Central Committee. But should I take it upon myself to "suppress self-criticism" by my personal authority then I assure you, dear Comrade Emelian, nothing will come of it besides the loss of this authority.[20]

Iaroslavskii then took up the accusation of cliqueishness, commenting in *Bol'shevik* that the recent discussion among Marxist historians showed "how *dangerous* the situation is for Bolshevik research into the facts of our past when one or another group of comrades declares revisionist anything that does not fit into its schema."[21]

Gorin, again taking up the cudgels for Pokrovskii, touched lightly on the possibility that Iaroslavskii's attitude indicated at least a tolerance of political deviation: it was no accident that in the past Pokrovskii's views had been attacked by oppositionists like Trotskii and the Bukharinist Slepkov.[22] This ploy—a standard but often very damaging one in Marxist scholarly debates during the cultural revolution—was later neatly reversed by Iaroslavskii, who managed to prove that Gorin had once included unacknowledged extracts from Trotskii's writings in his own work.[23]

Pokrovskii was a founding member of the Communist Academy and, in this period, chairman of its presidium. But the academy grew very rapidly from 1928, and as it did so some of the former *esprit de corps* was lost. New members—especially those who were not of the Old Bolshevik intelligentsia—were not necessarily as respectful of Pokrovskii's authority and intellectual stature as the old ones. Among the new members to whom the Old Bolshevik intellectual tradition was alien was L. M. Kaganovich, elected in 1929. Kaganovich headed the Academy's Institute of Soviet Construction. But from 1930, as head of the Moscow Party committee and a secretary of the Central Committee, he also stood second or third in the hierarchy of the Party leadership.

At the plenum of the Communist Academy held in June 1930, Pokrovskii's leadership of the academy was subjected to a barrage of criticism, mostly emanating from Kaganovich's Institute of Soviet Construction. A. I. Angarov accused him of overlooking the achievements of that institute. Pashukanis (who had headed the Institute until Kaganovich took over, and remained a member) charged that the Presidium of the Academy had failed to assert leadership in ideological discussions and hinted that Pokrovskii should resign on the grounds of his ill health.[24]

The Communist Academy was, in fact, ridden with ideological quarrels, the best documented in Western literature being the attack on the philosopher Deborin by a group of junior colleagues.[25] Several of these quarrels were resolved in 1931 (the year of the show trial of the Mensheviks) by the ousting of an "elder statesman" of the profession—Deborin in philosophy, Rubin in economics—on the grounds not only of intellectual heresy but also of previous membership in the Menshevik Party. Pokrovskii had not been a Menshevik, but he had not been an entirely orthodox Bolshevik either.[26] As an elder statesman of the Marxist historical profession, his position was undoubtedly precarious. To clinch a case against him, he reasoned, his opponents would "have to prove that a *'pokrovshchina'* in history is the same as a *'rubinshchina'* in economics or a *'deborinshchina'* in philosophy."[27] He hoped they could not do it, but the analogy weighed on his mind.

Pokrovskii supported Deborin in the 1930 dispute of philosophical "dialecticians" (Deborin's group) and "mechanists," while Iaroslavskii and Pashukanis opposed him.[28] But he was not unaware that Deborin's aggressive stance had alienated many of his Marxist colleagues and thus contributed to his downfall. Seen in this light, Pokrovskii's own aggressive stance and the faction-fighting among Marxist historians appeared ominous. Pokrovskii wrote to Gorin:

> We search out heresy everywhere and will soon find ourselves in the situation of the Deborinites. They, of course, also sought out heresy everywhere and thought that they didn't have to do any work. And then the screws were put to them [*ikh prizhali*]. And they will put the screws to us if we do not come to our senses in time. . . .[29]

But Pokrovskii was caught in a vicious circle. Both his group and his opponents' were accustomed to bombard the Central Committee and its *kul'tprop* departments with complaints and calls for arbitration. Pokrovskii could not end this unilaterally even if, as seems likely, he sensed the danger of airing the historians' dirty linen in front of the party leadership. So the Pokrovskyites continued to complain. In one such letter to the Central Committee, Gorin wrote:

> Slander, double-dealing, irresponsible public defamation of one's opponents... have, unfortunately, been conventional means of struggle.... They vote for our resolutions but in practice sabotage them; they declare their full political confidence in Comrade Pokrovskii... and simultaneously disseminate underground "cribs" [*shpargalki*] which discredit Pokrovskii politically....[30]

In January 1931 Kaganovich, in his capacity as Secretary of the Central Committee, requested a report from Pokrovskii on the state of the historical front, and, shortly after this, Pokrovskii received a note from three members of the Communist Academy Presidium (one of them being Pashukanis) alleging the existence and concealment of theoretical errors and an absence of self-criticism among Marxist historians.[31] In a state of great alarm, Pokrovskii prepared an eighteen-page complaint denouncing opponents by name and defending his historical views.[32] This he sent to Kaganovich, to the other secretaries of the Central Committee and to Molotov, chairman of the All-Union Sovnarkom.

Specifically, what Pokrovskii wanted was a censure of Iaroslavskii[33] and, presumably, his removal from the historical field. He did not get it, nor did the campaign against him cease. His closest associates were removed, Gorin being transferred from the Institute of History and the Society of Marxist Historians to become President of the new Belorussian Academy of Sciences, despite Pokrovskii's protest to Molotov that this would be "a catastrophe for the Society, and risks its disintegration."[34]

Nevertheless, Pokrovskii himself kept his job. His leadership of the Communist Academy was reaffirmed in a Central Committee resolution of March 1931, expressing both criticism and approval of the academy's work.[35] Obviously it was a compromise resolution. Equally obviously, it offered no solution for the hostilities, now very deep, existing within the Communist Academy leadership and the Marxist historical profession.

A new crisis followed the Central Committee's resolution almost immediately. This time it directly involved Iaroslavskii, not Pokrovskii, and the issue was the extremely thorny one of Lenin's attitude toward German social-democracy and the Second International in the prewar period. In 1930 a number of discussions on this subject had been held in the Institute of History, revealing that all interpretations were controversial, including that offered in the recently published volume of Party history edited by Iaroslavskii. The Istpart journal *Proletarskaia revoliutsiia* published a long article by A. Slutskii, a former Menshevik, now a candidate member of the Party.[36] This provoked a fierce rejoinder in the same journal by K. Pol, a former student of Bubnov in the Institute of Red Professors, who detected Trotskyism in Slutskii's work.[37] Slutskii sought to reply in the journal of the Society of Marxist Historians, *Istorik-marksist*. The editorial board was divided on the wisdom of publishing the reply, and Iaroslavskii, who supported publication,[38] found himself in a minority. In retaliation, Iaroslavskii held up publication of the journal. Only two issues of *Istorik-marksist* appeared in 1931, none after August. *Proletarskaia revoliutsiia* was in a similar situation, with the June issue still not in the press in the second half of October.

Iaroslavskii's strategy may have been to produce an insoluble conflict among Marxist historians and thus precipitate intervention from above, but if so, he miscalculated the nature of the intervention. During the late summer a stalemate prevailed, with discussion in the Institute of History scheduled for the autumn, and Pokrovskii unavailingly protesting to the Central Committee about the withholding from publication of *Istorik-marksist*.[39] Slutskii and his opponent for the discussion (S. S. Bankte) prepared papers, and these were duplicated and circulated. "One may suppose that the abstracts . . . fell into the hands of I. V. Stalin," writes a Soviet historian who has had access to relevant unpublished materials.[40] In any case, in the latter part of October, Stalin wrote a letter to the editors of *Proletarskaia revoliutsiia*[41] protesting against the publication of Slutskii's original article—and "blows of steel" fell on the Marxist historians.

Stalin's letter did not constitute intervention on behalf of a faction, although we are told that when the Communist Academy struggle reached the Central Committee Pokrovskii's authority was sustained,[42] and the letter did contain criticism of Iaroslavskii's work.[43] What the letter conveyed was lack of patience with historians. How *could* they argue about "whether Lenin was or was not a real Bolshevik?"[44] (This was Stalin's interpretation of Slutskii's contention that Lenin had underestimated the danger from the "opportunist" centrists of the German Social-Democratic Party.) How could they write political history without understanding politics? ("Who, save hopeless bureaucrats, can rely on written documents alone? Who, besides archive rats, does not understand that a party and its leaders must be tested primarily by their deeds, and not by their declarations?"[45]) And finally, what could possibly be the point of publishing articles like Slutskii's? "Perhaps for the sake of a rotten liberalism, so that the Slutskii's and other disciples of Trotskii may not be able to say that they were being gagged? A rather strange sort of liberalism, this, exercised at the expense of the vital interests of Bolshevism. . . ."[46]

The effect of Stalin's letter was to send the historians (and indeed all other Marxist scholars) into a flurry of self-criticism. A host of meetings was convoked immediately; in time, Stalin's letter was discussed in every institute of the Communist Academy and every Party organization in the country. The Society of Marxist Historians demanded a review of all existing historical literature, and students of the Institute of Red Professors were formed into brigades preparing assessments of large portions of the existing literature for publication in the press. More than one hundred thirty speakers were dispatched throughout Moscow to deliver reports, and even more were later sent to outlying Republics. According to I. I. Mints (now an Academician, then a young Communist historian associated with the Iaroslavskii group), "extermination of cadres of historians began. Many historians were slandered, then repressed. Many were compelled to admit 'errors.'"[47]

Although Iaroslavskii had been mentioned disapprovingly in the letter, his group took the initiative in the meeting of the Party fraction of the Society of Marxist Historians, and apparently were almost successful in pushing through a resolution upholding their position.[48] In the end, however, the resolution went against them: the authors of the four volume *Istoriia VKP (b)* edited by Iaroslavskii were censured for cliqueishness (*gruppovshchina*)[49]—despite the fact that, according to Stalin in the letter, they had erred on "matters of principle." Shortly thereafter, Iaroslavskii recanted before the Central Committee and in letters to the editors of *Pravda* and *Bol'shevik*.[50] His disciple Mints also recanted, but still lost his position as Party Secretary in the Institute of Red Professors. Of Iaroslavskii's other associates, A. L. Sidorov and N. L. Rubinstein "went off to do practical work" for a few years, and Dubrovskii suffered a similar short-term eclipse.[51]

The Pokrovskii group was criticized for its inability to foster self-criticism within the Society of Marxist Historians, and, while Pokrovskii's own "basic leadership" was deemed sound, his followers Gorin, Fridliand, and Vanag suffered recriminations, and "materials harmful to Pokrovskii" were quietly circulated (though not published) among historians.[52]

But neither group was ousted from the leadership of the profession at this time (1931–32). Iaroslavskii's apologies were accepted early in 1932,[53] and he was soon receiving personal instructions from Kaganovich and Stalin as to just how he should revise his *Istoriia VKP(b)* and how he should present Stalin's role in that history.[54] Mints went to work for Iaroslavskii in the Commission on the History of the Civil War—a lesser, but still respectable, assignment. Pokrovskii died in April 1932, but was succeeded as director of the Institute of History and chief editor of *Istorik-marksist* by his close associate, N. M. Lukin, a specialist in European history, who had taken over Gorin's place at Pokrovskii's side after the latter's banishment to Belorussia. As before, the current tasks of the historical profession (excluding the realm of Party history, which Iaroslavskii's group continued to dominate) were enunciated by members of the Pokrovskii school, notably Lukin and Pokrovskii's former students, N. N. Vanag and A. M. Pankratova.

By now, of course, the reader is anxiously awaiting the denouement of Pokrovskii's posthumous fall from grace in a "savage campaign," which, Medvedev tells us, was carried out under Kaganovich's direction. The public repudiation of Pokrovskii came only in 1936.[55] But his disgrace was known to historians from the decree "On the teaching of civil history" issued by the Party Central Committee and the Council of People's Commissars on May 16, 1934. This decree, celebrating narrative history and condemning schematism, was implicitly directed against the Pokrovskii school of Marxist historical writing, but did not mention Pokrovskii by name. It was, however, accompanied by two further decrees (August 8 and 9, 1934) on implementation of the May 16 decree, signed by Stalin, Kirov, and Zhdanov, and circulated only among a small group of historians.[56]

There are various ways of interpreting this denouement. It can be seen as a belated victory for the Iaroslavskii faction, backed by Kaganovich: Iaroslavskii became a member of the Academy of Sciences; his associates staffed the editorial boards of the leading historical journals; and Iaroslavskii—together with a defector from the Pokrovskii camp, A. M. Pankratova, who had suffered a brief period of exile in the mid-thirties— prepared the two volumes of denigration of Pokrovskii that appeared after his public condemnation.[57]

It can also be seen as a decisive intervention on the part of the leadership, a decision to subordinate the recalcitrant historians once and for all to firm control from above. Stalin, Kaganovich, Kirov, and Zhdanov are all reported to have taken a hand in the redirection of historical research and teaching in 1934, and Stalin's involvement in the writing of the *Short Course* of Party history published in 1938 indicates that he, at any rate, had decided that Party history was too important to be left to Party historians. Undoubtedly historical writing, like other forms of mass and elite communication, was important to Stalin and almost as important to his lieutenants; and this was especially true of the field of Party and revolutionary history.

But there is another dimension. The posthumous denunciation of Pokrovskii was surely a part of the wider trend of repudiation of the Communist intellectuals who were prominent in cultural revolution— Averbakh in literature, Shulgin in educational theory, Pashukanis in law, and so on. This repudiation was accompanied by a conservative turn in cultural and social policy, which Timasheff characterized as "The Great Retreat" (see Hough, this volume). Looking at the historical profession in this general context, we may note that the change of course occurred comparatively late; and moreover that it was a direct outgrowth not of the historical faction fights but of the reorientation of *education* policy (see Lapidus, this volume) initiated in 1931: the 1934 decree specifically concerned the teaching of history, and the advice given at about the same time to a delegation of historians at a Kremlin reception concerned the writing of textbooks.[58]

In history, the "great retreat" is usually identified with the renewed celebration of the Russian national tradition—that is, it is described in ideological terms. But in practical terms it also had a meaning: a reacceptance of the old "bourgeois" historians into the leadership of the profession. Again, in comparative terms, this reacceptance came late. The old technical specialists had been rehabilitated by Stalin in 1931; and by the next year they were already occupying official positions and publishing in official journals their uninhibited denunciations of the damage done during cultural revolution to the training of specialists. But from 1934, at any rate, the non-Marxist historians were back in positions of eminence and respect in the profession, writing the textbooks, publishing in the journals, and, ultimately, collaborating with Iaroslavskii in the denunciation of Pokrovskii and, effectively, of the whole effort to create a Marxist historical tradition.

The cultural revolution and subsequent "great retreat" radically changed the historical profession. From the mid-thirties, all historians had to pay lip service to Marxism, just as they did (despite the contradiction involved) to the glories of the Russian national tradition. The old factions were dissolved, or went underground. The profession did not become monolithic, an impossibility in an imperfect world. But it became more uniform and at the same time more docile. The hierarchical framework that emerged was more formal and richer in punitive sanctions than a professional hierarchy based simply on deference to achievement. Yet, insofar as it was a hierarchy for the whole profession, professional achievement was one (though not the only) means of commanding deference within it. This was a very different situation from that of NEP, when historians belonged to one of the two opposing ideological camps, or of the cultural revolution, when the Marxist camp achieved dominance only to undermine its own position by faction-fighting. The Marxist historians had not consolidated "hegemony" during the cultural revolution. However, in trying to do so and failing, they may have inadvertently helped provide the preconditions for professional integration.

Pashukanis and the Withering Away of Law in the USSR

Robert Sharlet

The first Soviet experiment in implementing the Marxist concept of *"otmiranie prava"* or the "withering away of law" began less than a month after the Bolshevik Revolution of 1917. The new regime's first legislation on the judiciary abolished the hierarchy of tsarist courts, which were soon after replaced by a much less complex dual system of local people's courts and revolutionary tribunals. [1] This initiated a process of simplification and popularization that in the immediate postrevolutionary days and months swept away most of the inherited tsarist legal system, including the procuracy, the bar, and all but the most basic laws needed to regulate a society. Even the remaining legal minimum was subject to interpretation by a new breed of judges, mostly untrained in law, who were encouraged to guide themselves by their "revolutionary consciousness" in applying the law. The Bolsheviks' objective was that even these remnants of a legal system would ultimately become superfluous and "wither away" or disappear after the anticipated short transitional "dictatorship of the proletariat." Their vision, formed by Marx and Engels and focussed by Lenin's *Gosudarstvo i revoliutsiia* (1917), was of a new society in which people would be able to settle their disputes "with simplicity, without elaborately organized tribunals, without legal representation, without complicated laws, and without a labyrinth of rules of procedure and evidence."[2] However, harsh reality quickly impinged upon this vision as civil war engulfed the country. Confronted with the imperatives of governing under the most difficult conditions, the Bolsheviks, as Hazard has conclusively demonstrated, deferred their dream of a new world and, as early as 1918, began the process of relegalizing the society, which culminated in a fully articulated legal system based largely on foreign "bourgeois" models during the early years of the New Economic Policy.

This study is devoted to the second Soviet experiment in the "withering away of law," which began during the NEP period with the slogan *"revoliutsiia prava"*[3] ("the revolution of the law"), gained momentum during the years of the "proletarian cultural revolution" and First Five-Year Plan, peaked during the Second Five-Year Plan, and came to a definitive halt only with the arrest and purge of the jurist E. B. Pashukanis and his associates beginning in January 1937.

As the author of *Obshchaia teoriia prava i marksizm* (1924), which presented his "commodity exchange theory of law," Pashukanis was the paramount figure in the second attempt to fulfill the Marxist vision of a world without legal coercion. At a time when Marxist jurists were struggling to develop a "Marxist" theory of law as a critique of the "bourgeois" legal system of NEP, Pashukanis' theory emerged as the most persuasive approach. It was soon accorded the status of *the* Marxist theory of law, and a school of "commodity exchange" jurists gathered under Pashukanis' theoretical leadership. The commodity exchange school of law included both jurists, and specialists in "soviet construction" (*sovetskoe stroitel'stvo*). Besides Pashukanis, the best known representatives of the school were P. I. Stuchka and N. V. Krylenko, both of whom were "Old Bolsheviks" as well as jurists.

The commodity exchange school of law was centered within the Communist Academy. Most of its adherents wrote for the Academy's law journal, *Revoliutsiia prava*, which began publication in 1927, and a number of them taught in the law section of the related Institute of Red Professors. In addition, the commodity exchange jurists occupied a network of strategic positions that enabled them to maximize and extend their influence over Soviet jurisprudence, including major academic positions, key publishing posts, official legislative drafting commissions, and executive rank in the justice apparatus. A few, notably Krylenko and Stuchka, even held higher Party office. Pashukanis exercised his leadership of the commodity exchange school from an interlocking series of prestigious academic and editorial positions in law and the social sciences, through which he increasingly projected his influence over legal research, codification projects, and legal education.[4]

The "revolution of law" initiated by the commodity exchange jurists preceded the call for a general "cultural revolution" in 1928. But their recognition that it was a part of the wider movement is indicated by Stuchka's adoption of the phrase "the cultural revolution of the law."[5]

There were differences within the commodity exchange school between Pashukanis' utopian goal orientation and Stuchka's more practical concern over the means for realizing their common dream of a future society free of legal coercion. However, during the late twenties these essentially theoretical differences were deliberately muted and carefully contained within the halls of the Communist Academy in order that a unified commodity exchange school could better confront its opponents on the "legal front" of the cultural revolution. By the end of the decade, Pashukanis and his "school" had effectively driven from the field all competing theories of law and successfully eliminated or extended their control over all nonaffiliated law journals, legal research institutes, and law faculties. This meant that all legal research and codification projects, as well as control over legal education, were henceforth concentrated within the Communist Academy's newly reorganized Institute of Soviet Construction and Law. Pashukanis, who headed the Institute, became the virtual leader of the Soviet legal profession.

The triumph of the commodity exchange school of Soviet jurisprudence meant greater emphasis on its long-term goal of the withering away of law. To its critics, this meant the spread of "legal nihilism," especially among Marxists, Communists, members of the intelligentsia, and even some officials. In 1929 *Pravda* reported what was probably a typical example of the growing contempt for the law: a local official had "found Soviet laws inconvenient for him and declared that no laws existed for Marxists."[6] Commenting on this example, a Soviet jurist wrote in 1929 that "in more serious and qualified circles, one comes across attempts to create *ad hoc* a whole theory on this subject,"[7] an allusion to Pashukanis' commodity exchange theory of law.

To appreciate the impact of the commodity exchange school on the second Soviet experiment in the withering away of law, a précis of Pashukanis' theory is necessary.[8] Pashukanis began from the premise that law was rooted in the institution of private property, and that its primary purpose was to facilitate and regulate the exchange processes of private enterprise. From this narrow premise was derived his complex theory of law as a uniquely "bourgeois" phenomenon. Since, for Pashukanis, law was the juridical expression of commodity exchange based on the principle of equivalency in the capitalist economy, his theory was known as the "commodity exchange theory of law." Conceptualizing all law as private law, Pashukanis derived public law from the equivalent relations of commodity exchange. Consequently, he represented the state in its capacity as guarantor of commodity exchange in the marketplace "as law and only law," while the state as an organization of class domination was designated a meta-juridical phenomenon beyond the scope of legal theory. Therefore, proceeding from Marxist principles, the commodity exchange theory anticipated the early "withering away" of law and of its state-guarantor as the socialist sector gained ascendancy over the capitalist sphere of the Soviet economy and the planning principle superseded the process of commodity exchange.

To elaborate, Pashukanis conceived of all legal relationships as contractual relationships reflecting the objective economic relationships of commodity exchange. Since commodity exchange was based on the equal relationship between property owners as legal persons with the right to acquire and alienate property in a market economy, the "form" or structure of the corresponding legal relationship was based on "equivalency," the principle that the contracting parties exchange with one another given commodities in equal amounts. From this point of view, even crime and punishment (and thus criminal law) was an expression of an *ex post facto* contractual relationship between a criminal and the state: the criminal, as one party to the "contract," committed a crime, and the state, as the other party, meted out punishment equivalent to the damage sustained by the victim.

For Pashukanis, even the state was reducible to private law. He conceptualized the state as a dual phenomenon—the "legal state," which manifested itself indirectly through legal norms based on the equivalency principle, and the "political state," which expressed its power directly by means of the "technical rules" of administration based on the principle of political "expediency."

Since Pashukanis considered the economic institution of commodity exchange to be peculiar to capitalism, he concluded that private law and its derivative, the legal state, were exclusively capitalist phenomena. He argued that law in Soviet society was "bourgeois law," which was primarily necessary for the regulation of the capitalist elements of the NEP economy. From his point of view, there neither was nor could be in the future any such phenomenon as "proletarian" or "socialist" law.

Pashukanis predicted that law (that is, private law and the legal state) would gradually begin to "wither away," as soon as its economic prerequisites of private property and commodity exchange were replaced by a public property economy based on the principle of economic planning. In Soviet terms, that meant the termination of the New Economic Policy, which Pashukanis and his associates anticipated, and which in fact took place at the end of the 1920s.

The impact of the commodity exchange school of law on the withering away process began to become apparent in the late twenties. Pashukanis and his colleagues assiduously devoted themselves to bringing about the realization of his prediction that private law and the legal state would gradually begin to wither away upon the elimination of the institutions of private property and the market. From their point of view, the prevailing political and economic trends were favorable. The doctrine of "socialism in one country," signaling the forthcoming end of the strategic retreat of the New Economic Policy, was first officially expressed in 1925 at the Fourteenth Party Conference. Later in the same year, the Fourteenth Party Congress adopted the policy of industrialization, which meant that a substantial growth of the socialist sector of the economy could be anticipated. In the language of the commodity exchange school of law, the imminent end of the New Economic Policy and the subsequent growth of the state sector meant a significant weakening of the juridical superstructure. By

1927 the Fifteenth Party Congress was calling for the construction of a socialist society, an objective that for Pashukanis and his colleagues required the gradual elimination of law. A. Ia. Estrin, speaking for the commodity exchange school, wrote in *Revoliutsiia prava:*[9]

> The basic conclusion which those of us working in the field of the theory and practice of Soviet law and in the work of legal construction can draw is that not only has the necessity of moving forward, decisively breaking away from the inertia of the juridical institutions and forms, . . . become acutely urgent, but now all the preconditions are present so that the achievements in the field of legal form and legal "superstructure" can conform to the achievements in the field of the planned construction of the "base."

The growth of the socialist base, Estrin argued, meant "the simplification and contraction" of the "legal form"—in other words, a withering away of the law.

It was a time, as Hazard has aptly expressed it, when "simplification of institutions and procedures seemed realistic and not utopian. . . ."[10] Another perceptive observer of Soviet jurisprudence described the climate of opinion around 1930, when, "under the influence of the successes of the Five-Year Plan, it was officially announced that socialism had won finally and irrevocably":[11]

> The line of reasoning which proves the inevitable disappearance of law under socialism by connecting law with the free exchange of commodities appealed chiefly to lawyers and generally educated people. Hundreds of thousands of single-minded communists, amongst them judges, investigators, and procurators, sincerely believed in the more orthodox assumption that socialism would make any state authority unnecessary, and in this way do away with law. Hearing from all sides that socialism had already won, many of them decided to draw the necessary conclusions.

"Withering away" was, of course, a familiar concept in the Marxist-Leninist vocabulary, but probably no one in the 1920s did as much to call attention to it and bring it into focus as did Pashukanis. Reviewing the first twelve years of Soviet legal development, Stuchka acknowledged Pashukanis' role in this connection. At the beginning of NEP, he wrote,

> The majority of communists referred to the law of the Soviet power skeptically, to say the least. When Lenin . . . initiated the laws concerning the

New Economic Policy, voices were openly heard saying: "Well, this is for them (the Nepmen) and not for us." And finally, when a genuinely scientific theory of law emerged here, . . . [the fact that it] held Soviet law in low esteem contributed significantly to its popularity.[12]

The concept of withering away had practical as well as theoretical implications, and the commodity exchange school, through the many strategic positions and editorships held by its adherents, was actively engaged in propagandizing the problems of the withering away of private law and the legal state on both levels. Considerable interest in the problems contingent upon the withering away process was reflected in a report to the Fifteenth Party Congress by N. M. Ianson, a prominent member of the Central Control Commission of the Party and of the Workers' and Peasants' Inspectorate, who was soon to succeed D. I. Kurskii as RSFSR Commissar of Justice. Ianson, reporting on an inspection of the lower judiciary, noted that the inspection had uncovered "a colossal quantity of litigation," which had caused "an enormous logjam." In language familiar to the commodity exchange school, Ianson criticized the fact that the defense of legality was being "converted into pedantry," at which point Krylenko, sitting in the audience, shouted "Right!" Ianson went on to warn against those "comrades with good juridical baggage" who were mainly concerned with "the forms of justice" and approached their duties with "a professional juridical bias." The legal system should be "linked with the requirements of life (voice: 'Right!'), with final expediency (applause)"; and the lower judiciary required "not just reforms . . . but even a small revolution."[13]

The spirit of the "revolution of the law" was also apparent among other government officials. One such official expressed the opinion that the legal system would be necessary only until there were enough administrators who could "decide each individual case according to its merits and the interests of the Soviet state."[14]

The idea of withering away was not confined to high political, administrative, and legal circles, but was even popularized for mass consumption. The article on "The Law" in *Malaia sovetskaia entsiklopediia* (1930) stated that

Law reaches its peak in bourgeois societies, as the most developed historical type of commodity producing society. . . . [Law will wither away] in the future society of communism, in which the class division will disappear and the planned regulation of the economy will fully replace the market regulation of production and exchange.... The regulation of the relations of production and exchange and all other social relations by means of the legal norm will be replaced by purely technical regulation....[15]

The commodity exchange school initially had its greatest impact on criminal law and procedure. As early as 1927, Krylenko began to draft new criminal codes consistent with the goal of withering away. That year Krylenko, under Pashukanis' influence, played a major role in drafting criminal codes for the Ukrainian and Armenian republics. Both of these codes were patterned after the Criminal Code of the RSFSR of 1926 and contained the "analogy" (see p. 181) and "social danger" principles, which, from the point of view of the commodity exchange school, were essential to the transition from equivalency to expediency.[16]

Pashukanis and Krylenko believed that the first step in the withering away of criminal law was the elimination of the most basic features of "bourgeois" criminal law from the Soviet codes. Consequently, they directed their attack against the "dosage system" of punishment and against the distinctions between intention, negligence, attempt, and participation.[17] According to Hazard, Pashukanis and Krylenko received the support of "practically every writer and researcher on criminal law in the Soviet Union."[18]

Pashukanis and his colleagues in criminal law had succeeded in replacing the term "punishment" with the words "measures of social defense" in the RSFSR Criminal Code of 1926. From their perspective, this was a modest step away from what Krylenko called the "price-list system" of code writing.[19] Next, the commodity exchange school began to argue forcefully within the Communist Academy in favor of the advantages of "direct action" (expediency) over "action by means of a general statute" (equivalency, or juridical action).[20] Pashukanis and Krylenko urged that a reformed Criminal Code of the RSFSR should have only one section—a general section laying down the fundamental principles that would guide the courts in the administration of justice. They argued that the section of the code that defined specific crimes in each article followed by a prescribed penalty should be eliminated. Their main concern at this point was that the judge should not be bound by narrow limitations, but that he should be able to "apply whatever penalty he thought necessary to assure the protection of society."[21]

In effect, the commodity exchange school proposed that repressive measures should not be equated with the type of crime committed or the individual's guilt, but should conform instead to the principle of expediency, which could mean a greater or lesser "measure of social defense," depending on the judge's discretion. Article 6 of Krylenko's draft criminal code of 1930 clearly reflects this objective of the commodity exchange school:[22]

> Measures of class oppression and of enforced educational influence may be applied to persons who have committed a certain delinquency as well as to persons who, in spite of not having committed a definite crime, justify the serious apprehension that they eventually may commit delinquencies, in consequence of their relations to criminal surroundings or of their own criminal past.

In 1931 the first national conference of Marxist jurists, dominated by the commodity exchange school, approved Pashukanis' and Krylenko's proposal to abolish the section of the criminal code dealing with specific crimes and punishments. The resolution of the conference stated that the substantial progress in industrialization and collectivization and the strengthening of the planning principle in general had

> created the conditions that have made it possible actually to attempt to eliminate the theory of value for value in criminal repression and to replace it by repression based on the principle of expediency as the guiding principle for the judge in each particular case.[23]

Along with the criminal law reforms, Pashukanis, Krylenko, and Estrin addressed themselves to the task of simplifying criminal procedure with a view to its eventual elimination. The interaction of autonomous contesting parties in the criminal process was regarded by the commodity exchange school as a reflection of market relationships and hence as a bourgeois phenomenon. In 1927 Krylenko had advocated "abolishing the Criminal Procedural Code [of the RSFSR] . . . and replacing it by a collection of technical rules. . . ."[24] There were indications by 1929 that the codifiers had been experimenting with the simplification of criminal procedure,[25] and a present-day Soviet legal historian (and contemporary of Pashukanis) has written that by characterizing "controversy" (*sostiazatel'nost'*) in criminal procedure as "bourgeois," the commodity exchange school adversely affected "the whole system of procedural guarantees and at the same time weakened interest in the scientific elaboration of Soviet procedure."[26]

Krylenko had a fairly explicit conception of the ways in which public order would be maintained after the eventual withering away of the court. Moral or educational measures would be applied to violators of the community rules. These measures would include suspended sentences, public censure, expulsion from the community, denial of the right to participate in social and political organizations, and deprivation of political rights. The elaborate pyramidal judicial system, with its different types of tribunals, would be abandoned, and control by the central authorities would cease. The judge would be guided by ethical rules that would reflect the society's complete achievement of socialism.[27]

This was a large order, but Pashukanis, Krylenko, Estrin, and others attempted to fulfill it. As a start, Krylenko felt that judicial behavior had to be changed so that judges would not approach the function of imposing punishment from "that damn idea of equivalence which sticks so firmly in the heads of all."[28] In effect, he and his colleagues wanted to introduce a new criminal code that would allow the judge to deal more "with the man" than with his actions.[29]

To facilitate the gradual simplification of the judicial process, the commodity exchange school, especially Krylenko, also promoted the further development and extension of the comrades' courts from the late twenties. The comrades' courts had first been organized in the Red Army, following the October Revolution, as peer courts for the punishment of minor offenses. However, it was in the course of the "revolution of the law" in the late twenties that the institution began to flourish.[30]

The jurisdiction of the comrades' courts was enlarged to include several heretofore criminal offenses and even civil suits. Up to this time, comrades' courts were primarily located in industrial enterprises, but from 1929 the institution was extended to housing associations and other residential units and, for the first time, into rural areas. This entailed further broadening of their jurisdiction into the traditional branches of family, land, labor, and housing law. The rural comrades' courts, for example, could hear child support cases and some alimony, land, and labor disputes; while the comrades' courts in housing developments had jurisdiction over thirteen categories of cases involving the use of housing facilities. The volume of cases heard by comrades' courts began to increase rapidly, with a comparable decline in the number of cases based on private complaints going through the regular "people's" courts.[31]

The process of the withering away of criminal law and procedure was also fostered by the encroachment of medicine, especially psychiatry, into the traditional jurisdiction of criminal law. In 1925, the first All-Union Conference of Psychiatry and Neurology resolved that

> the idea of imputability... must be eliminated from Soviet legislation and replaced by the idea of socially dangerous conditions produced by the neuropsychiatric deviation of the criminal.[32]

In subsequent years, the concept of legal responsibility was eroded in practice: legal criteria for insanity, involving will and intellect, were ignored. Harold J. Berman and Donald Hunt, in their study of forensic medicine in the Soviet Union, observed that "although the Criminal Code provided for legal tests of insanity, the tests actually applied were medical-psychiatric tests of mental illness."[33] Psychiatric criteria were very widely applied. For instance, drug addicts were not considered legally reponsible, and sometimes even slightly intoxicated persons who had committed criminal acts were considered nonimputable. By 1929 the criminal law specialist I. P. Trainin was writing that strong emotional excitement caused by a serious insult "might well serve as a basis for a finding of nonresponsibility on the ground of 'pathological affect.'"[34]

In civil law, the impact of the commodity exchange theory became apparent only at the very end of the twenties, partly because the theorists themselves assumed that nothing could be done in this area until a basic political decision was taken to abandon the economic relations of NEP. Nevertheless, there was discussion of civil law among the commodity exchange group during the twenties, with Stuchka rather than Pashukanis taking the leading role. Ultimately, the theorists contemplated, the civil law regulating the exchange of commodities both within and between the private and public sectors of the mixed economy of the NEP period would be converted into a series of technical rules (or, in Stuchka's terminology, "economic law") dictated by the imperatives of administering a publicly owned and operated industrial economy. "Sale and purchase is a bourgeois institution," Stuchka told a conference of justice officials in 1929. "Socialism does not recognize sales and purchases. It recognizes only direct supply."[35] Under socialism, state enterprises would gradually succeed individuals as the predominant subject of a right or juridical person.[36] It was anticipated that the Five-Year Plan would produce "a new contraction of law in favor of administrative regulation";[37] and in 1929 the Sixth All-Russian Congress of Workers of Justice adopted a resolution that stressed the necessity to begin "to reduce and simplify our civil law."[38]

With spontaneous action of the market curbed and the principle of economic planning extended, preparations for the withering away of civil law proceeded more rapidly. L. Ia. Gintsburg published the first "Program" or syllabus for economic law in 1929. The second edition of the program, which went to press in mid-1930, stated that the Civil Code of the RSFSR was rapidly withering away and being replaced by economic law, or technical rules. Quoting Pashukanis, Gintsburg observed that the intensive growth of planning was causing the "'displacement of legal form,'" which meant that the importance of "the formal juridical aspect in the organization of the social exchange of material things" was being reduced.[39] Outlining the process of the withering away of civil law, Gintsburg wrote that

> the social exchange of material things will be effected . . . not by the mechanism of separate, uncoordinated equivalent civil law contracts, each of which is the result of an agreement between autonomous economic wills, but by a system of organized and reciprocally coordinated acts originating from the single center for planned targets.[40]

By 1930 the impact of the commodity exchange school of law on the Soviet legal system was already becoming noticeable, especially in criminal and civil law and procedure and the administration of criminal justice. It had become rare "to encounter a direct defense of the system of legal principles that corresponds to the capitalist economic structure," noted an editorial in one of the group's journals in the summer of 1930. In the opinion of the journal, rationalization, collectivization, and the extension of planning had now made it possible to begin to eliminate legal regulation from all sectors of society—although, as it admitted, much still remained to be done in this respect.[41] An Englishman visiting the Soviet Union in the same year was told by a high official of the RSFSR Commissariat of

Justice that he expected that "all litigation, civil or criminal, would disappear within the next six or seven years...."[42]

But Pashukanis' and Krylenko's hopes that their draft criminal code would be adopted in 1930 were disappointed (in spite of which they continued to produce new drafts annually from 1930 to 1935). However, their drafts did have an effect on the administration of criminal justice, since they encouraged the belief that the 1926 Code was soon to be replaced.[43] It was reported that these draft codes "were more generally distributed in some areas than were copies of the criminal code in force": official commentators on the RSFSR Criminal Code actually advised judges to disregard certain of its provisions; and this apparently led to numerous errors in sentencing, with the courts giving insignificant penalties for stealing, disorderly conduct, and evasion of alimony payments, while meting out heavier penalties for lesser offenses.[44] Some Russian Republic courts even disregarded the laws on a wholesale basis, for which they were criticized by the Supreme Court of the RSFSR.[45] As Hazard reported,

> Encouragement of complete disregard of the precise provisions of the [criminal] code [of 1926] led to a broad application of the section promoting application by analogy to punish an act for which there was no definite section. The court practice had led to the result that no citizen could foretell what was a possible criminal act, since the analogies section might be applied to cover any act.[46]

In the field of criminal procedure, the "triumph of the simplifiers" was the Tadzhik Criminal Procedural Code of 1935, which contained only 154 articles.[47] The impact of the commodity exchange school on the judiciary was especially dramatic. Judges actually began to close their courts in some places, and Vyshinskii recalled in 1934 that

> only two years ago... the Chairman of the Mordov Regional Court issued a circular to all the subordinate courts urging the necessity of closing the organs of justice, in view of the fact that we were already entering the stage of socialism.... Only a year ago another judge wrote to the [RSFSR] Commissariat of Justice inquiring whether it was not time to close all the organs of justice in connection with the creation of a classless society....[48]

A second area in which the commodity exchange school had great impact was legal education. The organization and content of legal education in turn had profound implications for the future of law in Soviet society. Just as Pashukanis and his colleagues attempted to influence the withering away of the extant legal system, so also they sought to cut off any future legal and administrative development at the source by reshaping legal education to conform to their conception of the kind of legal personnel appropriate to preside over the gradual withering away of law.

The priority tasks in Soviet legal education as Pashukanis described them in 1927 were the struggle against "bourgeois" legal scholarship and a Marxist reorientation of teaching in the university faculties of Soviet law. He observed that there was only a thin stratum of Marxist scholars on the teaching staffs in the departments of state and law. The Law Department of the Institute of Red Professors—in effect a competitor of the old university faculties of law—had only recently been established and did not yet have many students. But Pashukanis was confident that the enrollment would grow and a new Soviet generation would receive "the correct Marxist methodological line for research on questions in the field of state and law."[49] The "line" to which Pashukanis was referring was, of course, the position of the commodity exchange school of law.

Pashukanis was especially concerned that bourgeois jurists tended to dominate the teaching of law in the Soviet Union. When the Collegium of the RSFSR Justice Commissariat adopted a resolution concerning the necessity of improving the Marxist character of law teaching and research, Pashukanis stressed that the resolution warned against placing jurisprudence "in strange hands, in the hands of specialists who neither have nor desire to have anything in common with Marxism-Leninism."[50] By 1928 Pashukanis observed that the core of Marxist jurists had grown sufficiently strong to dispense with bourgeois law professors. His group supported the purging of non-Marxist and bourgeois jurists from the legal superstructure, and especially from the law schools (on the university purge as a general phenomenon, see Lapidus, this volume, pp. 91–92). After the purge of bourgeois professors from the Soviet Law faculty of Moscow University in 1929–30 two adherents of the commodity exchange theory expressed the opinion that this had strengthened the Marxist position and cleared the way for reconsideration of traditional ideas on legal education "which had been uncritically received from bourgeois jurisprudence."[51] During this period many bourgeois jurists, especially the group around the journal *Pravo i zhizn'* and those connected with the Institute of Soviet Law, were accused of "smuggling bourgeois doctrines into Soviet jurisprudence and were expelled from the universities. . . ."[52]

By mid-1930, sufficient progress had been made in eliminating bourgeois professors from Soviet legal education for the commodity exchange school to be able to turn its attention to the bourgeois legal advisors in the state apparatus. M. Dotsenko cautioned that "the dangerous bourgeois juridical world view" still permeated the state apparatus because of a shortage of Marxist cadres.

> The actual 'carriers of evil' are primarily the enormous army of legal advisors to various [governmental] institutions, right up to the central institutions, and the so-called scientific advisers who are educated in juridical dogmatism and who not only apply the seal of their metaphysical world view to series of legislative acts . . . but also propagate their "scientific theories" through Soviet journals and particular institutes in which they artificially breed the bacteria of the juridical world view for mass consumption.[53]

Simultaneously, while eliminating bourgeois jurists from the law schools and advocating their removal from the state apparatus, the commodity exchange school was in the process of reconstructing the organization and content of legal education. The curriculum of the Law Department of the Institute of Red Professors served as their laboratory and provided the basic pattern that guided the Marxist reorganization of legal education in the Soviet Union. This curriculum included the commodity exchange school's version of Marxist methodology and law, the main themes of bourgeois jurisprudence, an analysis of major bourgeois legal institutions, and an examination of the doctrines of Marx, Engels, and Lenin on law and the state.[54]

Marxist course "programs" were drafted or at least planned by commodity exchange school men for every branch of law, including legal history.[55] The two syllabi most central to the process of the withering away of law and state were Gintsburg's *Programma po khoziaistvenno-administrativnomu pravu* and Iezuitov's and Rezunov's *Uchenie o sovetskom gosudarstve*. Gintsburg's program was the first on the new branch of "economic law" that was to supersede civil law; and the pronounced influence of the commodity exchange school may clearly be seen, for example, in its third topic: "The expanded socialist offensive, the transformation of exchange relations, and the fate of the Civil Code."[56] The new syllabus on the state prepared by Iezuitov and Rezunov was based on the premise of "a unified Marxist doctrine of the Soviet state," which was, in effect, a doctrine of the "political state"; and the authors rejected all "attempts to theoretically represent the Soviet state as a legal state."[57] Again, the influence of Pashukanis' and Stuchka's ideas was clear.

Under Pashukanis' leadership, the influence of the commodity exchange school was extended to correspondence courses in law. The Correspondence Division of the Institute of Red Professors, established in 1929, had a law section[58] whose journal was edited by Pashukanis (who at this time held the position of Rector of the Institute of Red Professors). The law section of the Correspondence Division was oriented toward the popularization of Marxist legal education, and its journal was especially designed to reach Party activists and teachers in Party schools and graduate schools, as well as the regular correspondence students.[59]

The freshman law student, whether in regular attendance or studying by correspondence, was quickly introduced to the basic positions of the commodity exchange school. His first course was the seminar on the general theory of law, taught by Pashukanis as, in effect, a seminar on the commodity exchange theory of law.[60] The occupations of Pashukanis' first class of correspondence students suggest the possible reach of his influence beyond the legal profession. The students included a military procurator in the Ukraine, an employee of the secret police in Belorussia, a high school teacher, a propagandist, and the assistant chief of the legal department of a credit bureau.[61]

Pashukanis' journal published grades and evaluations of student papers that indicate the type of intellectual monopoly to which the commodity exchange school aspired. On the theory of law, student papers were generally criticized for deviating from the commodity exchange interpretation and praised for following it. The result was that the papers sounded like regurgitations of Pashukanis' ideas, or fulsome affirmations that "the most correct point of view is the conception of Comrade Pashukanis, who first developed a Marxist understanding of the legal form of production relations. . . ."[62]

There was, however, one basic disadvantage to the position of the commodity exchange school: by talking about the withering away of law its members were cutting the ground from under their own profession. Law students noted that the prospects for a career in law were beginning to look dim and passed resolutions expressing doubt that they should continue their studies.[63] Vyshinskii later reported that the prevailing nihilism toward law had had an especially "pernicious" effect on "the organization of legal education and the training of legal personnel."[64]

From 1930 very few students specialized in criminal law.[65] Those who took the new "economic law" courses that replaced courses in civil law emerged in some ways poorly equipped. As Hazard noted, lawyers, graduates of the law school, practicing attorneys, and judges knew very little about the legal rights of individuals, although they were extremely proficient in resolving disputes between two state enterprises.[66]

The subject of the legal state was gradually disappearing from the curricula of the law schools. The course on the Soviet governmental system at Sverdlov Communist University was dropped at the end of the academic year 1929. The study of Soviet government was also increasingly ignored in the Soviet law faculty of Moscow University and in the preparatory section of the Institute of Red Professors. As an editorial in *Revoliutsiia prava* reported in 1929,

> The study of the Soviet Constitution, the governmental machinery of the proletarian state, is little by little being dropped from the curricula of our institutions of higher learning and the Party graduate schools.[67]

By mid-1930, one of Pashukanis' associates observed that "one often hears it said that there is no reason to get absorbed in the study of the state, since it . . . is withering away in the period of the dictatorship of the proletariat."[68]

The efforts of Pashukanis and the commodity exchange school of law had a major impact on Soviet jurisprudence, and by the end of the 1920s the impact had extended to the practice of law and the system of legal education. Pashukanis saw the introduction of the First Five-Year plan as a turning point.[69] As he wrote late in 1929:

> The role of the pure juridical superstructure, the role of law, is now diminishing, and from this one can infer the general rule that [technical]

regulation becomes more effective as the role of law becomes weaker and less significant.[70]

Hazard reports that Pashukanis boldly predicted that the withering away process would reach a decisive stage by the end of the Second Five-Year Plan.[71]

In the 1930s, an atmosphere of legal nihilism permeated the Soviet legal system.[72] Although the closing of local courts was eventually stopped, the comrades' courts continued to absorb more and more of the case load of the people's courts. The percentage of persons judged by the people's courts of the RSFSR on private complaints, beginning in 1929, fell to 26.9 in 1931, 16.9 in 1932 and 6.5 in 1933, "when social [i.e. comrades'] courts were formed everywhere."[73] Legal education had fallen into very low esteem. Hazard, reporting on his student days in Moscow, wrote:

> In 1934 we had an old building in bad repair, poorly decorated, unheated so that we sat in lectures fully clothed for the street. We had a schedule which changed so often without notice that it became a joke, and no one even knew from one semester to the next what would be the subjects which would be taught. Our students were men and women in their late twenties or early thirties, and they came for the most part because they had tired of other work they had previously been doing.[74]

Satisfactory though all this was from the point of view of withering away of law, there were problems for Pashukanis and the commodity exchange school.[75] Stalin and the Party leadership rejected the idea that the state itself was withering away (see Fitzpatrick, this volume, p. oo and note 65). In 1930–31, the Marxist legal profession underwent a process of recantation and self-criticism comparable with that occurring in other fields affected by cultural revolution. The major events of this phase were Pashukanis' "self-criticism" in late 1930, and the First All-Union Congress of Marxist Specialists on the State and Law, called in early 1931 and presided over by Pashukanis, which met to discuss the reconstruction of jurisprudence in conformity with the new emphasis on the strong state and the repudiation of "withering away" theories.

Pashukanis remained the unchallenged doyen of Soviet jurisprudence, but his "commodity exchange theory of law" did not fare so well. The imposition of positivist elements deprived it of much of its theoretical coherence as a sociology of law. As Pashukanis abandoned economics and turned to politics as the source of law, the state became, in theory as well as fact, the author of legal norms. In Pashukanis' revised theory, law was an expression of the policy of the state. While he accepted the necessity of strengthening the state to carry out the political tasks of the day, he did not draw the same conclusion for law, which he insisted should be characterized by maximum "flexibility" befitting the policy of a revolutionary state. He continued to resist the idea that there could be a "socialist law," believing that once the law of the proletarian state had been used to facilitate the transition from socialism to communism, it was destined to wither away.

The emphasis given by Pashukanis and his colleagues to "flexibility" in the law was consistent with their previous emphasis on "simplification" of the law. In this spirit, Pashukanis and Krylenko continued until 1935 to draft new codes of "criminal policy and law" based on the principle of "political expediency," while Pashukanis and Gintsburg at the same time continued to work for the supplanting of civil law with "economic law" reflecting the "technical rules" of the Five-Year plans and based on production units as juridical persons. Both of these tendencies were influential in Soviet legal education during the first half of the thirties.

In short, the political situation had changed but the views of the Pashukanis group, in essence, had not. The contradiction became manifest in 1935–36, with the drafting, public discussion, and ratification of the new Constitution of the USSR. The implications for law of the new constitution were immediately clear: the Soviet system required a strong and stable criminal law for the protection of public property, and a predictable and differentiated civil law for the protection of the new constitutional right of "personal property." A stable legal system, in turn, required the systematic legal education of a sufficient number of professionally trained lawyers.

The "Stalin Constitution" was ratified in late 1936; Pashukanis was arrested and disappeared in early 1937. This ended the second Soviet experiment in the withering away of law, and cleared the way for a new drive for legal "stability" headed by A. Ia. Vyshinskii, who succeeded Pashukanis as the effective leader of the Soviet legal profession. It was a denouement that, in view of Pashukanis' views on the principle of political "expediency," had its own irony. Almost immediately after Pashukanis' arrest, economic law was dropped from the law curriculum for the spring semester of 1936–37, and civil law restored. In the following years, the proposed codes of the Pashukanis school, especially the criminal codes, were subjected to exhaustive criticism by Vyshinskii and his associates. By 1941 new textbooks and course syllabi had been written by the Vyshinskii group for nearly every major branch of "Soviet socialist law," reincorporating many of the features that the Pashukanis school had eliminated in the interest of legal flexibility and simplicity.

Finally, Vyshinskii, as the new doyen of Soviet jurisprudence, redefined the theory of law as part of the general theory of "Soviet socialist state and law." The inference to be drawn from this was that law would wither away only with the withering away of the state. But for the foreseeable future, the state had to remain strong in view of the "capitalist encirclement." In effect, the new theoretical formulation postponed the "withering away of law" indefinitely.[76]

Little Heroes and Big Deeds: Literature Responds to the First Five-Year Plan

Katerina Clark

Most Western commentators have seen literature under the Five-Year Plan as moving toward a disastrous culmination: the end of literature as an autonomous activity and the drastic lowering of literary standards in the Stalinist thirties. However, the opposite could be argued: it was precisely in the aftermath of the First Five-Year Plan that writers and literary critics showed a renewed concern about literary quality. In literature, as in so many other spheres, the First Five-Year Plan period represented the high point of a radical utopianism that threatened traditional literary values. Utopian tendencies were already noticeable in the literary debates of the twenties, but it was only under the peculiar conditions of the Five-Year Plan that they received widespread application. The change of policy in 1932–34, however, checked rather than further institutionalized this radical movement.

As we know, under the First Five-Year Plan the Soviet Union underwent rapid planned industrialization and collectivization. But that general description cannot convey the period's peculiar flavor. It was a time of extremism, of dramatic gestures, of contrasts and paradoxes. On construction sites, for example, teams of self-sacrificing volunteers rubbed elbows with gangs of forced laborers and illiterate peasant recruits. But the singularity of the period lay in the fact that—as in Akhenaton's Egypt, Peter the Great's Russia, or France in the Great Revolution—utopian striving was the prerogative not of dreamers in garrets or holy men in the desert, but of the government itself.

The focus of this utopian striving was not just the industrial revolution, but a "cultural revolution" as well. However, the key myths of the age were so colored by a fervor for industrialization that they were usually expressed in terms of the factory model. Society itself was conceived as a machine, whose separate parts were harmoniously interrelated and regulated. In Five-Year Plan novels, even those dealing with the kolkhoz, one can find countless uses of the machine metaphor for society.[1] For instance, in a novel by Ia. Ilin, Soviet society is likened to a large factory in which the work of every department contributes to the running of the "Great Conveyor Belt" (*Bol'shoi konveier*, 1934). Some writers were so carried away by the Five-Year Plan cult of technology that they depicted industrial machines as actually impressing their own rhythms and harmonies on the psyche of the workers who operated them.[2]

The machine metaphor, of course, had to allow for the role of the Party as guiding force and vanguard. Typically, in a novel by V. Ilenkov, Soviet society is a "train" and the Party its "Driving Axle" (*Vedushchaia os'*, 1931). But, although the "driving axle" is indispensable, it is not the only part of the mechanism; and during the First Five-Year Plan the media stressed the crucial importance to society of *all* the separate parts making up the whole. Such values inform the following passage from *The Driving Axle*, in which one worker reproaches another for paying too much attention to "the axle":

> Let us take the train, for example: it has a furnace, and wheels, and driving gear, and assorted minor bolts—everything has its own place. And that is how a train manages to carry thousands of tons. But the bolts are important, and the whistle is important, and the smokestacks,—and all equally so. But you like only the driving axle. That's not the right approach.[3]

It should come as no surprise to learn that when, in the course of the novel, a giant express crashes, an investigation reveals that the cause of the disaster was negligence and sabotage in turning out minor parts of the driving axle. Furthermore, it is the little men of the factory who uncover the problem, while the head of the factory Party organization plays only a subordinate role.[4]

In literature, the First Five-Year Plan was an age of the minor parts, the masses or, in Gorkii's phrase, the "little men." Gone was the age of Gogol and Chekhov, when little men were represented in literature as pathetic creatures. They were now, as Gorkii put it, raised to their full "human dignity," to a "realization of the importance of the 'little men' in the world," and to a position in which they could fulfill their "creative" potential.[5] They were valuable, however, not in themselves but as the bolts and whistles of the great train of society. The nearest, although decidedly more primitive, analogy Gorkii could find for them was the millions of molluscs whose creative work over time built up great coral reefs.[6] But, "little men" though they were, they shared in the great achievements of the age; and for this reason their deeds were also "great."[7]

In Gorkii's essay, the society in which "little men" accomplish "great deeds" is contrasted with the old oppressive bourgeois society dominated by "great men."[8] His views here are typical of the First Five-Year Plan rhetoric, which celebrated the achievements of the masses rather than those of exceptional individuals.

A second characteristic was the emphasis on rapid and radical change. "We are fifty to one-hundred years behind the most advanced countries," Stalin told a meeting of Soviet managers in February 1931. "We must cover that distance in ten years."[9] The writers took their cue to collapse time, and *the topos* of literature in the period became the observation of millennial change. In Ilin's *The Great Conveyor Belt*, the construction site is transformed in a mere two weeks,[10] while in V. Kataev's novel *Time, Forward!* the hero finds that the terrain changes so radically every *day* that he has to change his route to work.[11] Some writers were not content to deal with days, months, or years, but preferred to invoke centuries and epochs. In the collectively written *People of the Stalingrad Tractor Factory*, the authors embellished Stalin's time model and claimed that in one year "we have advanced 200 years."[12] The hero of Leonov's *Sot'* perceives the leap (in a local context) as from the sixteenth century to the twentieth;[13] while in another example of collective authorship, *The History of the Construc-*

tion of the White Sea–Baltic Canal, the Five-Year Plan advance is described as a movement not from one century to another but from one epoch to another—from the "wooden age" to the "iron age."[14]

With the great leap forward of industrialization and collectivization, society had to be remade. Verbs expressing *re*making and *re*doing (*perestraivat'*, *perekovat'*, *peredelat'*, *pererozhdat'*, *perelozhit'*, *perevospitat'*, and so on) are characteristic of the language of the period. However, the list of things to be changed included not just the terrain, but also man himself. In keeping with the dominant industrial imagery, social institutions were seen as a sort of assembly line for retooling a human product and turning out the new Soviet man.

The main instrument for this retooling was labor—in factories, on construction sites, or in collective farms. Indeed it was widely believed that the experience of production could transform not only the masses of society, but individual deviants—the "alien elements" inherited from capitalism, "wreckers," hooligans, and criminals.

One of literature's functions in these years was to provide illustrations of these human transformations. And so in a book about a new tractor factory, for instance, the author is delighted to note that as a result of the workers' participation in socialist labor they no longer drink or swear in their leisure time.[15] The most dramatic illustrations can be found in books about "alien elements." One such source, and a particularly rich one, is the book commissioned to celebrate the White Sea—Baltic Canal project, an undertaking that used thousands of convict laborers. On almost every page the authors describe how the "human raw materials" were "reworked"[16] (largely through hard labor and exposure to "culture"— libraries, lectures, classes in basic literacy and technical skills, and so on).[17] They admit that with such poor quality materials, there was bound to be a high proportion of *brak* or faulty products: after all, "human material is much more difficult to work over than wood, stone, or metal".[18] Nevertheless, they claim, large numbers of the humans reworked in this way turned out as award-winning products.[19]

The book provides a whole series of individual biographies attesting to the power of socialist labor. Perhaps the most striking of these is the case of engineer Magnitov, a former bourgeois. The authors relate how, after Magnitov began to labor on the canal, he developed a quicker pulse and faster thought processes and nervous reactions: "He begins to take on the new tempo, to adjust his reason to it, his will and his breathing."[20] Once changed so radically, the engineer had trouble associating his former self with its present version. The authors reported: "Engineer Magnitov thinks of the old engineer Magnitov, and for him that person is already alien. Magnitov calls that person 'him'."[21]

In this period, the idea of radical transformation of human beings was so compelling that the RAPP theorist Averbakh maintained that everyone should undergo transformation, even the proletarians.[22] But in literature the alchemy was most commonly used to turn base bourgeois into revolutionary gold: to quote the title of B. Iasenskii's Five-Year Plan novel, "man changes his skin"—even bourgeois man, or, in this particular case, the Western technical adviser. Despite the prevalence of ideas of class determinism in the wake of the Shakhty trial, the literature of the period includes many examples of remarkable instant transformation and class inversion similar to engineer Magnitov's.[23]

The radical mood and industrial orientation of the Five-Year Plan period affected not only literary themes but the prevailing concepts of literature itself. Many of those involved believed that literature should be put at the service of the Five-Year Plan, and that it should be organized by analogy with industrial production. The most zealous of them attempted to find literary equivalents for each new official policy in the economic or political sphere: when the government launched a campaign to encourage "shock workers" in industry, many critics declared that literature should have them too; and when *Pravda* urged all industrial plants to fulfill the "Promfinplan," then *Literaturnaia gazeta* asked writers to do likewise.

These responses on the part of the writers to the demands of the age can be interpreted in different ways. Perhaps the millennial sentiment of the period was infectious; perhaps the pressures of class war obliged writers to offer palpable proof of their Five-Year Plan zeal; perhaps they were merely acting as seemed expedient. They were not, whatever else was the case, following a central "Party line" on literature, since the Party never gave any explicit instructions for the writers to follow.

In Western commentary, the literary extremism of these years is usually ascribed to the infamous "proletarian" literary association RAPP (see Fitzpatrick, this volume, pp. 28–29), which was responsible for many of the Five-Year Plan slogans for literature and took a bullying role toward other literary groups. Our contention, however, is that RAPP's power was not a cause but a symptom of the prevailing atmosphere of extremism. The salient features of RAPP's stance throughout the twenties—its crusade against the torchbearers of traditional intellectualism and "nonproletarian" elements, its xenophobia, and its insistence that literary activity should be subordinated to the interests of the whole society—all made the organization a natural leader of cultural revolution. But the radical policies it advanced for literature during the Five-Year Plan were hardly exclusive or original to RAPP, nor were they the most iconoclastic of the day.[24] In short, the narrow focus of literary factionalism does not provide the only, or even necessarily the best, context in which to view the literary dynamic of these years.

Large sections of the literary community wanted to find a way of participating in the experience of socialist construction, as the engineer Magnitov had done. They set out to *remake* the institution of literature, and even to *remake* themselves. In other words, the radical reconceptualization of the role of the writers, which has normally been associated with the events of 1932–34, was actually more characteristic of this earlier period. Moreover, the reconceptualization was not limited to Communist functionaries and self-styled "proletarians": it came from non-Party members of the literary profession as well.[25]

In the new concept, literature had to become a part of the general mobilization for industrialization. It had to be integrated into the broad-based cultural revolution. It had to be of, by, and for those "little men" and their "great deeds." This meant rejecting as "bourgeois" the old concept of literature as aesthetic, literature as the product of individual genius, literature as a privileged or distinctive language. It also meant rejecting as light-minded the notion that literary works should entertain their readers.[26]

The writers' first task was to find a way of associating literature with the industrialization effort. Contemporary slogans made the task seem very simple: "We Shall Include the Writer in Socialist Construction!"[27] "Writers Join the Battle for the Promfinplan!"[28] "Put All the Might of our Creative Resources Behind Socialist Construction!"[29] and "For Coal! For Iron! For Machines! Each Literary Group should Work For These!"[30] But how the literary word could produce more coal was in reality a difficult question to answer.

One school of thought held that literature should be restructured by analogy with industrial production. Most areas of the economy had their own production plans, so why not literature?[31] Typical of the schemes proposed was one that envisioned publishing houses functioning within literature as factories did within industry, each writer being hired by a particular publishing house that would then assign him work.[32] Such schemes met with little approval in the literary world.[33] But if they did not affect the substance of literary life, they did have an effect on literary style. For instance, a public announcement that Pasternak was working on his long poem *Spektorskii* was couched as his "Production Plan for 1931."[34]

But if literature never acquired a meaningful "plan," some individual writers did have considerable success in reorienting their work toward production *themes*. Implementation of the old "social command" theory (that is, that topics of contemporary relevance should be assigned to particular writers[35]) became a very real issue. Not all the radicals were for strict adherence to the "social command": the RAPP leader Averbakh himself had reservations about the theory.[36] Nevertheless, in the literary practice of the period something very close to "social command" emerged.

"Literature should not be a single step away from the practical affairs of socialist construction!" urged *Literaturnaia gazeta*.[37] The demand for proximity was taken very literally: writers who wanted to write on factories, for example, were expected to do field work in factories. From late 1929 many literary organizations (such as *Literaturnaia gazeta* and RAPP) began to organize writers into "brigades" and sent them on assignment to construction sites, kolkhozy, and factories.[38]

Most critics felt that it was not a time for the consideration of "eternal" questions.[39] Writers should not only describe the achievements of socialist construction, but choose forms and subjects that would prove helpful to those engaged in the industrial effort. They should study economics and technology;[40] and their works should provide a medium for the exchange of information on industrial experience.[41] They should write simple tales and sketches explaining economic policies and depicting model workers. So rigid was the insistence on immediate practical relevance that the literary group "Pereval" was disbanded for the heretical suggestion that a literary work should be judged on the basis of the author's "mastery of literary skills" rather than its topicality.[42] Even RAPP ran into trouble on this question. Its theoreticians were attacked for their statements that literature should use "psychological realism" in its depiction of the "living man." Critics argued that to pay attention to human psychology was only to lose sight of more important concerns.[43]

As Five-Year Plan fever took hold, critics interpreted the demand that literature "should not be a single step away from socialist construction" to mean that it should imitate the accelerated tempos of the industrialization effort. They suggested that writers should try to finish each work as rapidly as possible: after all, they said, it was necessary to "catch up and surpass" the capitalist West in book production as well as industry.[44] Writers should overcome the old prejudices about "nurturing" the material and striving for a polished product, for with that approach the product would be obsolete before it was finished.[45]

It was even argued that books should have a direct effect on production itself. Occasional slogans in the literary press reminded writers that "The Book Is An Instrument of Production,"[46] and "In Order to Conduct a Successful Spring Sowing Campaign We Must Arm Each Kolkhoz Member With A Book, and Likewise Every Sovkhoz Worker and Each Poor- and Middle-Peasant Household."[47] At a rather higher level of sophistication, a joint appeal of the Education Commissariat and the Federation of Soviet Writers described the writer's function as "raising the morale high, inspiring the masses for the struggle, ruthlessly exposing indifference, stagnation and desertion, all of which undermine the plan."[48]

The literary press placed great emphasis on the writers' part in the national campaign to raise the cultural and educational level of the masses. To this end, it was held, writers should provide a literature that was within the price range and intellectual reach of the newly literate. Publishing houses began putting out series of cheap mass editions.[49] Journals undertook campaigns to increase their readership.[50]

The masses were not only important to the literary profession as readers, but as potential writers as well. Overnight, as it seemed, the ranks of the profession were swelled by an influx of workers and peasants. RAPP regarded the training of these novices as the most important of its current tasks,[51] and was so zealous in prosecuting it that in 1931 it was able to report an 80 percent increase in membership over the past year, bringing its numbers to ten thousand.[52]

Literary circles were the main channel of recruitment for beginning writers. They were organized at each enterprise and run by an experienced writer or critic. Their products were then published in the wall-newspapers and broadsheets of the enterprise itself. But in order to give the more talented of the new recruits a wider public, a whole host of new journals, special anthologies, columns in the regular periodicals, and writing projects were set up. The existing Soviet institution of worker-, peasant-, and soldier-correspondents (the *rabkor, sel'kor,* and *voenkor*) was expanded, so that thousands of "little men" had the task of reporting to the outside world on local progress in the Five-Year Plan and cultural revolution.

The rationale of this movement was that worker-writers could function as intermediaries between the educated and the masses, and as such provide "levers" of the cultural revolution.[53] These were just the "first beginnings."[54] As the movement grew, those millions of "little men" would come, as Gorkii hoped, to realize their creative potential under socialism. Some theorists were even bold enough to claim that these newcomers to literature would eventually prove finer writers than any that had come before them.[55]

For the militants of the literary world, the ultimate goal of this mass recruitment was to abolish traditional literature and supplant the old-style professional writers. This view was to some extent influenced by the strident anti-intellectualism that accompanied the campaign against the bourgeois intelligentsia. The demand that a literature should be provided for the masses became a demand that *all* literature should be mass literature,[56] or even that all literature should be accessible to the semiliterate![57] Groups vied with each other to prove their greater commitment to the masses. Even RAPP, the traditional stronghold of opposition to bourgeois intellectualism, was reproached for the fact that articles in its journal *On the Literary Front* were too abstruse to be understood by the mass reader.[58]

The mass reader was called to sit in judgment on the professional writer's efforts. Many theorists suggested that the mass reader's response should be the ultimate test of a work's worth[59]—and therefore of whether a given writer should be published, or his works given wide circulation.[60] Workers assumed *shefstvo* or supervision over the activities of literary groups.[61] No doubt a good part of this was window-dressing. But it raises an interesting question about the *kto-kogo* of ideological influence: were the writers supposed to be molding the masses, or to be molded by them?

The literary journals abounded with triumphant and extravagant progress reports on the battle between "mass-ism" (*massovost'*) and the traditional prejudices of the profession. "This is a struggle against those illusions of grandeur which still persist in our literary community," declared the RAPP critic Ermilov in 1930.[62] In the same year, M. Kozakov claimed that the effects of the campaign against traditional literature had been so far-reaching that the very "contours of the writer's psyche have changed."[63] A common refrain of these years was expressed in the slogan "We must break the writer's individualism!"[64]

While the writer was urged to abandon the position of "independent observer" and become a "writer-fighter" (*pisatel'-boets*),[65] the new conception of his role in fact incorporated a number of specific and fairly mundane tasks—organizing libraries in the enterprises, running the literary circles, helping with the wall-newspapers, lecturing, arranging public debates and exhibitions, composing slogans and appeals to the workers, and finding worker representatives for the major literary committees.[66]

The writer, in other words, was to be "remade" as a journalist, technical expert, cultural worker, teacher, librarian, and public relations officer. Often, the articles on his new role neglected even to mention the possibility that he should be writing his own works—and when, after all, would he find time to do so? Self-effacement on the part of the established writers was considered essential for their reconstruction. But, with such a degree of self-effacement, literature as traditionally understood seemed to be withering away.

It should not be glibly assumed that this "withering away" was a purely artificial process generated from above. There was a genuine, if very diffuse, desire on the part of many writers to transform their own status in some way, to participate in the construction of the new society and to achieve a more direct link with the masses. Russian history provides precedents for this: the dispatch of the writers to Soviet enterprises during the Five-Year Plan can be seen as an industrial version of *narodnichestvo*, a resurgence of the impulse that sent the intelligentsia to the people in the 1870s.[67] In both cases, the educated went "to the people" to bring them enlightenment and to teach. But they also went to learn, to dissolve their own class prejudices, and to establish contact with those whom they perceived to be the crucial element in contemporary society.

Just as the nineteenth-century "repentant nobleman" sought to compensate for his material and social privileges, so the Five-Year Plan writer hoped to share his *cultural* advantages with the less privileged. No explanation made in terms of ambition or political and economic pressures could account, for instance, for the fact that the novelist Marietta Shaginian spent four years on a construction site working as a laborer to atone for her bourgeois past and truly enter into the spirit of the new age. [68]

Few writers appear to have stood entirely apart from this widespread movement. They were, of course, under strong moral pressure to join it, and the degree of commitment and the amount of time spent in the field varied enormously with the individual. [69] Hints of the resentment that some writers felt can be found in the fiction of the period. [70]

Whatever the balance between enthusiasm and coercion in the movement "to the people," the effect was that the authorial ego began to play a much more modest role than usual in composing a text. One symptom of this was the vogue for collective writing: writers' brigades, factories, and other enterprises were encouraged to publish collective accounts of their experiences and achievements. Organizations vied with each other in the number of authors they were able to engage in such projects: in late 1931 the enterprising factory "Red Triangle" was able to boast a book produced by a collective of fifteen hundred authors and one hundred editors (though the achievement was somewhat less impressive when it was noted that the factory had a labor force of fifteen hundred with one hundred senior personnel and, furthermore, that the well-known writers Slonimskii and Lavrenev were currently there on assignment). [71]

There were, however, problems with the principle of equal creative opportunity for all. In the first place, it produced a literature that was neither individualistic nor individualized, making heavy use of conventional formulas and schemes. In the second place, and perhaps appropriately, the literature of "little men" was primarily a literature of "little forms" (*malye formy*). Most believed that *the* genre for the times was the *ocherk* or sketch, a short form that stands on the borders between literature and journalism. Theorists promoted it because an *ocherk* was within the technical reach of a beginning writer and was so short that one could be rushed off quickly whenever a new achievement or policy was to be celebrated. [72]

Yet this did not mean that the literary world agreed on the necessity of abandoning the old literary genres and opting wholeheartedly for journalistic forms. Only certain avant-garde groups such as those contributing to Novyi lef drew such radical conclusions. Novyi lef advocated a "literature of fact" to replace the outmoded literature of the imagination,[73] but since by the end of the twenties most "proletarian" literary factions were hostile to everything coming out of that journal, this idea was consistently attacked in the most powerful organs of the literary press.[74] And in fact, for all their objections to the high literature of the past, proletarians tended to take the conservative position on formal and aesthetic questions.

It was the novel that suffered most in this period. As the Novyi lef theorists realized,[75] the novel was really the genre of an individualist age, but this age was singularly anti-individualist. The trend of opinion was running strongly against a writer's particularizing a protagonist by "psychologizing" (despite RAPP's theories of the "living man"[76]), and it was equally unfashionable to single out one protagonist as a hero.[77]

There was, nevertheless, a widespread feeling that the monumental achievements of the Five-Year Plan required a monumental literature. Most theorists assumed that the ocherk was only a beginning, and that the new literature would shortly develop its own "long form." In this belief, they began to speculate on what form the novel of the future should take. The consensus was that it should be "deheroized," oriented to the emerging future society or to production,[78] and "apsychological in its very structure."[79]

The campaign to remake the novel was launched by an attack on some of the classics of Soviet literature, notably Gladkov's 1925 novel Cement. In this novel, Gladkov had given Soviet literature its first major hero of socialist construction, Gleb Chumalov, whose battle to bring a cement factory back into production had been greatly applauded in the twenties. By 1929, however, critics had begun to point out that Chumalov's individual zeal and dramatic initiatives had confused and undermined "the entire production unit."[80] In one review, a disturbed Marietta Shaginian asked:

> What was it precisely that the young worker [i.e. Chumalov] restored, and against which forces did he struggle? The answer is quite clear: he restores a cement factory which was closed by Glavtsement, and struggles against the economic council and a number of other central bodies (Soviet planning

organs) which authorized the closing of the factory. . . . [Thus] the best works written in those times [the mid-twenties] attacked the earliest attempts at planning and, in romanticizing covert tendencies toward economic anarchy, revolted against planning. . . .[81]

Although Gladkov was, in fact, one of the chief proponents of the earlier theory of "revolutionary romanticism," which called for a "heroic" presentation of the positive characters in literature, he did his best to adapt to the changing fashion. But rather than abandon heroes altogether, in his Five-Year Plan novel *Energy* (1932),[82] he mass-produced them. *Energy* has an unwieldy cast of construction heroes who are presented *seriatim* in small groups to conduct philosophical dialogues and monologues on Soviet construction. These stolid, awkward digressions make a shambles of the plot line. Nevertheless, *Energy* was so often cited as a model for the construction novel that it can be described as one of about four "official" novels of the First Five-Year Plan.

Another of these "official" novels was Marietta Shaginian's *Hydrocentral* (1930–31). Here the author was so preoccupied with the technology of construction and the roles of the "little men" on the site that the result is less a novel than a bloated *ocherk*. Sholokhov's *Virgin Soil Upturned* (1932)[83] and Panferov's *Brusski* (1930–33),[84] which complete the list, concentrate on the topical issue of collectivization; but the necessity of following the twists and turns of official policy in this sphere meant considerable sacrifice of consistency of characterization and plot.[85]

As this account indicates, there were major problems in adapting the novel to Five-Year Plan requirements as they were currently understood in the literary world. If novelists were to present a picture of the "whole" in which no individual assumed a great place, they were faced with a chronic problem of low reader interest. The same was true of their attempts to introduce specificity through technological detail, for these details were often of the most minor and prosaic kind. Above all, the novels suffered from the prohibition on individual heroes. In the post-1932 period, the plot line of a Soviet novel usually centered on a hero figure, a leader. But during the First Five-Year Plan the cult of "little men" was so tyrannical that a writer was liable to attack if he so much as focussed his story on the *foremen* of an enterprise rather than the ordinary workers.[86] There was a multiplicity of little heroes in the Five-Year Plan novel, and the result was a profusion of subplots in search of a central plot or, worse still, the absence of any plot at all.

Two possible solutions to the problem of reader interest remained—the colorful villain, and the redemption story. The first would seem to have been particularly appropriate in view of the "wreckers" and "saboteurs" disclosed by the Shakhty trial and those that followed it; and indeed at no other time was Soviet literature so obsessed with its villains. But the results from a literary point of view were disappointing. In keeping with the utopian spirit of the time, "villains" were the alien elements that threatened the purity of the new society. Their function in the novel was often not to provide action or suspense, but rather to serve as symbolic demarcations of the boundaries between "us" and "them".[87] Foreigners (who were not usually presented as villains, or even as active protagonists) were treated in a somewhat similar way: they appear in almost all the industrial and construction novels of the period as foils for the Soviet viewpoint. They were merely devices for motivating long-winded philosophical dialogues that were essentially digressions from the main development of the plot.[88]

The redemption theme was very popular with writers in this period. It can be found in two main variants. The first of these charts a lost soul's progression from Tsarist beginnings to fulfillment under socialism, passing as he does through a way station of degradation and antisocial crime. He finds his salvation in socialist labor, which he first encounters in a children's home,[89] a forced labor colony,[90] or a Soviet enterprise.[91] This lost soul can be either bourgeois or proletarian-gone-astray-under-capitalism. But in the second variant on the redemption theme the protagonist is the bourgeois professional—content with his lot under Tsarism, passively resistant to the new regime but settling for a quiet, comfortable life and, finally, sharply challenged by the recognition that he is eminently replaceable by a new "Red specialist." This challenge leads either to his conversion and integration into the construction effort,[92] or to futile sabotage and arrest[93] (which is often only a less direct path to the same end).

Such novels arguably represent a nadir in Soviet literature, but it was short-lived. Well before the concluding year of the First Five-Year Plan, the utopian impulse in literature was beginning to falter. The committed writers were divided among themselves and engaged in bitter faction fights.

The results of the programs involving worker and writer participation were disappointing.[94] Above all, the literary community was beginning to realize the dangers of the Five-Year Plan emphasis on quantity rather than quality,[95] and on topicality rather than more enduring themes.[96] A very large investment of man-hours, money, and paper had produced a mass of slight and poorly written anthologies. These bore such engaging titles as *The First Writers' Brigade in the Urals* (1930) and *The Struggle for the Promfinplan in the Third Year of the Five-Year Plan* (1931). But, as the RAPP leaders Averbakh and Fadeev began to perceive, they had "no resonance" and did not "infect" their readers.[97]

From the end of 1930, the literary press shows a progressive retreat from the extreme positions adopted by the literary militants over the past three years.[98] New slogans appeared: "Let Us Turn Our Attention To Creative Writing!"[99] "For Artistic Quality!"[100] "For the *Big* [italics mine] Art of Bolshevism!"[101] and "Show the Country Its Heroes!"[102] There were critical appraisals of the literature of novice writers. An article of February 1931, for example, described their works as "overrated," "in general rather primitive," and "schematic."[103] Critics complained that, in the Five-Year Plan literature in general, there was too much "glossing-over of reality," and that it was often shoddy and hastily written.[104] It was said that topicality and the cult of technology had excluded not only human interest from literature but even ideology (!)[105] In May 1931 RAPP called on the writers to depict the "heroes" of the Five-Year Plan in their works.[106] And, from the beginning of 1931, the literary journals broke out of their previous isolationism and began to take an interest in developments in contemporary Western literature.

These changes can be explained in various ways. In the first place, Maksim Gorkii was to return permanently to the USSR in the spring of 1931, and it is clear from the comments in the literary journals that the writers were expecting him to play a leading role in literature. By April the strains of deference to Gorkii had built up to the slogan "Work Gorkii Style!"[107] This probably meant, in effect: pay more attention to literary craftsmanship. In a programmatic article "On literature" published that January, Gorkii declared:

> It is not always the subject-matter which plays a decisive role in a work, but real mastery of the art always plays that role. . . . It is my opinion that one

should learn not only from the classics, but even from the enemy if he has wit. To learn is not just to imitate, but to command the techniques of literary mastery. [108]

In other words, ideas that less than a year ago had been considered heretical were coming back into currency.

In the second place, literature was affected by developments in the broader political sphere. In June 1931 Stalin rejected "vulgar egalitarianism" (*uravnilovka*) in favor of wage differentials, and announced a new policy of "encouragement and concern" toward the old intelligentsia. [109] Under these circumstances, the "proletarian hegemony" of RAPP was no longer appropriate, and neither was a literary preoccupation with the undifferentiated working-class masses.

In literature, the slogan arising out of Stalin's speech was "Let Us Turn Our Attention to Literary Technique!"[110] This was to some extent ambiguous because of the two meanings of the Russian word "*tekhnika*": a year earlier, one suspects, the slogan might have been interpreted as a reference to *industrial* technology. There were, indeed, important elements of continuity between the literary orientation of the First Five-Year Plan and the Second. The pathos of industrialization continued to engage much of the writers' attention. Literary organizations continued to send "brigades" of "shock-worker" writers to the factories, and writers were still periodically enjoined to look to their "tempos" of literary production. But after 1931 these latter activities were conducted on a very much reduced scale and with little fanfare.

The major upheaval in literary life, which occurred only in 1932, was the dissolution of RAPP and other independent literary organizations and the founding of a single Union of Soviet Writers. Western commentators have seen these events as a final nail in the coffin of literary autonomy. There is, however, a good deal of evidence to suggest that the Party's action in dissolving RAPP was prompted by a desire to halt RAPP's persecution of independent writers' groups and of non-Party writers in particular;[111] and that the intention was not to oppress the literary profession but to rid it of ugly and counterproductive faction fighting. Certainly the relatively broad composition of the initial Writers' Union committees lends support to such an interpretation.

This is not to deny that the post-1932 reorganization was designed to provide an institutional framework for literature that would guarantee a high degree of ideological conformity. But it must also be recognized that the excesses of the First Five-Year Plan period had damaged literature, and that some aspects of the damage were of particular concern to the Party leadership. Among the deficiencies of the Five-Year Plan literature was its low degree of acceptability in the world outside the Soviet Union. With Gorkii's return, the Party leadership clearly wanted international recognition of Soviet accomplishments in the cultural field. It achieved this in some measure through the presence of a number of non-Communist foreign writers of international fame at the First Congress of Soviet Writers, held in 1934 in a spirit of conciliation and respect for the literary tradition.

We can chart the changing orientation of literature through a series of critical responses to a major RAPP novel of socialist construction mentioned earlier in this article—Ilenkov's *The Driving Axle*. The novel was originally hailed as a model for proletarian writers by Serafimovich, the grand old man of proletarian literature, writing in *Pravda* early in 1932.[112] But by mid-March of that year it was under attack at a meeting organized for the purpose at the House of Proletarian Literature. Just as the criticisms of Gladkov's *Cement* in 1929 were part of a campaign against heroization in the novel, so were these attacks on *The Driving Axle* indications that the literary reign of the "little man" of socialist construction was coming to an end. Of the various criticisms of the novel published at this time,[113] Gorkii's is probably the most indicative of the general change—especially if one compares it with his earlier essay on the literary role of "little men." Gorkii wrote:

> The tempos of our life will not allow rushed work and writing tossed off anyhow in the hope of getting it done as soon as possible. . . . Among the proletarians, you still find ideas which are harmful to their interests. For instance, we came up with the doctrine of the necessity for an "organized lowering of culture." Echoes of this theory have not yet died in the noise of construction, and the impulse to simplify in literature is one such echo of the anti-proletarian, anti-culture heresy. . . .
>
> The Soviet day sings out loudly and to the whole world of the gigantic, heroic and talented work of your class. It sings of the human hero, who gives birth to the collective heroism of the class. This grandiose work and this hero is still not being described in literature.[114]

In Ilenkov's novel, Gorkii wrote, "the mechanical role of the 'driving axle' as a part of the train obscured . . . the work of the political axle."[115] This was not to be a fault of future Soviet literature, in which the guiding role of the "political axle"—the Party, and especially its leadership— becomes abundantly clear.[116] On the other hand (and leaving aside the quality of the literature itself), it would also be impossible in the future for Soviet critics to ignore the question of literary quality, and—as at least one critic did in the Five-Year Plan years[117]—to give wholehearted endorsement to a work that was acknowledged to contain *major* compositional and stylistic defects.

Reading Zhdanov's famous address to the 1934 Writers' Congress with the immediate historical context in mind, it seems inappropriate to put too much stress on his frequently quoted formula that writers should be "engineers of human souls."[118] The thought, if not the precise words, was extremely familiar to writers who had lived through the First Five-Year Plan period; and it must have sounded less like a threat than a slight anachronism.

What was perhaps more significant was his emphasis on the crucial importance of literary technique for the Soviet writer,[119] and his view of the place of heroes in Soviet literature. It was in the decaying West, Zhdanov argued, that one found a preference for little heroes, minor writers, and modest themes. Soviet literature, in contrast, reflected the great themes and heroism of the Soviet construction achievement. The hallmark of the new Soviet literature, Zhdanov said, was to be "heroization."[120]

This indeed turned out to be the case. The "little man" as a central concern of Soviet writers disappeared along with other manifestations of the First Five-Year Plan cultural revolution. It was the turn toward the hero that would define Soviet literature for decades to come.

Visionary Town Planning during the Cultural Revolution

S. Frederick Starr

Toward the end of the First Five-Year Plan, the Young Guard Press in Moscow published a children's book entitled *The Green City*. In the postscript, the author addressed the question of whether his youthful readers would soon inhabit the verdant anti-cities that he had just described in detail:

> Kids! Everything I have said about the Green City is no fairy tale. We don't have such towns yet, but across the country communities for workers are being built, new Green Cities. . . . These will put an end to the old dirty villages. [1]

The creation of such settlements would also spell the end for cities as they had been known for centures, as Lenin's widow, Krupskaia, had only recently argued:

> . . . today there are no technical impediments to disbursing more or less equally over the whole country all the treasures of science and art that for centuries have been hoarded in a few centers. [2]

A grandiose vision, perhaps, but one that the 1930 edition of the Shorter Soviet Encyclopedia could uphold in the most matter-of-fact terms.[3] And why not? As the editor of a collection of statements on the subject coolly explained that same year: "Today the realization of 'utopias' is dictated to us by life itself."[4]

Are these merely fantasies of isolated dreamers who were out of touch with the realities of what an American journalist termed "Russia's Iron Age"?[5] After all, class war and political repression had made science-fiction novels too dangerous for publishers to touch by 1931,[6] and visionary painting, which had thrived during the more pacific era of the New Economic Policy, scarcely survived the first year of the Five-Year Plan. Surely, town planning must have fallen quickly into line as well.

To an extent that seems astonishing today, it did not, but in fact produced scores of proposals that make such utterances as those quoted above appear mild indeed. These proposals were as diverse as they were imaginative. Members of the State Academy of Artistic Sciences were treated to reports on cities to be planned purely by mathematics;[7] leaders of Moscow's Communal Economic Administration earnestly studied proposals for applying some mysterious "Biogeometric Principle" to the reconstruction—or better, obliteration—of Moscow;[8] while leading journals reported extensively on various plans for the manufacture of one-person, portable dwellings to house the "liberated" members of former families. Far from being isolated instances of temporary madness, these were all seriously conceived efforts to exploit town planning as "the mightiest factor for organizing the psyche of the masses," in the words of one widely publicized declaration.[9]

In a similarly utopian spirit, the Moscow architect Konstantin Melnikov submitted plans for a town conceived as a behaviorist laboratory for engendering a collective spirit in the labor force.[10] Publishing Melnikov's project—along with several others with similarly startling features—the journal *The Building Industry* (*Stroitelnaia promyshlennost*) announced that the proposed Green City near Moscow would be the first of a "whole series" of leisure towns.[11] Actually, it was not the first, nor was there just one series. Before a Communist party edict hobbled the movement (or movements) in June 1931, a host of specialists had put forward their schemes for radically transforming the Soviet way of life through utopian town planning and architecture. Even private citizens got into the act. Some composed draconian house-rules enforcing communality in collectivized dwellings;[12] others—complete amateurs—made bold to submit their proposals for replanning Moscow in connection with the construction of a Palace of Soviets; and, in a very different milieu, a congregation of Evangelical Christians drafted a prospectus for their new community of Evangelsk, which they named "The City of the Sun" after Campanella's sixteenth-century utopia.

Absorbing the apocalyptic mood of the Five-Year Plan, the authors of such schemes confidently expected that the new world of which they dreamed would be ushered in within their own lifetimes. Whereas in 1923 the architect Alexander Lavinskii had advanced his "Concretized Utopia" without suggesting any specific timetable,[13] in 1929 Leonard Sabsovich could declare flatly that the nonurban existence that he envisaged would be realized within a decade and a half, a projection that he felt compelled to halve within the year.[14] Sabsovich's extreme optimism was exceptional, but even Sabsovich's critics agreed that the time to plan for the new era was at hand. Opposition leader Grigorii Zinoviev, who in 1917 had opposed Lenin's plan for a Bolshevik coup as reckless, but who had subsequently aligned himself with the Party's "super-industrializers," warned against

> . . . that sober scepticism with which excessively "practical" people now meet plans for the construction of socialist cities. "Where?" they ask. "How?" "That will never be." "Only in 100 years," etc. Such *petit bourgeois* prejudice must be sternly rejected.[15]

The radically new life style might well necessitate certain transitional measures to help people adjust to it, as the architect Moisei Ginsburg conceded, but such measures would foster rather than check the forced-march pace of resettlement.[16]

In 1928–30, it indeed seemed that a new world was at hand. Visionary planners excitedly awaited its advent, and in their projects and theoretical writings attempted to describe its wondrous aspects. But as they did so, it became clear that there existed among them sharp differences of view on just what the new social setting would be like. From a few minor disagreements in 1928, these polemics rapidly broadened into full-blown debates at the Communist Academy in 1929,[17] then rapidly descended to name-calling, which reached something of a nadir when one official in the planning field referred to certain of his colleagues as Trotskyites, Fascists, and "cubo-futurist bastards."[18] When a Moscow architect reported in the French press that Soviet city planners had divided into warring camps, he was by no means exaggerating.[19]

Feuds among leading Soviet planners dominated the professional press of the day to such an extent that subsequent commentators have found it all but impossible to perceive any common elements among the contending visions of the future. Instead, the thrust of historical analysis has been toward identifying the various factions and seeking connections between each of them and the principal heresies of the day. Thus, the two leading factions have been identified as the right and left wings of the movement,[20] though the application of such terms to the realm of town planning is at best problematical and at worst simply erroneous. Meanwhile, the contours of the movement as a whole, and even its existence as a single phenomenon, have scarcely been recognized.

Among all the debates that divided Russia's visionary town planners, none was aired more publicly than that between the so-called urbanists and disurbanists. Approaching the movement today, it is the polemic between these two factions that dominates the published record. No brief overview can do justice to the entire range of issues over which the two groups differed, nor, for that matter, can the full extent and significance of the common ground between them be adequately conveyed in any telegraphic summary. But even a brief overview will suffice to indicate the degree to which the contending schools of "urbanism" and "disurbanism" both rose in response to a single set of economic, social, and ideological circumstances and were both, at bottom, antiurban visions of the future.

The chief theorist of the so-called urbanist perspective was no urbanist at all. It was this man, Leonard Moisevich Sabsovich, who in 1930 delightedly claimed that "soon our biggest cities will be the most backward places to live in the USSR,"[21] and that all existing cities would be "swept from the face of the earth."[22] A year earlier Sabsovich had emerged from his post as a member of *Gosplan's* "Commission on a General Plan" to publish a book entitled *The USSR in Fifteen Years: A Hypothesis for a General Plan for Building Socialism in the USSR.*[23] His main hypothesis, as we have noted, was alluringly simple: since the economic and social transition to Communism would be completed within a decade and a half, the settlements and dwellings appropriate to the new world would have to be ready by then.

The broad outlines of Sabsovich's vision of the future derived straight from Engels and Marx: the abolition of large cities; the destruction of isolated farmsteads; and the resettlement of all people in totally collectivized settlements that would be neither cities nor countryside. The specifics of his vision were his own, however, and were based on his analysis of the social impact of a new source of energy: electricity. True to the traditional Russian emphasis on large-scale economic units, Sabsovich assumed that electrification would be most effectively applied to fairly extensive enterprises. Hence, he believed that electricity should and would lead to the establishment of grandiose laundry facilities, baths, kitchens, and bakeries serving whole blocks or towns, rather than to the manufacture of small applicances for use in individual apartments.[24] Accordingly, he foresaw the construction of numerous collectivized settlements (but not cities) with populations of some forty to sixty thousand persons each.[25] This picture, presented in a series of public lectures and radio talks during 1928 and 1929, was soon to be hailed by everyone from the Commissar of Enlightenment, A. V. Lunacharskii,[26] to the chief economist for the First Five-Year Plan, S. G. Strumilin.[27]

How would Sabsovich's conception come into being? Here again, his strategy depended upon electrification, for he expected that there would soon be created a single, integrated power grid covering the entire nation. Once established, this grid would permit small agro-industrial towns to spring up wherever manpower was needed to exploit resources. Thus, electricity would bring about the disburdenment of existing cities and the dispersion of the population across the land in much the way that Krupskaia had envisaged. Indeed, this is precisely what was already occurring with the creation of five new towns near Stalingrad,[28] and with the construction of the communities of Avtostroi near Nizhnii Novgorod, Traktorstroi near Kharkov, Dnepropetrovsk in the Ukraine, and a host of other towns then under scaffolding. Inevitably, Sabsovich claimed, such factory towns would completely supplant the old urban centers and, with the withering of the centralized state under Communism, transform the Soviet Union into a federation of small towns of equal size, linked by electric-powered mass public transportation.[29]

Thus, the "urbanists'" vision was urbanistic only in the very limited sense of retaining a network of nodal points in an otherwise completely decentralized national plan of settlement. Had other planners not rejected even this degree of agglomeration, Sabsovich and his followers would surely never have been called urbanists in the first place. But such other planners did exist, and were attracting adherents among the same audiences that Sabsovich was addressing.

The chief theorist of the "disurbanist" perspective was the sociologist M. Okhitovich, who set forth his conception in a brief paper on "The Socialist Means of Population Dispersion and a Socialist Type of Housing" delivered at the Communist Academy on October 1, 1929, and in a more rigorous, yet at the same time more evocative, essay published by *Contemporary Architecture* four months later.[30] Like Sabsovich, Okhitovich believed passionately in theory. But where Sabsovich sought to ground every postulate in writings by the Communist fathers, Okhitovich would usually point to his own first principles. Chief among these was his definition of a city as "a knot of communication: a knot of roads and rivers." "What distinguishes a city from the country?" he asked.

> The conjunction of crossing roads and rivers. A village, as distinct from a city, always consists of ONE ROAD. If a village has more than one, a quantum jump has occurred, crafts have been separated from landworking, etc. . . . It is no longer a village. It is the BEGINNING of a city and the END of a village, its collapse.[31]

With this bold assertion, Okhitovich was off and running. Like Marx, he averred that the history of mankind was a tale of unfolding economic relationships, but, unlike Marx, he considered ownership of the means of production to be only one among several social determinates, and not even the central one. That role he assigned jointly to the source of energy and the means of transportation. Thus, in describing the peasant village, he cites the monopoly of animate sources of energy and the primitive system of transport, rather than the manorial or communal ownership of land. With the introduction of new sources of power and new means of communication into rural areas, the village would disappear, which was precisely what Okhitovich believed to be happening in the USSR. Similarly, if one could introduce new forms of energy and transport in urban areas, the city would become unnecessary, which he also believed to be occurring as he wrote:

> It is the revolution in the transmission of energy which is the condition that allows us to hope for the abolition, on the one hand, of the unbelievable isolation [of the peasant village] and the hypertrophied tedium [of the big city] on the other.[32]

Like Lenin, whom he considered his guide, Okhitovich identified electrification as the source of the energy that would usher in the Communist era. Every source of power, large or small, would henceforth feed into a single, nationwide grid from which every user of energy, large or small, could take as much as he required and at any point at which it was needed. In contrast to Sabsovich, who saw electricity as strengthening collective social units at the expense of the individual, Okhitovich saw it as serving the individual as well as society as a whole. Just as the unification of all sources of power into one system would create bonds among all users of energy, so the ability to transmit electrical energy to the most remote spot would render possible the liberation of each member of society from the impersonal urban centers to which he had previously been condemned by wood and coal power.

This simultaneous liberation of society and the individual would also be promoted by new modes of transportation: airplanes, electric-powered trains, and especially the automobile. The tendency of interurban trains to strain the boundaries of the old closed city was seen by Okhitovich as but a foretaste of things to come. With the full development of the dawning modes of transportation, society would become wholly "destationized."[33] No function would be pinned to any one place, and those central places at which functions had formerly been concentrated—towns and cities— would simply die. Individual functions and individual human beings would for the first time be free to move anywhere.

A conspicuous trait of the antiurban movement as a whole and of the so-called disurbanist strain in particular was an infatuation with fluidity and open-endedness. As symbols of motion, railway stations figure prominently in town plans of the era;[34] airplanes and dirigibles zoom freely over architectural renderings by Ivan Leonidov and Konstantin Melnikov; drawings of proposed cities and even of individual buildings were often presented as oblique aerial views with the horizon stretching dramatically into the distance. A spiral-shaped city by T. Varentsov[35] and a plan by N. Ladovskii for a "dynamic city" in the form of a parabola[36] are especially vivid, but otherwise characteristic, manifestations of this mood. But no one surpassed Okhitovich in his enthusiasm for "destationizing" life, and no one produced a more specific program for achieving it.

Having defined cities as places where two or more routes come together, but having asserted also that electricity, electric trains, and the automobile were rendering obsolete all large agglomerations of people, Okhitovich moved on logically but astonishingly to project the coming socialist form of settlement as a "linear city" consisting solely of continuous bands of parallel transportation lines covering the entire country without beginning or end. In this manner would be created a "socialist dispersion settlement, which is neither city nor countryside."[37]

Judged by his own statements rather than those of certain of his followers who sought to temper his excesses, Okhitovich was indeed a radical antiurbanist, and nowhere is this clearer than in his proposals for housing. Like all leading planners, including Sabsovich, Okhitovich was a collectivizer. He devoutly believed that in the immediate future all bourgeois types of property and personality would vanish, thereby removing the last impediments to the flowering of the human psyche. But, whereas Sabsovich and the "urbanists" spoke of the merging of individual interests into a communal whole and therefore advocated the construction of large col-

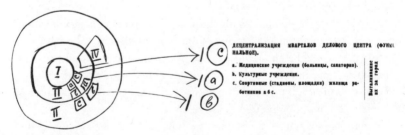

Okhitovich's plan calls for the radical decentralization of urban centers by functions: *a.* medical institutions (hospitals, sanatoriums); *b.* cultural institutions; *c.* sports facilities (stadiums and playing fields); housing for workers, *a, b, c.* SOURCE: M. Okhitovich, "K probleme garoda," *Sovremennaia arkhitektura,* 1929, no. 4, p.132.

lectivized housing units, Okhitovich and his followers did not hesitate to assert that the collectivization of support facilities would serve primarily individual ends. "The stronger the collective links," he wrote, "the stronger becomes the individual personality [*lichnost*]."[38] Okhitovich insisted that the communal houses of which others dreamed were part of the

These portable housing "cells" for single persons, devised by N. Sokolov and M. Ginsburg, represent the culmination of the anarcho-individualist tendency in Soviet architecture during the cultural revolution. SOURCE: N. Sokolov, "Opyt arkhitekturnogo myshleniia," *Sovremennaia arkhitektura*, 1929, no. 3, p.95.

problem of bourgeois civilization and not its cure, since they could not help but keep the human personality in captivity. In their place, he proposed to build small separate structures capable of housing one person each—the family having long since passed from the scene. As a further guarantee that society's institutions would not hamper the liberated individual, male or female, Okhitovich insisted that these individual housing cells be "destationized." Just as movable harvesters and oil-drilling equipment marked the destationization of the economy, so portable houses would reflect the destationization of society. "The house of the future," he concluded, would be "a standardized, motorized, easily transportable, small and hence inexpensive structure."[39]

Acting under the direct influence of Okhitovich's astounding pro-

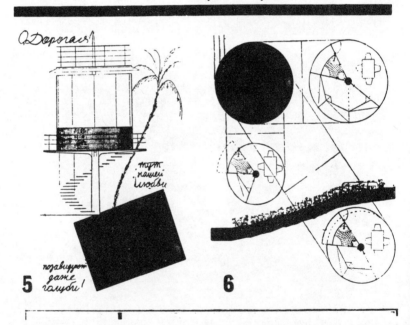

сти их, к тому, что все лепилось в один запутанный клубок.

Another view of portable housing "cells" by Sokolov and Ginsburg. Elevation and floor plans, showing interior fixtures. SOURCE: N. Sokolov, loc. cit.

nouncement, several architects and theorists began elaborating it in detail and translating it into actual building designs. Thus, we have Moisei Ginsburg proposing a series of portable housing cells to be raised up on stilts,[40] and Iurii Larin (who otherwise followed Sabsovich's lead) polemicizing in favor of movable houses consisting of little but a bed and wash basin set on seven square meters of floor space.[41] Others meanwhile had set about to apply further aspects of Okhitovich's theories to plans for whole settlements.[42] Long before they could have had any concrete assurance that their visionary ideas might be implemented, the radical "disurbanists" had drafted detailed blueprints to guide the builders of linear settlements and portable housing cells, and had expounded the place of their projects in the history of mankind.

ANTIURBANISM AND UTOPIAN REVOLT

From the foregoing it can be seen that, for all their obvious differences, both "urbanists" and "disurbanists" were part of a single movement, the principal thrust of which was to liquidate once and for all large cities in Russia. They differed on whether to consider agglomeration as bad in any form, and on the extent to which individuation should be encouraged within a collectivized setting. But in their hostility to the metropolis and in their belief that cities could be replaced at once with highly decentralized forms of settlement, the visionary planners shared a common outlook and one that constituted a prominent ideological current within the Cultural Revolution.

It will be readily noted that on many points this program closely resembles orthodox Communist prescriptions for the society of the future. The merging of city and countryside, the withering of the capitalist city, the overcoming of the "idiocy of rural life"—all are safely grounded in Marx's works and in the writings of Marx's Russian followers, including Lenin. But, at the same time, there are several points on which the planners ranged beyond the parameters of orthodox Marxist discussion in order to express views that were decidedly their own.

First among the distinctive features of Russia's visionary planners is the sheer depth of their hostility to cities. In lecture after lecture, on page after page, they railed against the city like a band of modern St. Johns raging against Babylon. Unlike Marx, they saw the fact that large metropolitan complexes had grown up under capitalism as only part of the trouble; for Russia's visionary planners, all cities were irretrievably evil, regardless of whether they were feudal, capitalist, socialist, or communist. In this spirit, Moisei Ginsburg attacked the slightly less radical Sabsovich as a compromiser who had failed to grasp the full wretchedness of all urban life:

> The idea of creating regional centers, like the idea of forming little centric towns, is unconditionally erroneous. In essence, it substitutes a small evil for a big one. Of course, a small evil is better than a big one, but the fact is that the idea of centralization in any form is such that it can only lead to the strengthening of the center.[43]

Nowhere, it should be noted, did Ginsburg or any other antiurbanist muster such vehemence in denouncing Marx's chief *bête-noir*, the "idiocy of rural life."[44]

A second point on which the visionary planners veered away from orthodox Marxist precepts was in their treatment of the problem of violence in history. The antiurbanists knew full well that Marx had held that the historical process unfolded through a series of violent clashes between the forces and counterforces within society. Nonetheless, they came out squarely against violence and the use of compulsion to achieve their object. Both Sabsovich and Okhitovich emerged as strong advocates of voluntarism in all things. Agro-industrial settlements must be designed so as to *attract* the peasantry to them, Sabsovich declared,[45] while Okhitovich proposed no stronger measures than "voluntary collectivization, supported by special benefits."[46] The architect Konstantin Melnikov went even further in his opposition to the use of force by designing for his Green City a special "Laboratory of Sleep," where a socialist mentality would be gently induced in thousands of sleeping citizens by washing them with sounds and smells that were to be scientifically selected for their collectivist associations.[47]

Such views on violence and change go a long way toward resolving the question of whether the antiurban ideologies should be linked with the "Left" or the "Right" deviation in Communist party affairs. On the one hand, Sabsovich and Okhitovich shared the Left's belief that change should be immediate and total. Stalin's henchman, Kaganovich, was therefore quite correct in linking them with the now heretical views of the fallen Trotskii.[48] On the other hand, though, their belief that violence was neither necessary nor desirable links them squarely with the Right, i.e., with the position of the discredited Bukharin. Neither of the Left nor Right in their own allegiances, the visionary planners wanted the best of both worlds.

In this 1929 drawing, M. Ginsburg and N. Sokolov exhort Soviet architects to "Think with your head and not with your ruler." These individuated cells set in a rural landscape are an extreme reaction against the regimentation and collectivization of both urban and rural life called for by the First Five-Year Plan. SOURCE: N. Sokolov, *loc. cit.*

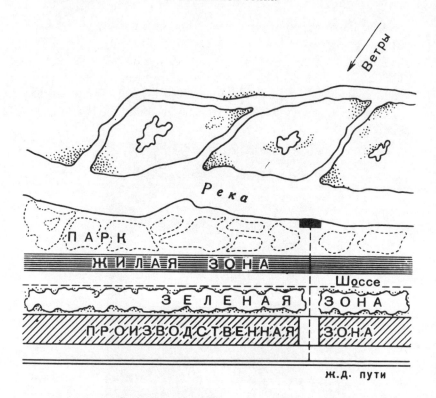

N. A. Miliutin: Residential zone, Stalingrad tractor plant. *Top to bottom:* Wind (arrow); River; Park; Living Zone; Green Zone; Production Zone. The town is arranged so that fresh air will waft across the river and through the park, and then to the housing area, which in turn is separated from the industrial zone by a green belt. SOURCE: M. G. Barkhin, ed., *Mastera sovetskoi arkhitektury ob arkhitekture,* Moscow, 1975, pl. 27.

However naïve their view on violence and change may seem in a Soviet context, it had ample precedents in the annals of political thought, notably in the visions of French utopian socialists of the early and mid-nineteenth century. Other aspects of the planners' work recall these same sources, as, for example, their negative emphasis on society as a tool for liberating the creative instincts of the individual and their passionate rejection of the city per se for the sake of the small town or countryside. And, in the last analysis, how greatly do Sabsovich's communal dwellings differ from

Fourier's phalansteries and how much does Okhitovich's "new form of settlement" differ from Proudhon's rural anarchy? Both comparisons were drawn at the time, as were equally telling analogies to the works of Rosseau, Lev Tolstoi, and the turn-of-the-century English utopian Ebenezer Howard.[49] Clearly, then, the radical planners represent a sudden blossoming of a very old revolutionary tradition that had once flourished in Russia but that had been submerged beneath the tide of positivism and then Bolshevism.

In its faith that human beings could be redeemed through contact with Nature, and its willingness to abandon large cities in order to bring this about, this other tradition was unabashedly romantic. Hence, we are not surprised to detect in our planners—especially Okhitovich and his followers—a strong streak of romantic individualism and antirationalism. When, in 1930, *Contemporary Architecture (SA)* published Okhitovich's proposals, its pages were enlivened by Alexander Rodchenko's elegiac photographs of sylvan scenes—a far cry from the coldly Constructivist design that had heretofore dominated the journal. "Think with your head and not with your ruler," counseled one member of the Union of Contemporary Architects in a note on his drawings of portable living units.[50] In the Green City proposal, Ginsburg followed this romantic plea by drawing ribbon settlements that meandered across the countryside in anything but a strict, linear fashion.[51] It is true that Nikolai Miliutin spurned such rhetoric as un-Communist.[52] But after comparing his own linear city to "a large steam-driven generating station," he turned around a few pages later to conjure up the image of happy toilers settling down after a day's work to read a book "in the garden or out on the terrace."[53] Some writers gave such romantic imagery a frankly anachronistic twist, as when the Commissar of Enlightenment spoke glowingly of inhabitants of the socialist city spending their days painting pottery, tooling beautiful bookbindings, and doing woodcarvings.[54] But Lunacharskii's rejection even of contemporary aesthetics as inappropriate for the life and architecture of new settlements is exceptional.[55] More often than not, the romantic ideal was grounded squarely in some future world.

Sabsovich and the "urbanists" would have been appalled at the charge of romanticism and individualism. They were not particularly rural in orientation, and they criticized Okhitovich for pretending to be "terribly r-r-revolutionary" while advocating nothing more than a backwards-looking, *petit bourgeois* form of "automobile socialism."[56] And yet the element of romantic individualism is strongly present in the writings of Sabsovich and his fellow "urbanists." For all their professed hostility to "individualism," the collectivity of which they spoke so fondly was less an end in itself than a modern and efficient means of stripping from the individual all the mundane impediments to his free ascent to higher realms. According to Sabsovich, the end of history would be attained when every person would be liberated to become, in effect, a Schilleresque hero, developing his individual genius by indulging in free play, *Spieltrieb*, in such areas as music, sculpture, sport, and "invention."[57] Of course, the state would long since have ceased to exist.

What impelled Russia's antiurbanists toward the romantic anarchism that flowered so luxuriantly during the years 1929 and 1930? What are the wellsprings of this individualism, which sounds like a diapason in the midst of the stridently collectivist cadences that characterize the rhetoric of Sabsovich and his followers? It is unfortunate that so few participants left sufficient personal papers on which to form a solid judgment on this critical issue, and that the living survivors do not include the most representative figures of the movement. But even in the absence of exhaustive evidence, it can be observed that, on many important points, the antiurbanists were moving in directions that were diametrically opposed to what has come to be regarded as the mainstream of Soviet development in those years.

Thus, there is something wildly incongruous about Moisei Ginsburg's platitude, issued early in 1930 as word of the brutality of the collectivization effort was reaching Moscow, that he wished nothing more than for peasants to be free to listen to skylarks.[58] Similarly, Sabsovich's dictum that "socialism has as its object the maximal development of the individuality of each person"[59] can only give pause when one recalls that at the time he pronounced it the economic planners were herding workers around the countryside at will in order to satisfy their lust for high productivity. By the same token, the idealization of rest and leisure in all the four entries to the Moscow Communal Economy's "Green City" competition, held the same year that "shock quarters" of steady overtime were being introduced to meet production quotas, seems to verge on the cynical.[60] And cynicism yielded to the grotesque when Moscow's leading architects and planners gave themselves up to the cult of Nature just as Nature herself was everywhere being presented as the savage force standing in the way of man's attaining his earthly dominion.

The list could be extended indefinitely. But to belabor the extent of the antiurbanists' apparent opposition to dominant currents of the day only begs the question of how they might have been driven to utopian revolt in the first place. Here again, available evidence permits little beyond a tentative hypothesis, namely, that the antiurbanists were themselves recent converts to the cause, having until 1928–29 staunchly supported precisely those policies against which they subsequently revolted. Paradoxically, the urbanists' stance arose in opposition to official developments in which they themselves had been directly involved.

For example, Moisei Ginsburg throughout the 1920s had been the leading exponent of standardization in Soviet architecture, by virtue of which he had been appointed director of the laboratory charged with working out prototypes for every town and building type to be constructed in the Russian Republic. He plunged into the task with his accustomed zeal, quickly working out plans for the super-collectivized *Stroikom* housing units. No sooner had he come out forthrightly for standardization than he began—tentatively through 1929 and without reservations by 1930—to develop other building types, which, though mass-produced, nonetheless permitted the maximum flexibility and diversity in their actual use. Simultaneously, he began advocating his "destationized" housing units and non-linear "linear" cities. So directly did these projects follow on the heels of his apotheosis of standardization that it is hard to escape the conclusion that Ginsburg had become fearful of the behaviorist implications of his own earlier work, and even of the *Stroikom* housing units that were the first fruit of his work with the Building Commission.

To take a second example, it is noteworthy that not one of the antiurbanists attempted to hide behind institutionalized facades, but each boldly put himself forward as the personal representatives of an ideal. It is scarcely coincidental that precisely as they were doing this the various professions of which they were a part—architecture, economics, sociology, etc.—were deeply embroiled in parallel crises that would soon culminate in their being transformed into tightly structured and highly depersonalized state agencies.

The avant-gardists among the architects had worked for a decade to impose their various doctrines on each other, to be sure, from their sanctuaries in academia or small-group practice. Then the cultural revolution threw their cozy world into disarray as proletarian architects threatened to do to them what they had unsuccessfully tried to do to each other for years.

With this, the utopian planners quickly discovered the value of diversity both in their architectural and professional life. Nikolai Ladovskii and his colleagues in the League of Architect-Urbanists (ARU) announced that no single pattern of settlement should be adopted for the whole country,[61] while avant-gardists of all shades of opinion took pains to protect their individual autonomy within the "All-Union Architectural and Scientific Society" (VANO),[62] established while the antiurbanist movement was at its peak in May 1930. Against this background, the antiurban utopianism and the individualistic style in which it was presented appears as the architects' wishful attempt to liberate themselves from the impending threat of being swallowed by an impersonal and centralized union dominated by their opponents.

On the basis of arguments presented thus far, it would be fair to conclude, at least tentatively, that antiurbanism constituted a many-sided utopian revolt against certain of the major forces molding Soviet life during the cultural revolution. At its most radical, antiurbanism opposed the power of large organizations, defended professional individuality, rejected the idea of a war against nature, and submitted collectivism to the measure of the individual. In each case, the movement was reactive, fleeing into unreality in the face of brutal policies with which its members could not effectively reckon because in many instances they themselves had once advocated them.

Now, had the antiurbanists really been so totally out of step with their times, they would surely have been denied official support. But this was scarcely the case. Every one of their theories was developed under the patronage of important state agencies, seriously considered at prestigious learned assemblies, and disseminated through official organs, newspapers, and journals and even over the radio.

Typical of the several agencies providing money and support for the antiurbanists' research was the State Institute for the Planning of Cities (*Giprogor*), founded in the Russian Republic in 1930 but promptly expanded to include branches in the Ukraine (*Giprograd*), White Russia, and elsewhere. [63] In the Donbass and Zaporozhe areas, where numerous towns were built embodying the most advanced conceptions of the day, the Giprograd agency built upon the work of two slightly older bodies, the "Bureau for Planning a Greater Zaporozhe" (f. 1928) and the Commission on Planning New Cities for the Donbass" (f. 1929), [64] which throughout 1929 and 1930 had listened sympathetically to such visionary planners as V. Lavrov, A. Vesnin, P. Aleshin, P. Amosov, etc.

Sabsovich, in his post in the State Planning Commission (*Gosplan*), Ginsburg, as head of *Stroikom's* construction laboratory, and Miliutin, as chairman of the "Section on Socialist Resettlement, Housing, and Way of Life" under the Communist Academy's Institute of Economics, were all in particularly good positions to make known their views. Each had at his disposal at least one house journal, while a series of general publications devoted to architecture, culture, economics, and the arts gave regular and positive coverage to the work of the antiurbanists. Beyond these forums, the staid and respectable Moscow Architectural Society made great efforts during this period to provide to all factions a public platform, which the antiurbanists put to good use.

No less important as patrons of the antiurbanists were such matter-of-fact institutions as the Moscow Communal Economic Administration, which sponsored the notorious "Green City" competition, the Central Communal Bank (*Tsekombank*), which financed nearly all the more visionary projects that were actually built, and certain leading industries. The city of Magnitogorsk, for example, was initially planned as a linear settlement by the steel industry, while several other industries combined efforts to draft plans for the linear town and satellite settlements at Stalingrad. [65] Nor were representatives of these various agencies and industries left to learn of the antiurbanists' designs from the press. A meeting at the All-Union Association of Workers in Science and Technology (*Varnitso*), at which Sabsovich spoke in July 1929, included leaders from *Giproshakht*, *Donugol*, *Avtostroi*, and other bureaucratic bodies charged with planning towns. After backing Sabsovich to the hilt, the entire assembly resolved to carry its campaign to the industrial world of the USSR. [66]

Not only did the antiurbanist theoreticians come into contact with official agencies that welcomed their views, but they found actual patronage as well. Thanks to this, they ceased to be mere "paper architects." During the first three years of the Five-Year Plan, such towns as Beketovka, Traktorstroi, Donugul, Magnitogorsk, Dzherzhinsk, Kominternovsk, Kuznetsk, Donetsk, and Zaporozhe—over sixty in all—were constructed *ex nihilo*, according to plans drawn up by specialists applying some or all of the antiurbanist precepts, [67] while several hundred older communities were substantially replanned. Admittedly, many of these turned out to be quite conventional, while the boldest departures were soon to be smothered under the standardized town plans imposed by the Second (and, on the architectural front, more extensive) Five-Year Plan. [68] Nonetheless, the concrete achievement was substantial by any measure, far greater than would have been the case had the antiurbanists' program been under some quarantine.

The support extended to the antiurbanists in their work would never have been forthcoming had the Communist party itself not at least tacitly accepted their vision. On the basis of everything we know of NEP policies and practices, this would have seemed most unlikely in 1927, one year before the visionary planning movement began; similarly, by 1931, the idea of Party support for the radical planners would have become ludicrous, for by that time the Party had already taken stern measures to suppress them as dangerous fanatics. Nonetheless, between these two dates antiurbanism was able to flourish precisely because it broadly corresponded with the utopian vision implicit in the Party's First Five-Year Plan. Never mind that the antiurbanists carried their program to the limits of Communist orthodoxy and beyond; for the brief interval 1928–30, they were safe.

The notion of support by the Communist party for the antiurban visionaries between 1928 and 1930 raises as many questions as it answers. Granted that it accounts for the extensive public discussion of radical town planning that was permitted in those years and for the degree of practical application of the planners' ideas that was allowed to go forward; it nonetheless poses the question of the Party's motives with ever greater force. Why, after all, did the Party permit such extreme sentiments to flourish and, indirectly, even provide institutional and financial support for them at the very time it was seeking to mobilize the country for the very practical task of industrialization? The answer goes far toward clarifying the attitudes not only of those Party officials responsible for town planning, but particularly of the visionary planners themselves.

THE PRACTICABILITY OF THE
ANTIURBAN VISION

It need hardly be said that the antiurbanist program partook of that strain of utopianism that existed within Marxism itself, the same strain that had surfaced so unexpectedly on the eve of 1917 in Lenin's *State and Revolution* and that burst into the open once more as the Cultural Revolution raised hopes that society would soon be completely transformed. Given this obvious source of justification for antiurbanist views, it is all the more surprising that neither the antiurbanists themselves nor their friends within the Party chose to cite it as justification for their position.

To be sure, the planners knew their Marx and Lenin and sprinkled their texts with appropriate citations from their more visionary works, as if to prove that they themselves were not the anarchic utopians they appeared to be. But, for the most part, both the theoreticians and Party writers preferred to base their case solidly on their reading of what was actually happening around them.

We have sampled the antiurbanists' ideological formulations, which they elaborated with undisguised zeal. At the same time, they were keenly sensitive to the charge of dealing only with "abstract and unreal 'theoretical' arguments," as Lazar Kaganovich put it at the June Plenum of the Central Committee in 1931.[69] Kaganovich's ability to back his attack with punitive measures against them did not help matters, but this was not the sole cause of their sensitivity. Rather, they seem to have been deeply convinced from the outset that, as one publicist put it, "The Socialist city is not a fantasy and not a utopia. It is a concrete and real task."[70] In support of this contention, both the planners and their backers within the Party brought forth massive evidence to demonstrate that every one of their prescriptions that others found to be utopian was actually coming to pass in the Soviet Union, thanks to the onward rush of the Great Leap Forward.

Why abandon the old, metropolitan centers? The answer was obvious to the antiurbanists: they were in the process of collapse anyway. And, indeed, a sympathetic German observer concluded after a tour of Soviet cities in 1928 that:

> ... Russian urban administrations are unable to keep in good repair the vast properties entrusted to their care. Consequently, with few exceptions,

> Russian urban dwellings give the appearance of extensive and frightening decay and dilapidation. . . . Sewer systems and water lines have been most gravely affected, especially in the northern cities . . . creating thoroughly disagreeable and unsanitary conditions.[71]

Even Lazar Kaganovich had to admit that the Soviet capital was on the brink of decay. A resident of a typical Moscow apartment reported to him that:

> When the house was taken over by the (housing) Trust, it began to fall into disrepair. One of the courtyards was turned into a dumpheap. The broken gates were not repaired. The furnaceman, a drunkard who did nothing whatever, was rewarded for economizing fuel. The house was practically unheated. . . .[72]

Most of the utopians lived in Moscow, and if some of them, like Moisei Ginsburg, were fortunate enough to be living in up-to-date structures of their own design, the decay was nonetheless constantly before their eyes. Was Moscow dying? Those who had been in the city during the Civil War knew full well the fragility of their great metropolis, for within the space of three years they had watched the population diminish by half and the unheated housing stock fall to gradual demolition by frost. As they read daily newspaper reports on the opening of vast new regions in the south and east, they could readily conclude that Moscow was indeed fated to pass away.

And if it should disappear, so what? Kaganovich, who was no friend of the antiurbanists, spoke movingly in 1931 of the fact that, for all its population, Moscow lacked most of the facilities normally associated with a major capital. Eighty-six percent of the houses of Moscow were of but one or two storeys, sixty-two percent of them being of wood construction.[73] Only forty-two percent of all inhabited structures were served by running water, the figure in some areas being as low as twelve percent. Eight percent of roadways were "improved," the remainder being cobblestone or gravel; subsurface canalization existed in only a few central areas and even there was rapidly decaying; the tramlines had become wildly disorganized; and regular garbage collection did not exist.[74] Leningraders might well feel that they had something to maintain. Muscovites by the late twenties, however, had good reason to conclude that their city was no city at all. And if the usual infrastructure of urban life did not exist, then there was little to regret in Moscow's passing.

But why build totally new settlements rather than capitalize on even that small investment that had been made in existing towns? The main reason, of course, was that the Five-Year Plan called for the development of new industrial areas, while collectivization demanded new forms of rural settlement. These national policies created a situation in which the antiurbanists' proposals could quite fairly be considered as practical responses to a client's request rather than as unsolicited strokes of pure imagination. In the case of Sabsovich, the link with national policy is especially clear, in that the Supreme Council on the National Economy specifically requested him to elaborate his views.[75] But the same case can be made for all the other antiurbanists as well.

That the utopian current was a direct product of the Five-Year Plan and was rendered intelligible by the plan's grandiose intentions can be seen from the antiurbanists' involvement with ongoing official discussions of electrification. Taken in isolation, the electro-centric civilization envisaged by Sabsovich and Okhitovich appears as an eccentric flight of fancy. But scores of articles published as the great dams of Dneprostroi and Magnitogorsk were nearing completion make it clear that educated Russians commonly believed their country to be on the brink of obtaining unlimited energy, and that this Promethean prospect literally compelled them to accept some sort of cultural revolution as inevitable and imminent. When a member of the State Commission on Electrification (*Goelro*) proclaimed that electricity constituted "the most important side of the building of socialism," he was outdoing Lenin's famous dictum in a manner that most contemporaries could only have approved.[76] The antiurbanists' doctrines on the decentralization of economic life, on the diffusion of the population into areas that were presently uninhabited, and on the impact of electrification on collective and individual life were safely within the bounds of what was widely accepted as reasonable discourse.[77]

Even a superficial reading of the west European and American architectural press would have convinced doubters that new cities were everywhere the great concern of the moment, and Soviet town-planners paid far closer attention to new work abroad than did most of their colleagues elsewhere. The Moscow Architectural Society trebled its subscriptions to foreign journals between 1927 and 1929,[78] and the Soviet architectural press was deluged with analyses of new towns abroad during the cultural revolution in a way it had never been during the NEP years. Okhitovich defended his proposals in terms of his reading of American and Australian experience,[79] while others framed their arguments in terms of new housing in places as diverse as Sweden, Holland, Germany, Czechoslovakia, New Zealand, and Japan.[80] Minneapolis was hailed as holder of the world record for downtown green space and cited as justification for tearing down parts of Moscow.[81] American green-belt towns were hailed as worthy experiments in the construction of small communities.[82] Stockholm provided an admired example of collective amenities in its new satellite towns. Thanks to their omnivorous study of planning around the world, the Soviet antiurbanists were confident that their proposals were precisely what the best minds abroad would come to if only they were fortunate enough to live in a socialist state.

The two main forms of settlement proposed by the antiurbanists could both be supported with reference to current developments in the Soviet economy. Sabsovich conceived his settlements as being simply a rationalized and standardized form of the factory towns that were springing up across the country as the Five-Year Plan progressed. On these grounds the distinguished economist Stanislav Strumilin gave them his support and worked out certain details of their organization with reference to those enterprises that he had helped being into being as chief architect of the Five-Year Plan.

Projects for generally linear forms of settlement, too, grained credibility as the Five-Year Plan founded industries in locations dictated primarily by sources of raw materials and access to power or rail transport but that were otherwise dissimilar to sites heretofore chosen for settlement. The expansion of Stalingrad through the creation of new industries stretching for twenty miles along the banks of the Volga River was but the most visible instance of this development. Avtostroi near Nizhnii Novgorod was another, while the new industries sited along the arterial roads leading from Moscow and other cities are a variant example. The idea of linear towns seemed particularly congenial for recreation areas in that it assured maximum privacy for each person. Hence, few reviewers registered surprise when Moisei Ginsburg applied it to the proposed "Green City" to be built in the woods northeast of Moscow.[83]

No aspects of the antiurbanists' programs seems more bizarrely utopian at first glance than their notions on housing, but these, too, gain a certain plausibility in the context of the First Five-Year Plan. Like it or not, collectivism was a fact wherever factories were built without first constructing adequate housing. Sabsovich's critics feigned shock when he proposed allotting only seven square meters per person, but far lower figures were common at Kuznetsk, Magnitogorsk, Dnepropetrovsk, Dzherzhinsk, and elsewhere.[84] In Moscow, where the average allotment had shrunk from 5.2 to 4 square meters between 1927 and 1930, communalization by necessity was already in practice.[85] In despair at the failure of municipal authorities to provide inexpensive canteens, workers set up their own collective kitchens, of which one planner counted some sixty-four in Moscow alone.[86] Once more, the "utopians" could claim to be merely imposing order on the chaotic new world that had emerged so suddenly after 1928.

It may seem farfetched to apply the same argument to Okhitovich's portable and individuated settlements, and it must be admitted that the disurbanists did not themselves do so. Yet never in Russian history had a higher premium been placed on the mobility of labor. The "destationization" of humanity may have been a cultural ideal for Okhitovich, but labor specialists at *Gosplan* took it to be an economic necessity. Similarly, Okhitovich's culturalist motives for favoring individual cottages do not alter the fact that solid economic reasons existed for opposing the construction of large communal habitations, given the limited supply and high cost of the materials needed for high-rise construction then. Experiments were going forth at the time on how to apply wood construction to large buildings,[87] but, until these succeeded, small structures had obvious practical advantages.

A final point on which the apparently utopian thinking of the antiurbanists was firmly rooted in reality was their view on the destruction of the family and the emancipation of women. On both points, of course, they merely followed with great literalness the precepts of Marx and Engels, and on both points, too, they were in substantial agreement with the Party. They differed only on the timetable. The radical planners' eagerness to construct towns and houses embodying these notions at once, with only a brief transitional period or no transition at all, becomes understandable in light of the fact that female employment was rapidly increasing during these years, that the fertility of urban females in Great Russia was declining, and that families were being ripped apart by overwhelming intergenerational tensions and by the demand for laborers at new factories, often situated at a distance from the old centers. Given this, and as the living space available to each family unit shrank in the late 1920s, the utopians felt quite reasonable in concluding that the family had indeed become an institution of the past. When Lunacharskii, in an essay on the culture of the socialist city, discussed the coming end of such categories as "my parents" and "our children," he could do so in the confidence that the last days were already at hand.[88]

The most vulnerable aspect of the antiurbanists' proposals was that they appeared to require immense investments that the society could ill afford to make. Yet, in this area, too, the antiurbanists did not doubt that it was not they but their critics who misunderstood the temper of the times. The first to make this point, predictably, was the economist Sabsovich, who touched on the issue in his address to the All Union Association of Workers in Science and Technology in 1929. He claimed that the linkage of agriculture with industry would reduce the cost to both sectors of foodstuffs and manufactured goods.[89] Further, he argued that collectivized services in the socialist city would drastically cut the cost of provisioning, not only to the collectivity but also the individual. Since the experience of factory kitchens constructed in Moscow, Leningrad, and Ivanovo-Vozheskensk had already proved this with respect to food, Sabsovich felt confident that similar economies would be achieved by collectivizing laundries and other facilities. Beyond this, he laid great stress on the increases in gross productivity to be achieved by enrolling the female population into economically productive work and on gains in the productivity of labor to be brought about thanks to the impact of improved conditions of life. Together, these factors would more than cover the initial investment and could, over the long run, cut back the cost of housing the population by one-half to two-thirds.

That Sabsovich did not bother to work out a more detailed budget for his proposals attests to his belief that his argument was so obviously correct as to make superfluous any more meticulous defense. The apparently successful implementation of antiurban ideas at the new community adjoining the Dneprostroi dam and at other settlements around the country, combined with the uncritical optimism prevailing during the first two years of the Plan, no doubt encouraged this attitude. By 1930, though, the overheated economy was showing serious signs of strain. Costs had to be reduced to the barest minimum, which in turn generated a desperate need for a more solid defense of the economics of antiurbanism. Sabsovich attempted to provide just this in a fairly detailed analysis of the problem published in 1930. Here for the first time an antiurbanist put actual figures on his claims. Here, too, he revealed that the key factor reducing costs would be the employment of women. With a higher proportion of the total community in the factory, he argued, one could reduce the population of each settlement from his earlier projection of sixty thousand down to fifteen to eighteen thousand.[90]

Meanwhile, the idea of putting a price tag on utopia had caught the imagination of the influential *Gosplan* economist Stanislav Strumilin, who promptly drafted an extended study on the financial aspects of the socialist city, which was published in the May 1930 number of the journal of the State Planning Agency.[91] By now a convinced believer in the antiurban dream, Strumilin did not challenge Sabsovich's claims so much as refine them. Indeed, his argument follows point by point that presented by Sabsovich a few months earlier, the major alterations being the addition of precise data drawn from Strumilin's own volume on *The Workers' Way of Life in Figures*[92] and a few points that had emerged in the course of a recent debate on antiurbanism among specialists involved in drafting the national economic plans.

On the basis of the actual experience with the "anti-cities" under construction at Stalingrad and with the newly formed state collective farm, "The Giant," Strumilin projected the optimal population for an agro-industrial settlement to be between twenty and sixty thousand. The towns of Novo-Kuznetsk and Shcheglovsk, at one hundred ten thousand and one hundred thousand, respectively, and the Gosplan's newly established standard figure of one hundred thousand he considered to press the absolute maximum.[93] Strumilin admitted that the initial expense of housing and basic facilities in the ideal city would exceed the present norm of eight hundred rubles per capita, but calculated that for a community of forty two thousand five hundred, the cost of producing food would be a twelfth of the existing norm in Moscow, and that heating, transportation, and a series of similar expenses would drop by like proportions. Adding the increased productivity of labor, the higher percentage of the labor force employed, and several other external factors, he arrived at a total long-term cost that was thirty eight percent of what it would have been had the same population and industries been placed in an existing metropolis.[94] Strumilin rested his case. The utter practicality of the socialist anti-city would carry the day against those who would "discredit the very idea of socialist construction in this sphere."[95]

VISION AND REALITY

Or would it? The antiurbanists could muster impressive evidence in support of the contention that their program was no visionary abstraction but a working blueprint for a world that was already coming into being. Doubtless, such evidence carried weight with many in their audience, but in the last analysis its chief function was to strengthen in the antiurbanists themselves the conviction that their new faith was not a cry for what *should* be but for what inescapably *would* be.

It is worth noting, however, that this type of argumentation became increasingly common as the Five-Year Plan wore on. In 1929 Sabsovich could pass down his revelations with scant concern for establishing their correctness on the basis of precise data. A year later, not only he but most of his supporters were culling economic and social statistics for evidence that the New Jerusalem was at hand. Okhitovich alone of the leading antiurbanists did not succumb to this urge, but stood fast in his belief that his theories required no further evidence in their support.

Does this indicate that the antiurbanists' hopes were, after all, quite unrealistic and that they were themselves increasingly conscious of this? The way in which they seem deliberately to have closed their eyes to certain crucial aspects of the world around them makes it hard to escape this conclusion.

How else could Strumilin, one of the economists best acquainted with the Five-Year Plan, have permitted himself to pretend in 1930 that the plan's recently expanded program for capital goods could be achieved while at the same time increasing household expenditures? To be sure, this had been assumed in the original plan approved in 1929, but by 1930 it had ceased to be so obvious and was, in fact, a point requiring explanation.[96]

Yet in Strumilin's calculations, as well as those by Sabsovich, Miliutin, and a number of others, he continued blithely to assume that savings effected through the introduction of communal facilities and the presence of two wage-earners in a family would automatically be passed on to consumers rather than be plowed back into capital investment by the state. The antiurbanists' expectation that the benefits of electrical technology would be passed at once to the consumer was based on the same assumption at a time when the press was filled with complaints over the scarcity of investment capital for producer goods.

It may well have been genuine naïveté that pervaded the thinking of those advocates of linear planning who refused to place a price on the capital investment in roads, railroads, and equipment that their proposal required. Blinded, perhaps, by their assumption that energy would henceforth be available in unlimited amounts and without cost, they might well have simply assumed that the high initial expenses would be more than offset by long-term savings. But if they can be given the benefit of the doubt on this point, it is inconceivable that the visionary planners could have completely missed the ample publicity being given to the new rail lines then under construction, lines that would place Moscow and other major centers more firmly than ever at the hub of a centripetal national network of transportation.

Most glaring of all was the systematic refusal of antiurbanists of every stripe to take serious cognizance of the massive urbanization taking place before their eyes. As late as 1926, the percentage of the Soviet population living in cities had not surpassed 1913 levels for the Russian Empire (18 percent), but over the next half decade a veritable flood of immigrants poured into cities large and small. Nizhnii Novgorod (Gorkii), where Miliutin was toying with linear cities, trebled in population; Kharkov, where ideas akin to Sabsovich's were being applied at a suburban tractor factory, doubled; Stalingrad, which all antiurbanists avidly claimed as their own, reached half a million; and Magnitorgorsk, where "urbanists" and "disurbanists" were contending, had already attained a population (one hundred forty-six thousand) in excess of what the reformers considered acceptable.[97] It was well and good for the utopians to point out that urbanization was proceeding most swiftly in towns with populations of only ten thousand to twenty thousand, and that the old centers were becoming relatively less important as new regions were being opened to settlement. But to define a great center like Moscow as a dying city was blatantly disingenuous: during the cultural revolution its population burgeoned from two to nearly four million persons.[98]

Reality was cancelling out utopia, and the utopians knew it. Sabsovich wrote a whole essay on the subject,[99] and a disciple of his, B. Strogova, complained bitterly about the shantytowns sprouting up on the periphery of Moscow like Latin American *barriadas*.[100] Yet, for all this, the theoreticians and planners did not really face up to the urban migration. They never attempted openly to assess its causes, let alone to consider its implications for their theories. To do so would have been fatal, just as it would have been fatal for them to acknowledge fully the costliness of their proposals or the Five-Year Plan's stress on forced nonconsumption.

To face squarely the urban migration would have required the antiurbanists to acknowledge that the mass of peasants trudging with their bundles from the Kiev and Kazan railroad stations had been driven to the metropolis by a force more fundamental and universal than their own optimistic theories, namely, by the desire of the rural poor everywhere to seek jobs and a better life in the city. This they could not possibly accept, neither as Communists nor as participants in that much broader movement of European intellectuals who, from the Enlightenment down to our own century, have believed the modern industrial city to be a transitory evil fated over time to wither in favor of some rural or rural-urban utopia.[101] Rather than confront evidence that challenged their entire teleological system, the antiurbanists increasingly heaped the blame for their troubles on the Soviet government. At their mildest, such planners would chide drafters of the Five-Year Plan for their failure in 1926 and 1927 to consider the impact of new industries upon cities and on housing resources.[102] In their more outspoken moods—which were frequent—they would criticize proposals to build a subway in Moscow, a "city without a future,"[103] belittle continued development of Moscow along the lines of the "urbanistic and bourgeois plan for a Great Moscow" devised as recently as 1925,[104] and flail the Five-Year Plan as a whole for designating so much of the new construction money for existing major centers and for projects devoid of revolutionary vision. As one spokesman put it, "Our construction of cities (and among them the new ones) is shot through with a petit bourgeois spirit of the most banal of banal sorts."[105]

Such statements attest to the utter deterioration of that degree of rapport that had existed between visionary theorists and the Party at the outset of the cultural revolution. Back in 1929, the planners had been in revolt against certain national programs, but they were in substantial agreement with others, notably those founded on a belief in the possibility of an immediate and total transformation of Soviet life. It was on this point that the Party and planners came to diverge by mid-1930.

In seeking to assign responsibility for this split, it must be recognized that there had been an unresolved tension within the Party itself between the desire to leap headlong into a utopian future and the need to build up all those human and material resources without which Russia would not meet even the minimum needs of the present. Visionary planners had never been overly concerned with this last need, and yet during 1930 it emerged as the Party's first priority. As this happened, the utopian strain within the Party's counsels withered and died.

This put the antiurbanists in the untenable position of continually reminding the Party of positions it had once endorsed but had subsequently rejected. The Party found this acutely embarrassing and set out at once to discredit the source of its irritation. *Pravda* began the attack in a brief statement in its May Day issue of 1930. It held up to ridicule both Sabsovich personally and the "disurbanists" generally for proposing to turn the Russian worker into a bad copy of the "aristocrats of German labor."[106] This was not yet an official denunciation, however, and in tone it did not even equal the biting invective the antiurbanists had been directing against the official policies. By May 16, though, the Central Committee had had a chance to look into the matter, and on that day it concluded that the utopians had to be called to task:

> The Central Committee observes that along with the growth of the movement for a socialist way of life there is a group of extraordinarily ill-founded, semi-fanatical and therefore extremely harmful attempts of certain comrades [Iu. Larin, Sabsovich, etc.] in one jump to leap all the barriers on the road to the socialist reconstruction of the way of life, [barriers] which are rooted . . . in the economic and cultural backwardness of the country. . . .[107]

Such irresponsible notions must be put aside, the Central Committee declared, for they were the work of "opportunists" and "leftist phrasemongers" bent upon luring the nation into squandering its precious resources.

This decree did not suffice to quell antiurbanism, which for several more months continued to be discussed quite openly. In October 1930 the campaign against the visionary planners took a new turn when they were accused of being linked with a number of politically unacceptable philosophies and groups. The most damaging of these was the accusation that the planners were heirs to an anti-Bolshevik current associated with the name of Alexander Chaianov, a former member of the Socialist Revolutionary Party. Chaianov, an agricultural economist by profession, was said to have called repeatedly for the establishment of an all-peasant *Sovnarkom* in the USSR.[108]

To be tarred with the brush of "Chaianovism" in 1930 was indeed serious, for it meant that one advocated a kind of anarchist "peasant democracy." All that remained was to blame these deparate wreckers for the widespread failure of town planners to meet their 1930 quotas, which was done in November of the same year.[109]

After this, Kaganovich's attack at the Plenum meeting of the Party in June 1931 was anticlimatic. It was not without importance, however: here for the first time a Party spokesman came out squarely in favor of large cities as against the small towns and linear settlements of the antiurbanists. As Kaganovich explained, Russia's cities had become "socialist" the moment power was transferred to the Bolshevik government in 1917.[110] Accordingly, to talk of socialism as being incompatible with urban life was absurd. After all, who could deny that the revolution had been made in the cities?

> Our cities played an extensive part in the revolution; they have won the adherence of the peasant masses in the historical struggle for communism. This is primarily true of the large cities, such as Leningrad and Moscow. And therefore the nonsense regarding the reduction, or the self-abolition, of the large centers is not worth serious attention.[111]

Stalin put it more directly when he affirmed "the leading role of the socialist city vis-à-vis the petit bourgeois village."[112] By this point, the antiurbanist vision was already dead.

What, if any, was the long-term impact of the radical planners' work?

By 1934 it appeared that the movement was quite forgotten. Ginsburg turned his back on the current entirely, Strumilin had returned to his technical functions, and Okhitovich was devoting his days to adapting Chernyshevskii's utopian novel *What Is To Be Done* for the stage. [113] Occasional denunciations of antiurban ideas still rang in the press, but now the concern of the day was to transform Moscow into a world capital with a population of five million. The so-called Stalin Plan for Moscow, approved in July 1935, transformed the city into a great metropolis, complete with wide access boulevards lined with huge apartment complexes of fourteen stories each. [114] Seeing these today, one suspects that the authors of the Stalin Plan were greatly relieved at having been freed of the need to pay obeisance to the utopian and anarchistic side of Marxism-Leninism.

At the same time, the antiurbanist decentralizers had left a dual legacy that endured throughout the otherwise centralizing era of Stalinism and in modified form has persisted down to our own day. They were the first to call for an outright prohibition on further construction in large cities, a demand to which the Party partially acquiesced in 1932 when it banned the construction of major new factories within Moscow proper. This edict, though it came on the heels of the collapse of antiurbanism as a movement, opened a way for the planning agencies—Giprogor, Giprograd, etc.—to apply certain of the ideas advanced by the utopians, if only in limited contexts. This was further encouraged the arrival in the USSR in October 1930 of two Pullman coaches full of German and Swiss town planners, including Hannes Mayer, Ernst May, and Hans Schmidt. [115] Even though antiurban utopianism was at that moment being subjected to scathing criticism, the German and Swiss planners were able to save at least some of its elements and to apply them at such towns as Perm, Nizhnii Kurinsk, and Birobidzhan. The plans were very much their own, but, because the Soviet utopians had taken inspiration in part from these very planners in the first place, their proposals retain many of the features that their more radical Soviet disciples had pushed to extremes. Encouraged in part by the Germans' success, a large group of moderate Soviet planners carried out numerous projects in the same vein. [116]

The other side of the visionary planners' legacy was negative, for their failure discredited the romantic naturalism for which they had stood. Henceforth, town planners in the Soviet Union had to demonstrate that they were above such Rousseauian idylls—that they were, like the Germans, hard-headed and "scientific." Through new programs for training city planners that were instituted at the time, these qualities were instilled in the younger Soviet planners. Only with the emergence of the most recent generation of planners, who have no fear of being tainted by the discredited ideals of the cultural revolution, has the work of reevaluating this visionary movement begun.

The Cultural Revolution and Western Understanding of the Soviet System

Jerry F. Hough

The First Five-Year Plan has been the center of great scholarly attention in the West, but the main focus of interest has been the transformation in the economic realm—the industrialization and collectivization drives. In the cultural, intellectual, and scientific spheres, as Sheila Fitzpatrick points out, scholars have emphasized the increased repression and political constraints of the First Five-Year Plan period, and, as a consequence, they have seen basic continuity with the even further repression characteristic of the later Stalin years. Indeed, from this perspective, the reemphasis on authority and the revival of the old cultural authorities in the Second Five-Year Plan period could be interpreted as essentially a continuation of the process initiated with the Shakhty trial of 1928—the movement toward an authoritarian regime in all senses of the term.

Although the late 1920s and early 1930s must have seemed an exhilirating period of freedom—in fact, of newly found freedom—for many of the radicals and dreamers who were "unleashed," no one would or could deny that these years involved increased repression for a much larger number of intellectuals. The cultural revolution did constitute the first break—what Joravsky would call "the great break"—with the NEP policy of inconsistent but often permissive censorship and uneasy toleration of intellectual diversity, and the fate of both traditional and radical rural sociologists during the cultural revolution was an all too clear indication of what might happen when the regime believed its central interests were at stake.

Nevertheless, the history of the Soviet Union cannot be limited to a history of the regime's censorship policy and its purges. The content of substantive policies, the values expressed in them, the interests that they satisfied and failed to satisfy—these too must be part of the political chronicle of the Soviet period, including the Stalin years. And if the subject of debate is the basic nature of the system, its inner dynamism, and even the structure of power within it, the question of the nature and source of substantive policies is a crucial one.

In the realm of substantive social and cultural policy, it is clear that we cannot speak of continuity through the Stalin period along a basic line established in 1927–28. The early and mid-thirties saw a second "great break"—a "Great Retreat," in Nicholas Timasheff's phrase.[1] In field after field, the regime not only repressed the radical Marxists, but also repudiated the programs with which they were associated. Wage egalitarianism was denounced, and the authority and status of professional and managerial personnel were strengthened. For the first time, large numbers of persons with higher education were admitted into the Party, while the Party purge of 1932–33 removed a large part of the big worker-peasant intake of previous years. Children of white-collar parents found it easier to enter higher education. Harassment of those formerly called "bourgeois specialists" diminished. The school curriculum became more traditional, academic standards were raised, and discipline was reemphasized. In history traditional Russian heroes—even some of the Tsars—returned to relative favor; in literature and art the Russian realists of the nineteenth century were extolled; in psychology the renowned non-Marxist Pavlov—an outspoken critic of the regime in the 1920s—was acclaimed. The destruction of churches and personal harassment of believers gave way to a calmer hostility. The Party leadership itself, now eager to be "cultured" (kul'turnyi) unconsciously began to assimilate many of the values of the old intelligentsia.

It is, of course, no new discovery that a change of policy occurred after 1931 in the social and cultural realm. The "Great Retreat" is one of the most discussed phenomena of the Stalin era, and many of the foremost analysts of the Soviet experience have tried to explain it. Trotskii spoke of the "revolution betrayed" by the bureaucracy and the enshrinement of the bureaucrat's middle-class values,[2] and Timasheff seemed to agree, although less pejoratively, in his reference to "the decline of Communism".[3] Barrington Moore and Merle Fainsod, perhaps influenced by Talcott Parsons, wrote of "the dilemmas of power" and of "the imperatives of industrialization."[4]

Yet, for all the discussion of the Great Retreat, none of the Western literature seriously asks the question, retreat from what? The period of the New Economic Policy of the 1920s was far from a period of revolutionary militance and insistence on ideological purity in terms of Party policy— and indeed the literature that sees the 1930s as an ideological retreat treats NEP in very much the same way. Whatever the degree of wage egalitarianism in the state enterprises during NEP, Lenin himself had instituted a system of privileges for the "bourgeois specialists"; and the social spectrum must also include the Nepmen, whose prosperity from private entrepreneurial activity was tolerated by the regime. Moreover, by 1921 the power of the trade union to defend the workers had already been defined in quite narrow terms, and, as Lenin and later Trotskii complained, the influx of Communists into important administrative positions had scarcely put an end to what they called "bureaucratism"—that is, a hierarchy of authority and status.

Throughout the 1920s, Marxist radicals attacked the cultural administration of Narkompros (the People's Commissariat of Enlightenment) for being too eclectic in its toleration of different art forms, including the most traditional, and, worst of all, for surreptitiously preserving the hated "bourgeois" gymnasium as the basic secondary school under a new name. And, it must be said, there was considerable justice in these criticisms. In addition, higher education continued to be dominated by "bourgeois scholars," and, despite some effort to the contrary, the proletarian component in institutions of higher education was in the 15–20 percent range during most of the twenties and had risen only to 25.4 percent in the 1927–28 school year.[5]

The central contribution of this book is, of course, to remind us that there was in fact reason to speak of a Great Retreat—that between NEP and the high Stalin years there was a distinctive period of militancy, imposition of Marxist orthodoxy, and revolutionary utopianism in the cultural-social realm. The "retreat" of the 1930s was, first and foremost, a retreat from the policies of the First Five-Year Plan period, rather than from the policies followed for the greater part of the 1920s.

It is always unfortunate when any major historical phenomenon slips from the view of historians, and for this reason alone a study of the First Five-Year Plan cultural revolution is a valuable contribution to our knowledge. In this case, however, the gap in the Western literature is not a trivial one, for the failure to understand the discontinuities between the First Five-Year Plan period and the Second has confused a number of extremely important issues in the interpretation of Soviet history. This confusion, moreover, has been a key element in the acceptance of a totalitarian model that distorts our understanding of the Stalin period almost as much as it does the years after Stalin's death.

I

As emphasized in the earlier essays of this volume (and in the discussion at the conference at which they were originally presented), the first consequence of the neglect of the cultural revolution has been a major oversimplification in the conventional analysis of "Stalin's revolution from above." By focussing on the industrialization-collectivization decision and on the factional struggle associated with it, one can easily form the impression that the only actors were a very small number of oligarchs and that the key decisions reflected the values of a tiny handful of men (maybe only one) in the face of an unexpected crisis. In this perspective, the society-state relationship is seen entirely in "we-they" terms—as an inert and unsuspecting society subjected to a Third Revolution by ruthless men who had gained unrestricted control of the political apparatus. Indeed, to the extent that the focus really is on the collectivization decision alone and that that decision is thought to have flowed from mistaken assumptions about the grain crisis, the entire "revolution from above" takes on a peculiarly arbitrary character.

As the conflicts of the cultural revolution demonstrate, however, NEP "society" itself was quite varied in character, containing significant numbers of radicals and militants as well as moderates and conservatives on nearly all policy questions. One need not be a Marxist to recognize that many workers must have felt suspicion and hostility toward bourgeois specialists and Nepmen, and that many poor peasants must have had a similar attitude toward more well-to-do peasants and rural tradesmen. Aside from class antagonisms in the countryside itself, many city-dwellers must have deeply distrusted the kulaks and been more than willing to interpret any grain shortage in terms of a conspiracy. Millions of unemployed urban workers and city-oriented rural youth yearned for the jobs that rapid industrialization would bring. And then there were those who disdained "bourgeois culture" in one form or another and who were determined to be "modern" in the Marxist sense of the term.

Surely it would be wildly misleading to suggest that Stalin was a passive barometer who was simply responding to societal pressures for change—even Party pressures for change—when he launched the Third Revolution. But if we are to understand the late twenties and early thirties, it would be equally wrong to assume that these pressures were irrelevant. As Adam Ulam emphasized twenty years ago,[6] Communist parties have succeeded in winning power not in advanced industrial countries, as their own ideology would suggest, but in countries at an early stage of industrialization. The explanation for this paradox must be found, Ulam argued, in the appeal that militant Marxism holds for many potentially modernizing elements in such countries—people who stand to benefit from industrial development and who unconsciously seek an ideology that posits both the inevitability of this development and the ultimate resolution of all discomforts associated with it.

If the Communist party's victory in Russia (victory not only in October, but in the Civil War that followed) must be understood in the terms Ulam suggests, and if for these reasons more of the country's modernizers were drawn to the Party after the revolution, then any treatment of the Third Revolution as a totally alien development ignores the societal forces that produced the revolution itself. The militants of the cultural revolution were an important part of NEP society, and nearly every Communist and a great number of young non-Communists shared, with varying degrees of ambivalence, the feelings they expressed. At least in their promotion of industrialization, they also had very considerable support even from the more sober-minded "practical" proponents of industrialization. By losing sight of much of the social dynamics of the period, we have isolated the political leadership from the social setting to which at least in some measure it was responding.

A second major consequence of the blurring of distinctions between the First Five-Year Plan period and the years that followed has been a deeply flawed conceptualization of Stalinism. The era has most often been analyzed in terms of the totalitarian model, which serves to highlight those features of the Stalinist system (and others like it) that are thought to distinguish it from more traditional types of authoritarian regime. In most variants of the model, the first distinguishing feature of the totalitarian system is the determination of the political leader to transform society and human nature on the basis of his ideological premises, while the second is his determination to institute an ever-tightening, all-encompassing network of controls in order to emancipate himself from all societal pressures and influences, including those coming from either a broadly or narrowly defined elite. In arguing that the totalitarian model provides a reasonable (if, of course, oversimplified) approximation of the Stalin regime, scholars point to the Third Revolution and its spirit of transformation as evidence of the first feature of the model, and to the growing restrictions on the expression of ideas and on other types of freedom, which reached a peak in the last years of Stalin's life, as evidence of the second.

Without any question, the Soviet political system did become progressively more authoritarian as Stalin aged (though there was some ebb and flow in the application of pressure, most notably during World War II). To be sure, the number of deaths resulting from the 1937–38 purge has often been grossly exaggerated,[7] and Hannah Arendt's image of a completely terrorized and atomized society has almost no relationship to the reality of the time. (The regime's "mobilization" program was really an unprecedented attempt to integrate, not atomize, a vast number of inexperienced workers and former peasants into a rapidly expanding urban sector.) Nevertheless, even if the picture of purge and terror embedded in the totalitarian model is discounted to a considerable degree, we are still left with the unquestionable fact that intellectuals and policy-oriented professionals in particular had to operate under increasingly rigid restrictions, and that criticism of the dictator and his basic political system became dangerous in the extreme. After the 1937–38 purge, the officials at the very top of the system must have felt a special sense of insecurity—as indeed, according to Khrushchev, they did.

Yet the scholarly literature speaks not simply of a system becoming more authoritarian, but of one becoming totalitarian. It emphasizes that the political leadership was engaged in a transformation of society and human nature on the basis of its ideological values and its self-imposed mission to prepare the way for the ultimate Communist stage of history. It is this image that needs to be reexamined. While the cultural revolution and other policies of the First Five-Year Plan period did indeed embody the transforming spirit suggested by the totalitarian model, much of this spirit (except that incorporated in the continuing drive to promote industrialization) disappeared with the repudiation of cultural revolution. The drive to transform man and society became in large part a drive to industrialize the country and to inculcate the values needed for the population to adjust to industrial society and to accept the legitimacy of the political system.

With the destruction of the old revolutionaries (and many of the young spokesmen of the cultural revolution) in the purge of 1937–38, the workers and peasants who had surged into higher educational establishments during the cultural revolution became the core of the "Class of 1938," which gained most from the holocaust. But, as Sheila Fitzpatrick pointed out, these men, like workers virtually everywhere, were culturally conservative, highly valuing respectability and *kul'turnost'*, and, paradoxically, their rise only solidified the support for the policy that brought the cultural revolution to an end. While many of the policies of the "Great Retreat" could be explained as the product of the "imperatives of industrialization," the regime went well beyond any requirements for the establishment of a well-functioning industrial order in its accomodation to the desire of the "new class" for status and rewards. Particularly in the postwar period, as Vera Dunham has shown in rich detail, even the yearning of this group for such symbols of middle-class respectability as lace curtains was given recognition in the literature of the time—a major change from the more austere Communist ethos of the 1920s and the First Five-Year Plan period.[8]

In short, as we contemplate the striking discontinuities in policy that occurred in the late 1920s and early 1930s, it becomes painfully clear that at no single time during the Stalin period did the Soviet Union actually correspond to the totalitarian model. The model's emphasis upon an ideologically determined drive to transform society applies reasonably well to the First Five-Year Plan period; and the emphasis upon tightening of control fits well with the authoritarianism and ideological rigidity of the latter Stalin years. However, taken together, the two major aspects of the model are an anachronistic combination. More important, they are essentially an inconsistent combination in human terms, for the type of person necessary to administer and carry through a continuous revolutionary transformation is too undisciplined and disrespectful to fit easily within— or be tolerated by—a system with rigid controls and an abhorrence of experimentation. This inconsistency is not a minor flaw in the totalitarian model, for the very persuasiveness of the model as an explanatory tool for the Stalin era has depended on it. It has only been this inconsistency that has permitted such a wide and diverse range of phenomena to fit the model so well.

II

If we focus upon the fact that there was an ideologically infused revolution in the cultural-social realm, which, to a large extent, was abandoned in the first half of the 1930s, a series of more specific problems also arise that have not been properly considered by Western historians. In the first place, what are the implications of the cultural revolution and its reversal for our understanding of Politburo-level politics and the power position of Stalin during this period?

It would be possible to interpret the cultural revolution as a purely tactical move by Stalin in his struggle against the Right Opposition, or as a reflection of Stalin's own class-war convictions (also expressed in the economic and foreign policy of the period), or as a result of an initiative taken by other members of the elite to apply to the cultural sphere slogans developed in policy areas in which Stalin had a more direct interest. In order to choose between these alternate interpretations with any assurance, we would need far better access to primary sources than we have at present. But what we can do, in the present state of our knowledge, is consider the implications of the various interpretations of Stalin's relationship to the cultural revolution for our analysis of the subsequent Great Retreat. We should realize that our explanation of the first phenomenon should be consistent with our explanation of the second.

In practice, such consistency has not always been achieved. Stalin's actions in the late 1920s have often been explained not in terms of ideological conviction but of political manipulation. The General Secretary is described as trying to outmaneuver the Right, making cynical use of the radicals to suppress the non-Marxists, manufacturing a war scare to discredit the opposition and/or convince the population of the need for sacrifices, and so on. Yet in the standard accounts of Politburo conflicts *circa* 1934, we find a quite different analysis of Stalin's political behavior and motivation. In regard to this period, Stalin is often described as taking an implacably hard-line position as a matter of deep conviction, only to be partially defeated by a faction headed by Kirov that was advocating more conciliatory policies.

Whatever Stalin's original attitude to the cultural revolution, the 1931–32 reversal of policy creates enormous difficulties for the view that Stalin was defeated by Kirov in 1934. The difficulties essentially involve the timing of the supposed conflict between Stalin and a "moderate opposition." It is hard to see why Kirov or anyone else should have challenged Stalin on such a platform in 1934, since in most realms (except foreign affairs) the reversal of policy was already in full swing. Even in the industrial sphere, the indicators of the Second Five-Year Plan were more realistic. In agriculture, the decision to recognize the private plot meant that collectivization was to be limited for the time being to the production of grain and technical crops.[9]

One could try to preserve the Kirov hypothesis by postulating that the defeat of Stalin occurred in 1931 rather than 1934,[10] but this solution too has serious problems. Certainly Stalin went out of his way to identify himself personally with the 1931 reversal of attitude toward the bourgeois specialists, to announce and claim credit for the new social and educational policies introduced from 1931, and even to involve himself in the disciplining of the Communist intellectuals through his letter to *Proletarskaia revoliutsiia*. Moreover, after Stalin had gained greater freedom of action with the purge of 1937, he never returned to the policies of the cultural revolution. (The comparison with Mao is instructive.)

Just as the collectivization decision seems to have been an unanticipated response to an unexpected grain crisis, so it may well be that the Great Retreat was an unanticipated response to the unexpected chaos of the First Five-Year Plan period—and to the discovery that militant agents of social transformation are likely to be as disrespectful of any new Communist establishment as they were of the old bourgeois one, and that they are wildly impractical in their demands for funds.

Nevertheless, there must have been a "politics" of this process of discovery. It would seem plausible to identify Molotov—Moscow secretary and Central Committee secretary from 1928 through 1930—as a leading protagonist and defender of the cultural revolution. On the other hand, top economic administrators like Ordzhonikidze and Kuibyshev might reasonably be expected to push for an end to "impracticality" and for the adoption of social policies that benefitted the managerial personnel. The "industrialists" attitudes may well have been shared by Kaganovich, given his later fifteen-year tenure as chief administrator of Soviet heavy industry. The introduction of the first Great Retreat policies closely followed Molotov's replacement as Moscow and Central Committee secretary by Kaganovich. (The hypothesis about Molotov's backing of the cultural revolution tends to be supported by the fact that from 1930 he was the Politburo's top foreign policy expert, and at Comintern level Soviet foreign policy retained a "class-war" content well after 1931, even when it was producing disastrous results in Germany.[11])

But this is scarcely the place to pretend to definitive conclusions about conflicts within the Politburo in the 1930s. We should, however, be aware that more serious scholarly study of politics within the Stalinist leadership might extend and indeed change the picture established forty years ago by Nicolaevsky's stimulating but unfortunately undocumentable reports in *Sotsialisticheskii vestnik*. Problems of access aside, there are some basic political facts that can and ought to be elucidated. We have not even bothered to sort out the official responsibilties of the various Central Committee secretaries and the deputy chairmen of the Council of People's Commissars during the late 1920s and the 1930s. As soon as we recognize the discontinuity of policy in the early 1930s, the need for an examination of the policies associated with it becomes abundantly clear.

The second set of problems suggested by an awareness of the cultural revolution and its repudiation revolves around the relationship of "state" and "society" in the Stalin period. As a number of essays in this volume have shown, the Party leadership was not acting in a social vacuum. One could contend that the partial coincidence between Party policy and the desires of many societal elements is basically irrelevant—that Stalin was responsive to no societal pressures and that it was happenstance that somebody turned out to be pleased with some of his policies—but such a view is difficult to sustain.

The exercise of political power is not limited to the casting of a ballot or the formation of a pressure group. A dissatisfied peasantry can provide a well-nigh impenetrable milieu for successful guerrilla action, and, in principle, it should be as difficult to herd peasants into collective farms as into strategic hamlets. Of course, force and coercion can be applied, but it must be applied by real people with real feelings and interests. "Instruments of control" can wither away—as, in fact, they have done in many revolutionary situations. When a political leadership takes steps that please the young, the talented, and the ambitious (the persons who must invariably provide the spearhead if any revolutionary movement is to be successful), when it provides them with upward mobility into the managerial-professional strata and rewards them once there, it is unreasonable to deny that political power is being recognized by the leadership and is producing at least an anticipatory response.

To be sure, one could put the label of "bureaucrats" upon the administrative-professional personnel of the Stalin period, forget about the rapidly growing skilled labor force, and see these "bureaucrats" as part of the state that was dominating and transforming society. Yet, if this is done, we should recognize that we have changed the basic assumptions of the classic totalitarian model, for that model included the professional-managerial personnel among the acted-upon rather than among the shakers of society.

Moreover, if the professional-managerial strata are included within the "state," the meaning of that term has been stretched virtually beyond recognition. Barrington Moore is surely right in saying that in any society industrialization is originally imposed on an unsympathetic and often hostile majority by a relatively small minority.[12] (Even 20 percent of the population is still a relatively small minority.) Without doubt, such a generalization is valid in the Soviet case. The fact that the pro-industrializing minority—the managers, the professionals, the skilled workers, and even many of the young peasants streaming into the city to become unskilled workers—were employed by the government does not make them different in kind from industrializing minorities in other countries.

Of course, even though Stalin functioned within a social context and may have perceived the need to ally himself with and respond to societal forces, he clearly did not need to function as an accommodating mediator or broker among the range of societal forces. By responding to a number of pressures from key groups, he "bought" the ability to suppress many other pressures—as well as many individuals associated with them. (His reign, like that of many authoritarian rulers, demonstrated once more that responsiveness to many of the values and desires of a broad societal group or groups does not necessarily mean civil rights for individuals within the group.)

It must also be remembered that Stalin's regime was an increasingly authoritarian one. Even in areas such as city planning, where the final outcome of the changes of the early 1930s seems to have been a reasonable balance of the interests and values of the professionals within the field, the rigidity of later years often meant that new professional judgments had little opportunity to influence policy, and that even moderate and "respectable" experimentation became extremely difficult. Any new "imperatives of industrialization" that were learned in the last fifteen years of Stalin's life had to wait until 1954–55 before becoming the subject of serious policy-making.

The generalizations advanced here on the relationship of "state" and "society" are undoubtedly too sweeping. In reality, both during the cultural revolution and afterwards, this relationship was a complex and varying one. In a specialized field such as psychoneurology, for example, the enthusiasts and "militants" of cultural revolution tended to be professionals. In education, the revolutionary activists were not only professionals but young politicians with a pre-1928 institutional base in the Komsomol— and their presence, of course, gave cultural revolution a different configuration from that of psychoneurology. Similar distinctions need to be made in regard to the Great Retreat policies, whose impact was obviously different in the field of history (where the leadership wanted a partial refurbishing of old national heroes, a task for which Marxist historians were obviously unsuitable) than in rural sociology (where the leadership was peculiarly afraid of the results of any scholarly research, whatever the approach and methodology).

But we resort to inadequate generalizations primarily because we still have so much to learn. We know more about "society" in the Stalin period than we do about the divisions within the political leadership, but our knowledge on this subject is also very meager. Even for the years of the cultural revolution, there are many professions and policy areas that could not be discussed within the framework of a single book, and the last twenty years of the Stalin period have hardly been touched as far as serious historical research is concerned. David Joravsky's monumental work on Lysenko[13] is one of far too few recent works that indicate what can be done despite problems of documentation. Yet whatever picture emerges in detail after a comprehensive scholarly examination, it will certainly reveal a more complex "state-society" relationship than we have ever realized in the past. It will, we hope, provide the basis for a much better model of the Stalin regime than the totalitarian model has proven to be.

NOTES

Fitzpatrick: Editor's Introduction

1. Lenin's most widely cited comments on cultural revolution are in his article "O kooperatsii" (1923). A compilation has been made by G. Karpov, *Lenin o kul'turnoi revoliutsii* (Moscow, 1967).

2. The standard exposition of the concept is given in Stalin's speech to the Eighteenth Party Congress (1938), in I. V. Stalin, *Sochineniia* I (XIV), ed. Robert H. McNeal (Stanford, 1967), and elaborated in *Bol'shaia sovetskaia entsiklopediia* XXIV (2d ed., Moscow, 1953), pp. 364–66. For a recent theoretical discussion, see M. P. Kim, "On cultural revolution as a general law of social development in the transitional period," in *Obshchie zakonomernosti perekhoda k sotsializmu i osobennosti ikh proiavlenii v raznykh stranakh* (Moscow, 1960).

3. The pioneering work was Max Eastman's *Artists in Uniform*, first published in 1934. Notable monographic studies are E. J. Brown, *The Proletarian Episode in Russian Literature, 1928–1932* (New York, 1953); David Joravsky, *Soviet Marxism and Natural Science, 1917–1932* (London, 1961); and Loren R. Graham, *The Soviet Academy of Sciences and the Communist Party, 1927–1932* (Princeton, 1967).

4. There are, of course, a number of works on Stalin and the purges. But for the student of Soviet society, the major Western studies remain A. Inkeles and R. Bauer, *The Soviet Citizen* (Cambridge, Mass., 1959), based on data of the Harvard refugee project, and Merle Fainsod, *Smolensk under Soviet Rule* (London, 1958), based on data from the Smolensk Archives.

Fitzpatrick: Cultural Revolution as Class War

1. Quoted *Narodnoe prosveshchenie*, 1928 no. 1, p. 26 (Stalin, political report of the Central Committee, Fifteenth Party Congress).

2. Quoted ibid., p. 7 (Rykov's report on the Five-Year Plan), and p. 14 (Molotov's report on work in the countryside).

3. *Pravda*, 30 November 1927, p. 1.

4. Roy A. Medvedev, *Let History Judge. The Origins and Consequences of Stalinism* (New York: 1971), p. 112.

5. The meeting was held in Moscow 30 May–3 June 1928 under sponsorship of the agitprop department, with other cultural and educational figures as invited guests. The full stenogram is in B. Olkhovyi, ed., *Zadachi agitatsii, propagandy i kul'turnogo stroitel'stva* (Moscow–Leningrad, 1928). Krinitskii's speech was also published separately as A. I. Krinitskii, *Osnovnye zadachi agitatsii, propagandy i kul'turnogo stroitel'stva* (Moscow–Leningrad, 1928). The quotations here are from

Krinitskii, op.cit., pp. 10, 17; *Pravda*, 8 June 1928, p. 5; *Kommunisticheskaia revoliutsiia*, 1928 no. 17–18, p.166.
   6. See Lutchenko, in *Voprosy istorii KPSS*, 1966 no. 2, p. 33.
   7. Kaganovich, *XVI syezd VKP(b)*. *Stenograficheskii otchet* I (Moscow, 1935), p.147.
   8. *Torgovo-promyshlennaia gazeta*, 11 March 1928, p.2 (Rykov); *Pravda*, 30 March 1928, p.3 (Kuibyshev); *Pravda*, 28 March 1928, p.1 (Ordzhonikidze). For the Ordzhonikidze reference, I am indebted to Kendall Bailes.
   9. Lutchenko, loc.cit.; Stalin, speech in *XVI syezd VKP(b)*. *Stenograficheskii otchet* I (Moscow, 1931), p. 293.
   10. On Tomskii's attack, see Lunacharskii in *Pravda*, 2 June 1928, p.7, and Gastev in *Pravda*, 7 June 1928, p.2.
   11. Bukharin, "The proletariat and questions of artistic policy," *Krasnaia nov'*, 1925 no. 4, p. 266.
   12. See, for example, Bukharin's speech in *Sud'by sovremennoi intelligentsii* (Moscow, 1925), p.27.
   13. "A class trial," *Pravda*, 19 May 1928, p.1.
   14. Krinitskii, op.cit., p.79.
   15. A. Avtorkhanov, *Stalin and the Soviet Communist Party* (London, 1959), p.29.
   16. The campaign against Sviderskii is described in detail in Sheila Fitzpatrick, "The emergence of Glaviskusstvo. Class war on the cultural front, Moscow 1928–29," *Soviet Studies*, October 1971.
   17. F. Vaganov, *Pravyi uklon v VKP(b) i ego razgrom (1928–30 gg.)* (Moscow, 1970), p.102.
   18. The exact date of Vyshinskii's appointment is not known, but he apparently began work in Narkompros in September (interview with Vyshinskii in *Pravda*, 25 September 1928, p.6).
   19. The volume edited by Khodorovskii, *Kakogo inzhenera nuzhny gotovit' nashi vtuzy* (Moscow, 1928), was a marshalling of specialist opinion in support of Narkompros's policy, which was currently under attack from Vesenkha. Khodorovskii's coeditor, P. S. Osadchii, was a witness and unindicted coconspirator in the "Industrial Party" trial, and several other contributors were accused or named during the Shakhty or Industrial Party trials. Vyshinskii described *Kakogo inzhenera* as one of "those historic documents on which investigation and subsequent prosecution in the affair of the Shakhti wreckers and the Industrial Party affair were based" (*Nauchnyi rabotnik*, 1930 no. 11–12, p. 25).
   20. *Komsomol'skaia pravda*, 15 November 1928, p.4.
   21. Conversation with Emil Ludwig on 13 December 1931, in I. V. Stalin, *Sochineniia* XIII (Moscow, 1951), p.121.
   22. Ibid., and comment on Communist literati (1925) in Stalin, *Sochineniia* VII (Moscow, 1947), pp. 42–43.
   23. For much of the NEP period, Bukharin was the Politburo's liaison with the Komsomol and spokesman on youth. However his lack of rapport with the Komsomol may be judged from his description of the typical Komsomol leader as an ignorant, manipulative little *apparatchik* (speech to Moscow Party conference, 1927, in *Krasnoe studenchestvo*, 1927–28 no. 11, p.32). As for the RAPP leaders,

Bukharin had not only disagreed with them but ridiculed them (see his "The proletariat and questions of artistic policy," *Krasnaia nov'*, 1925 no. 4).

24. *Vestnik Kommunisticheskoi Akademii*, 1929 no. 35–36, pp. 227 ff., 297 ff.

25. The new appointments of Bukharin and Kamenev were announced in *Komsomol'skaia pravda*, 1 June 1929, p. 4.

26. For evidence of Bukharin's development of tendencies to "technocratic thinking" in his new job, see Kendall E. Bailes, "The politics of technology: Stalin and technocratic thinking among Soviet engineers," *American Historical Review*, April 1974.

27. Such rumors are, by their nature, difficult to reconstruct. At the agitprop meeting in May 1928, Krinitskii suggested that Lunacharskii's interest in commercial profit for the Soviet film industry was "a mistaken transfer of NEP principles into the field of ideology" (Krinitskii, op. cit., p. 23). At a teachers' congress in 1929, Lunacharskii was obliged to give a long self-justification in answer to a question on his charging "fantastic" fees for public lectures (TsGAOR 5462/11/12, pp. 45–46). He was reprimanded by the Central Control Commission of the Party for holding up the Leningrad-Moscow express train to suit his own convenience (*Pravda*, 22 June 1929, p. 3). Other rumors concerned his wife (a stage and cinema actress), his contacts with the acting and literary world, his frequent trips abroad, and an unelucidated diamond smuggling scandal involving one of his or his wife's acquaintances.

28. See Loren R. Graham, *The Soviet Academy of Sciences and the Communist Party, 1927–1932* (Princeton, 1967), pp. 114–15. Bukharin was elected to the Academy in February 1929, Lunacharskii in January 1930.

29. T. H. Rigby, *Communist Party Membership in the U.S.S.R. 1917–1967* (Princeton, 1968), p. 116.

30. For examples, see Sheila Fitzpatrick, "The 'soft' line on culture and its enemies," *Slavic Review*, June 1974, which discusses the conflict between leadership policy toward the bourgeois specialists and Communist rank-and-file attitudes.

31. The average monthly salary of employees in the central administration of the RSFSR in the first quarter of 1926–27 was 150.95 rubles, as against 60.02 for workers in census industry (*Itogi desiatiletiia sovetskoi vlasti v tsifrakh 1917–1927* [Moscow, (1927)], p. 342). In 1925, after a double salary raise, university professors could earn 200–250 rubles a month by the customary practice of holding two to three jobs (each with a six-hour teaching load). But, as the professors complained, their salary "still remains lower than the salary of qualified specialists—engineers, chemists, agronomists, bank employees and so on—who work in the so-called productive commissariats" (*Nauchnyi rabotnik*, 1925 no. 1, p. 177).

32. A vivid picture of the cafe milieu, from a disapproving but fascinated RAPP perspective obviously based on personal observation, is given in V. Kirshon and A. Uspenskii's topical play *Konstantin Terekhin (Rzhavchina)* (Moscow, 1927).

33. For information on anti-Communist and other organizations in the schools, see E. Strogova in *Komsomol'skaia pravda*, 1 April 1928, p. 2; I. Chernia in *Kommunisticheskaia revoliutsiia*, 1928 no. 17–18; *Narodnoe prosveshchenie*, 1928 no. 5, pp. 25, 32, 39. On the Esenin cult, see *Upadochnoe nastroenie sredi molodezhi. Eseninshchina* (Moscow: Communist Academy, 1927), and M. Koriakov, "'Eseninshchina' and Soviet youth," *Vozrozhdenie* (Paris) XV (1951).

34. M. Gorev in *Izvestiia*, 13 June 1929, p.4; F. Oleshchuk in *Revoliutsiia i kul'tura*, 1928 no. 10 (31 May), p.21.
35. See report of Second Congress of Scientific Workers of the USSR, *Izvestiia*, 13 February 1927, pp. 3–4; and report of XIII All-Union Congress of Soviets (speeches of Pozern and Lezhava) in ibid., 17 April 1927, pp. 5–6.
36. A. Lunacharskii, "The intelligentsia and its place in socialist construction," *Revoliutsiia i kul'tura*, 1927 no. 1, p.32.
37. Loren R. Graham, *The Soviet Academy of Sciences and the Communist Party*, pp. 120–30.
38. *Smolensk Archives*, WKP 33: gubkom bureau, 11 June 1928.
39. Bailes, "The politics of technology," loc.cit., p.446.
40. *Rabochaia gazeta*, 17 April 1929, p.8. For other reports of intensified *spetseedstvo* and flight of engineers after the Shakhty trial, see S. A. Fediukin, *Velikii oktiabr' i intelligentsiia* (Moscow, 1972), pp. 386–87.
41. The Vakhitov soap factory in Kazan presents an interesting case, because its Communist director *had* in 1926 exercised local initiative against a group of engineers and been rebuked for "harassment." As a result, the Kazan Party organization was slow to draw implications from the Shakhty trial, despite the fact that the local GPU had unmasked a plot closely modelled on the Shakhty scenario, and had to be rebuked for its failure to harass the engineers. Data from *Deiatel'nost' partiinoi organizatsii Tatarii po osushchestvleniiu leninskikh idei stroitel'stva sotsialistiskogo obshchestva* (Kazan, 1971), pp.201–202.
42. K. V. Gusev and V. Z. Drobizhev, eds., *Rabochii klass v upravlenii gosudarstvom (1926–1937 gg.)* (Moscow, 1968), pp.144–45.
43. The Central Committee published no instructions on purging, but in July 1928 the Smolensk gubkom obviously received verbal encouragement from the Central Committee rapporteur (Lominadze) to do so (*Smolensk Archives*, WKP 33, meeting of plenum of Smolensk gubkom, 16 July 1928). Narkompros RSFSR tried to discourage purging or, when this proved unsuccessful, to restrict it according to guidelines published in *Ezhenedel'nik Narodnogo Komissariata Prosveshcheniia RSFSR*, 1929 no. 15, pp.18–19. There was open conflict on the question between the Ukrainian Narkompros and Ukrainian Party Central Committee (see Mikhailov, in *Kul'turnaia revoliutsiia v SSSR 1917–1965* [Moscow, 1965], p.325).
44. "Fighting tasks of the cultural revolution," *Pravda*, 5 February 1929, p.1.
45. *Narodnoe prosveshchenie*, 1929 no. 3–4, p.20.
46. Ibid., p.51.
47. Stalin, *Sochineniia XI* (Moscow, 1949), pp.72, 78–79, 127–36.
48. On the war games of the Komsomol Cultural Army, see L. S. Frid, *Ocherki po istorii razvitiia politiko-prosvetitel'noi raboty v RSFSR (1917–1929 gg.)* (Leningrad, 1941), p.141.
49. The *kul'tpokhod* was announced at the Eighth All-Union Congress of the Komsomol in May 1928. The best source is V. A. Kumanev, *Sotsializm i vsenarodnaia gramotnost'* (Moscow, 1967).
50. *Komsomol'skaia pravda*, 14 December 1928, p.4.
51. See Central Committee resolution "On the Saratov *kul'tpokhod*," cited

Kumanev, op.cit., p.191, from *Pravda*, 13 October 1929; Kaganovich and Bub-nov, in *XVI s"ezd VKP(b)*. *Stenograficheskii otchet*.

52. Broido in *Na putiakh k novoi shkole*, 1930 no. 1, p.57.

53. *Novye formy i metody prosvetitel'noi raboty* (Moscow: Narkompros RSFSR, 1929), pp.13–14.

54. "Fighting issues of public education," *Pravda*, 30 August 1929, p.1; Orgburo resolution of 5 August 1929 "On the directing cadres of educational workers," *Narodnoe prosveshchenie*, 1929 no. 12, p.12.

55. *Biulleten' Narodnogo Komissariata po Prosveshcheniiu RSFSR*, 1930 no. 19, pp.21 ff.

56. Central Committee resolution "On current tasks of cultural construction in connection with the results of the Second All-Union Party Meeting on Educa-tion," 25 July 1930, in *Biulleten' Narodnogo Komissariata po Prosveshcheniiu RSFSR*, 1930 no. 23, p.5.

57. I. Trifonov, *Ocherki istorii klassovoi bor'by v gody NEPa 1921–1937* (Moscow, 1960), p.174.

58. Day by day reports on the purge of Narkompros appeared in *Vecherniaia Moskva* through December 1929–January 1930.

59. *Narodnoe prosveshchenie*, 1929 no. 10–11, p.144.

60. Compare, for example, the Opposition line on problems of working-class youth described in *Molodaia gvardiia*, 1926 no.9, pp.99–100, with opinions ex-pressed by Milchakov (one of the minority of *anti*-Opposition members of the Komsomol Central Committee in 1926) in ibid., 1926 no. 4, p.83; or the expressed opinions of the RAPP leader Averbakh with the Opposition line on literature, which he is attacking, in *Na literaturnom postu*, 1928 no. 8, p.10.

61. Examples of RAPP's insubordination include its attacks on Gorkii; Aver-bakh's repeated refusal to accept a Central Committee posting outside Moscow during the cultural revolution (S. Sheshukov, *Neistovye revniteli. Iz istorii literaturnoi bor'by 20-kh godov* [Moscow, 1970], pp.223, 322–23, 335); his support of the Shatskin-Sten criticism of bureaucratic attitudes in the Party; and his failure as editor of the RAPP journal *Na literaturnom postu* to publish, or even for some months to comment upon, the Central Committee resolution of April 1932 dissolv-ing RAPP.

62. Averbakh, in L. Averbakh et al., *S kem i pochemu my boremsia* (Moscow-Leningrad, 1930), p.4.

63. *Krasnaia nov'*, 1927 no. 6, p.242.

64. Rene Fulop-Miller, *The Mind and Face of Bolshevism* (London and New York, 1927). The book describes virtually every Communist visionary who could be met in Moscow *circa* 1924 (vastly overestimating their importance at that time). However, many of the men and ideas the author mentions really did become influential during the cultural revolution.

65. Stalin, Political Report of the Central Committee to the Sixteenth Party Congress, in his *Sochineniia* XII (Moscow, 1949), pp.369–70: "We, are for the withering away of the state. And at the same time we stand for the strengthening of the dictatorship of the proletariat, which is the mightiest and most powerful of all state powers that have existed up to the present time. The highest development of

state power with the purpose of preparing conditions for the withering away of state power—that is the Marxist formula. Is that 'contradictory'? Yes, it is contradictory. But it is a contradiction of life itself, and it wholly reflects Marx's dialectic." Even after Stalin's statement, ideas of the withering away of the state, of social classes, and of the distinction between mental and physical labor and town and countryside continued to circulate. Two years later, Molotov had to explain again that no such radical transfiguration could be expected during the Second Five-Year Plan (*XVII konferentsiia Vsesoiuznoi Kommunisticheskoi Partii (b). Stenograficheskii otchet* [Moscow, 1932], pp.145-48).

66. See comment by A. S. Bubnov in his *Statyi i rechi* (Moscow, 1959), pp.358-59. The relevant legislation is in *Biulleten' Narodnogo Komissariata po Prosveshcheniiu RSFSR*, 1931 no. 12, pp.2-3; 1931 no. 14-15, pp.21-26; 1933 no. 11, p.7; 1933 no. 13, p.6.

67. A report on the workers' delegation to Narkompros is in *Komsomol'skaia pravda*, 6 February 1929, and of the Narkompros collegium meeting at the 'Geofizika' factory in *Izvestiia*, 26 February 1929.

68. N. de Witt, *Education and Professional Employment in the USSR* (Washington, D. C.: National Science Foundation, 1961), p.783.

69. Calculated from *Sotsialisticheskoe stroitel'stvo SSSR. Statisticheskii ezhegodnik* (Moscow, 1934), pp.406, 410.

70. K. V. Gusev and V. Z. Drobizhev, eds., *Rabochii klass v upravlenii gosudarstvom (1926–1937 gg.)* (Moscow, 1968), p.157.

71. *Sotsialisticheskoe stroitel'stvo SSSR* (Moscow, 1934), p.410.

72. See *Za promyshlennye kadry*, 1933 no. 8–9, p.76; Vsesoiuznyi komitet po vysshemu tekhnicheskomu obrazovaniiu pri TsIK SSSR, *Biulleten'*, 1933 no. 9–10, p.7; A. N. Veselov, *Professional'no-tekhnicheskoe obrazovanie v SSSR* (Moscow, 1961), p.285.

73. See, for example, comments by Iakovleva, Pokrovskii, and Krupskaia in *Narodnoe prosveshchenie*, 1929 no. 3–4, pp. 30,43,51.

74. *Sotsial'nyi i natsional'nyi sostav VKP(b). Itogi vsesoiuznoi partiinoi perepisi 1927 goda* (Moscow, 1928), pp.41, 45.

75. Speech of 23 June 1931, in I. Stalin, *Sochineniia* XIII (Moscow, 1951), pp.69–73.

76. "On some questions of the history of Bolshevism," *Proletarskaia revoliutsiia*, 1931 no. 6; also in Stalin, *Sochineniia* XIII (Moscow, 1951), pp.84–102.

77. Central Committee resolution of 25 March 1931 "On the complete cessation of mobilization of workers from the bench for current campaigns of local Party, soviet and other organizations," *Partiinoe stroitel'stvo*, 1931 no. 7, p.63. The resolution also forbade reduction of the working day for factory workers engaged in part-time study or any public or social activities.

78. Bubnov, speech of 23 April 1931, in *Kommunisticheskoe prosveshchenie*, 1931 no. 12, p.18.

79. For example, in his speech to the conference of Marxist rural scholars, 27 December 1929, in Stalin, *Sochineniia* XII, pp.141 ff.; and in his verbal encouragement to the young Communist Academy radicals Iudin and Mitin to attack the ex-Menshevik philosopher Deborin (see David Joravsky, *Soviet Marxism and Natural Science 1917–1932* [London, 1961], p.262).

80. Stalin wrote in a letter to the proletarian dramatist Bill-Belotserkovskii on 2 February 1929: "I consider the very posing of the question of 'rightists' and 'leftists' in our literature... incorrect. The concept of 'right' and 'left' in our country is a Party concept or, more exactly, an inner-Party concept. 'Rightists' and 'leftists' are people deviating to one side or other of the pure Party line. Therefore it would be strange to apply these concepts to such a non-party and incomparably wider field as literature." (Stalin, *Sochineniia* XI [Moscow, 1949], p.326.)

81. For further discussion on this point, see my article "Culture and politics under Stalin: a reappraisal," *Slavic Review*, June 1976.

82. According to one source, between January 1930 and October 1933, 666,000 worker-Communists were promoted to administrative or managerial positions or sent to higher education (I. F. Petrov ed., *Kommunisticheskaia partiia - um, chest' i sovest' nashei epokhi* [Moscow, 1969], pp.221–22). I am indebted to Jerry Hough for this reference.

83. Vera S. Dunham, *In Stalin's Time. Middleclass Values in Soviet Fiction* (London and New York, 1976).

84. See *Vsesoiuznoe soveshchanie zhen khoziaistvennikov i inzhenerno-tekhnicheskikh rabotnikov tiazheloi promyshlennosti. Stenograficheskii otchet* (Moscow, 1936).

Lewin: Society, State, and Ideology during the First Five-Year Plan

1. F. Lorimer, *The Population of the Soviet Union: History and Prospects* (Geneva, 1946), pp. 38–39, 40.

2. Ibid., p.22.

3. L. M. Spirin, *Klassy i partii v grazhdanskoi voine v Rossii, 1917–1920* (Moscow, 1968), p.301.

4. Ibid., p.386.

5. Ibid., pp.386–87. His material is from the Central Party Archives.

6. O. I. Shkaratan, *Problemy sotsial'noi struktury rabochego klassa SSSR* (Moscow, 1970), pp.351–54.

7. Ibid., p.256. He explains these phenomena as well as the oppositions inside the party at that time—notably the Workers' Opposition—as results of vacillations under the pressure of "spontaneous forces" (*stikhiia*).

8. A. A. Matiugin and D. A. Baevskii eds., *Izmeneniia v chislennosti i sostave sovetskogo rabochego klassa* (Moscow, 1961), p.83.

9. Mikhail Zoshchenko (1895–1958), author of many humorous stories of life under NEP; Ilia Ilf and Evgenii Petrov were joint authors of the satirical novels *The Twelve Chairs* (1928) and *The Little Golden Calf* (1931).

10. Computed by Sovnarkom's Committee for the Assessment of the Tax Burden, published in *Statisticheskii spravochnik SSSR za 1928 god* (Moscow, 1929), pp.42–43, where we also took our figures on the social groups. The figures deal with "employed" (without their families). The figures are rounded off throughout this paper, since we are interested only in the order of magnitude.

11. I. Magidovich, in *Statisticheskoe obozrenie*, 1928 no. 11, p.80.

12. *Statisticheskii spravochnik SSSR za 1928 god*, pp.796–97.

13. A. Ya. Levin, *Sotsial'no-ekonomicheskie uklady v SSSR v period perekhoda*

ot kapitalizma k sotsializmu: goskapitalizm i chastnyi kapital (Moscow, 1967), p.23, for the year 1925–26.

14. Magidovich, in *Statisticheskoe obozrenie*, 1928 no. 11, p.87. All such figures have to be treated with considerable caution. People were prudent and left undeclared everything they could. But the scope of the capitalist sector is certainly reflected here realistically.

15. The chairman of the agriculture department in Ivanovo-Voznesensk *gubernia*, himself of peasant stock, stated quite clearly: "The peasant is used to seeing in the government an alien force." Quoted in M. P. Kim, ed., *Sovetskaia intelligentsiia: istoriia formirovaniia i rosta* (Moscow, 1968), p.140.

16. See the excellent paper by V. P. Danilov, "The rural population of the USSR on the eve of collectivization," *Istoricheskie zapiski*, 1963 no. 74, p.96.

17. See M. Lewin, "Who was the Soviet kulak?", *Soviet Studies*, 2, XVIII (1966).

18. Iu. V. Arutiunian, *Sotsial'naia struktura sel'skogo naseleniia SSSR* (Moscow, 1971), p.26.

19. *Stat. spravochnik . . . za 1928 g.*, p.42.

20. V. P. Danilov, "Towards a characterization of the social and political circumstances in the Soviet countryside on the eve of collectivization," *Istoricheskie zapiski*, 1966 no. 79, p.37; N. A. Ivnitskii, *Klassovaia bor'ba v derevne i likvidatsiia kulachestva kak klassa* (Moscow, 1972), pp.71, 74.

21. Ivnitskii, *Klassovaiia bor'ba . . . klassa*, p.65.

22. In 1928 there were only 233,000 specialists with higher education, and among them only about 48,000 engineers. A further 288,000 people had secondary specialized education. See *Trud v SSSR, Statisticheskii sbornik* (Moscow, 1968), pp.251, 262.

23. R. Pethybridge, *The Social Prelude to Stalinism* (London, 1974), p.196. The quotation is taken from the title of a chapter in this book.

24. See table in Kim, *Sovetskaia intelligentsiia*, p.134.

25. Strumilin's computation, quoted in L. Averbakh, *Na putiakh kul'turnoi revoliutsii*, 3d ed. (Moscow, 1929), p.72.

26. Rykov and Lunacharskii quoted in Averbakh, *Na putiakh kul'turnoi revoliutsii*, pp.64 and 68 respectively.

27. Arutiunian, *Sotsial'naia struktura*, p.38. In 1924 a peasant child would have, on the average, two to three years schooling, children in cities—3.1 years per child. Such data give a fair picture of the low starting point, in terms of popular education, the regime had to build on.

28. Averbakh, *Na putiakh*, p.166.

29. Averbakh, ibid., pp.186–87, quoting Trotsky's "anti-Leninist" opinion from *Literatura i revoliutsiia*.

30. According to Kim, ed., *Sovetskaia intelligentsiia*, p.174, workers and peasants occupied half the places in higher educational institutions ("*vuzy*"— rendered as "universities" in text). The other half—and after 1926 even more— went to "employees" and "others" (i.e., children of the propertied classes, past and present).

31. Quoted in M. P. Kim, ed., *Kul'turnaiá revoliutsiia v SSSR, 1917–1965* (Moscow, 1967), p.95.

32. Oblomov is the hero of a nineteenth-century novel of that title by I.

Goncharov—a "superfluous man" who sinks into idleness and lethargy on his provincial estate.

33. Quoted in Averbakh, *Na putiakh*, p.121.

34. Ibid., p.176.

35. R. Pethybridge, *The Social Prelude to Stalinism*, p.350; and see his chapter on "Illiteracy."

36. M. A. Vyltsan, *Sovetskaia derevnia nakanune velikoi otechestvennoi voiny* (Moscow, 1970), p.142; Lorimer, *The Population of the Soviet Union: History and Prospects*, p.112, states that the overall growth rate, 1926–39, was 1.23% a year. This was very high when compared with other countries, but it was much higher in the USSR itself in 1926 and 1927 as well as, probably, in 1938. Tsarist Russia saw its population grow by 1.74% a year during the period 1897–1914.

37. *Sotsialisticheskoe stroitel'stvo v SSSR* (Moscow 1935), p. xlviii, claims a population of 165,748,400 at the end of 1932, but the 1939 census found only about 5 million inhabitants more. Something must have been very wrong. The 1937 census was disavowed by the government; many statisticians were purged as "wreckers."

38. For information on *otkhod* in those years see A. M. Panfilova, *Formirovanie rabochego klassa SSSR v gody pervoi piatiletki* (Moscow, 1964).

39. *Narodnoe khoziaistvo SSSR v 1956 g.* (Moscow 1957), p.656; Arutiunian, in A. P. Dadykin, ed., *Formirovanie i razvitie sovetskogo rabochego klassa 1917–1961* (Moscow 1964), pp.113–15; M. Iu. Pisarev, *Naselenie i trud v SSSR* (Moscow, 1966), p.68 and passim.

40. M. Ia. Sonin, *Vosproizvodstvo rabochei sily v SSSR i balans truda* (Moscow 1959), p.143; *Statisticheskii spravochnik SSSR za 1960 g.* (Moscow, 1961), p.110. It is quite revealing to read Stalin saying in June 1931 (Stalin, *Sochineniia* XIII [Moscow, 1951], p.53): "There is no longer any 'flight of the peasant to the city' or 'spontaneous movement [*samotëk*] of the labor force.'" Soviet scholars had to repeat this outrageous misrepresentation for years. What was really happening was pandemonium—both "flight" and "spontaneous movement" as never before.

41. A. V. Kornilov, *Na reshaiushchem etape* (Moscow, 1968), pp.158–59; Panfilova, *Formirovanie*, p.80.

42. S. Ordzhonikidze, *Stat'i i rechi* II (Moscow, 1956), pp. 411–12.

43. For some data on this see Ordzhonikidze, ibid.; *Pravda*, 15 November 1931; *Spravochnik partiinogo rabotnika* vypusk 8 (Moscow, 1934), pp.846–49; *Bol'shevik*, 1934 no. 7, p.16.

44. Nicholas S. Timasheff, *The Great Retreat. The Growth and Decline of Communism in Russia* (New York: E. P. Dutton and Co.), 1946.

45. Ivnitskii, *Klassovaia bor'ba*, p.242.

46. N. I. Nemakov, *Kommunisticheskaia partiia—organizator massovogo kolkhoznogo dvizheniia (1929–32)*, pp.159, 168. The category of *lishentsy* was abolished in 1935 (see *Pravda*, 30 December 1935).

47. *Sobranie zakonov i rasporiazhenii raboche-krest'ianskogo pravitel'stva SSSR* 1930, no. 50, art. 524. This is an interesting document in which the sociologist and historian may study the condemned capitalist elements, most of whom never saw much of any "capital" in their lives.

48. *Sobranie zakonov* 1930, no. 19, art. 212, lists such actions as "abuses" and

forbids them, but this could not have had any effect since the same people could easily be persecuted under other headings.

49. S. Bulatov, in *Sovetskoe gosudarstvo*, 1933 no. 4, p.71.

50. Data in *Statisticheskoe obozrenie*, 1928 no. 2, p.80; on capital value per average shop or commercial enterprise, see A. Ia. Levin, *Sotsioekonomicheskie uklady*, p.125.

51. A full list of offenses that either increased considerably or became the object of a special campaign, and therefore looked particularly ominous, is given in *Sovetskaia Iustitsiia*, 1932 no. 34, p.13.

52. O. I. Shkaratan, *Problemy sotsial'noi struktury*, p.264.

53. A. Stepanian, in V. S. Semenov, *Klassy, sotsial'nye sloi i gruppy v SSSR* (Moscow, 1968), pp.20–21.

54. *Sovetskaia Iustitsiia*, 1932 no. 2, p.15.

55. *Sobranie zakonov* 1932, no. 78, art. 475, and no. 45, art. 244.

56. Quoted in J. Azrael, *Managerial Power and Soviet Politics* (Cambridge, Mass., 1966), pp.247–48.

57. Kaganovich, in *Bol'shevik*, 1936 no. 13, p.54.

58. Kirov, *Izbrannye stati'i i rechi* (Moscow, 1957), pp.700–707.

59. In my article "Taking Grain," in C. Abramsky, ed., *Essays in Honour of E. H. Carr* (London, 1974), I describe the mechanism of the procurements and their effect on the development of the *kolkhozy*.

60. Arutiunian, *Sotsial'naia struktura*, p.158.

61. Ibid. One quarter of the peasants still could not read in 1939.

62. Iaroslavskii, quoted in Kim, ed., *Kul'turnaia revoliutsiia*, p.248.

63. S. Syrtsov, in *Bol'shevik*, 1930 no. 5, pp.47–49, which is the source of the summary that follows.

64. "*Okazënivanie krestian*" is the term used by a peasant delegate in VI *s"ezd sovetov*, bulletin, 1931 no. 20, p.3. He explained that this meant depriving them of the results of their labor, and said that kulaks laughed at the *kolkhozniki* because they were now "on rations" (*na paike*).

65. Machine Tractor Stations (MTS) were set up in 1929 to consolidate tractor and machinery holdings and service the *kolkhozy*. Later they also assumed functions of political supervision over the *kolkhozy*.

66. A. Ia. Iakovlev, *Voprosy organizatsii sotsialisticheskogo sel'skogo khoziaistva* (Moscow, 1933), p.184. Sheboldaev is quoted from XVII *konferentsiia VKP(b)*, *Stenograficheskii otchet* (Moscow, 1932), p.208.

67. L. Kaganovich, in *Na agrarnom fronte*, 1933 no. 1, p.40.

68. The Central Committee decision is in *Partiinoe stroitel'stvo*, 1933 no. 5, p.62. The document illustrates the kind of menacing language the Central Committee was then using.

69. N. V. Krylenko was Commissar of Justice of the RSFSR.

70. *Sovetskaia Iustitsiia*, 1932 no.5–6, p.16. The same periodical (1933 no. 15) adds more categories of typical transgressions of the "crude administrative" variety: forcing the *kolkhoz* to feed all kinds of parasites favored by the raion bosses; imposing illegal corvees; preempting money from the bank accounts of the *kolkhozy*; taking cattle away from them, and so on.

71. S. Krasikov, *Sergei Mironovich Kirov* (Moscow, 1964), p.176.

72. Summarized from *Sputnik kommunista v derevne*, 1933 no. 2, p.48.

73. Kirov is quoted from Krasikov, *Sergei Mironovich Kirov*, p.176; Stalin from *Partiinoe stroitel'stvo*, 1933 no. 5, p.3.

74. There was even a formal prohibition against creating mutual aid funds from *kolkhoz* resources: it could be done only on the basis of private contributions from the *kolkhozniki*—see *Sputnik kommunista v derevne*, 1933 no. 2, p.48.

75. *Sotsialisticheskoe zemledelie*, 1933 no. 16–17, p.9.

76. Arutiunian, *Sotsial'naia struktura*, p.57.

77. Ordzhonikidze speaking at the Seventeenth Party Conference in 1932, in *Stat'i i rechi* II, p.340.

78. Quoted in Kim, ed., *Sovetskaia intelligentsiia*, pp.48, 56.

79. V. I. Lenin, *Sochineniia*, XL, 5th ed. (Moscow, 1962), pp.199, 218.

80. Kim, ed., *Sovetskaia intelligentsiia*, pp.126–27; S. A. Fediukin, *Velikii oktiabr' i intelligentsiia* (Moscow, 1972), p.377.

81. The Shakhty trial of engineers for wrecking and sabotage was held in May–June 1928. See Fitzpatrick, "Cultural revolution as class war," this volume.

82. Kim, ed., *Sovetskaia intelligentsiia*, p.127, admits that such fears were well founded, but he puts the blame on "Makhaevite tendencies" among workers and exempts policy makers from any share in it.

83. *Pravda*, 17 August 1931.

84. Suicides were committed even in such inconspicuous places as Rzhev, where intellectuals could not have been too numerous. The party leadership was disturbed by the phenomenon. See *Smolensk Archives* WKP 55 (document dated July 1930).

85. Kim, ed., *Sovetskaia intelligentsiia*, pp.324–25.

86. M. Iu. Pisarev, *Naselenie i trud SSSR* (Moscow, 1966), p.41.

87. Figures from the 1930 survey are in M. P. Kim, ed., *Industrializatsiia SSSR 1929–1932* (Moscow, 1970), p.571; data on the 1933 survey are in *Sotsialisticheskoe stroitel'stvo SSSR* (Moscow, 1935), p.522.

88. This is an assessment for the year 1937 made by S. L. Seniavskii, *Izmeneniia v sotsial'noi strukture sovetskogo obshchestva 1938–1970* (Moscow, 1973), p.299. According to him, by 1940 the intelligentsia (in which he includes only specialists with higher or secondary professional education) constituted only 3.3% of the employed population, whereas the "non-specialized officials" constituted 13.2% of the total employed work force.

89. *Sobranie zakonov* 1931, no. 44, art. 322.

90. Iu. B. Borisov, in Kim, ed., *Kul'turnaia revoliutsiia*, p.138. Such figures can be used only as indications of trends; their exactitude is very questionable.

91. V.I. Kuzmin, *Istoricheskii opyt Sovetskoi industrializatsii* (Moscow, 1963), p.149.

92. The preference for "crude leadership" does not mean that every manager actually was a despotic type. There certainly were many of the traditional Russian "paternalist" type and some, a minority, of "businesslike" frame of mind and style (*delovye*), compromising and conniving. Whatever the typology, their power and privileges were common to the whole category, especially in the more important enterprises and establishments.

93. G. Shklovskii, in *Revoliutsiia prava*, 1930 no. 7, p.89.

94. Ibid.
95. Ibid., pp. 59–61.
96. P. I. Stuchka, in *Revoliutsiia prava*, 1930 no. 10, p. 19.
97. Ordzhonikidze, *Stat'i i rechi* II, pp. 228–29.
98. "You can dig there as much as you like, they won't give you exact data." Ibid., p. 228.
99. These are quotations from P. Postyshev's speech in Kharkov, in *Partiinoe stroitel'stvo*, 1933 no. 5: he was expressing the generally accepted tenets of what was then "the Bolshevik art of leadership."
100. Syrtsov, *O nedostatkakh i zadachakh* (Moscow-Leningrad, 1930), p. 15 (speech of February 1930).
101. *Bol'shevik*, 1934 no. 21, p. 12.
102. *KPSS v resoliutsiiakh s"ezdov i konferentsii* II (Moscow, 1957), pp. 541, 546.
103. L. F. Morozov and V. P. Portnov, *Organy partiino-gosudarstvennogo kontrolia 1923–1934* (Moscow, 1964), pp. 139–42.
104. S. Ikonnikov, *Sozdanie i deiatel'nost' obedinënnykh organov TsKK-RKI v 1923–1934 godakh* (Moscow, 1971), p. 212.

Lapidus: Educational Strategies and Cultural Revolution

1. An element of ambiguity arises in using the term "cultural revolution," which has both a general and a specific connotation, and describes a broad developmental process as well as a specific historical episode. The two connotations, moreover, are not necessarily congruent. As Sheila Fitzpatrick points out in her introductory essay, the proletarian cultural revolution of 1928–32 in the USSR departed in its scope, methods, and goals from the Leninist conception of cultural revolution as a process of gradual ideological transformation. This redefinition was subsequently repudiated, and the Leninist usage was restored. To avoid confusion, the term will be capitalized when used to refer to the events of 1928–32.

2. See Kenneth Jowitt, "An Organizational Approach to the Study of Political Culture in Marxist-Leninist Systems," *The American Political Science Review*, LXVIII, 3 (September 1974). For a more general treatment of conflicting perspectives and strategies with respect to cultural revolution in the USSR, see Gregory Massell, *The Surrogate Proletariat: Moslem Women and Revolutionary Strategies in Soviet Central Asia 1919–1929* (Princeton, 1974); and Gail Warshofsky Lapidus, *Women in Soviet Society: Equality, Development and Social Change* (Berkeley and Los Angeles, 1977), chapter 3. For a comparative perspective, see Massell's "Family Law and Social Mobilization in Soviet Central Asia: Some Comparisons with Communist China," *Canadian Slavonic Papers*, no. 2–3 (Summer 1975), and Richard Fagen, *The Transformation of Political Culture in Cuba* (Stanford, 1969).

3. For the view that the struggle to create a new type of "socialist man" is a special case of the more general transformation of traditional attitudes, values, and behavior in the process of modernization, see the suggestive paper by Alex Inkeles, "The Modernization of Man in Socialist and Non-Socialist Countries," presented at symposium on The Social Consequences of Modernization in Socialist Countries, Salzburg, Austria, September 1972.

4. For several examples among many, see George Bereday, William Brickman, and Gerald Read, eds., *The Changing Soviet School* (Cambridge, Mass., 1960); Alex Inkeles, *Social Change in Soviet Russia*, chapter 1 (Cambridge, Mass., 1968); Jaan Pennar, Ivan Bakalo, George Bereday, *Modernization and Diversity in Soviet Education* (New York, 1971).

5. Merle Fainsod, *How Russia is Ruled* (Cambridge, Mass., 1963), p.111.

6. Richard Lowenthal, "Development vs. Utopia in Communist Policy," in Chalmers Johnson, ed., *Change in Communist Systems* (Stanford, 1970).

7. *KPSS v rezoliutsiiakh i resheniiakh s"ezdov, konferentsii i plenumov TsK* (Moscow, 1954), I, p.419.

8. A. V. Lunacharskii, *O narodnom obrazovanii* (Moscow, 1958), p.523.

9. For a discussion of the mechanisms used to influence the social composition of educational institutions, the shifting policies that guided their use, and the outcomes of these efforts, see Gail Warshofsky Lapidus, "Socialism and Modernity: Education, Industrialization and Social Change in the USSR," in P. Cocks, R. Daniels, and N. Heer, *The Dynamics of Soviet Politics* (Cambridge, Mass., 1976); James McClelland, "Stalin's Changing Educational Goals: Proletarianizing the Student Body," *Past and Present* (forthcoming); David Lane, "The Impact of Revolution on the Selection of Students for Higher Education: Soviet Russia, 1917–1928," *Sociology* (London, 1973); and Oskar Anweiler, "Educational Policy and Social Structure in the Soviet Union," in Boris Meissner, ed., *Social Change in the Soviet Union* (Notre Dame, Ind., 1972).

10. *Narodnoe prosveshchenie v RSFSR k 1928/29 godu: Otchet NKP za 1927/28 uchebnyi god* (Moscow, 1929), p.65. The statistical data must be used with great caution, as the pressures for proletarianization encouraged the misrepresentation of social status. Even allowing for a substantial inflationary effect, however, McClelland's careful analysis confirms the trend toward increasing worker representation, partly at the expense of the peasant cohort.

11. *KPSS*, I, pp.419–20.

12. Nadezhda Krupskaia, *Pedagogicheskie sochineniia v desiati tomax*, VII, p.12 (Moscow, 1959).

13. Sheila Fitzpatrick, "The 'Soft' Line on Culture and Its Enemies: Soviet Cultural Policy, 1922–1927," *Slavic Review*, June 1974.

14. Sheila Fitzpatrick, *The Commissariat of Enlightenment: Soviet Organization of Education and the Arts under Lunacharsky* (Cambridge, 1971), p.220.

15. Ibid., p.215.

16. Lunacharskii, *O narodnom obrazovanii*, p.438.

17. *Narodnoe prosveshchenie*, 1925, 10–11; V. N. Shulgin and M. V. Krupenina, *V bor'be za marksistkuiu pedagogiku*, and the writings of Shulgin discussed at greater length in this paper.

18. Lunacharskii, *O narodnom obrazovanii*, pp.403–405.

19. See the discussion in Sheila Fitzpatrick, this volume, pp.9–11.

20. For an editorial encouraging the purges, see *Pravda*, 5 February 1929. The opposition of Lunacharskii is expressed in *Narodnoe prosveshchenie*, 1929, 3–4, 4–5, and *Pravda*, 1 April 1929; of Krupskaia in *Pravda*, 8 June 1929, *Na putiakh k novoi shkole*, 1930, 4–5. A resolution of Sovnarkom opposing the expulsions is included in *Direktivy VKP*, p.149.

21. For a detailed account, see Merle Fainsod, *Smolensk under Soviet Rule* (Cambridge, Mass., 1958), pp.343–63.

22. Ibid., p.345.

23. Ibid., pp.355–56.

24. Nicholas DeWitt, *Education and Professional Employment in the USSR* (Washington, 1961), p.655.

25. See, for example, Krupskaia's remarks at the meeting of the Narkompros collegium, December 1929, in *Spornye voprosy marksistkoi pedagogiki* (Moscow, 1930), p.49.

26. *KPSS*..., p.519.

27. F. F. Korolev, *Narodnoe khoziaistvo i narodnoe obrazovanie v SSSR* (Moscow, 1961), p.24.

28. *Spornye voprosy*, p.33.

29. This effort to systematize Shulgin's views draws on a variety of his writings over a number of years. Because its purpose is to present a schematic overview rather than to explore the particular context in which each work was written and the specific problems that it addressed, it tends to minimize shifts of emphasis and approach that would emerge more sharply in a chronological treatment. Shulgin's writings include a long series of essays published in *Na putiakh k novoi shkole*, as well as *Osnovnye voprosy sotsialnogo vospitaniia* (Moscow, 1926); *O novom uchebnike* (Moscow, 1927); *Obshchestvennaia rabota shkoly i programmy GUS* (Moscow, 1926); *V bor'be za marksistkuiu pedagogiku* (with M. V. Krupenina) (Moscow, 1929); "Vospitanie narodnikh mass s tochki zreniia revoliutsionnogo proletariata," in A. G. Kalashnikov, ed., *Pedagogicheskaia Entsiklopediia*, vol. I (Moscow, 1927); and V. N. Shulgin, ed., *Problemy nauchnoi pedagogiki: pedagogika perikhodnoi epokhi* (Moscow, 1930). The most illuminating western treatments of Shulgin's ideas and their significance are Oskar Anweiler's *Geschichte der Schule und Pädagogik in Russland vom Ende des Zahrenreiches bis zum Beginn der Stalin-Ära* (Berlin, 1964), pp.414–28, and a chapter in a forthcoming study by Sheila Fitzpatrick, *Education and Social Mobility in the Soviet Union: A Political History of Soviet Education, 1921–1934.*

30. *Spornye voprosy*, pp.1–19.

31. Ibid., p.34.

32. The relevant decrees are gathered in *Direktivy VKP (B) i postanovleniia sovetskogo pravitel'stva o narodnom obrazovanii, 1917–1947* (Moscow, 1947), pp.151 ff.

33. Kenneth Jowitt, *Revolutionary Breakthroughs and National Development* (Berkeley and Los Angeles, 1971), p.115.

34. For statistics on enrollments by field of specialization, see Nicholas DeWitt, *Education and Professional Employment in the USSR* (Washington, D.C., 1961), p.638.

35. For a discussion of the changes in psychological theory underlying the reorientation of educational policy, see Raymond Bauer, *The New Man in Soviet Psychology* (Cambridge, 1955).

36. For an illustration of the new ethos, see George Counts, trans., *I Want to be Like Stalin* (New York, 1947).

Joravsky: The Construction of the Stalinist Psyche

1. Lenin, *Sochineniia* (4th ed.) XLIV, p.227.
2. See A. I. Solzhenitsyn, *The Gulag Archipelago* (New York, 1973), p.328, for the quotation from Lenin, and passim, for Solzhenitsyn's views on the cultural revolution.
3. For a lead into the large Soviet literature on the cultural revolution, see "Kul'turnaia revoliutsiia," *Sovetskaia istoricheskaia entsiklopediia* VIII (1965), pp.279–86, with bibliography. The main official writer is M. P. Kim. See, for example, Kim, ed., *Sovetskaia intelligentsiia (Istoriia formirovaniia i rosta 1917–1965 gg.)* (Moscow, 1968). For an antiestablishment historian who dissents from the stress on continuity and insists on a sharp break between the Leninist and Stalinist phases, see Roy Medvedev, *Let History Judge* (New York, 1972). Relaxation of the strict controls on Soviet historiography would undoubtedly lead to a major debate on this theme.
4. A. Amalrik, *Will the Soviet Union Survive until 1984?* (New York, 1970).
5. I am summarizing here the picture of the great break that I offered in Joravsky, *Soviet Marxism and Natural Science, 1917–1932* (New York, 1961), pp.233–314, and in *The Lysenko Affair* (Cambridge, Mass., 1970), passim.
6. See Joravsky, *Soviet Marxism and Natural Science*, ch. 17.
7. E. Kol'man, "Politics, economics and mathematics," *Za marksistsko-leninskoe estestvoznanie*, 1931 no. 1, p.27. This is a speech Kol'man gave to the Society of Materialist-Dialectical Mathematicians on November 29, 1930. It is reprinted in his *Na bor'bu za materialisticheskuiu dialektiku v matematike* (Moscow, 1931).
8. See, for example, Kommunisticheskaia Akademiia, Institut vysshei nervnoi deiatel'nosti, *Vysshaia nervnaia deiatel'nost'; sbornik trudov instituta* (Moscow, 1929), pp.ix–x, for a confession of continuing failure in the search for a distinctively Marxist approach. See also Kornilov's frank talk in the introduction to *Psikhologiia*, 1928 no. 1, p.3. See also Kornilov's introduction and his opening article in *Problemy sovremennoi psikhologii* (Moscow, 1928), vol. III of *Uchenye zapiski Instituta eksperimental'noi psikhologii*.
9. See P. O. Efrussi, *Uspekhi psikhologii v Rossii* (Petrograd, 1923), for an account of the Congress on Psychoneurology in Moscow, January 10–15, 1923, at which Kornilov launched the drive. His "Contemporary psychology and Marxism," *Pod znamenem marksizma*, 1923 no. 1, contains the "themes of my speech . . ., where I raised, for the first time in the Russian literature, the problem of 'psychology and Marxism'." The quotation is from *Psikhologiia i marksizm* (Moscow, 1925), p.233. At the Second Psychoneurological Congress, January 3–10, 1924, Zalkind was the most effective orator pleading for a Marxist psychology. See the account in G. Daian, "The Second Psychoneurological Congress," *Krasnaia nov'*, 1924 no. 2 (19), pp. 163–64. Cf. *Vrachebnaia gazeta*, 1930 no. 1, p.52, for Zalkind saying that the struggle for Marxism in psychology began in 1919, and "seriously" in 1922, in "the psycho-physiological section of the Institute of Communist Education, which was created on the initiative of APO-TsK," i.e., the Agitprop Division of the Central Committee. That explicit link with Agitprop, claimed for the first time in 1930, is not evident in the publications of the twenties.

10. Very extensive searches by Soviet scholars have not turned up, for example, a single reference to Pavlov in the prerevolutionary writings of Marxists, or a single reference to Marxism in the prerevolutionary writings of Pavlovians. Plekhanov and the other Russian radicals who came to intellectual maturity in the 1870s had some interest in the philosophical aspects of psychology, but Lenin's generation had almost none. The whole matter will be examined in detail in a book that I am now writing on the history of the Pavlov school from the 1860s to the 1950s.

11. See below, p.123.

12. See below, pp.124 ff., for the first steps toward the deification of Pavlov. For the "Pavlov Sessions" of 1950–51, see Akademiia Nauk SSSR, *Nauchnaia sessiia, posviashchennaia problemam fiziologicheskogo ucheniia Akademika I.P.Pavlova, 28 iiunia-4 iiulia 1950 g.* (Moscow, 1950), and Akademiia Meditsinskikh Nauk SSSR, *Fiziologicheskoe uchenie Akademika I.P.Pavlova v psikhiatrii i nevropatologii; materialy... zasedaniia... 11–15 oktiabria 1951 g.* (Moscow, 1951).

13. For recent signs of Soviet scholars struggling to hold to these legends while taking cognizance of facts that tend to undermine them, see M. Ia. Iaroshevskii, *Istoriia psikhologii* (Moscow, 1966), and A. V. Petrovskii, *Istoriia sovetskoi psikhologii* (Moscow, 1967).

14. See Joravsky, *Soviet Marxism and Natural Science.*

15. For a brief, frank characterization of the schools, see Iu. V. Frankfort, "On the struggle for Marxist psychology," *Krasnaia nov'*, 1927 no. 10, pp.169–96.

16. See the account in *Zhurnal nevropatologii i psikhiatrii*, 1930 no. 3, pp.98–107.

17. Ibid. Cf. Zalkind's different figures in *Pedologiia*, 1930 no. 2, pp.161–62.

18. See items noted in notes 16 and 17. Cf. *Vrachebnaia gazeta*, 1930 no. 1, p.52.

19. See *Zhurnal nevropatologii i psikhiatrii*, 1930 nos. 3 et seq., for the Society's journal under the new leadership.

20. See, for example, B. M. Rozentsvaig, "The bases for the establishment of psycho-neurological clinics," *Moskovskii meditsinskii zhurnal*, 1929 no. 11–12, pp.85–95; V. A. Giliarovskii, "Urbanization and the rise of pathological elements in the neuro-psychic milieu," in *Psikhonevrologicheskie nauki v SSSR* (Moscow, 1930), pp.334–35; and V. V. Dekhterev, "Establishment of clinics as a basis of struggle with exhaustion of the nervous system," *Klinicheskaia meditsina*, 1930 no. 19–20, pp.1094–99.

21. Gannushkin, "On protecting the health of the Party *aktiv*," *Revoliutsiia i kul'tura*, 1930 no. 4.

22. Rokhlin, "Mental-health work among the Party *aktiv*," *Zhurnal nevropatologii i psikhiatrii*, 1930 no. 3, p.25. Rokhlin repeated this apothegm in a number of publications.

23. See, for example, A. B. Zalkind, "Illnesses of the Party *aktiv*," *Krasnaia nov'*, 1925 no. 4, pp.187–203. For a collection of his articles on this subject, see Zalkind, *Rabota i byt obshchestvennogo aktiva* (Moscow, 1930). Cf. Zalkind, *Umstvennyi trud; Gigiena i ratsionalizatsiia umstvennoi deiatel'nosti* (Moscow, 1930).

24. See Rokhlin, *Trud, byt i zdorov'e partiinogo aktiva* (Dvou, 1931), espe-

cially chapters 5 and 6. Note his references to previous publications by other authors.

25. Ibid., p.131, for a summary of five studies of the *aktiv* in scattered places. Those suffering from nervous illnesses ranged from a low of 41.5% to a high of 88.7%. Cardiovascular disorders ranged from a low of 12.0% to a high of 75.0%. Earlier editions of Rokhlin's book were more forthright than this 1931 edition in their discussion of such problems.

26. See Iv. Strelchuk and Rumshevich, "The life and everyday round of mentally-ill persons in the village," *Zhurnal nevropatologii i psikhiatrii*, 1930 no. 5, pp.123–30. For grim figures on the inadequacy of psychiatric institutions, see L. Prozorov, "A survey of the state of affairs in psychiatric care in the RSFSR," ibid. no. 4, pp.120–23; no.3, pp.109–10; and no. 4, pp.127–28.

27. L. M. Rozenshtein, "The social-prophylactic trend in psychiatry," ibid., 1930 no. 4, p.5; and Rozenshtein, "The mental health movement in the USSR and its tasks in connection with reconstruction," *Vrachebnaia gazeta*, 1931 no. 2, p.123. The phrase, "factories producing chronic inmates," is attributed to a Western specialist.

28. Ibid.

29. Rokhlin, op.cit. in note 24, p.9.

30. Ibid., pp.7–8.

31. The original articles appear in *Trudy Psikhiatricheskoi Kliniki MGU* (1926), which was unavailable to me. For Gannushkin's confession see his "On the protection of the health of the Party *aktiv*," *Revoliutsiia i kul'tura*, 1930 no. 4, pp.43–44.

32. *Psikhonevrologicheskie nauki v SSSR* (Moscow, 1930), pp.301–304. Note on pp.301–302 the denial that transfer of workers from manual to mental labor can cause mental illness.

33. Gannushkin, op.cit. in note 31; and V. A. Vnukov, "The decisive links in the protection of the health of cadres," *Revoliutsiia i kul'tura*, 1930 no. 4, pp.40–43.

34. See, for example, *Zhurnal nevropatologii i psikhiatrii*, 1930 no. 3, pp.22–23.

35. Ibid., 1931 no. 1, p.3. Cf. no. 2, p.83, for a report of a long publication delay following the Commissar's speech, leading people to believe that he had suspended the journal. Compare the biographies of M. F. Vladimirskii and N. A. Semashko, in *Deiateli SSSR* and elsewhere, for a striking example of the different types of public health officials before and after the great break.

36. The editors of *Zhurnal nevropatologii i psikhiatrii* were slightly heretical in their apology, in 1931 no. 1, p.3. They pointed out that the offensive articles they had printed were originally speeches at the Behavioral Congress of January 1930, that they were sent to press before the *razvoroshenie* (turning upside down) of the Commissariat of Health in the spring of 1930, and before the *razvoroshenie* of "theoretical positions" in February–March 1931.

37. S. I. Subbotnik, "For a Bolshevik attack on the theoretical front of psychoneurology," ibid., 1931 no. 2, pp.8–17. Note that Commissar Vladimirskii had singled out Subbotnik for criticism. Ibid., 1931 no. 1, p.3.

38. Ibid., 1931 no. 2, p.14. The "conscious or subconscious enemy" was V. V. Dekhterev, op.cit. in note 20.

39. Subbotnik, op.cit. in note 37, p.14. Note the attack on former Health Commissar Semashko, on the same page.

40. He then signed himself "Propper." See his biography in *Biograficheskii slovar' deiatelei estestvoznaniia i tekhniki* I (1958), pp.260–61. The other two new leaders were V. N. Kolbanovskii and M. B. Krol. Note that all three had a medical background, unlike Kornilov, who was a school teacher before he became an experimental psychologist.

41. Grashchenkov (Propper), "Results of the discussion on the natural science front and the struggle on two fronts in medicine," *Zhurnal nevropatologii i psikhiatrii*, 1931 no. 5, p.13. See nos. 1 and 2 for the first installments of this long statement of the new position.

42. M. B. Krol, "Successes of Soviet neuropathology over 15 years," *Sovetskaia nevropatologiia, psikhiatrii i psikhogigiena*, 1933 no. 1, p.1.

43. S. I. Kaplun, *Obshchaia gigiena truda* (Moscow, 1940), pp.91–92.

44. Krol, op.cit. in note 42.

45. See Giliarovskii, "Achievements of Soviet psychiatry for the past 15 years and its immediate prospects," *Sovetskaia nevropatologiia, psikhiatrii i psikhogigiena*, 1933 no. 1, pp.8–17, for a review that seems to show real progress, until one reads Giliarovskii very carefully, with special attention to his omissions.

46. The two specialists were A. R. Luriia and I. D. Sapir. On Luriia, see Joravsky, "A Great Soviet Psychologist," *New York Review of Books*, 16 May 1974. Isai Davidovich Sapir, 1897–?, was a major figure in Soviet psychiatry and in Marxist discussions until 1931, when he was discredited. He disappeared in the mid-thirties.

47. I have gotten this impression from a hasty skimming of the journals. See especially the index of articles, 1901–1930, in *Zhurnal nevropatologii i psikhiatrii*, 1931, nos. 6 and 8.

48. In June 1932 there was a major conference on schizophrenia. See *Sovetskaia nevropatologiia, psikhiatriia i psikhogigiena*, 1932 no. 8, pp.454–56, for a brief report. Cf. Vygotskii, "On the problem of schizophrenia," ibid., pp.352–65. The record of the conference, *Sovremennye problemy shizofrenii* (Moscow, 1933) has been unavailable to me. For an anonymous history of the problem of schizophrenia, with special reference to Soviet controversies, see *Sobranie dokumentov samizdata* XXII, nos. 1101 and 1104.

49. The phrase is Maiakovskii's. See *The Bedbug, and Selected Poetry* (New York, 1960), p.220.

50. Vygotskii, "The science of psychology," in *Obshchestvennye nauki v SSSR, 1917–1927* (Moscow 1928), p.40, saw psychotechnics as *the* practical goal of psychological science, "i.e., the mastery in deed of human behavior, the subjection of it to the control of reason." A high point was reached in September 1931, when Moscow was host to the Seventh International Psychotechnical Congress (or International Congress of Applied Psychology, as it is also known). See its *Résumés des rapports* (Moscow, 1931) and *Tezisy dokladov . . .* (Moscow, 1931). Cf. reports in *Izvestiia*, 1931, Sept. 9, 10, 11, and 15. The early thirties was the time when A. K. Gastev and his institute studying the "Scientific Organization of Labor" reached the peak of their activity, before he was arrested and the institute closed down. See

his biography in *Kratkaia literaturnaia entsiklopediia* II (1964), pp.83–84. At the same time, one can see the beginning of the end in such polemics as A. B. Aleksandrovskii, "Against bourgeois tendencies in industrial psychology and the physiology of labor," *Za marksistsko-leninskoe estestvoznanie*, 1931 no. 2, pp.34–49.

51. See "For *partiinost'* in the hygiene and physiology of labor," *Pravda*, 16 June 1931. See *Vestnik Kommunisticheskoi Akademii*, 1930 no. 39, for an attack on the concept of an optimum rather than a maximum workload. (Thanks to Sheila Fitzpatrick for that reference.) S. I. Kaplun, the leading authority in the field of "labor hygiene," and a chief target of the attack in *Pravda*, was already backing away from his earlier views at the time of the First All-Union Psychotechnical Congress, May 1931. See his speech in *Vrachebnaia gazeta*, 1931 no. 13, pp.1014–18. See the 1940 edition of his textbook, *Obshchaia gigiena truda*, pp.75–76, for his argument that "on the whole, the problem of fatigue as a mass, usual phenomenon, is already undoubtedly gone (*bezuslovno sniata*)".

52. See *Sovetskaia psikhotekhnika*, 1930 no. 2–3, p.232, for a resolution adopted at the Behavioral Congress.

53. See especially the report of the First All-Union Psychotechnical Congress, May 1931, in *Vrachebnaia gazeta*, 1931 no. 13, pp.1014–18.

54. See, for example, A. B. Aleksandrovskii, op.cit. in note 50, p.41. Studies of national character were condemned in the strongest terms. See, for example, M. B. Krol, "Behavioral 'science' in the service of the national-democrats," *Zhurnal nevropatologii i psikhiatrii*, 1931 no. 1, pp.25–34.

55. V. A. Artemov, "On the question of a social industrial psychology" in *Psikhonevrologicheskie nauki v SSSR* (Moscow, 1930), p.208.

56. For a convenient translation, see Joseph Wortis, *Soviet Psychiatry* (Baltimore, 1950), pp.242–45. Cf. Raymond Bauer, *The New Man in Soviet Psychology* (Cambridge, Mass., 1952), ch. 8.

57. Akademiia Meditsinskikh Nauk SSSR, op.cit. in note 12, p.393. The speaker was K. K. Platonov.

58. I. B. Galant, "Results of mental examination of 335 Red Army men," *Zhurnal nevropatologii i psikhiatrii*, 1931 no. 2, pp.18–20.

59. Ibid., p.20. The article was printed with strong editorial disapproval in the fleeting period when the new Bolshevik editors were balancing between offering autonomous professional advice and catering to official prejudices. For another example, see ibid., 1931 no. 1, p.41, where L. M. Rozenshtein offers "psychohygiene" as "an ally of the command, educational and political service of the Army."

60. Frolov, "What is the physiology of military labor?" in N. A. Zelenov, ed., *Voprosy fiziologii voennogo truda i voenno-professional'nogo otbora* (Moscow, 1928), pp.9–30. The article seems to me a largely meaningless translation of conventional wisdom about army morale into Pavlovian terms.

61. See *Sovetskaia psikhotekhnika*, 1930 no. 2–3, p.232; Aleksandrovskii, op.cit. in note 50, p.43; and *Zhurnal nevropatologii i psikhiatrii*, 1931, *prilozhenie*, p.20.

62. Iu. P. Frolov, *Vysshaia nervnaia neiatel'nost' pri toksikozakh ... Dlia voennykh vrachei i toksikologov* (Moscow, 1944).

63. See *Periodicheskaia pechat' SSSR, 1917–1949; bibliograficheskii ukazatel'*,

vol. I, vypusk 1, pp.79–84; vypusk 2, items 3, 79–87, 96–97; vol. VII, pp.84–90. The count includes only journals; that is, it excludes nonperiodical serials. It makes some arbitrary distinctions between educational journals that may be considered psychological journals and those that may not.

64. The one journal in psychiatry and neuropathology was *Zhurnal nevropatologii i psikhiatrii*, which has undergone repeated changes of title. The one in pedagogy was *Sovetskaia pedagogika*. *Sovetskaia psikhonevrologiia*, published in the Ukraine, is a possible third journal: it survived until 1941. It is also noteworthy that psychological publications survived better in Georgia than elsewhere. Finally, it should be noted that the publications of the country's two leading pedagogical institutes were an outlet for articles by psychologists.

65. For a survey of them, see relevant sections of Raymond Bauer, op.cit. in note 56; Petrovskii, op.cit. in note 13; Josef Brozek and Dan Slobin, *Psychology in the USSR: An Historical Perspective* (White Plains, N.Y., 1972); and *Psikhologicheskaia nauka v SSSR* (Moscow, 1959–60), 2 vols.

66. T. I. Rainov, "Alienation of action," *Vestnik Kommunisticheskoi Akademii*, 1925–26, nos. 13, 14, and 15.

67. That is how the Congress was perceived by the reflexologist A. G. Ivanov-Smolenskii. See his *Estestvoznanie i nauka o povedenii cheloveka* (Moscow, 1929), pp.93 ff.

68. See the letter from the Institute, in *Psikhologiia*, 1928 no. 2, p.175. To be precise, the Communist Academy was represented by its Society of Materialist Psychoneurologists, which was not as Pavlovian as the Academy's Institute of Higher Nervous Activity.

69. That is Vygotskii's characterization of the whole school, of which Kornilov was the leading figure. See Vygotskii, op. cit. in note 50, p.37.

70. A. B. Zalkind, "The First Congress for the Study of Human Behavior," *Zhurnal nevropatologii i psikhiatrii*, 1930 no. 6, p.22.

71. A. B. Zalkind, "The First Congress for the Study of Human Behavior," *Pedologiia*, 1930 no. 2, pp.161–62.

72. A. B. Zalkind, "The behavioral congress and Soviet psychoneurology," *Vrachebnaia gazeta*, 1930 no. 7, p.503. Cf. Zalkind's article on the eve of the Congress, which concludes with something like a threat: institutes and societies that do not send delegates will be showing their *"ideinoobshchestvennaia bednost'."* Ibid., 1930 no. 1, p.53.

73. Zalkind estimated 1400 specialists plus 1600 guests. Op.cit. in note 70, p.22. Another account reports 3000 people, about half from Leningrad. *Sovetskaia psikhotekhnika*, 1930 no. 2–3, p.225.

74. A. V. Lunacharskii, "Art as a form of human behavior," in *Psikhonevrologicheskie nauki i sotsialisticheskoe stroitel'stvo SSSR* (Moscow, 1930), pp.222–49.

75. For the speeches of Karev and Luppol, see ibid., pp.15–77. For the attacks on them by Stalin's young zealots, see Joravsky, *Soviet Marxism and Natural Science*, pp.250–53. The perceptive reader may note that I have refrained, throughout the present article, from making distinctions of age among the various parties to the psychoneurological controversies. In this respect the philosophical controversies were different; they pitted young, comparatively ignorant Stalinists against

older, comparatively sophisticated Marxists. The psychoneurological specialists who were demoted in 1931 were frequently as young as those who took their places, or even younger. Suffice it to note that M. B. Krol, b.1879, became the Party's chief psychiatrist, while S. L. Rubinshtein, b.1889, became the most respected philosophical interpreter of psychology. V. N. Kolbanovskii, b.1902, took the place of K. N. Kornilov, b.1879, as the chief of experimental psychology, and N. I. Grashchenkov, b.1901, became chief neurologist, but one can hardly make a rule of those cases. I. N. Shpil'rein, b.1891, L. S. Vygotskii, b.1896, A. R. Luriia, b.1902, I. D. Sapir, b.1897, A. B. Zalkind, b.1888, and I. F. Kurazov, b.1897, were among the most severely chastised and demoted in the aftermath of the 1931 "discussion."

76. A. A. Iushchenko, "For Bolshevik self-criticism on the front of psychoneurology," *Zhurnal nevropatologii i psikhiatrii*, 1931, *prilozhenie*, p.26. Note his explicit tribute to Kol'man for "the timely intervention" that ensured a correct line in the "discussion." For an official summation, see the resolution, "Results of the discussion on reactological psychology," *Psikhotekhnika i psikhofiziologiia truda*, 1931 no. 4–6, pp.387–91. Also printed in *Psikhologiia*, 1931 no. 1, pp.1–2.

77. See, for example, Kornilov, "The contemporary state of psychology in the USSR," in *Problemy sovremennoi psikhologii* III (1928), p.24.

78. See, for example, V. M. Bekhterev, *Kollektivnaia refleksologiia* (Petrograd, 1921), and the review, by V. Nevskii, in *Pod znamenem marksizma*, 1922 no. 3, pp.55–61. Bogdanov may be said to have had social psychology as his central preoccupation in most of his writing. See especially his *Nauka ob obshchestvennom soznanii* (Petrograd, 1923), and his *Tektologiia: vseobshchaia organizatsionnaia nauka*, 3 editions, 1922–1928.

79. See I. F. Kurazov, *Vvedenie v istoricheskuiu psikhologiiu* (Moscow, 1931). Cf. the "*rezkii otpor*" cited in *Pod znamenem marksizma*, 1934 no. 5, pp.188–89. For Vygotskii and Luriia, see their joint effort, *Etiudy po istorii povedeniia: obez'iana, primitiv, rebenok* (Moscow, 1930). For the official reaction, see Joravsky, op.cit. in note 46. Recently it became possible for Luriia to publish the results of his 1931–32 studies of peasants. See his *Ob istoricheskom razvitii poznavatel'nykh protsessov* (Moscow, 1974). I wish to thank Michael Cole for calling my attention to this book, indeed for lending it to me.

80. See, for example, the resolution cited in note 76.

81. S. I. Kaplun, "Marx and questions of labor hygiene," *Gigiena i bezopasnost' truda*, 1933 no. 2; Kaplun, "Lenin and questions of labor hygiene," ibid., 1934 no. 1–2; S. G. Gellershtein, "On the psychology of labor in the works of K. Marx," *Sovetskaia psikhotekhnika*, 1933 no. 1; S. L. Rubinshtein, "Problems of psychology in the works of Karl Marx," ibid., 1934 no. 1. To get a sense of the great difficulty in squaring experimental psychology with the views of Karl Marx, see his famous rejection of any approach to psychology except the study of history. A convenient reprint, together with a collection of other excerpts on "existence and consciousness," is in Bottomore and Rubel, eds., *Karl Marx: Selected Writings in Sociology and Social Philosophy* (New York, 1964), pp.72–73, et passim.

82. S. L. Rubinshtein, *Osnovy obshchei psikhologii* (Moscow, 1946), as quoted in T. I. Iudin, *Ocherki istorii otechestvennoi psikhiatrii* (Moscow, 1951), p.413.

83. Compare *Pod znamenem marksizma* in the years to 1931, when articles on psychology were quite frequent, with the same journal, 1931 et seq. Ditto for *Vestnik Kommunisticheskoi Akademii*.

84. See Kh. Koshtoiants, "Physiology and the theory of development," *Pod znamenem marksizma*, 1932 no. 5–6; Koshtoiants's report on the International Congress of Physiology in Rome, ibid., 1932 no. 9–10, pp.238–49; N. Nikitin, "Natural science about man, and socialism," ibid., 1933 no. 6; L. Karlik, "Some results of the work of Professor Speranskii's school," ibid., 1934 no. 3, and so on. See ibid., 1936 no. 9, pp.87–99, for a report of a conference at which the official ideologists, paying heavy respect to Pavlov's school of physiology, demanded that experimental psychology justify its existence. Cf. *Za marksistsko-leninskoe estestvoznanie*, 1931–32, for many articles on physiology, and none on psychology except for an attack on V. M. Borovskii in 1931 no. 1 (foreshadowing the virtual destruction of comparative or animal psychology). There were also a few articles on psychotechnics in the journal.

85. For one of the last examples, heavily mixed with uncritical admiration of Pavlov's physiological hypotheses, see N. I. Propper (Grashchenkov), "The reflexological trend in physiology," ibid., 1932 no. 3–4. An expanded version is his "Refleksologiia," *Bol'shaia meditsinskaia entsiklopediia* XXVIII (1934), pp.737–55.

86. As quoted by M. R. Mogendovich, "The last stage of the Bekhterev school," *Psikhologiia*, 1931 no. 1, p.102.

87. Among the first to spread the word were V. M. Borovskii, "Conditioned reflexes from the viewpoint of comparative psychology," in *Problemy sovremennoi psikhologii* III (1928), pp.26–36; Borovskii, "What is new in the study of reflexes," *Pod znamenem marksizma*, 1930 no. 2–3; and I. S. Beritov (or Beritashvili), *Individual'no-priobretennaia deiatel'nost' tsentral'noi nervnoi sistemy* (Tiflis, 1932), which is a revised and expanded version of a 1927 monograph. For a summary of the criticism, together with an effort to save the experimental data accumulated by Pavlov's school, see Jerzy Konorski, *Conditioned Reflexes and Neuron Organization* (Cambridge, 1948). Konorski was a student of Pavlov's.

88. The most explicit and firm denial has been excluded from both editions of his collected works. See *Psikhiatricheskaia gazeta*, 1917 no. 8, pp.200–205, for his discussion with the Petrograd Philosophical Society. That his repudiation of materialism was common knowledge in the twenties is evident in the remarks of Pokrovskii, quoted below, p.125.

89. Originally in Bukharin's long reply to Pavlov's criticism of Marxism, in *Krasnaia nov'*, 1924 nos. 1 and 2; widely quoted, e.g. by Vygotskii, op.cit. in note 50, p.32. At the same time Marxist critics of Pavlov could quote Bukharin's rebuke to those who equated Marxism and reflexology. For that, see Bukharin's speech to the Fifth Comintern Congress, *Pravda*, 29 June 1924.

90. Quoted by I. D. Sapir, *Vysshaia nervnaia deiatel'nost' cheloveka* (Moscow, 1925), p.156.

91. *Vestnik Kommunisticheskoi Akademii*, 1926 no. 16, pp.286–87.

92. Ibid.

93. For evidence of his defiance and ridicule, see Bukharin's 1924 article cited

in note 89, and see Kornilov's virtual call for Pavlov's arrest in March 1930. Quoted below, p.126.

94. For Pavlov's stand against the Bolshevization of the academy, see Loren R. Graham, *The Soviet Academy of Sciences and the Communist Party* (Princeton, 1967), pp.116–18.

95. See his biography in *Fiziologicheskaia shkola I. P. Pavlova* (Leningrad, 1967), pp.254–56.

96. The official record of the Congress consists of two volumes, *Psikhonevrologicheskie nauki v SSSR* (Moscow, 1930), and *Psikhonevrologicheskie nauki i sotsialisticheskoe stroitel'stvo SSSR* (Moscow, 1930). I wish to thank Sheila Fitzpatrick for calling my attention to the second volume. L. N. Fedorov's speech was published as "The method of conditioned reflexes in the study of higher nervous activity," *Chelovek i priroda*, 1930 no. 4.

97. N. I. Grashchenkov (Propper), "The school of Academician Pavlov at the behavioral congress," *Zhurnal nevropatologii i psikhiatrii*, 1930 no. 3.

98. *Pedologiia*, 1930 no. 3, pp.422–23.

99. Ibid.

100. See, for example, the resolution cited in note 76.

101. Among the new top Party specialists in the psychoneurological sciences, Krol showed awareness of the discrepancy between Pavlov's hypotheses and neurophysiology, but Grashchenkov did not.

102. See *Materialy k istorii Vsesoiuznogo Instituta Eksperimental'noi Meditsiny* (Moscow, 1941).

103. Ibid., p.10–11.

104. *Izvestiia*, 16 October 1932.

105. Stalin, *Sochineniia* XIII, p.410.

106. *Izvestiia*, 18 October 1932. The quoted words are those of V. N. Popov, chief of the sector of scientific institutes of the Commissariat of Health.

107. See, for example, Karlik's article cited in note 84. There is a very large literature by and about Speranskii. For a convenient introduction see A. D. Speransky, *Basis for the Theory of Medicine* (New York, 1944).

108. See, most notably, his 1934 response to birthday greetings from the Sechenov Society of Physiologists: "Yes, I am glad that together with Ivan Mikhailovich [Sechenov] and an army of dear co-workers, we won the whole indivisible animal organism—instead of a mere half of it—for the mighty power of physiological research. And that is entirely our indisputable Russian service to world science, to general human thought." Pavlov, *Polnoe sobranie sochinenii* I (1951), p.13. For Pavlov's conscious estrangement from the mainstream of neurophysiology, see A. F. Samoilov, "A general characterization of I. P. Pavlov as a scientific researcher," *Zhurnal eksperimental'noi biologii*, series B, 1925, no. 1–2, pp.7–8, 19.

109. For a convenient reprint, with the photograph, see Pavlov, *Polnoe sobranie sochinenii* I (1951), p.19.

110. For an early expression of this theme, see Mitin's tribute to Pavlov, in *Pod znamenem marksizma*, 1936 no. 2–3, p.41. Note that the preceding tribute by Maksimov comes close, but still ascribes "mechanistic materialism" to Pavlov.

Solomon: Rural Scholars and the Cultural Revolution

1. For a discussion of the dating of the cultural revolution by current Soviet writers, see Sheila Fitzpatrick, "Cultural Revolution in Russia, 1928–1932," *Journal of Contemporary History*, January 1974, pp.33–35.

2. In varying degrees, this interpretation may be found in David Joravsky, *Soviet Marxism and Natural Science, 1917–1932* (New York, 1961); Edward J. Brown, *The Proletarian Episode in Russian Literature, 1928–1932* (New York, 1953); Konstantin Shteppa, *Russian Historians and the Soviet State* (New Brunswick, N.J., 1962); and Raymond Bauer, *The New Man in Soviet Psychology* (Cambridge, Mass., 1952).

3. David Joravsky, "The Construction of the Stalinist Psyche," this volume.

4. Sheila Fitzpatrick, "The 'Soft' Line on Culture and its Enemies: Soviet Cultural Policy, 1922–1927," *Slavic Review*, June 1974, p.269.

5. Sheila Fitzpatrick, "Cultural Revolution as Class War," this volume.

6. For a more detailed treatment of this controversy, see Susan Gross Solomon, *The Soviet Agrarian Debate: A Controversy in Social Science, 1923–1929* (Boulder, Colorado, 1977).

7. In the main, this research took the form of statistical studies conducted under the aegis of the *zemstva*. For synopses of these studies, see N. A. Svavskii and Z. M. Svavitskii, *Zemskie podvornye perepisi, 1880–1913 gg.* (Moscow, 1926); N. A. Svavitskii, *Zemskie podvornye perepisi; obzor metodologii* (Moscow, 1961); E. Volkov, *Agrarno-ekonomicheskaia statistika Rossii* (Moscow, 1923).

8. Rural social studies in America followed a similar path of development.

9. The academy was originally known as the Petrovskii Agricultural Academy. In 1923, it was renamed in honor of K. A. Timiriazev, who had taught in the department of botany and physiology and earned the gratitude of the Bolshevik leadership by announcing his support for the new regime. For a recent Soviet account of the history of the academy, see *Moskovskaia Sel'skokhoziaistvennaia Akademiia imeni K.A.Timiriazeva 1865–1965* (Moscow, 1969).

10. A. V. Chaianov, *Petrovsko-Razumovskoe v ego proshlom i nastoiashchem: putovoditel' po Timiriazevskoi Sel'skokhoziaistvennoi Akademii* (Moscow, 1925), p.47. A conscious effort was made to recruit students of proletarian background. As a consequence, between 1917 and 1927, the percentage of students of working class and peasant background jumped from 39.6% to 79.5%. O. M. Targulian, "The Academy over 10 years," *Puti sel'skogo khoziaistva*, 1927 no. 10, p.52.

11. Targulian, loc.cit., p.58.

12. The research and pedagogic functions of this Institute were under the aegis of RANION; the administration of the Institute was under the jurisdiction of Glavnauka RSFSR.

13. For this institution, such ties were a novelty. In the Tsarist period, the Timiriazev Academy had a reputation for radicalism; indeed, between February and June of 1894, it was closed down by the authorities. *Moskovskaia Sel'skokhoziaistvennaia Akademiia*, p.64.

14. This journal, which began publication in 1925 and ceased in 1929, was formed by the fusion of two journals: *Sel'skoe i lesnoe khoziaistvo*, the journal of the Commissariat of Agriculture, and *Uspekhi agronomii*, the journal of the Timiriazev Academy.

15. Party policy toward the social sciences in the NEP period was two-pronged. The long-term objective was to foster the growth of a Marxist science of society; the short-term goal was to support existing inquiry whatever the ideological inclinations of the social scientists. Prior to 1926, the Party concentrated on the short-term objective. But beginning at mid-decade, as the pool of Marxist social scientists began to increase, the long-term goal began to displace the short-term one. See Fitzpatrick, "The 'Soft' Line," loc.cit., pp.267–88; Leonard Schapiro, *The Communist Party of the Soviet Union* (New York, 1964), pp.341–43.

16. The case for the founding of this section was made to the June 1925 meeting of the Presidium of the Communist Academy by V. P. Miliutin, who became the first head of the section ("Minutes of the general meeting of members of the Communist Academy, 2 June 1925," *Vestnik Kommunisticheskoi Akademii*, 1925 no. 12, p.369). 1925 was a year of great expansion for the Communist Academy. In addition to the Agrarian Section, three other research sections were created ("Short report on the activity of the Communist Academy," *Vestnik Kommunisticheskoi Akademii*, 1926 no. 15, p.305).

17. The Agrarian Section made a conscious attempt to attract young Marxist students doing their graduate work in the Timiriazev Academy ("Activity of the Communist Academy, January–June 1926." *Vestnik Kommunisticheskoi Akademii*, 1926 no. 17, p.305). As a consequence, the section, which began with a staff of twenty-eight researchers, expanded rapidly.

18. For an assessment of the extent to which and the ways in which governmental policy commitments influenced work in Soviet rural studies, see Susan Gross Solomon, "Controversy in Social Science: Soviet Rural Studies in the 1920's," *Minerva*, Winter 1976, pp.554–82.

19. Some of these scholars were included in Jasny's book on leading Soviet economists of the 1920s. Naum Jasny, *Soviet Economists of the Twenties: Names to be Remembered* (Cambridge, 1972), pp.196–204.

20. Some Western historians have suggested that during the period of the Provisional Government, the Organization-Production scholars were affiliated with the Socialist Revolutionary Party. See, for example, E. H. Carr and R. W. Davies, *Foundations of a Planned Economy, 1926–1929*, I, Part 1 (London, 1969), p.20; Herbert J. Ellison, "The Socialist Revolutionaries," *Problems of Communism*, June 1967, p.7; Basile Kerblay, "A. V. Chayanov: Life, Career, Works," in *A. V. Chayanov on the Theory of the Peasant Economy*, ed. D. Thorner, B. Kerblay, and R. E. F. Smith (Homewood, Ill., 1968), pp.xxxvi-xxxvii. We were not able to find any evidence to corroborate this claim. In fact, at a conference called in 1930 to discuss deviance among academics, the members of this group were not denounced as "former SRs," whereas other scholars were so labelled; moreover, a recent Soviet article on the period lists the Chaianov group as "members of the Organization-Production school" while it denounced other scholars as "former SRs" (N. K. Figurovskaia, "The bankruptcy of the 'agrarian reform' of the bourgeois Provisional Government," *Istoricheskie zapiski* LXXXI [1968], pp.30–31).

21. For a biographical essay on Chaianov and an extensive bibliography of his works, see Kerblay, "A. V. Chayanov: Life, Career, Works," loc.cit.

22. For a discussion of "cosmopolitanism" in scholarship, see Alvin Gouldner, "Cosmopolitans and Locals: Towards an Analysis of Latent Social Roles," part one,

Administrative Science Quarterly, December 1957, pp.281–306; part two, *Administrative Science Quarterly,* March 1958, pp.444–80.

23. Kritsman was a Marxist historian who had been active in both politics and scholarly life since the early postrevolutionary days.

24. On the average, the Agrarian-Marxists were fifteen years younger than their rivals. In 1925, they averaged twenty-four years of age; at the same point in time, the Organization-Production Scholars averaged thirty-nine years of age.

25. A few of the Agrarian-Marxists were still doing graduate work in the Timiriazev Academy as late as 1926–27 (*Biulleten' Gosudarstvennogo Nauchno-Issledovatel'skogo Instituta Sel'sko-Khoziaistvennoi Ekonomii,* 1927 nos. 1 and 2, p.62).

26. This journal was founded in 1925 and continued publication until 1935. For the first half of its life, its editor-in-chief was L. N. Kritsman.

27. Gouldner, "Cosmopolitans and Locals," loc.cit. There was some contact between the Agrarian-Marxists and their Marxist colleagues living outside Russia. For example, two members of the Kritsman group made a visit to the Institute for Social Research in Frankfurt.

28. In the field of rural inquiry—unlike in other fields of Soviet culture—the cultural revolution did not occasion eccentric or utopian thinking. In the period 1928–31, the study of the countryside was treated in deadly earnest.

29. For an account of the work experience of these scholars, see Kerblay, "A. V. Chayanov: Life, Career, Works," loc.cit.; George L. Yaney, "Agricultural Administration in Russia from the Stolypin Reforms to Forced Collectivization: An Interpretative Study," in James Millar, ed., *The Soviet Rural Community* (Urbana, Ill., 1971), pp.3–35.

30. As early as 1912, Chaianov expressed his "lack of interest" in studying questions of the national economy. A. V. Chaianov, *Len i drugie kul'tury v organizatsionom plane krest'ianskogo khoziaistva nechernozemnoi Rossii,* I (Moscow, 1912), p.vii.

31. These scholars did not deny the utility of the Marxists' studies of interfarm relations, but they urged that such studies be regarded as supplements rather than as alternatives to their own microeconomic approach. See N. P. Makarov, *Krest'ianskoe khoziaistvo i ego evoliutsiia* I (Moscow, 1920), p.54.

32. The explanation of the family farm put forward by the Organization-Production scholars contained an early version of the backward-sloping supply curve of labor—a fact noted by anthropologists in the West. See J. Boeke, *The Structure of the Netherlands Indian Economy* (New York, 1942), p.18.

33. The demographic account was most fully elaborated in A. V. Chaianov, *Biudzhety krest'ian Starobelskago uezda* (Moscow, 1915).

34. The scholars' failure to consider these inequities stemmed from the fact that they considered the family farm to be inseparably linked to the repartitional commune.

35. The most important of these works were: A. V. Chaianov, "Peasant Farm Organization," in A. V. *Chayanov on the Theory of the Peasant Economy,* pp.29–271; A. N. Chelintsev, *Teoreticheskie obosnovaniia organizatsii krest'ianskogo khoziaistva* (Kharkov, 1919); A. N. Chelintsev, *Sel'sko-khoziaistvennye raiony evropeiskoi Rossii kak stadii sel'sko-khoziaistvennoi evoliutsii i kul'turnoi uroven'*

sel'skogo khoziaistva v nikh (Moscow, 1911); A. V. Chaianov, *Osnovnye idei i formy krest'ianskoi kooperatsii* (Moscow, 1919); A. V. Chaianov, *Opyt izucheniia izolirovannogo gosudarstva* (Moscow, 1921); A. V. Chaianov, "Optimal sizes of agricultural land-holdings," *Problemy zemleustroistva, optimal'nye razmery zemledel'cheskogo khoziaistva, kolichestvennyi uchet effekta zemleustroistva* (Moscow, 1922).

36. A. V. Chayanov, "On the Theory of Non-Capitalist Economic Systems," in A. V. *Chayanov on the Theory of the Peasant Economy*, pp. 1–29. This seminal article was originally published in German and never appeared in Russian.

37. The principal theorist of the group was L. N. Kritsman. Kritsman's younger colleagues saw themselves as empirical researchers and were quite content to work within the theoretical framework he elaborated.

38. According to a Western historian of Soviet Russia, this theory was held by the majority of educated Russians and by Russian policy-makers at the beginning of the twentieth century. T. Shanin, *The Awkward Class* (Oxford, 1972), p. 1.

39. Kritsman set forth his theory in two short articles written in 1925. See L. N. Kritsman, "Lenin and the path to socialism," L. N. Kritsman, *Proletarskaia revoliutsiia i derevniia* (Moscow, 1929), pp. 13–29; L. N. Kritsman, "The union of the proletariat and the majority of the peasantry in the USSR after the victory of the revolution," ibid., pp. 24–46. As Kritsman freely acknowledged, these articles owed much to Lenin's 1923 articles on cooperation.

40. Kritsman, "Lenin and the path to socialism," loc. cit., p. 45.

41. These projects came to fruition in the second half of the 1920s by which point they belonged clearly to the corpus of work done by the Agrarian-Marxists. For a list of these works, see footnote 45 below.

42. A. V. Chayanov, "Peasant Farm Organization," loc. cit. The first five chapters of this work had been published under a different title in 1923. However, the last two chapters were written specifically for the 1925 edition and were devoted expressly to the macroeconomic question.

43. These scholars advocated a cooperative scheme according to which the family farm would remain the basic unit of cultivation but would perform only those aspects of farming that were most efficiently carried out by a single farm; other tasks would be performed by a group of farms integrated horizontally. A. V. Chaianov, *Osnovnye idei i formy krest'ianskoi kooperatsii* (Moscow, 1927).

44. For an example of these findings, see *Sel'skoe khoziaistvo na putiakh vostanovleniia*, ed. L. N. Kritsman (Moscow, 1925).

45. The most important of these works were L. N. Kritsman, *Klassovoe rassloenie v sovetskoi derevni* (Moscow, 1926); Ia. A. Anisimov, I. Vermenichev and K. Naumov, *Proizvodstvennaia kharakteristika krest'ianskikh khoziaistv razlichnykh sotsial'nykh grupp* (Moscow, 1927); I. Vermenichev, A. Gaister, and G. Raevich, *710 khoziaistv Samarskoi derevni* (Moscow, 1927); A. Gaister, *Rassloenie sovetskoi derevni* (Moscow, 1928).

46. For the full stenographic report of the meeting, see N. P. Makarov, "Differentiation of the peasant farm," *Puti sel'skogo khoziaistva*, 1927 no. 4, pp. 103–13; A. N. Chelintsev, "On the question of differentiation of the peasant farm," ibid., pp. 113–32; A. V. Chaianov, "On differentiation of the peasant farm," *Puti sel'skogo khoziaistva*, 1927 no. 5, pp. 109–22; N. D. Kondratev, "On the question

of rural differentiation," ibid., pp.123–40; Ia. A. Anisimov, "Differentiation of the peasant farm," *Puti sel'skogo khoziaistva*, 1927 no. 6, pp.126–28; S. Uzhanskii, "Differentiation of the peasantry," ibid., pp.129–36; N. N. Sukhanov, "On differentiation of the peasant farm," ibid., pp.137–47; "Discussion of the paper on differentiation of the peasant farm," *Puti sel'skogo khoziaistva*, 1927 no. 9, pp.118–33; I. Vermenichev, "On differentiation of the peasantry," *Puti sel'skogo khoziaistva*, 1928 no. 1, pp.105–13. A detailed analysis of the debate can be found in Solomon, *The Soviet Agrarian Debate.*

47. The affinities between the Organization-Production analysis and an equilibrium model of development have been pointed out in Shanin, *The Awkward Class*, p.108.

48. For example, see the plan for agriculture drawn up at the end of 1924 by the Commissariat of Agriculture. *Osnovy perspektivnogo plana razvitiia sel'skogo i lesnogo khoziaistva* (Moscow, 1924).

49. Carr and Davies, *Foundations of a Planned Economy* I, part one, p.17.

50. With an eye for the jugular, the Agrarian-Marxists set out to refute the proposition that the family farm was a biological organism with its own internally determined cycle of growth and decay. M. Kubanin, *Klassovaia sushnost' protsessa drobleniia krest'ianskikh khoziaistv* (Moscow, 1929).

51. Several members of the Kritsman group attempted to develop a Marxist approach to the study of farm structure, a topic over which the Chaianov group had hitherto exercised a virtual monopoly. See V. Liubako and K. Naumov, "On the the question of the construction of organizational plans of sovkhozy," *Puti sel'skogo khoziaistva*, 1927 no. 12, pp.3–8; Ia. Anisimov, "Formulation of certain questions about the organization of agriculture in the past," *Puti sel'skogo khoziaistva*, 1928 no. 1, pp.3–17; Ia. Anisimov, "Basic premises of the Organization-Production school in the study of the organization of the peasant farm," *Puti sel'skogo khoziaistva*, 1928 no. 2, pp.3–15; Ia. Anisimov, "Toward the formulation of certain questions about the organization of agriculture applicable to the circumstances of the USSR," *Puti sel'skogo khoziaistva*, 1928 no. 4–5, pp.16–26.

52. The Organization-Production scholars had refined the use of budgets as a technique of research in the study of farm structure. Until 1927 they had expressed great pride in their innovation, but now they began to minimize its importance. See A. V. Chaianov, *Biudzhetnye issledovaniia: istoriia i metody* (Moscow, 1929); A. V. Chaianov, *Krest'ianskoe svekloseianie tsentral'no-chernozemnoi oblasti* (Moscow, 1929).

53. The scholarship that lent itself most readily to this purpose was that on the agricultural regions of Russia. See A. N. Chelintsev, "Agricultural regions, the regional perspectives on agriculture and the trend of agricultural policy measures," Part one, *Puti sel'skogo khoziaistva*, 1927 no. 9, pp.35–57; Part two, *Puti sel'skogo khoziaistva*, 1927 no. 11, pp.42–62; A. N. Chelintsev, "Toward a methodology of agricultural micro-regionalization," *Puti sel'skogo khoziaistva*, 1928 no. 4–5, pp.26–46.

54. The last expression of gratitude by the Agrarian-Marxists to their teachers occurred in 1927. See Anisimov, Vermenichev and Naumov, *Proizvodstvennaia kharakteristika*, p.31. Even at this point, the young researchers were less than fully gracious about the help they had received. For their part the Organization-

Production group acknowledged their debts to their rivals in terms that were excessively flattering. See Chaianov, *Biudzhetnye issledovaniia*, p.295.

55. A. V. Chaianov, "Methods of compiling organizational plans of agricultural enterprises under the conditions of the Soviet economy," *Biulleten' Gosudarstvennogo Nauchno-Issledovatel'skogo Instituta Sel'sko-Khoziaistvennoi Ekonomii*, 1928 no. 1–4, pp.5–15; A. N. Chelintsev, "On the structural principles and productive types of kolkhozy," *Puti sel'skogo khoziaistva*, 1928 no. 11, pp.22–38.

56. The members of this group had expressed their skepticism about the viability of large-scale socialist agriculture in the immediate postrevolutionary period. See A. V. Chaianov, "The concept of profitability of the socialist farm," *Metody bezdenezhnogo ucheta khoziaistvennykh predpriiatii* (Moscow, 1921). As late as 1925, they continued to express the same skepticism. See Chaianov, "Peasant Farm Organization," loc.cit., p.267.

57. For a detailed discussion of the atmosphere that surrounded the Shakhty trial, see Kendall Bailes, "Stalin and the Revolution From Above: the Formation of the Technical Intelligentsia, 1928–1934" (Unpublished Ph.D. dissertation, Columbia University, 1971).

58. The extent to which behavior can be conditioned by the anticipation of developments was discussed in Samuel Stouffer et al., *The American Soldier: Adjustment During Army Life* I (Princeton, 1949), p.411.

59. *KPSS v rezoliutsiiakh* II (7th ed., Moscow, 1957), p.437, as cited in Moshe Lewin, *Russian Peasants and Soviet Power* (London, 1968), p.206.

60. Chaianov, "Methods of compiling organizational plans of agricultural enterprises," loc.cit. Chaianov reinforced his image as a technical expert with a chapter on agriculture that he contributed to a collection of essays published in 1928 under the title *Life and Technology in the Future* (A. V. Chaianov, "The possible future of agriculture," in A. Kolman, ed., *Zhizn' i tekhnika budushchego* [Moscow, 1928], pp.260–85). The same attempt to divorce politics from expertise was evident in Chelintsev's work of this period. See Chelintsev, "On the question of differentiation," loc.cit.; and "On the principles of construction," loc.cit.

61. "Activity of the Communist Academy," *Vestnik Kommunisticheskoi Akademii* XXX (1929), p.252.

62. That charge came out of a meeting of the Central Committee department of agitation and propaganda held from May 30 to June 3, 1928. Fitzpatrick, "Cultural Revolution in Russia," loc.cit., pp.41, 47.

63. For a biography of Shefler, see *Puti sel'skogo khoziaistva*, 1928 no. 6, p.113.

64. *Moskovskaia Sel'skokhoziaistvennaia Akademiia*, p.138.

65. "Excerpt from the minutes of the meeting of the RANION presidium on the merging of the Institutes of Agricultural Economy and Land Consolidation and Resettlement," dated 1 February 1929, in *Organizatsiia sovetskoi nauki v 1926–1932 gg. Sbornik dokumentov* (Leningrad, 1974), p.315.

66. The effects on a community of scholars of an insistence on credentials has been discussed in Robert K. Merton, "Insiders and Outsiders: A Chapter in the Sociology of Knowledge," *American Journal of Sociology*, July 1972, pp.9–48.

67. Chelintsev, "On the structural principles and productive types of kol-

khozy," loc.cit., p.27; A. V. Chaianov, "From class-based peasant cooperation to socialist reconstruction of agriculture," *Sel'sko-khoziaistvennaia zhizn'*, 15 February 1929, pp.2–3.

68. See, for example, O. M. Targulian, "Kolkhoz construction according to Chelintsev and self-collectivization according to Chaianov," *Puti sel'skogo khoziaistva*, 1930 no. 9, pp.8–25. According to Targulian, the sins of the Chaianov group were grievous. While the Party was commending the kolkhozy on ideological grounds, Chelintsev persisted in measuring the performance of those farms by the normal standards of efficiency. And, while the Party was stressing the pervasiveness of social antagonisms in the countryside, Chaianov was writing about the peasants moving peacefully and voluntarily into collectives ("self-collectivization"); indeed, Chaianov insisted that only through a voluntary movement could technological revolution be accomplished without a social catastrophe. See A. V. Chaianov, "The today and tomorrow of large-scale farming," *Ekonomicheskoe obozrenie*, 1929 no. 9, pp.39–51.

69. This journal was the organ of four institutions: the RSFSR Commissariat of Agriculture, the All-Union Commissariat of Agriculture, the Timiriazev Academy, and the Lenin Agricultural Academy.

70. For these charges, see the record of a conference called in 1930 to denounce the "Kondratev group," whose membership was alleged to include the leaders of the Organization-Production school. *Kondrat'evshchina* (Moscow, 1930). A recent book by a Soviet author provides some more detailed information on the charges against the group. Apparently, the so-called party was alleged to have had nine underground groups in Moscow, centered mainly in the Commissariats of Agriculture and Finance, in the newspaper *Bednota*, in the Timiriazev Academy, and in research institutes on agricultural economics. Further networks were uncovered in the provinces with Socialist Revolutionaries and kulaks being among the members. Roy Medvedev, *Let History Judge* (New York, 1971), pp.113–14.

71. The conference was reported in some detail in the journal of the Agrarian Institute (formally Section) of the Communist Academy ("Analysis of the peasant household," part one, *Na agrarnom fronte*, 1929 no. 7, pp.96–106; part two, *Na agrarnom fronte*, 1929 no. 8, pp.83–106). This was not the first time that members of the Kritsman group had been criticized, but it was the first time that an attack had been directed against their credentials as Marxists.

72. M. Sulkovskii, "An experiment in the making of a seminar program on agricultural economics for socio-economic higher educational institutions," *Na agrarnom fronte*, 1929 no. 10, pp.146–55.

73. The full stenographic report of the conference was published in 1930. *Trudy pervoi vsesoiuznoi konferentsii agrarnikov-Marksistov* (Moscow, 1930).

74. See "The first Urals oblast conference of Marxist agrarian scholars," *Na agrarnom fronte*, 1929 no. 11–12, pp.211–14; "Meeting of Communist agrarian scholars under the agitprop department of the Central Committee of the Belorussian Communist Party," ibid., pp.215–18; *Trudy pervoi vsesoiuznoi konferentsii agrarnikov-Marksistov*, pp.104–107.

75. *Trudy*, p.430.

76. The delegates heard an address on rural policy by M. Kalinin. However, the

discussion of collectivization at the December meeting stemmed not from Kalinin's speech, but from that of the economist Iu. Larin, who argued that the kolkhozy were not fully socialist forms of agriculture.

77. By late 1929, cross-fire among Marxist researchers was common throughout the country, and consequently the December meeting was witness to a series of regional disputes. The main confrontation, however, was that within the Moscow contingent; here S. M. Dubrovskii, the Deputy Director of the International Agrarian Institute of the Peasant International, was ranged against Kritsman and his followers.

78. In adding this injunction, Stalin took the opportunity of unmasking certain "bourgeois prejudices" that, he claimed, were still current in Marxist rural research. *Trudy*, pp.434–46.

79. Ibid., pp.446–48.

80. Interview with S. M. Dubrovskii, 6 May 1969.

81. Apparently a "criticial" discussion of Kritsman's work was planned for early 1931, but there is no record of such a discussion's having been held. "On the work of the Agrarian Institute of the Communist Academy," *Na agrarnom fronte*, 1930 no. 10, p.113.

82. See, for example, the recantation by Sulkovskii, ibid., pp.146–47.

83. "From the editors," *Na agrarnom fronte*, 1932 no. 1, p.4.

84. This is best illustrated by the fate of G. A. Studenskii. In the first half of the 1920s, Studenskii was affiliated with the Organization-Production group, although he had certain theoretical differences with the group's leaders. At mid-decade, Studenskii attempted to steer a middle course between the Organization-Production and Agrarian-Marxist groups. See G. A. Studenskii, *Opyt issledovaniia organizatsii krest'ianskogo khoziaistva tsentral'no-chernozemnoi oblasti* (Moscow, 1926); G. A. Studenskii, *Problemy organizatsii krest'ianskogo sel'skogo khoziaistva* (Samara, 1927). Such a course proved impossible, and Studenskii was castigated by both groups. Toward the end of the decade, Studenskii apparently decided to throw in his lot with the Kritsman group; his bid was not accepted, for he was regarded as having been tainted by his early association with the Organization-Production scholars.

85. As has been pointed out, the latitude accorded to non-Marxist scholars in this period was not guaranteed in law, but it had the sanctity conferred by repeated practice. Fitzpatrick, "The 'Soft' Line," loc.cit.

86. For a discussion of the growth of subspecialties as a response to scientists' dissatisfaction with the allocation of resources and prestige in their fields, see Warren O. Hagstrom, *The Scientific Community* (New York, 1965).

87. Fitzpatrick, "Cultural Revolution as Class War," this volume.

88. Some scholars have suggested that the type of conflict that arises in a field may be related to the form of socialization to which novices are subjected. Jonathan R. Cole and Stephen Cole, *Social Stratification in Science* (Chicago, 1973), pp.77–78.

Enteen: Marxist Historians during the Cultural Revolution

1. RANION—the Russian Association of Social Science Institutes, founded in 1921—was an array of a dozen or more research institutes, including the Institute

of History, which were also centers for graduate-school instruction. Combining Marxist and non-Marxist historians in its staff, and having the function of training Marxist students for scholarly careers, RANION was a chief testing ground for the policy of "using non-Communist hands in the building of Communism."

2. "How the new scientific generation is really being trained (behind the wings at RANION)," *Vecherniaia Moskva*, 6 February 1928.

3. V. Zeimal and P. Pospelov, "The IKP Party cell in the struggle for the general line," *Pravda*, 1 December 1931.

4. See "Dispute on D. M. Petrushevskii's book," *Istorik-marksist*, 1928 no. 8, pp.79–129; Pokrovskii's criticism of Tarle in ibid., 1928 no. 7, pp.3–17; Tarle's rejoinder, ibid., 1928 no. 9, pp.101–107. On Zhebelev, see Loren R. Graham, *The Soviet Academy of Sciences and the Communist Party, 1927–1932* (Princeton, 1967), pp.104–108, and L. Hamilton Rhinelander, "Exiled Russian scholars in Prague: the Kondakov Seminar and Institute, *Canadian Slavonic Papers/Revue Canadienne des Slavistes* (1971), vol. XVI, no. 3, pp.331–52.

5. See Pokrovskii's article "Class war and the ideological front," 7 November 1928, and his criticism of Tarle cited above.

6. The emigré Russian historian Rostovtsev protested against Pokrovskii's election to the Presidium of the Congress, and this incident made a deep impression on Pokrovskii, who subsequently often alluded to it as an example of class conflict in scholarship. For reports on the Congress, see Pokrovskii, in *Vestnik Kommunisticheskoi Akademii* (1929) no. 30, pp.231–37; and Samuel Harper, "A Communist view of historical studies," *Journal of Modern History*, 1929 no. 1, pp.77–86.

7. See my article "M. N. Pokrovskii as an organizer of scholarship," *Jahrbücher für Geschichte Osteuropas* (1974), vol. 22, pp.56–57.

8. *Pravda*, 13 July 1929; *Vestnik Kommunisticheskoi Akademii* (1929) no. 32, pp.211–12.

9. *Vestnik Kommunisticheskoi Akademii* (1929) no. 33, p.274; (1930) no. 37–38, p.156, and no. 42, p.163; *Bor'ba klassov*, 1931 no. 1, p.120; *Plan rabot Kommunisticheskoi Akademii za 1928–1929 gg.* (Moscow, 1929), p.79.

10. Teodorovich, "On *Narodnaia volia*," *Katorga i ssylka* (1929) no. 57–58, pp.7–44.

11. "Theses for the 50th anniversary of *Narodnaia volia*," *Pravda*, 9 April 1930.

12. Teodorovich, *Istoricheskoe znachenie partii narodnoi voli* (Moscow, 1930), pp.240–46.

13. P. O. Gorin, *M. N. Pokrovskii, bol'shevik-istorik* (Minsk, 1933), p.113.

14. Ibid., p.102.

15. Ibid., p.101.

16. A. P. Nosov and A. N. Zakharikov, *Nekotorye voprosy bor'by KPSS za marksistskoe osveshchenie istorii bol'shevisma 1928–1932* (Moscow, 1962), pp.62–63.

17. *Istoriia VKP (b)* (4 vols., Moscow, 1926–30). According to A. L. Sidorov, one of the authors, these volumes were the chief product of "Iaroslavskii and his school" (*Istoriia SSSR*, 1964 no. 3, p.136). The contributors (with the exception of Piontkovskii) made up the nucleus of Iaroslavskii's faction: they were T. Kramol-

nikov, N. Elvov, O. Rimskii, I. Mints, I. Nikitin, A. Roos, D. Baevskii, A. Vaks, A. Sidorov, D. Kin and S. Piontkovskii.

18. Teodorovich, *Istoricheskoe znachenie narodnoi voli*, p.249.

19. Sokolov, "On the historical views of M. N. Pokrovskii," *Kommunist*, 1962 no. 4, p.75.

20. Nosov and Zakharikov, op.cit., p.75. The ellipses are probably theirs, not Pokrovskii's.

21. Iaroslavskii, in *Bol'shevik*, 1930 no. 3–4, p.122.

22. *Voprosy prepodavaniia leninizma, istorii VKP(b)*, *Kominterna* [stenographic report of the 1929 conference on the teaching of Leninism, Party history, and the Comintern] (Moscow, 1930), pp.183–85.

23. Iaroslavskii, "On the 1905 Revolution," *Istorik-marksist* (1931) no. 21, pp.151–52.

24. *Vestnik Kommunisticheskoi Akademii* (1930) no. 39, pp.14–90, especially pp.34–36.

25. See David Joravsky, *Soviet Marxism and Natural Science, 1917–1932* (London, 1961), chs. 14 and 16.

26. Pokrovskii had left the Bolsheviks with the V*pered* group in 1909, rejoining only in the middle of 1917.

27. L. V. Ivanova, *U istokov sovetskoi istoricheskoi nauki. Podgotovka kadrov istorikov-marksistov 1917–1929* (Moscow, 1968), p.180.

28. See Gorin's remarks in *Vestnik Kommunisticheskoi Akademii* (1930) no. 42, pp.62–65 and 148–49.

29. Gorin, M. N. *Pokrovskii, bol'shevik-istorik*, p.107.

30. Quoted Sokolov, from Central Party Archives, in *Kommunist*, 1962 no. 4, p.77. Ellipses are, most likely, by Sokolov.

31. Ibid. The members of the Communist Academy Presidium were Pokrovskii, Kaganovich, Miliutin, Kerzhentsev, Pashukanis, Ostrovitianov, Bubnov, Varga, Gaister, Deborin, and O. Iu. Schmidt.

32. The archives contain five separate drafts of the letter. Though one of them is signed by Kaganovich and Molotov, for some reason there is disagreement among Soviet specialists as to which is the final draft (interview with A. P. Nosov, Moscow, December 14, 1966). It seems that Pokrovskii denounced his opponents by name and that some drafts contain more names than others. Passages from the letter of summaries of it have appeared in six recent works: Nosov and Zakharikov, op.cit., pp.87–88; Sokolov, in *Kommunist*, 1962 no. 4, pp.75–78; Sokolov, preface to M. N. Pokrovskii, *Izbrannye proizvedeniia* I (Moscow, 1966), p.67; Ivanova, op.cit., p.180; Sidorov, in *Istoriia SSSR*, 1964 no. 3, p.63; and E. A. Lutskii, "The development of M. N. Pokrovskii's historical conception," in *Istoriia i istoriki* (Moscow, 1965).

33. Nosov and Zakharikov, op.cit., p.88.

34. Gorin, M. N. *Pokrovskii, bol'shevik-istorik*, pp.109–10.

35. "Resolution of the Central Committee of VKP(b) of 15 March 1931 on the report of the Presidium of the Communist Academy," *Pravda*, 20 March 1931.

36. "Bolsheviks on German Social Democracy in the period of its pre-war crisis," *Proletarskaia revoliutsiia*, 1930 no. 6, pp.37–72.

37. "Bolsheviks and the pre-war Second International," *Proletarskaia revoliutsiia*, 1931 no. 2–3, pp.22–58, and no. 4–5, pp.35–79.

38. Iaroslavskii, "To the editorial board of *Bol'shevik*," *Bol'shevik*, 1931 no. 21, p.68; and also *Problemy marksizma*, 1931 no. 8–9, p.14.

39. Sokolov, in *Istoriia SSSR*, 1969 no. 5, p.47.

40. *Evropa v novoe i noveishee vremia* (Moscow, 1966), p.505.

41. "On some questions in the history of Bolshevism," *Proletarskaia revoliutsiia*, 1931 no. 6. The letter was also published in a multitude of other journals, and is translated in Stalin, *Problems of Leninism* (Moscow, 1962), pp.483–97. It is the subject of a recent article by John Barber, "Stalin's letter to the editors of *Proletarskaya revolyutsiya*," *Soviet studies*, January 1976, pp.21–41.

42. Sidorov, in *Istoriia SSSR*, 1964 no. 3, p.136.

43. Stalin wrote: "Even some of our historians—I mean historians without quotation marks, Bolshevik historians of our Party—are not free from mistakes which bring grist to the mill of the Slutskiis and Voloseviches. In this respect even comrade Iaroslavskii is not, unfortunately, an exception: his books on the history of the CPSU (b), despite their merits, contain a number of errors in matters of principle and history." (Stalin, *Problems of Leninism*, p.497)

44. Ibid., p.483.

45. Ibid., p.492.

46. Ibid., p.484.

47. *Vsesoiuznoe soveshchanie istorikov* (Moscow, 1964), p.75.

48. See Mints's public recantation, in which, among other things, he confessed the error of voting for an incorrect resolution on November 10 that interfered with the mobilization of historians (*Bol'shevik* 1931 no. 23–24, p.135); and report in *Vestnik Kommunisticheskoi Akademii*, 1932 no. 1–2, p.42.

49. *Vestnik Kommunisticheskoi Akademii*, 1932 no. 1–2, p.45.

50. *Pravda*, 10 December 1931; *Bol'shevik*, 1931 no. 21, pp.84–86.

51. *Istoriia SSSR*, 1964 no. 3, p.136; *Istoricheskie zapiski* (1967) no. 80, p.223.

52. *Istorik-marksist*, 1932 no. 23–24, pp.8–9; Sidorov, in *Voprosy istorii*, 1967 no. 3, p.35.

53. Nosov and Zakharikov, op.cit., pp.100–101.

54. *Sovetskaia istoricheskaia entsiklopediia* VII (Moscow, 1965), p.717.

55. "The teaching of history in our school," *Pravda* 27 January 1936.

56. For an informative discussion of the unpublished decrees, see M. V. Nechkina, in *Istoriia SSSR*, 1962 no. 2, pp.73–74.

57. *Protiv istoricheskoi kontseptsii M. N. Pokrovskogo* and *Protiv antimarksistskoi kontseptsii M. N. Pokrovskogo* (Moscow-Leningrad, 1939–40).

58. A. I. Gukovskii, "How I became a historian," *Istoriia SSSR*, 1965 no. 6, pp.96–97.

Sharlet: Pashukanis and the Withering Away of Law in the USSR

1. See *Dekrety sovetskoi vlasti* I (1957), pp.124–26.

2. J. Hazard, *Settling Disputes in Soviet Society: The Formative Years of Legal Institutions* (New York, 1960), p.vi.

3. See the editorial "Our tasks," *Revoliutsiia prava*, 1925 no. 1, p.3.

4. See R. Sharlet, "Pashukanis and the Rise of Soviet Marxist Jurisprudence, 1924–1930," *Soviet Union*, 1974, vol. I, no. 2, esp. pp.112–15.

5. P. I. Stuchka, "Culture and law," *Revoliutsiia prava*, 1928 no. 2, p.20. Stuchka's emphasis was on the gradual reduction of legal compulsion in the society.

6. Quoted in P. N. Galanza, "The psychological theory of law and Marxism," *Uchenye zapiski Kazanskogo Gosudarstvennogo Universiteta* (1929), vol. 89, book 1, p.116.

7. Galanza, loc.cit.

8. For an English translation of E. B. Pashukanis' *Obshchaia teoriia prava i marksizm*, see *Soviet Legal Philosophy* (Cambridge, Mass., 1951), ed. J. Hazard and trans. H. Babb. For a critical analysis of the initial construction and subsequent development of his theory, see Sharlet, "Pashukanis and the Commodity Exchange Theory of Law, 1924–1930" (Ph.D. diss., Indiana University, 1968), chs. I and III. A contemporary Soviet evaluation of the Pashukanis school is given in M. S. Strogovich, "On the treatment of certain legal problems in the works of P. I. Stuchka, N. V.Krylenko and E. B. Pashukanis" in S. N. Bratus', ed., *Voprosy obshchei teorii sovetskogo prava* (Moscow, 1960), p.397. (Academician Strogovich was a contemporary of Pashukanis, and in this article he partially "rehabilitated" the conception of a theory of law separate from the theory of the state.)

9. A. Ia. Estrin, "XV Congress of the Party and questions of law," *Revoliutsiia prava*, 1928 no. 2, p.13.

10. Hazard, *Settling Disputes in Soviet Society*, p.487.

11. S. Dobrin, "Soviet Jurisprudence and Socialism," *Law Quarterly Review* (1936) vol. 52, pp.420–21.

12. Stuchka, "Twelve years of the revolution of the state and law" (1929), in Stuchka, *Izbrannye proizvedeniia po marksistsko-leninskoi teorii prava* (Riga, 1964), p.461.

13. XV *syezd VKP (b). Stenograficheskii otchet* I (1961), p.527.

14. Paraphrased in R. Schlesinger, *Soviet Legal Theory* (2d ed., London, 1951), p.202.

15. N. I. Cheliapov, "The Law," in *Malaia sovetskaia entsiklopediia* VI (Moscow, 1930), pp.811–12.

16. See Hazard, *Settling Disputes in Soviet Society*, pp.222, 393, 487; J. Starosolskij, "The Principle of Analogy in Criminal Law: an Aspect of Soviet Legal Thinking" (unpublished manuscript, 1954), p.36.

17. See Hazard, "The Abortive Codes of the Pashukanis School," in D. D. Barry, F.J. M. Feldbrugge, and D. Lasok, eds., *Codification in the Communist World* (Leyden, 1975), pp.158–67.

18. Hazard, "Reforming Soviet Criminal Law," *Journal of Criminal Law and Criminology* (1938) vol. 29, p. 160. The most active supporters were Estrin, Ia. V. Staroselskii, G. I. Volkov and S. Ia. Bulatov.

19. Ibid., p.164, note 20.

20. Stuchka, "Twelve years of the revolution of the state and law," loc.cit., p.461.

21. Hazard, "Reforming Soviet Criminal Law," loc.cit., p.165.

22. *Proekt novogo ugolovnogo kodeksa RSFSR* (Moscow, 1930), p.33.

23. *Sovetskoe gosudarstvo i revoliutsiia prava*, 1931 no. 4, p.132.

24. N. V. Krylenko, "It is time!", *Revoliutsiia prava*, 1927 no. 4, pp.88–89.

25. See Hazard, *Settling Disputes in Soviet Society*, pp.393–94.

26. N. N. Polianskii, *Ocherk razvitiia sovetskoi nauki ugolovnogo protsessa* (Moscow, 1960), p.40.

27. See Hazard, *Settling Disputes in Soviet Society*, pp.434–35.

28. N. V. Krylenko, *Reforma ugolovnogo kodeksa* (Moscow, 1929) p.64.

29. See Dobrin, "Soviet Jurisprudence and Socialism," loc.cit., p.419.

30. See A. Ia. Vyshinskii, *Sudostroistvo v SSSR; Sudy obshchestvennoi samodeiatel'nosti* (2d ed., Moscow, 1935), chs. 2–6.

31. See H. Berman and J. Spindler, "Soviet Comrades' Courts," *Washington Law Review* (1963), vol. 38, pp.849–52.

32. Quoted in H. Berman and D. Hunt, "Criminal Law and Psychiatry: The Soviet Solution," *Stanford Law Review* (1950), vol. 2, p.640.

33. Ibid., p.642.

34. Ibid., p.643.

35. Qutoed in L. Ia. Gintsburg, *Programma po khoziaistvenno-administrativnomu pravu* (1st ed., Moscow, 1929), p. 5.

36. See S. I. Raevich, in *Sovetskoe pravo. Zapiski Instituta Sovetskogo Prava* (1929), vyp. 2, p.171.

37. Iu. Geiman, "Economic law approaching the 12th anniversary of October," *Ezhenedel'nik sovetskoi iustitsii*, 1929 no. 44, pp.1029–30.

38. Quoted in Gintsburg, op.cit., p.3.

39. Ibid., p.5 and Gintsburg, *Programma po khoziaistvenno-administrativnomu pravu* (2d ed., Moscow, 1931), p.7.

40. Gintsburg, op. cit. (2d ed., 1931), p.5.

41. Editorial, "On the legal front," *Biulleten' zaochnoi konsul'tatsii Instituta Krasnoi Professury*, 1930 no. 8, pp.3–4. This journal was edited by Pashukanis and staffed by adherents of the commodity exchange school.

42. D. Pritt, "The Russian Legal System," in M. Cole, ed., *Twelve Studies on Soviet Russia* (London, 1933), p.165.

43. Hazard, "Housecleaning in Soviet Law," *American Quarterly on the Soviet Union* (1938) vol. I, no. 1, p.15.

44. Hazard, "Reforming Soviet Criminal Law," loc.cit., pp.166–67.

45. *Sbornik postanovlenii plenuma Verkhovnogo Suda RSFSR* (Moscow, 1932), p.31.

46. Hazard, "Reforming Soviet Criminal Law," loc.cit., p.166.

47. Hazard, *Settling Disputes in Soviet Society*, pp.393–94. The new Uzbek and Turkmen Codes of Criminal Procedure also contained very few articles—175 and 180 respectively. In contrast, the extant RSFSR Code had 465 articles.

48. *Za sotsialisticheskuiu zakonnost'*, 1934 no. 5, p.16.

49. Pashukanis, "On the law department of the Institute of Red Professors," *Revoliutsiia prava*, 1927 no. 3, pp.160–61.

50. Pashukanis, "On the theoretical training of workers of Justice," *Revoliutsiia prava*, 1928 no. 4, p.92.

51. V. Iezuitov and M. D. Rezunov, *Uchenie o sovetskom gosudarstve* (Moscow, 1931), vyp. 2, pp.2–3.

52. See V. Gsovski, "The Soviet Concept of Law," *Fordham Law Review* (1938) vol. 7, p.28, note 104, for the names of twenty-seven legal scholars who were affected.

53. M. Dotsenko, "Training of scientific cadres in socialist construction," *Biulletin' zaochnoi konsul'tatsii Instituta Krasnoi Professury*, 1930 no. 8, p.36.

54. Pashukanis, "On the law department of the Institute of Red Professors," loc.cit., p.161.

55. These course programs or syllabi were prepared by members of the Section for the Preparation of Cadres of the Institute of State, Law and Soviet Construction of the Communist Academy. Overarching all these syllabi was A. K. Stal'gevich's *Programma po obshchei teorii prava* (Moscow, 1929), which embodied Pashukanis' general theory of law.

56. Gintsburg, *Programma po khoziaistvenno-administrativnomu pravu* (2d ed., Moscow, 1931), p.9.

57. Iezuitov and Rezunov, *Uchenie o sovetskom gosudarstve*, pp.9–10.

58. The purpose of the law section was the preparation of qualified Marxist researchers in the field of Soviet law and construction for scientific research institutes, Marxist teachers of Soviet law for Party schools and graduate schools, and theoretically equipped Communists for supervisory work in institutions concerned with questions of Soviet law and construction. *Biulleten' zaochnoi konsul'tatsii Instituta Krasnoi Professury*, 1930 no. 2, p.64.

59. Editorial "On the question of training Marxist-Leninist scientific cadres," *Biulleten' zaochnoi konsul'tatsii Instituta Krasnoi Professury*, 1930 no. 5–6, p. 3.

60. See the syllabus for the freshman seminar on the general theory of law in *Biulleten' zaochnoi konsul'tatsii Instituta Krasnoi Professury*, 1930 no. 2, pp.65–69. In general, the seminar themes were similar to the chapter headings of Pashukanis' *Obshchaia teoriia prava i marksizm*, with the exception of the "class" theme, which was not emphasized in the book.

61. *Biulleten' zaochnoi konsul'tatsii Instituta Krasnoi Professury*, 1930 no. 2, pp.98–104.

62. Quoted A. Bystrova and L. Gittel', "A short review of the work of the seminar on the general theory of law," *Biulleten' zaochnoi konsul'tatsii Instituta Krasnoi Professury*, 1930 no. 1, p.46.

63. *Sovetskoe gosudarstvo*, 1934 no. 2, p.40.

64. A. Ia. Vyshinskii, *K polozheniiu na fronte pravovoi teorii* (Moscow, 1937), p.18.

65. *Biulleten' zaochnoi konsul'tatsii Instituta Krasnoi Professury*, 1930 no. 2, pp.98–104.

66. Hazard, "Housecleaning in Soviet Law," loc.cit., p.13. Hazard wrote: "Law concerning the rights of the individuals was relegated to a few hours at the end of the course in economic-administrative law and given apologetically as an unwelcome necessity for a few years due to the fact that capitalist relationships and bourgeois psychology had not yet been wholly eliminated."

67. "The Five-Year Plan and the Soviet state," *Revoliutsiia prava*, 1929 no. 4, p.9.

68. O. Dzenis, "Current problems of the state," *Biulleten' zaochnoi konsul'tatsii Instituta Krasnoi Professury*, 1930 no. 8, p. 6.

69. "The Five-Year Plan and the Soviet state," *Revoliutsiia prava*, 1929 no. 4, p.6.

70. Pashukanis, "Economics and legal regulation," *Revoliutsiia prava*, 1929 no. 5, p.37.

71. See Hazard, "Housecleaning in Soviet Law," loc.cit., p.12.

72. Interview with a Soviet jurist in Moscow, 1964. The respondent specifically referred to the draft criminal and criminal procedural codes inspired by the commodity exchange theory of law as examples of the tendency toward legal nihilism.

73. Berman and Spindler, "Soviet Comrades' Courts," loc.cit., p.852.

74. From a letter of John N. Hazard from Moscow dated 6 September 1937, in D. Barry, W. Butler, and G. Ginsburgs, eds., *Contemporary Soviet Law* (Leyden, 1974), pp. xxv-xxvi.

75. For an analysis of the criticism and revision of Pashukanis' commodity exchange theory of law, and a discussion of the decline of the commodity exchange school, see Sharlet, "Pashukanis and the Commodity Exchange Theory of Law, 1924–1930" (Ph.D. diss., Indiana University, 1968), chs. V–VII.

76. Vyshinskii, gen. ed., *The Law of the Soviet State*, trans. H. Babb, Intro. by J. Hazard (New York, 1948), p.52. For the impact of Vyshinskii's redefinition, see R. Sharlet, "Stalinism and Soviet Legal Culture," in *Stalinism: Essays in Historical Interpretation*, ed. R. C. Tucker (New York, 1977), pp.155–79.

Clark: Little Heroes and Big Deeds

1. See, for example, L. Leonov, "*Sot'*," *Novyi mir*, 1930 no. 4, pp.27–28, and no. 5, p.36; F. Panferov, "*Bruski*" (part II), *Oktiabr'*, 1929 no. 7, pp.25 and 29; 1929 no. 9, p.38; 1930 no. 2, p.111.

2. e.g., F. Gladkov, "*Energiia*," *Novyi mir*, 1932 no. 1, p.8; no. 2, p.112; no. 7–8, p.105.

3. V. Ilenkov, "*Vedushchaia os'*," *Oktiabr'*, 1931 no. 9, p.15.

4. Ilenkov, op.cit., *Oktiabr'*, 1931 no. 11–12, p.59.

5. M. Gorkii, "On little men and their great work," in his *O literature* (Moscow, 1955), p.339.

6. Ibid., p.337.

7. A similar idea is expressed in Gladkov's *Energiia* (see *Novyi mir*, 1932 no. 1, p.15).

8. Gorkii, op.cit., p.339.

9. I. Stalin, "On the tasks of the industrialists," in his *Sochineniia* XIII (Moscow, 1951), p.37.

10. Ia. Ilin, *Bol'shoi konveier* (Moscow, 1934), p.76.

11. V. Kataev, "*Vremia vpered*," *Krasnaia nov'*, 1932 no. 1, p.16.

12. *Liudi stalingradskogo traktornogo* (Moscow, 1934), p.415.

13. *Novyi mir*, 1930 no. 1, p.26.

14. *Belomorsko-Baltiiskii kanal imeni Stalina* (Moscow, 1934), pp.180–82.

15. *Liudi stalingradskogo traktornogo*, p.406.

16. *Belomorsko-Baltiiskii kanal imeni Stalina*, p.402.

17. Ibid., pp.153–58, 338–40.

18. Ibid., p.402.

19. Ibid., pp.35–38.

20. Ibid., p.356.

21. Ibid.

22. "Cultural revolution and contemporary literature. Resolution on the report of comrade L. Averbakh at the First All-Union Congress of Proletarian Writers," *Na literaturnom postu*, 1928 no. 13–14, pp.4–5.

23. A qualification has to be made here. It is not until after the reversal of policy on bourgeois specialists of July 1931 that one encounters such transformations of bourgeois characters. However, since novels take some time to write, most Five-Year Plan novels were in fact published after this date.

24. At this time RAPP was actually a very broad-based literary organization, and I refer here only to the Moscow leadership—L. Averbakh, Iu. Libedinskii, A. Fadeev, V. Ermilov, and others. The position of these men was less extreme than that of their Leningrad rivals of the "Litfront" faction of RAPP. In particular, they questioned the insistence on topicality (Averbakh, "Aristocratic prejudices," *Na literaturnom postu*, 1930 no. 7 [April], p.3); and complained about the poor quality of the "mass literature" being published (Averbakh, "On the orientation of the masses and the danger of a dominance of peasant limitations," *Na literaturnom postu*, 1929 no. 14 [July], p.13). See also M. Gelfand and I. Zonin, "Discussion on the creative method," *Pechat' i revoliutsiia*, 1930 no. 4 (April), pp.5–10.

25. For example, the theorists of *Novyi lef* (see below, p.200).

26. *Literaturnaia gazeta*, 1930 no. 3 (20 Jan.) and no. 9 (3 March).

27. *Literaturnaia gazeta*, 1930 no. 2 (13 Jan.).

28. Ibid., 1930 no. 40 (9 Sept.).

29. Ibid., 1930 no. 41 (14 Sept.).

30. Ibid., 1930 no. 42 (19 Sept.).

31. See "The Literary Five-Year Plan," in H. Borland, *Soviet Literary Theory and Practice During the First Five-Year Plan* (New York, 1950), pp.20–37.

32. "For union of writer and publishing house" (editorial), *Literaturnaia gazeta*, 1930 no. 8 (24 Feb.).

33. "Can writers be equated with toilers?", *Literaturnaia gazeta*, 1930 no. 6 (10 Feb.).

34. *Literaturnaia gazeta*, 1930 no. 61 (24 Dec.).

35. See H. Borland, op.cit., pp.26–33.

36. L. Averbakh, *Kul'turnaia revoliutsiia i voprosy sovremennoi literatury* (Moscow-Leningrad, 1928), p.64. For different viewpoints, see *Pechat' i revoliutsiia*, 1929 no. 1, pp.19–65.

37. *Literaturnaia gazeta*, 1930 no. 44 (24 Sept.).

38. Ibid., 1929 no. 18 (19 Aug.).

39. Z. Elsberg, in *Literaturnaia gazeta*, 1929 no. 16 (6 Aug.), p.2; I. Grossman-Roshchin, in *Na literaturnom postu*, 1929 no. 15 (May), pp.4–5.

40. *Literaturnaia gazeta*, 1930 no. 10 (10 March) and no. 48 (19 Oct.).

41. Ibid., 1930 no. 48 (19 Oct.).

42. "Pereval and the art of our times," and "The end of Pereval (from the editors)," *Literaturnaia gazeta*, 1930 no. 16 (29 April).

43. See, for example, T. Kostrov, "On realism, the 'living man' and the style of proletarian literature. Comrade Ermilov's brigade on the path to Rome," *Literaturnaia gazeta*, 1930 no. 13 (31 March).

44. *Na literaturnom postu*, 1929 no. 10 (May), p.2.

45. "The literature of a great epoch" (editorial), *Pravda*, 1930 no. 91 (2 April).

46. *Literaturnaia gazeta*, 1929 no. 11 (1 July).

47. Ibid., 1930 no. 5 (3 Feb.).

48. Ibid., 1930 no. 41 (14 Sept.).

49. Ibid., 1930 no. 39 (4 Sept.).

50. Ibid., 1930 no. 24 (27 June).

51. "For proletarian cadres, for Bolshevik tempos (for the First Oblast Conference of MAPP)," *Na literaturnom postu*, 1930 no. 2 (Jan.).

52. V. Kirshon, "The first results of the call of shock-workers into literature," *Literaturnaia gazeta*, 1931 no. 49 (10 Sept.).

53. K. Zelinskii, "On the literary pages of mass publications," *Literaturnaia gazeta*, 1930 no. 3 (20 Jan.).

54. "New literary cadres" (editorial), *Literaturnaia gazeta*, 1930 no. 49 (24 Oct.).

55. Fadeev, in *Na literaturnom postu*, 1930 no. 11 (June), p.1.

56. Ibid., 1928 no. 13-14, p.8.

57. M. P., "Face to the millionth reader," *Literaturnaia gazeta*, 1930 no. 39 (4 Sept.).

58. [Workers], "A breakdown in GIKhL," *Literaturnaia gazeta*, 1931 no. 15 (19 March).

59. "We have to break the writer's individualism," *Literaturnaia gazeta*, 1929 no. 16 (6 Aug.), and V. Tsepotev, "A review of criticism from below," *Na literaturnom postu*, 1929 no. 8 (April), p. 44.

60. "Union of writers. The governing board meets," *Literaturnaia gazeta*, 1929 no. 32 (25 Nov.).

61. Editorial, *Literaturnaia gazeta*, 1930 no. 36 (20 Aug.), and "For workers' supervision over the writers' organizations. Appeal of workers from the Vladimir Ilich factory," *Pravda*, 5 August 1930.

62. *Literaturnaia gazeta*, 1930 no. 49 (24 Oct.).

63. "The contours of the writer's psyche have changed," *Literaturnaia gazeta*, 1930 no. 48 (19 Oct.).

64. "We have to break the writer's individualism," *Literaturnaia gazeta*, 1929 no. 16 (6 Aug.).

65. Editorial, *Literaturnaia gazeta*, 1930 no. 44 (29 Sept.).

66. See, for example, report from AMO factory, *Literaturnaia gazeta*, 1930 no. 5 (3 Feb.); editorial, ibid., 1930 no. 36 (20 Aug.); D. Kalm in ibid., 1930 no. 3 (18 Jan.).

67. The critic M. Chumandrin refers to this movement as a "going to the people" (*khozhdenie v narod*) in *Na literaturnom postu*, 1930 no. 17, p.60.

68. Z. V. Udonova, *Marietta Shaginian* (Moscow, 1960), p.34.

69. Note Gladkov's bitter remarks about writers who spend the briefest possible time at factories and construction sites, in *Literaturnaia gazeta*, 1929 no. 16 (5 Aug.).

70. See, for example, V. Kataev, *"Vremia vpered,"* *Krasnaia nov'*, 1932 no. 4, p.44; L. Leonov, "Skutarevskii," *Novyi mir*, 1932 no. 7–8, p.113; L. Korelin, in *Na literaturnom postu*, 1930 no. 23–24, pp.32–33 (complaining of such sentiments among the established writers).

71. "1,500 authors and 100 editors," *Literaturnaia gazeta*, 1931 no. 56 (17 Oct.).

72. A. Reviakin, "Notes of a rural correspondent," *Literaturnaia gazeta*, 1930 no. 5 (3 Feb.); "letter of Viktor Shklovskii to A. Fadeev," ibid., 1929 no. 1 (22 April); I. Zhiga, "A transitional genre," ibid., 1930 no. 29 (15 July).

73. N. Chuzhak, ed., *Literatura fakta: pervyi sbornik rabotnikov LEF* (Moscow, 1929), p.11.

74. See, for example, L. Averbakh, *Kul'turnaia revoliutsiia i voprosy sovremennoi literatury*, pp.120–22.

75. S. Tretiakov, "The new Lev Tolstoi," in Chuzhak, ed., *Literatura fakta*, pp.29–31.

76. These theories required Soviet writers to present their characters with psychological realism—that is, without undermining the work's ideological message, to give an account of the protagonists' inner thoughts and motives. Members of the Litfront faction consistently opposed this view.

77. V. Friche, "On the question of novel-like genres of proletarian literature," *Pechat' i revoliutsiia*, 1929 no. 9 (Sept.), p.11.

78. *Na literaturnom postu*, 1929 no. 13 (July), p.54; *Pechat' i revoliutsiia*, 1929 no. 9 (Sept.), pp.6–7; ibid., 1930 no. 9 (Sept.), pp.17–19.

79. Friche, *Pechat' i revoliutsiia*, 1929 no. 9 (Sept.), p.10.

80. Z. Elsberg, *Literaturnaia gazeta*, 1929 no. 16 (5 Aug.).

81. "On the Five-Year Plan and writers' competition," *Literaturnaia gazeta*, 1929 no. 16 (5 Aug.).

82. The reference is to those sections of *Energiia* that were published during the First Five-Year Plan.

83. The novel was not actually finished until 1960. The reference here is to those sections that first appeared in 1932.

84. The novel was completed in 1937. The reference here is to those sections published between 1928 and 1933.

85. See, for example, the changing treatment of the villain Lukich in Sholokhov's *Podniataia tselina* or of Iashka Chukhliav and Kirill Zhdarkin in Panferov's *Bruski*.

86. "Na proverku!", *Literaturnaia gazeta*, 1929 no. 16 (5 Aug.).

87. See, for example, F. Gladkov's *Energiia*, L. Leonov's *Skutarevskii*, Ia. Ilin's *Bol'shoi konveier*.

88. This fault is to be found even in V. Kataev's *Vremia vpered*, otherwise the best Five-Year Plan novel in terms of plot development.

89. Nikanor, in Ia. Avdeenko, *Ia liubliu* (Moscow, 1933).

90. *Belomorsko-Baltiiskii kanal imeni Stalina*, especially pp.152–64, 323–42, and 248–62.

91. B. Iasenskii even uses this formula to describe the conversion of an American working-class engineer in his *"Chelovek meniaet kozhu,"* *Novyi mir*, 1932 nos. 10–12.

92. *Belomorsko-Baltiiskii kanal imeni Stalina*, pp.122–38.

93. Kraiskii and Akatuev in Ilenkov's V*edushchaia os*'; Petrygin in Leonov's *Skutarevskii*.

94. "At the meeting of MAPP and *Litgazeta*," *Literaturnaia gazeta*, 1931 no. 19 (9 April); report of A. Isbakh, *Na literaturnom postu*, 1930 no. 15–16 (Aug.), p.294.

95. See S. Sheshukov, *Neistovye revniteli: iz istorii literaturnoi bor'by 20-kh godov* (Moscow, 1970), p.294.

96. T. Trifonov, *Literaturnaia gazeta*, 1931 no. 14 (14 March).

97. A. Fadeev, *Literaturnaia gazeta*, 1932 no. 5 (28 Jan.); L. Averbakh, *Na literaturnom postu*, 1931 no. 25, p.7.

98. L. Averbakh, "On the theme of literature today," *Izvestiia*, 15 Dec. 1930.

99. *Literaturnaia gazeta*, 1931 no. 14 (14 March).

100. Ibid., 1931 no. 7 (4 Feb.).

101. Ibid., 1930 no. 20 (14 April).

102. Ibid., 1930 no. 25 (10 May).

103. Iu. Iuzovskii, *Literaturnaia gazeta*, 1931 no. 10 (23 Feb.).

104. "Breakdown in GIKhL," *Literaturnaia gazeta*, 1931 no. 16 (19 March).

105. I. Makarev, "Showing heroes—the general theme of proletarian literature" (report to the September plenum of RAPP), *Na literaturnom postu*, 1931 no. 35–36 (Dec.), p.59.

106. "Show the country its heroes!" (editorial), *Literaturnaia gazeta*, 1931 no. 25 (5 May).

107. *Literaturnaia gazeta*, 1931 no. 22 (24 April).

108. Ibid., 1931 no. 6 (31 Jan.).

109. I. Stalin, *Sochineniia* XIII (Moscow, 1951), p.55–59: speech to the industrialists of 23 June 1931.

110. Editorial, "Literary technique," *Literaturnaia gazeta*, 1931 no. 13 (9 March).

111. See Sheshukov, op.cit., pp.313–36; A. K. Romanovskii, *Iz istorii podgotovki pervogo vsesoiuznogo syezda pisatelei* (Moscow, 1958), pp.9–10.

112. "A living factory," *Pravda*, 1932 no. 51 (21 Feb.).

113. For example, "Open letter to V. Ilenkov, A. Serafimovich and E. Panferov's group: on the novel *The Driving Axle*," *Literaturnaia gazeta*, 1932 no. 13 (17 March).

114. Gorkii, *O literature*, pp.565–67.

115. Ibid., p.564.

116. From approximately 1932, the leader-figures in Soviet novels grew in stature and began to play a much more forceful role in directing the production effort. This change caused some problems for the Five-Year Plan novels whose publication spread over a number of years, and accounts for the lack of consistency in the characterization of positive heroes (e.g., Kirill Zhdarkin in Panferov's *Bruski*).

117. I. Mashbits-Verov, reviewing *Bruski*, *Oktiabr'*, 1930 no. 8 (Aug.), pp.197, 208–209.

118. *Pervyi syezd pisatelei. Stenogramma* (Moscow, 1934), p.4.

119. Ibid., p.5.
120. Ibid., p.4.

Starr: Visionary Town Planning during the Cultural Revolution

1. E. Evenbach, *Zelenyi gorod* (Moscow, 1931), postscript.
2. N. Krupskaia, "Cities of the future," in B. Lunin, ed., *Goroda sotsializma i sotsialisticheskaia rekonstruktsiia byta* (Moscow, 1930), p.9.
3. V. Bashinskii, "Planirovka gorodov," *Malaia sovetskaia entsiklopediia*, VI (Moscow, 1931), pp.571–72.
4. B. Lunin, *Goroda sotsializma*, introduction, p.3.
5. W. H. Chamberlin, *Russia's Iron Age* (New York, 1933).
6. A. F. Britikov lists thirty-eight science-fiction novels published between 1924 and 1927 and only eleven for 1928–1931 (*Russkii-sovetskii nauchno-fantasticheskii roman* [Moscow, 1970], p.86).
7. B. Sakulin's proposal in this vein is considered in E. A. Stanislavskii, *Planirovka i zastroika gorodov Ukrainy* (Kiev, 1971), p.110, and K. N. Afanasiev, ed., *Iz istorii sovetskoi arkhitektury, 1926–1932* (Moscow, 1970), p.115, note 12.
8. *Iz istorii sovetskoi arkhitektury, 1926–1932*, p.123.
9. "First declaration of the Association of Urbanist-Architects," *Ezhegodnik literatury i iskusstva na 1929 g.* (Moscow, 1930), p.541. Reprinted in *Iz istorii sovetskoi arkhitektury, 1926–1932*, p.125.
10. K. S. Melnikov, 'Prockt "Zelenyi gorod,"' MS, Melnikov archive, Moscow; abbreviated reports on Melnikov's project and others in the same competition are published in "The experiment of a socialist garden city," *Stroitel'naia promyshlennost'*, 1930 no. 5, especially pp.450–58.
11. Ibid., p.450.
12. "Instruction on the settlement of the communal house," *Goroda sotsializma*, pp.140–43.
13. A. Lavinskii, "Materialized Utopia," *LEF*, 1923 no. 1, pp.61 ff.
14. L. N. Sabsovich, *SSSR cherez 15 let, gipoteza general'nogo plana* (Moscow, 1929); and idem., "Not gradually, but immediately. Are we taking the right path?," *Goroda sotsializma*, pp.46–47.
15. G. Zinoviev, "From Utopia to real life," *Revoliutsiia i kul'tura*, 1930 no. 1, pp.4–6.
16. M. Ginsburg had frequently advanced this idea during the late 1920s in his journal *Sovremennaia arkhitektura*, and later elaborated it in detail in his book *Zhilishche; Opyt piatiletnei raboty nad problemoi zhilishcha* (Moscow, 1934), wherein he advocates the provisional retention of apartments of varying sizes for various-sized families.
17. Reported by V. Ia. Belousov, "The reconstruction of everyday life and the problem of socialist resettlement," *Nashe stroitel'stvo*, 1930 no. 11–12, pp.451–52.
18. N. A. Miliutin, "Basic questions of the theory of Soviet architecture," *Sovetskaia arkhitektura*, 1932 no. 2–3, p.3.
19. A. Pasternak, "Les problemes de l'édification des villes socialistes en U.R.S.S.," *L'Architecture d'Aujourd'hui*, 1931 (November), pp.5–9.
20. Perhaps the earliest effort in this line is that of the German critic Leonie

Pilewski, "Neuer Wohnungsbau in der Sowjetunion," *Die Form*, 1931 no. 3, p.102.

21. L. Sabsovich, "Why must we and can we build socialist cities?" *Revoliutsiia i kul'tura*, 1930 no. 1, pp.17 ff.

22. L. Sabsovich, "Not gradually, but immediately," loc.cit., p.48; *Gorod budushchego i organizatsiia sotsialisticheskogo byta* (Moscow, 1929), pp.21-23.

23. L. Sabsovich, *SSSR cherez 15 let; gipoteza general'nogo plana stroitel'stva v SSSR* (Moscow, 1929).

24. Ibid., pp.28 ff.

25. Sabsovich, "Agro-industrial cities," in *Goroda budushchego*, p.72.

26. A. Lunacharskii, "The architectural design of the socialist city," *Revoliutsiia i kul'tura*, 1930 no. 1, pp.56-60; "Culture in socialist cities," *Revoliutsiia i kul'tura*, 1930 no. 1, pp.38-40.

27. S. G. Strumilin, "The problem of socialist cities," *Planovoe khoziaistvo* 1930 no. 5, especially pp.98-100; idem., "The problem of socialist cities," *Izvestiia*, 21 and 24 June 1930.

28. T. Khvesin, "How we are building socialist Stalingrad," *Revoliutsiia i kul'tura*, 1930 no. 1, pp.67-70.

29. B. Strogova refers to Moscow's replacement by a "union of towns" ("An octopus city or a union of towns?", *Goroda budushchego*, p.146).

30. M. Okhitovich, "The socialist means of resettlement and the socialist type of housing," *Vestnik Kommunisticheskoi Akademii*, 1929 no. 35-36, pp.335-38; idem., "Notes on the theory of resettlement," *Sovremennaia arkhitektura* (SA), 1930 no. 1-2, pp.7-13.

31. Okhitovich, "Notes on the theory of resettlement," loc.cit., p.9.

32. Ibid., p.9. See also M. Okhitovich, "What is the city dying of?", *Stroitel'stvo Moskvy*, 1930 no. 1; and "On the problem of the city," *Sovremennaia arkhitektura* (SA), 1929 no. 4.

33. Okhitovich, "The socialist means of resettlement and the socialist type of housing," loc.cit., pp.337-38.

34. See the visionary train station described by A. Zelenko, "The city of the near future," *Revoliutsiia i kul'tura*, 1930 no. 1, pp.29-35.

35. This project of 1928 is misdated by Kenneth J. Frampton in his otherwise perceptive discussion of it in "Notes on Soviet Urbanism, 1917-1932," *Architects' Year Book* XII (1968), pp.243-44.

36. *Iz istorii sovetskoi arkhitektury, 1926-1932*, p.128.

37. M. Okhitovich, "Not a city, but a new type of settlement," *Ekonomicheskaia zhizn'*, 7 December 1929.

38. Okhitovich, "Notes on the theory of resettlement," loc.cit., p.13.

39. Okhitovich, "The socialist means of resettlement and the socialist type of housing," loc.cit., p.338.

40. *Sovremennaia arkhitektura*, 1930 no. 6, p.26.

41. Iurii Larin, *Zhilishche i byt* (Moscow, 1931), pp.4-5.

42. Ginsburg spoke in defense of Okhitovich at the Communist Academy in 1929 (*Vestnik Kommunisticheskoi Akademii*, 1929 no. 35-36, p.338). Leonidov and Pasternak publicly associated themselves with Okhitovich's theories with their

plan for Magnitogorsk in 1930 (P. A. Aleksandrov, S. O. Khan-Magomedov, *Ivan Leonidov* [Moscow, 1971], pp.55 ff.).

43. M. Ginsburg, "The socialist reconstruction of existing cities," *Revoliutsiia i kul'tura*, 1930 no. 1, pp.50–54.

44. Le Corbusier perceived this accurately when he wrote Ginsburg that "Deurbanization is a false interpretation of Lenin's principles. Lenin said 'If you want to save the peasant, you must bring industry to the village'. Lenin did not say 'If you want to save the city dweller'. The two problems must not be confused, and yet they are confused." *Sovremennaia arkhitektura*, 1930 no. 1–2; translation from A. Kopp, *Town and Revolution* (London, 1970), appendix 6, p.252.

45. Sabsovich, *Gorod budushchego*, p.58.

46. Okhitovich, "Not a city, but a new type of settlement," loc.cit., p.153.

47. S. Frederick Starr, *Konstantin Melnikov: Solo Architect in Mass Society* (Princeton, 1977), ch.VII.

48. L. Kaganovich, *Socialist Reconstruction of Moscow and Other Cities in the USSR* (New York, n.d.), pp.85–87.

49. F. Svetlov, S. Gornyi, "The socialist city in the classless society," *Planovoe khoziaistvo*, 1934 no. 2, p.158.

50. This drawing from *Sovremennaia arkhitektura* is reproduced in *Iz istorii sovetskoi arkhitektury, 1926–1932*, p.113.

51. "Questions of planning; the experiment of a socialist garden city," *Stroitel'naia promyshlennost'*, 1930 no. 5, pp.452–53.

52. N. Miliutin, *Sotsgorod*, trans. Arthur Sprague (Cambridge, Mass., 1975), p.22.

53. Ibid., p.36.

54. Lunacharskii, "Culture in socialist cities," loc.cit., pp.39–40.

55. Lunacharskii, "Architectural design of the socialist city," loc.cit., p.60.

56. Sabsovich, "The maddened petty-bourgeois or the auto salesman," *Goroda sotsializma*, pp.157–58.

57. Sabsovich, *Gorod budushchego*, pp.34–35.

58. *Sovremennaia arkhitektura (SA)*, 1929 no. 6, pp.30–31.

59. Sabsovich, *Gorod budushchego*, p.39.

60. At one point Sabsovich spoke of workers vacationing for half of each year (*Gorod budushchego*, pp.34–35).

61. "Second declaration of the Urbanist Architects," *Sovetskaia arkhitektura*, 1931 no. 1–2, pp.19–20; reprinted in *Iz istorii sovetskoi arkhitektury, 1926–1932*, p.132.

62. "Declaration of the All-Union Architects' Scientific Society," *Sovremennaia arkhitektura*, 1930 no. 3, p.1.

63. *Sbornik zakonov USSR* (Kharkov, 1930), no. 21, p.206.

64. *Sbornik zakonov USSR* (Kharkov, 1929), no. 24, p.199; *Sbornik zakonov USSR* (Kharkov, 1930), no. 46.

65. A. Pozdneev, "Organization of the construction of new cities," *Planovoe khoziaistvo*, 1930 no. 12, pp.295–304.

66. Protocol of the Combined Industrial-Technical and Social-Cultural Sections, July 11, 1929, in Sabsovich, *Gorod budushchego*, p.63.

67. See Maurice Frank Parkins, *City Planning in Soviet Russia* (Chicago, 1952), chs. 2–3.

68. V. E. Poletaev, "Housing construction in Moscow in 1931–34," *Istoricheskie zapiski*, 1960 no. 66, pp.6–8.

69. L. Kaganovich, "On the Moscow city economy and the development of the urban economy of the USSR," *KPSS v rezoliutsiiakh i resheniiakh syezdov, konferentsii i plenumov TsK IV* (Moscow, 1970), pp.557–58. Official translation, *Socialist Reconstruction of Moscow and Other Cities in the USSR* (New York, n.d.), p.82.

70. N. Chernia, "Cities of socialism," *Revoliutsiia i kul'tura*, 1930 no. 1, p.11.

71. P. Martell, "Legislation Concerning Residential Development in the Soviet Union," in Lissitzky, *Russia: An Architecture for World Revolution* (trans. Eric Dluhosch, London, 1970; translation modified by the author against original in *Wohnungswirtschaft* XXIII [Berlin, 1928], pp.140–41.

72. Kaganovich, *Socialist Reconstruction of Moscow*, p.26.

73. Ibid., p.21.

74. Ibid., pp.39, 47, etc.

75. Sabsovich, *Gorod budushchego*, pp.10–12.

76. G. Lonov, "The new plan of electrification," *Planovoe khoziaistvo*, 1932 no. 5, p.85.

77. See, for example, G. Krzhizhanovskii, "On the activity of GOELRO," *Planovoe khoziaistvo*, 1930 no. 12, pp.39–47; S. I. Tokachev, "Application of electrical energy to domestic life," *Planovoe khoziaistvo*, 1930 no. 12, pp.193–96.

78. *Ezhegodnik* MAO (Moscow, 1930), p.16.

79. Okhitovich, "Not a city, but a new type of settlement," loc.cit., p.155.

80. V. Mirer, "Planning of towns in Holland," *Kommunal'noe delo*, 1930 no. 4; V. Mirer, "Town planning in Czechoslovakia," *Kommunal'noe delo*, 1930 no. 7; M. Nefedov, "Replanning of Nanking," *Kommunal'noe khoziaistvo*, 1931 no. 10; B. L. Kogan, "Housing construction of the city of Frankfurt," *Nashe stroitel'stvo*, 1930 no. 11–12, pp.462–69; O. Vutke, "Rapid building in housing construction," *Nashe stroitel'stvo*, 1930 no. 11–12, pp.473–78; A. Krasinovskii, "The ideas of Corbusier," *Kommunal'noe delo*, 1929 no. 11; V. Mirer, "Replanning of the city of Tokyo," *Kommunal'noe khoziaistvo*, 1929 no. 21–22, etc.

81. *Stroitel'stvo Moskvy*, 1931 no. 1, pp.35 ff.

82. L. Vygodskii, "What is new in urban construction and planning. The expansion of Stockholm," *Kommunal'noe khoziaistvo*, 1929 no. 7–8, pp.134–37.

83. "Questions of planning. The experiment of the Garden City," *Stroitel'naia promyshlennost'*, 1930 no. 5, pp.452–53.

84. *Bauwelt* XXI (1931), p.703.

85. Ibid., and *Sovremennaia arkhitektura*, 1927 no. 1, p.12.

86. Kaganovich estimated in 1931 that Moscow needed 50% more canteens and restaurants (*Socialist Reconstruction of Moscow*, p.30). Iu. Larin, "Urban life and the collectivization of everyday living," *Sovetskoe stroitel'stvo*, 1930 no. 5, p.21; and idem., "Socialist reconstruction of everyday life," *Zhilishchnaia kooperatsiia*, 1930 no. 4, p.8.

87. A. Pozdneev, "Organization of the construction of new cities," loc.cit., p.299.

88. A. Lunacharskii, "Culture in socialist cities," *Revoliutsiia i kul'tura*, 1930 no. 1, pp.35–37.

89. Sabsovich, *Gorod budushchego*, pp.55–56.

90. Sabsovich, "Not gradually, but immediately," loc.cit., p.53.

91. Strumilin, "The problem of socialist cities," *Planovoe khoziaistvo*, 1930 no. 5, pp.98–100. See also his article in *Izvestiia*, 21 and 24 June 1930.

92. S. G. Strumilin, *Rabochii byt v tsifrakh* (Moscow-Leningrad, 1926).

93. Ibid., pp.107–10.

94. Ibid., pp.88–92. Cf. Miliutin's adaptation of Strumilin's figures, *Sotsgorod*, pp.116–17.

95. Ibid., p.106.

96. See Holland Hunter, "The Overambitious First Soviet Five Year Plan," *Slavic Review*, 1973 no. 2, pp.249–52.

97. A. G. Rashin, "Growth of urban population in the USSR (1926–1959)," *Istoricheskie zapiski*, 1960 no. 66, p.273.

98. Ibid. By 1934, the population of Moscow had reached 4,183,000.

99. L. Sabsovich, "Growth of urban population and socialist reconstruction of everyday life," *Na planovom fronte*, 1930 no. 6.

100. B. Strogova, "An octopus city or a union of towns," loc.cit., p.144.

101. On this current, see Carl E. Schorske, "The Idea of the City in European Thought: Voltaire to Spengler," in *The Historian and the City*, ed. Oscar Handlin and John Burchard (Cambridge, 1963), pp.95–114.

102. A. Puzis, in debate at the Communist Academy on 1 October 1929, *Vestnik Kommunisticheskoi Akademii*, 1929 no. 35–36, p.340.

103. B. Strogova, "An octopus city or a union of towns," loc.cit., p.144; and Sabsovich, *Gorod budushchego*, p.47.

104. Strogova, op.cit., p.147.

105. N. A. Miliutin, "Struggle for the new life-style and Soviet urbanism," *Goroda budushchego*, p.116.

106. Mikhail Koltsov, "On the threshold of your home," *Pravda*, 1 May 1930, p.6.

107. *Pravda*, 17 May 1930.

108. E. Iaroslavskii, "The Dreams of the Chaianovs and Soviet reality," *Pravda*, 18 October 1930. On the accusations against Chaianov and others involved in the "Kondratev affair," see Susan Solomon's article in this volume, pp.145–46 and note 70.

109. M. V. Kriukov, "A year of struggle on the construction front," *Stroitel'stvo Moskvy*, 1930 no. 11, pp.9–11.

110. Kaganovich, *Socialist Reconstruction of Moscow*, p.82.

111. Ibid., p.98.

112. From *Voprosy Leninizma*, cited by F. V. Popov, ed., *Planirovka sotsialisticheskoi rekonstruktsii gorodov* (Moscow, 1934), p.26.

113. M. Okhitovich, *Chto delat'?* (Moscow, 1934).

114. *General'nyi plan rekonstruktsii goroda Moskvy* (Moscow, 1935).

115. Claude Schnaidt, *Hannes Meyer: Bauten, Projekte und Schriften* (Teufen, 1965), pp. 27 ff.; Hans Schmidt, "Die Tätigkeit deutscher Architekten und Spezialisten des Bauwesen in der Sowjetunion in den Jahren 1930 bis 1937," *Wissenschaftlichte Zeitschrift der Humboldt-Universität zu Berlin*, 1967, Heft 3, pp. 383-400; J. Buekschmitt, *Ernst Mai* (Stuttgart, 1963).

116. See, for example, V. G. Davidovich, T. A. Chizhykova, *Aleksandr Ivanitskii* (Moscow, 1973), pp. 63-79.

Hough: The Cultural Revolution and Western Understanding of the Soviet System

1. Nicholas S. Timasheff, *The Great Retreat: The Growth and Decline of Communism in Russia* (New York, 1946).

2. Leon Trotsky, *The Revolution Betrayed* (New York, 1937).

3. The phrase is the subtitle of Timasheff's *The Great Retreat*.

4. Barrington Moore, Jr., *Soviet Politics: The Dilemma of Power* (Cambridge, Mass., 1950); Merle Fainsod, *How Russia is Ruled* (Cambridge, Mass., 1953), pp. 104-109.

5. This paragraph is drawn from Sheila Fitzpatrick, *Education and Social Mobility in the Soviet Union* (forthcoming).

6. Adam B. Ulam, "The Historical Role of Marxism and the Soviet System," *World Politics*, October 1955, pp. 28-29.

7. Merle Fainsod and Jerry F. Hough, *How Russia is Ruled* (3d ed., Cambridge, Mass., 1978), ch. 5.

8. Vera S. Dunham, *In Stalin's Time* (London and New York, 1976).

9. For example, in 1937, a year in which the socialist sector of agriculture did particularly well, the private sector provided 52 percent of the country's potatoes and vegetables, 71 percent of its meat, 57 percent of its fruit, and 71 percent of its milk. Jerzy F. Karcz, "From Stalin to Brezhnev: Soviet Agricultural Policy in Historical Perspective," in James R. Millar, ed., *The Soviet Rural Community* (Urbana, Ill., 1971), p. 54. Figures such as these are often cited to prove the efficiency of the private sector, but, particularly in the early decades, they demonstrate even more that the production of these crops was collectivized only to a limited degree.

10. Kendall E. Bailes, *Technology and Society under Lenin and Stalin* (Princeton, 1977), ch. VII.

11. See the discussion in Sheila Fitzpatrick, "Domestic Factors in Soviet Foreign and Comintern Policy, 1928-1934" (paper delivered to conference on Domestic Factors in Soviet Foreign Policy, Ann Arbor, Michigan, April 1976).

12. Barrington Moore, Jr., *The Social Origins of Democracy and Dictatorship* (Boston, 1966).

13. David Joravsky, *The Lysenko Affair* (Cambridge, Mass., 1970).

THE CONTRIBUTORS

Katerina Clark is Assistant Professor of Russian in the Slavic Department of the University of Texas at Austin. She has recently published an essay, "Utopian Anthropology as a Context for Stalinist Literature," in Robert C. Tucker, ed., *Stalinism* (New York: Norton, 1977), and is currently working on a book on the structure and evolution of the Soviet novel.

George M. Enteen is Associate Professor of History at the Pennsylvania State University. His articles on historiography have appeared in *Jahrbücher für Geschichte Osteuropas, Survey, Soviet Studies,* and *Slavic Review,* and he is the author of a forthcoming study of Pokrovskii.

Sheila Fitzpatrick is Associate Professor of History at Columbia University. She is the author of *The Commissariat of Enlightenment. Soviet Organization of Education and the Arts under Lunacharsky, October 1917–1921* (London and New York: Cambridge University Press, 1971) and of a forthcoming study of Soviet education policy 1921–1934, *Education and Social Mobility in the Soviet Union.*

Jerry F. Hough is Professor of Political Science at Duke University. He is the author of *The Soviet Prefects* (Cambridge, Mass.: Harvard University Press, 1969) and *The Soviet Union and Social Science Theory* (Cambridge, Mass.: Harvard University Press, 1977), and coauthor of Merle Fainsod and Jerry F. Hough, *How Russia is Ruled* (3d ed., Harvard University Press, forthcoming).

David Joravsky is Professor of History at Northwestern University. He is the author of *Soviet Marxism and Natural Science, 1917–1932* (London: Routledge and Kegan Paul, 1961) and *The Lysenko Affair* (Cambridge, Mass.: Harvard University Press, 1970). He is currently working on a history of the Pavlov school from the 1860s to the 1950s.

Gail Warshofsky Lapidus is Assistant Professor of Political Science and Sociology, University of California at Berkeley. She is the author of *Women in Soviet Society: Equality, Development and Social Change* (Berkeley and Los Angeles: University of California Press, 1977).

Moshe Lewin is Professor of Soviet History and Politics, Centre for Russian History and East European Studies, University of Birmingham, England. He is the author of *Russian Peasants and Soviet Power* (London: Allen and Unwin, 1968; New York: Norton, 1976), *Lenin's Last Struggle* (New York: Random House, 1968) and *Political Undercurrents in Soviet Economic Debates* (Princeton, N.J.: Princeton University Press, 1974).

Robert Sharlet is Professor of Political Science at Union College, Schenectady, New York. He is coauthor (with Z. I. Zile and J. C. Love) of *The Soviet Legal System and Arms Inspection* (New York: Praeger, 1972) and, most recently, of an essay, "Stalinism and Soviet Legal Culture," in Robert C. Tucker, ed., *Stalinism* (New York: Norton, 1977). He is currently writing a book on *Pashukanis and Revolutionary Legal Theory in the USSR, 1917–1937.*

Susan Gross Solomon is Associate Professor of Political Economy at the University of Toronto. She is the author of *The Soviet Agrarian Debate: A Controversy in Social Science, 1923–1929* (Boulder, Colo.: Westview Press, 1977).

S. Frederick Starr is Secretary of the Kennan Institute for Advanced Russian Studies at the Woodrow Wilson International Center for Scholars, Washington, D.C. His publications include *Decentralization and Self-Government in Russia* (Princeton, N.J.: Princeton University Press, 1972) and *Melnikov: Solo Architect in Mass Society* (Princeton, N.J.: Princeton University Press, 1976).

INDEX

305

crime, 44, 54, 60, 61; re-education of criminals, 55, 192–93, 202
cultural revolution: in China, 1, 2, 24, 37, 78–79, 80, 96, 249; contemporary Soviet definition of, 2, 255n.2; First Five-Year Plan definition of, 8–9, 14–15, 90; Lenin on, 2, 8, 9, 11, 255n.1; proletarian and pseudoproletarian elements in, 4, 32–34; and Right Opposition, 13–17; Stalin on, 2, 36, 255n.2; Western scholars on, 4, 78–81, 105–108, 129–30, 241, 255n.3, 269n.3; and youth, 5, 11

Deborin, A. M., 162, 260n.79
Dotsenko, M., 183
Dubrovskii, S. M., 166, 285n.77
Dunham, Vera, 40, 247

education, 5, 38, 40, 70–71, 78–104; administration of, 26–27, 85; anti-Communist organizations in schools, 20; FZU schools, 33–34; investment in, 9, 50, 89; psychological and aptitude testing, 118–19; rabfaks, 83, 92; reorganization after cultural revolution, 35, 99–104, 167; social purging in schools, 23–24, 91–92; "withering away" of school, 30, 89, 93, 94–99
—higher education: social discrimination in, 23, 35, 73, 83, 91, 101; worker *vydvizhenie* to, 3–4, 33–34, 51, 71, 92
Engels, F., 30, 108, 109, 110, 169, 183, 211, 231
Ermilov, V. V., 198
Esenin, S., 19, 20, 51, 257–58n.33
Estrin, A. Ia., 174, 178

Fadeev, A. A., 36, 203
Fainsod, Merle, 80, 243
Fedorov, L. N., 125–26, 127
Fitzpatrick, S., 130, 151
Fourier, Charles, 221
Fridliand, Ts., 159, 166
Frolov, Iu. P., 119
Fulop-Miller, Rene, 30

Gannushkin, P. B., 113, 115
generational conflicts, 5, 11, 17–18, 29, 133–34, 143, 156, 274–75n.75, 280n.24, 25
Giliarovskii, V. A., 116
Ginsburg, M., 209, 215, 216, 217, 218,

219, 221, 222, 223, 228, 239, 297n.16, 298n.42
Gintsburg, L. Ia., 180, 183
Gladkov, F., 200–201, 205
Golovanov, N., 25
Gorin, P. O., 159, 161, 162, 163, 166
Gorkii, Maksim, 105, 126, 127, 191, 197, 203, 205, 206
Gosplan (State Planning Commission), 53, 68, 210, 225, 231, 233
Grashchenkov, N. I., 116, 126, 275n.75, 277n.101
Grinko, G. F., 88
Gusev, S. I., 30

Hazard, John, 170, 174, 176, 181, 185, 186
Howard, Ebenezer, 221

Iagoda, G. G., 15
Iakovlev, I. Ia., 64
Iakovleva, V. N., 24
Ianson, N. M., 175
Iaroslavskii, E., 160, 161, 162, 164, 165, 166, 167, 168, 288n.43
Iasenskii, B., 193
Iavorskii, B. L., 31
Iezuitov, V., 183, 184
Ilenkov, V., 190, 205, 206
Ilf and Petrov, 47, 261n.9
Ilin, Ia., 190, 191
industrialization, 9, 10, 11, 98, 243, 245, 247, 251–52; and education, 9, 89; as literary theme, 194, 200–201, 203; and social mobility, 38; tempos, 12–13
Institute of Red Professors, 29, 36, 156, 157, 161, 164, 165, 170, 182, 183, 184
intelligentsia: Communist, 28, 31–32, 36–37, 167; Lenin on, 8, 12, 68, 69; "new Soviet," 11, 70–73; privileges of, 19–20, 38, 73; and regime, 5–6, 7, 18–19, 21, 67–68, 104, 110–11; Stalin on, 9, 11, 16, 34; technical and scientific, 9, 21. *See also* professions
—"bourgeois," 4, 8, 9, 12, 19, 37, 47, 69–70, 192–93, 202; accusations against, 12, 15, 22, 69–70, 146, 238, 258n.41, 284n.70; rehabilitation of, 34, 35–36, 73, 167–68, 242
Iudin, P. F., 36, 260n.79

Joravsky, David, 130, 253
Jowitt, Kenneth, 100